Deschutes

ARE WE THERE YET?

ARE WE THERE YET?

The American Automobile
Past, Present, and Driverless

Dan Albert

W. W. NORTON & COMPANY
Independent Publishers Since 1923
NEW YORK LONDON

For information about permission to reproduce selections from
this book, write to Permissions, W. W. Norton & Company, Inc.,
500 Fifth Avenue, New York, NY 10110

For information about special discounts for bulk purchases, please contact
W. W. Norton Special Sales at specialsales@wwnorton.com or 800-233-4830

Manufacturing by LSC Communications Harrisonburg
Book design by Lovedog Studio
Production manager: Lauren Abbate

ISBN 978-0-393-29274-9

W. W. Norton & Company, Inc., 500 Fifth Avenue, New York, N.Y. 10110
www.wwnorton.com

W. W. Norton & Company Ltd., 15 Carlisle Street, London W1D 3BS

1 2 3 4 5 6 7 8 9 0

In honor and loving memory of,

1968 Ford Country Sedan, 1969 Buick Special wagon, 1972 VW Beetle BEV, 1975 Oldsmobile Custom Cruiser, 1978 Olds Cutlass Supreme, 1978 Dodge D100 Adventurer, 1984 Dodge Ram, 1985 Saab 900S, 2000 BMW 323i, 2007 F150, 2008 Honda Odyssey

CONTENTS

ARE WE THERE YET?

Introduction

A NATION OF DRIVERS

The author's 1985 Saab 900S, somewhere on a journey across America.

W E HAD SOME FRIENDS ON THE CAPE. THEY WERE ALWAYS so generous with us. They'd invite us for dinners of steaks and wild mushrooms that they had foraged themselves. There was vodka. But when we would try to reciprocate they always demurred. So if Sasha Gessen's son needed a car, I would give him a car. It wasn't pure generosity on my part though. My mother had been nudging me, and then nagging me, to get a new car. We were about to bring home a new baby. "Daniel," she would say, "the Saab is fifteen years old. You need something safer. Don't you want something newer?" I put my foot down. Then she went to work on my wife. I lost, two against one.

Admittedly, plastic bits were falling off, and the body was still a little bent where it had been rear-ended. Yes, it wouldn't stay in third gear without a bungee cord, but the Saab had never let us down. My future wife and I had taken it on a six-week grand tour of America, down winding hollows in West Virginia and across the South Dakota prairie. At Great Sand Dunes National Park in Colorado, a kangaroo rat had bedded down on the warm engine overnight and the violent blowout of its little body popped a belt off when I turned the key. The ranger lent me a wrench and I put it back on. Guts and hair coated the engine compartment, but the musky smell through the air vents dissipated in a few days. It was gone by the time we reached the California coast, where we parked next to a campsite by the beach and watched whales swim along the shore in the late-afternoon sun.

When we returned to Michigan, I followed the maintenance schedule in the *Saab 900 8 Valve Official Service Manual*, refreshing belts, flushing coolant, and an oil change every 3,000 miles. I fixed minor problems (some of which I may have caused). I did the brakes and changed the clutch. Saab made planes for the Swedish Air Force and only turned to building cars after World War II when the warplane business went soft. As airplane designers, they were free from automotive conventions. They put the engine in backwards to make it easier to change the clutch and they put the ignition switch on the floor between the bucket seats, I assume because that's where you insert the key to start the engine on a Swedish warplane. So, it was a quirky car, a fun car, even a rare car out in flyover country. After West Virginia, we crossed several states before seeing another one. But, that was many years before the plastic bits and the bungee cord. Anyway, who wants to wrestle a car seat into a two-door hatchback.

So, my Saab became Keith's Saab and he dropped $500 on it to ensure that it could make the run between New York and the Cape for steaks and mushrooms. Anyone who has made that trip regularly—indeed any trip along the Boston-Washington corridor— knows highway dysfunction at its worst. Traffic swarms the cities like a chaos of angry bees and you quickly become one of the angriest. The trip from here to there can take an easy four hours, or miserable seven, but it's hard to know which when you depart. "Traffic is unbearable," people say, but of course it isn't. Millions choose to bear it every day. My (our) 1985 Saab definitely didn't like stop-and-go traffic, in which it tended to run hot. It preferred the open road, where the aerodynamic body made it possible for a mere 115 horses to cruise at seventy-five miles an hour with ease.

Keith continued to care for the Saab. When it developed leaks, he fed it fluids. He dutifully swapped it from one side of the street to the other in observance of alternate side parking. New Yorkers get by without a car, and the city doesn't make car ownership easy, or cheap, but a car can definitely come in handy. Keith moved house twice and reports that each time he found that he had exactly two Saab's worth of stuff. They seemed a good fit, Keith and the quirky Saab. Then Sasha's son killed my (our) car. It ran well enough, he tells me, until the night of the *n+1* Issue 2 party. This would have been February 2005. I'll let him tell the rest, because I can't bear to:

> Chad and I were in charge of liquor procurement, and we drove the Saab to this place in Sunset Park, under the BQE, where you could get beer pretty cheap, and we managed to fit 36 cases of beer in the car! We actually had an argument over whether it'd be possible—I didn't think they would fit, Chad thought they would, and Chad was right. What we didn't realize was that this was too much weight for the Saab. The wheels were audibly rubbing against the wheel wells, and maybe something else was going on. Anyway, we made it back to our place and parked, but after that the Saab wouldn't move. The engine started, but the car wouldn't move. And there wasn't much time left until the party! Luckily our managing editor's boyfriend was in a band and they had a van and we borrowed that.

From there the story devolves into tow trucks, lost paperwork, and a bicycle. I know he was sad, so I don't blame him. "If you have tears, prepare to shed them now," he had said, before bending to the tale of the Saab's final days. And it's only a machine, after all.

I'm assuming it was in thanks for letting him share the Saab's final years, or a foreshadowing of guilt, that he asked me to write for his new magazine's website. I sent him a piece about how Governor Arnold Schwarzenegger wanted to terminate my 1976 Buick Estate wagon. Keith made the piece much better, put it up on the website, and here we are.

*   *   *   *

THIS IS A BOOK about our relationships to cars and through cars and the stories we tell about those relationships, both as individuals and as a nation. How we understand the history of the American automobile and make sense of our automobile-dependent present will determine the driverless future.

My Saab story is uniquely my own, but hardly unique. Whether Americans ride in a car daily or almost never, they inhabit a nation, the landscape, society, culture, and economy of which were remade during the twentieth century around the privately owned automobile. That uniquely American experience of teaching our children to drive bonds us together. It is a fraught moment, a time of uncommon closeness between parents and their adolescents yearning to be free. They suddenly need their parents in a way they haven't since puberty. For parents, it is bittersweet. We see our roles reversed and our babies moving freely in the world for the first time. Their operator's license will identify them as first-class citizens, with all the privileges of a driver. Second-class citizens, those too poor, too old, or too infirmed to have a car, still must inhabit the landscape the automobile has wrought and remain dependent. Deadening sprawl has made walking, cycling, and even motorized mass transport logistically impossible. Like it or not, automobility is our national way of life.

I don't pretend that every American experiences automobility the same way. "Driving while black" is not the same as driving while white. A person driving a new luxury coupe with a 50,000-mile warranty and free routine maintenance experiences a different automobility than someone living life on the economic margins and driving a twenty-year-old sedan with a leaky radiator. And it goes almost without saying that the car culture is deeply gendered. Men are heavily overrepresented in every aspect of the automobile economy. Car guys fetishize sports cars and regale each other with tales of double-clutching; they are the hobbyists who customize their cars or restore them, and shade-tree mechanics who change their oil and their brake pads. But I have learned that there are millions of incognito car guys—both men and women—driving among us. While she was tapping my vein for an IV, a middle-aged nurse in scrubs outed herself as a car guy: she averred that she'd never surrender her BMW convertible with its stick shift for a driverless car. My oldest daughter can't change a tire or check the oil. Evidently she doesn't even know how to put gas in the van. But often, when I ask her where she was last night, she replies, "Driving. It's relaxing." She shuns my footsteps rather than following in them, but she's a car guy as well. A best-selling, eco-conscious, lefty novelist I know asked me for car buying advice. He cares deeply about climate change and so had settled on a choice between two high-mileage options for his first brand-new car: a diesel VW Golf and a Toyota Prius hybrid.* He had run through careful greenhouse gas calculations based on how he planned to use the car. By assuming more highway driving than city, long trips, not short, he was able to make the carbon footprint for the two cars come out even. Those calculations were a tell. He was never going to buy a Prius, a soporific rolling appliance. Eco-conscious, yes, but also a devotee of what Volkswagen called *Fahrvergnügen*, "driving pleasure." He wanted dispensation more than advice. I told him to let his car-guy soul buy the Golf and he did.

Of course, there are car guys the world over. The United States accounted for 63 percent of the world's vehicles in 1960, 23 percent in 2000, and less than 14 percent in 2014. "More than one billion

---

* This was many years before Volkswagen's diesel cheating crimes.

vehicles populate the earth today," calculates Daniel Sperling, professor of engineering and environmental science and policy at the University of California, Davis. "The globe is accelerating toward a second billion, with South and East Asia leading the way and Russia, Eastern Europe, and South America following along." Not only do consumers embrace the luxury, flexibility, and status of automobile ownership, national leaders pursue automobile manufacturing as a path to prosperity and industrial prowess. They know it worked out well for the United States. The Chinese now produce 30 million cars a year and the rate of car ownership there increased fivefold between 2004 and 2014. President Xi Jinping has made automobile production central to his "Made in China 2025" industrial policy.

Yet America, where the ratio of cars to people reached 816 per 1000 in 2014, has always been an outlier. There are 239 million cars and light trucks registered in the United States, more cars than drivers to drive them. The US was by more than a generation the first mass-motorized society in the world. The reasons for that big head start are several. The modern automobile was invented in Europe, where it was considered a rich man's toy. In America, however, a culture of consumption and a free and open society with relative income equality generated a fertile mass market. Henry Ford pursued that mass market with missionary zeal for low, low prices. He developed a system of mass production based on interchangeable parts, the moving assembly line, and total control of labor to serve that line. Ford alone produced nine million cars in the five years between 1921 and 1925, and as what Marx's disciple Antonio Gramsci would label "Fordism" spread, the rest of the industry doubled that number. High productivity let workers enjoy material abundance—a middle-class lifestyle—and unprecedented mobility. Auto production consumed North America's abundant natural resources, converting iron, coal, and forests into motorcars and domestic oil into gasoline. The car also demanded space, another natural resource this continental nation has in abundance. The automobile converted virgin land to productive use: bigger homes, consolidated schools, office parks, and shopping malls. Add to this economic activity new business opportunities from gas stations and motels to drive-in movies and auto repair shops. The total value realized by motorizing America in the 1920s, economists say, is unknowable.

Once created, automobility had to be expanded, adapted, and defended for it to survive. When expansion slowed in the middle 1920s, automakers invented the car loan and easy credit to re-inflate the market. When traffic violations and adjudicating car crashes clogged the courts in the 1930s, a new form of automotive jurisprudence was invented. To combat congestion, we built more roads. To combat urban smog, we added catalytic converters. When the cost in human lives became too dear, we added seat belts, airbags, and crumple zones to make car crashes more survivable. In the face of climate change, we're not abandoning our cars; we're electrifying them. Likewise, the driverless car will revolutionize automobility to allow it to thrive for another century.

A deep understanding of American automotive history and the American car culture is critical to cutting through the self-serving explanations for the driverless car and getting to the truth. One line of thought holds that technological advances will finally fulfill the long-held dream of a driverless car orders of magnitude safer than driven cars. In fact, the technology to create driverless cars has existed for more than half a century. In the 1950s RCA and GM ran driverless cars on test tracks. In the 1990s, federally supported research demonstrated "hands off, feet off" driving could be relatively easily achieved. Realizing the safety benefits of automation, it turns out, doesn't take much computing power at all. In any case, high technology is not the only answer to achieving most of these noble ends. For example, speed governors, parking fees, and higher gas taxes have all been available to make driving safer, rescue the city, and protect the environment over the years. The various problems supposedly endemic to the current model of automobility do not arise naturally from the technology of the driven car. That they have not been solved before speaks not to inadequate technology but to choices made about the relative value of, for example, speed, economic efficiency, and human life.

Another line of thought holds that Americans hate driving, that we're really bad at it, and that owning a car is too expensive. Millennials love their phones more than their cars. So, young people are getting licenses later in life, or not at all, gravitating to walkable neighborhoods, and opting for new and environmentally friendly mobility solutions like app-hailed rides, shared electric scooters, and bicycles. Yet, the ubiquity of chauffeur-driven cars available by ride-hailing app allows them to enjoy an automobile lifestyle once available only to the wealthy.

These evolving consumer choices and generational shifts have developed within a structural transformation of American capitalism. The driven car has gone from being the very engine and facilitator of economic activity to a knot in the system, something to be cut out. When they arrived on the scene 120 years ago, the automobile and motor truck smoothed the flow of commerce and capital and wove the country together into a single market. A major theme of the current mobile revolution—by that I mean the iPhone and the cloud, not the driverless car—has been replacing physical travel with virtual transport. Kids can attend class without going to school, shoppers can buy anything they desire without leaving the house, and many people can "work" from anywhere. The automobile and road once reduced friction in the flow of commerce. They made it easier to get out and make things and buy things—indeed, the automobile itself was the consumer product most desired and the one whose production reaped the most profits. Now, automobile production has become, in the aggregate, unprofitable. The FANGs—Facebook, Amazon, Netflix, Google—are Wall Street's money machines. They have made commerce nearly frictionless, thereby beating the automobile at its own game. With the driverless car, moving through space becomes as frictionless, effortless, and unreal as moving through the cloud. The robot car is the ultimate mobile device.

Kids today may eschew driving, but even many people already behind the wheel seem to have quit driving.

Small steps that made driving ever easier—from electric starters to automatic transmissions and computerized engine management to antilock brakes—were nothing compared to the giant leap of satellite navigation, GPS, made in 1996. Being directed by a humanoid voice from a mobile phone may seem a natural evolution of the paper map. But a map was something you pored over and studied, something you *consulted*. GPS must be *obeyed*. Furthermore, GPS navigation keeps us fixed in time and space. In other words, it used to be that when we drove we had a general sense of where we were and when we would get there. On the road, however, we were neither precisely here nor exactly there. We were in motion. Similarly, although we could glean from the map a rough idea of how long a trip should take, the precision of the paper map became a nebulous time bubble on the road, a dynamic approximation rather than a precise moment.

When I was a kid sitting in the wayback of our Olds Custom Cruiser and posed that profound philosophical question, "Are we there yet?" my dad answered with something vague. I knew it was a long trip, but never had myself fixed in time. I stared out the window, listened to the rhythm of the tires over the expansion joints, and watched the cars go by. I wasn't here, or there, but in between, en route. My kids ask and I give them our arrival time down to the GPS minute. The road was once an open-ended adventure, full of wrong turns and serendipitous discoveries. Now the phone knows every mile and every minute before we leave the garage.

Finally, GPS is just one aspect of the persistent connectivity provided by mobile phones. Now work, family obligations, rich media and social marketing follow us into the car. Once we were incommunicado, inhabiting an interstitial space that was neither work nor home. We were neither workers nor consumers but drivers. It is said that this persistent, cloud-enabled connectivity distracts the driver and causes crashes. For many "drivers," driving has become the distraction. Driving is now so easy, so passive, that many people gave it up long ago. Yet there they sit, behind the wheel. These zombie drivers feed on Facebook updates, insistent texts, and any number of other interruptions.

Yet, the driverless car enters the obdurate auto-centric landscape built up over a century. No matter how many presidents and senators intone, "My infrastructure bill . . . ," we have neither the will nor the capacity to tear it all up and start again. Nevertheless, the end of driving in America will have profound consequences for how we organize our lives.

But enough of this heaviness. We're hitting the road circa 1893, having jacked a car from France and customized it for the freedom-loving, democratic U.S. of A. The American automobile of 1910 is cheap and cheerful, ready to take us off-road through the heartland (where even the roads are off-road). When we tire of our rattletrap Model T, we'll trade it in for a 1925 Chevrolet, no money down, in any color we like. With the roads now paved and the American automobile transformed from an open carriage to a glass-enclosed, all-weather machine, we'll start seeing cars everywhere. I don't pretend the road will always be easy. When the Depression hits, we'll barely be able to afford gas. Detroit won't even build cars during World War II and we'll be ordered not to drive for the duration. Automobile plants will win the war for the Allies, though. Afterwards, our years of automotive deprivation will be rewarded with a powerful and beautiful new breed of American automobiles. During the golden decade of the 1950s, we'll ride superhighways into space. As we enter the 1960s, the road gets bumpy with critics popping out from behind every bit of shrubbery. The car blows smog out the tailpipe and there seem to be a lot of wrecks and dead bodies on the road, they will say. From then on, Detroit will suffer a protracted decline, ending in bankruptcy. Automobility will survive, however, and by the twenty-first century we'll be driving bigger, more powerful cars farther and faster than ever. Then things get murky and I lose sight of the road ahead. Somewhere along the way, the car became unfixable and the kids quit wanting to drive it. Soon, it will motor along on its own.

We'll go from muddy roads to superhighways, from horseless buggies to driverless EVs. Like any road trip, it is going to be fun. We'll discuss car books, car movies, how cars are made and how they work. We'll cast a critical eye on all the cars we come across on the road. Since it's a long trip, I'll probably get to talking about myself, what it was like to ride in the wayback, about my adventures in car repair, and the exquisite joy of teaching my daughter to drive. I will even tell a joke or two, probably three, some even worse than the others. I've been traveling this road for more than thirty years. So, buckle up and relax. I'll drive.

PART ONE

Chapter 1

THE FIRST REVOLUTION:
Let's Review

The privileged classes relished the thrill and danger of automobiling, making victims of the pedestrian masses. The press reported on these tragedies but also promoted automobile racing.

MOST PEOPLE REASONABLY EXPECT A BOOK ABOUT THE evolution of the automobile to begin with the invention of the automobile itself. I've disappointed enough people in my life already, so I give you the Jesuit Rat Car of 1672. In that year, missionary Ferdinand Verbiest created a steam wagon to bring the Emperor of China to Jesus, but the car was only big enough to carry a rat.

If you don't like the Jesuit Rat Car as an automotive first, you might consider Nicolas-Joseph Cugnot's cannon hauler of 1769. A product of the French army's skunk works, it was canceled in beta testing. In 1790, Nathan Read got the first American patent for a steam-powered wagon, a remarkable feat because the US Patent Office itself had yet to be invented. Perhaps that counts. In London,

Richard Trevithick set a Georgian coach body atop a steam boiler and eight-foot wheels, creating the first giraffe-less carriage. In 1805, American Oliver Evans drove his harbor dredge, the Orukter Amphibolos, down the streets of Philadelphia in hopes of enticing investors for a car business. Philadelphia cobblestone street paving gave horses purchase but shook the Orukter so violently that the wheels broke. Let's call his the first amphibious car.

Samuel Morey patented an engine in 1826 and then proceeded to show it off by strapping it onto a buckboard wagon. According to an eyewitness, Morey tripped while trying to mount the wagon. The engine "ran across the street, through the gutter, over the sidewalk, and turned a somersault, a complete wreck." This may explain why it took nearly two hundred years to try driverless cars again. Richard Dudgeon built his first steam minibus in 1853 and his 1866 model still sits in the Smithsonian collection. It did thirty miles an hour in New York City and out onto Long Island. He invented it, he later wrote, to end the abuse and mistreatment of horses. Sylvester Hayward Roper of Roxbury, Massachusetts, built steam carriages starting in 1859. At a scant 650 pounds, the Roper's two horsepower carriage could reach 25 mph and cost a penny a mile to run. In the 1850s, heavy steam-powered vehicles were developed to travel overland for use as plows and portable saw mills. These "traction engines" would later evolve into tractors. In 1878, the state of Wisconsin offered an XPRIZE award of $10,000 (about $200,000 today) for anyone who could develop a "cheap and practical substitute for the use of horses . . . on the highway and the farm." There were several entries, but only two specially built machines finished the race. They were far lighter and less cumbersome than the agricultural traction engines on which they were based. The "Oshkosh" beat the "Green Bay," but the governor (foreshadowing the penurious Scott Walker) reneged on the prize. Eventually the winning crew got half the money, but they were still steaming mad.

Any one of these "firsts" from the seventeenth century through to the mid-1870s might have evolved into the automobiles we know today. None was perfect, some far from it, but then new machines rarely are. The first electronic computers filled entire rooms and had no memory. Windows 95 crashed as often as a drunken driver. Sure, the Jesuit Rat Car had its problems, but imagine how many rats it would have carried after 250 years of development by the people who gave the world fireworks. Automotive pioneer Hiram Percy Maxim noted in his autobiography, "We have had the steam engine for over a century. We could have built steam vehicles in 1880, or indeed in 1870. But we did not. We waited until 1895." According to historian Clay McShane, "The pre-1890s steamers failed mostly because of regulation, not mechanical inefficiency." Local governments passed outright bans on driving steam contraptions on city streets for fear of boiler explosions.

Early automotive historians such as John Bell Rae argued that steam and electricity were not the right technology. But no sudden technological breakthrough explains the automobile's arrival in the 1890s either. Around 1860 Nikolaus Otto developed the four-stroke (Otto cycle) engine that cars still use today. The lightweight wheels and frames that would become crucial to the gasoline automobile had been developed for bicycles in the 1860s as well. A patent application filed in 1879 for the gasoline automobile would later be declared valid and recognized by all of the major manufacturers. But it would still be twenty years before the dawn of the Automobile Age.

Rather than looking in vain for an *ur* automobile or the mythical figure who invented it, we should instead ask why the technology was taken up when it was. Why did the American automobile suddenly seem like such a good idea in the 1890s? Within the space of a few years, not one or two odd inventors, but dozens, began showing off experimental autos. The largely forgotten William Morrison of Des Moines, Iowa, drove his electric car down the streets of Chicago in 1891. The famous brothers Charles and Frank Duryea of Springfield, Massachusetts, ran the first internal-combustion (IC) automobile in the United States in 1893. The Stanley brothers produced their first steam automobile in 1897. They sold 200 Stanley Steamers during the following two years—outselling all other makes. Of the 4,200 vehicles produced by 1900, fewer than 1,000 had IC engines. The balance was shared about equally by steamers and electrics.* Inventors were coming out of the woodwork. They dreamed up contraptions and Americans bought them. By 1899, commentators and industry experts saw that the motorcar was destined to revolutionize American life in profound ways.

Today, the feel of change is again in the air. Mary Barra, CEO of General Motors, has said, "Today, we are at the start of . . . a revolution in the auto industry." The best way to understand the present revolution is to examine the original automobile revolution. So, let's review.

America First types may be disappointed to learn that it was France that had the first car culture. Reporting on the bicycle and automobile show at Madison Square Garden in January 1899, a *New York Times* journalist noted that the normally avant-garde US was "far behind the European countries in adopting the bicycle and motor vehicles. France has paid the most attention to the latter, and motor carriage racers were very popular there a decade ago." He boastingly and presciently added, "Yet, though late in beginning, it will take us but a short time to make up lost ground, and then we will lead the world in this as we do in about all things else." American inventors learned from European inventions by reading journals such as *American Machinist* and *Scientific American*. We even adopted the French word, *automobile*; the English term, "motor car," now sounds quaint.

When the Duryea Brothers were still puttering about at the experimental stage, companies such as Panhard et Levassor, Roger (which sold the German Benz in France), Peugeot, De Dion-Bouton, and Bollée were in production and selling cars at a profit. These cars had exciting innovations. Frenchman Léon Serpollet's steam car had a

---

* By 1900, there were 109 manufacturers who produced 4,192 vehicles. Steam cars accounted for 1,681 of these; 1,575 were electric, and 936 had internal-combustion engines. See Rudi Volti, *Cars and Culture: The Life Story of a Technology* (Baltimore, MD: Johns Hopkins University Press, 2006).

flash boiler. Without it, steam cars took as long as a watched pot to get going. Benz introduced the steering wheel in 1891. The Americans still used tillers. On visiting the nation's first stand-alone automobile show in 1900, a journalist for *Horseless Age* was relieved to find "few have adopted that foreign freak, the wheel." A car with a wheel would be "a nerve racker of the worst kind" while a tiller makes automobiling "a most fascinating pleasure." The simple tiller worked well enough on lightweight, relatively slow-moving American cars. Using a tiller to manage the bigger motors and higher speeds of the contemporaneous European models, however, would have been quite nerve-racking indeed. While the Americans were still hiding their transverse motors under the seat, Panhard et Levassor came up with the standard layout of a longitudinally mounted engine in the front. There was much smacking of heads because, of course the engine belonged in the front. That's where the horses had been. The *Système Panhard* provided the room for the engine to grow in size and power.

The first American car owners were Europeans by another name, that is, members of the trans-Atlantic elite who steamed back and forth in first-class cabins. They bought their cars like baubles, opulent toys for keeping up with the Rothschilds next door. These machines appealed especially to young men of inherited wealth. *Motor World* reported in 1903 that John Jacob Astor owned fifteen automobiles, including a $17,000 Mors from France (equivalent to half a million dollars today). In all, the magazine counted fifty machines in the stables of five families worth a total of $250,000 (the equivalent of $7 million today). By 1905 Astor had twenty. In the interim, Astor's first cousin Margaret Laura Astor became a widow. Her husband, William Eliot Morris Zborowski, Count de Montsaulvain, died driving his Mercedes in a race up a hill in Italy. His mechanic was thrown clear of the wreck and survived. In 1905, Cornelius K. G. Billings, an avid horse racer with an inherited fortune, sold off all his horses and proceeded to spend $30,000 a year keeping his ten cars.

With impunity, these heirs used the public streets running from

Paris to Lyon, the mountain roads of Palermo, Italy, and the country lanes of Nassau County, New York, as their private race tracks.

William Kissam Vanderbilt II, Willie, was a notorious madman among the automobiling sportsmen. He bought his first car in 1899; many more followed. In 1902, he handily beat Baron Henri de Rothschild and set a world record. "With my 40 H.P. Mercedes I broke the world's kilometer record . . . at the rate of 111 kilometers an hour," he recorded in his racing diary. Two years later he set a new record of 148 km/h (92 mph) at Daytona, which is nuts. He sponsored the Vanderbilt Cup races on Long Island. He tore dangerously around the cottages of Newport, Rhode Island, but always went free when the police nabbed him. His chauffeur took the rap.

Marxian analysis is of little use in understanding the sudden enthusiasm for the automobile among the super wealthy. These men were so rich that their automotive consumption happened almost beyond the realm of capital and labor. But some Freudian analysis might help. Driving a gasoline automobile at the turn of the last century combined manly command of explosive power, the titillation of speed, and its inherent threat of violent death. William Vanderbilt confided to an interviewer (whom he perhaps mistook for his analyst) that his inherited wealth was "as certain death to ambition as cocaine is to mortality." Racing gave Willie a thrill and excitement his life otherwise lacked.

A motoring journal expanded on this theme: "In Europe it is openly recognized that the main excuse for the speed mania is the desire to feel new sensations and juggle away the emptiness of a purposeless life." In and of itself, that was a good thing, for civilization is all about "new sensations" which bring "spiritual progress." The problem, however, was that the men doing the racing were the idle rich. The scions had no hand in actually building and repairing the cars. "They are like savages with firearms," the editorial concluded its "Anti-speed Philosophy."

Filippo Tommaso Marinetti's *Manifesto of Futurism*, written in 1909, took this psychological hypothesis one step further, embracing the link between automobiling, violence, and the search for life's meaning. Marinetti's manifesto did more than merely outline an aesthetic philosophy—it laid the groundwork for fascism. War is "the world's only hygiene," he wrote. Violence, Marinetti predicted, would usher in a new age of Italian glory. But it all began with a car crash.

Having pulled an all-nighter, Marinetti and his friends rush to their automobiles. He describes "crushing [watch dogs] beneath our burning wheels." A pair of wobbly cyclists cause him to crash into a ditch, but he's thrilled: "Oh, maternal ditch, half full of muddy water! A factory gutter! I savored a mouthful of strengthening muck which recalled the black teat of my Sudanese nurse!" Climbing out from under the wreck, he "felt the white-hot iron of joy deliciously pass through my heart!" Willie and Filippo, they are the joy riders, the boy racers, the ones who fed on the automobile's latent violence. For Marinetti, crashing wasn't an accident to be avoided. It was the whole point of the exercise.

The deadly exploits of super-rich automobilists were a site of political debate in Europe. The views of the European press followed the political leanings of their publishers. A socialist paper, for example, condemned Count Zborowski's hill climb racing. He was quite welcome to kill himself, the paper allowed, but threatening the public in the process demonstrated the arrogance of wealth.

In the United States, newspaper publishers like James Gordon Bennett of the *New York Herald* sponsored races, confident that by covering the event they could sell more papers. In 1896, *Cosmopolitan* magazine offered a $3,000 purse ($100,000 today) for a race that ran from New York City to Irvington, about twenty-five miles away. The crowds at the starting line were so huge, the police had to be called in to maintain order. Cyclists followed along, with the inevitable accidents not far behind. In one case, "a wheelman [cyclist] was run into and seriously hurt by one of the horseless carriages," *Scientific American* reported. "The operator was arrested."

Although they reported on the races in the sport and society pages, both the motor press and mainstream newspapers in the United States condemned the reckless speeders. In 1902, the *New York Times* editorialized against plans announced by "certain young billionaires" to build a speedway running from Long Island City, just over the river from Manhattan, out to Hempstead. The editors mocked the "gilded youth" who bought the most expensive cars precisely because they were expensive. They wrote that rather than being slapped with a fine the speeder should be "imprisoned or put to death by electricity or the rope." The argument against the private road then took a sarcastic tack. The thrill of high-speed automobiling involved mainly "the chase . . . the great satisfaction and excitement in seeing how closely he can miss his fellow-citizens who are riding or walking or driving on the same thoroughfares through which he recklessly whizzes." Since the road would be closed to other traffic, that thrill of running down pedestrians would be lost.

The public was equally conflicted, or divided. Many put down their newspapers and headed out to watch the races, as they did for the *Cosmo* contest. Spectators lined the routes of high-speed races on public roads, despite, or perhaps because of, the obvious danger. On the other hand, as the monstrous cars trickled down from the 0.1 percent to the merely rich, more and more of them tore through town, killing anyone who got in their way. A 1909 *Puck* centerfold, "Privileged Sport," captures the mood. A chauffeur, bent over the wheel, barrels through the city in the boss's big machine. Relaxing in the rear are his wealthy employers in their motoring costumes. (Automobilist clothing for both men and women included a long duster of heavy cloth, fur, or leather, tall boots, and gauntlets. A scarf obscured the face but for goggled eyes. The full kit lent a monstrous and inhuman air.) Newspaper clippings surround the car like smoke: "ANOTHER BOY DIES UNDER MOTORCAR," "AUTO CUTS DOWN CHILD," "TWO GIRLS RUN DOWN BY SPEEDING TAXICAB." These headlines were both typical and common in the newspapers of the day.

Such incidents were skirmishes in a war of colonization. Before the automobile, city streets were multifunctional spaces, used for commerce and recreation as well as travel. The upper classes used automotive violence to drive the working classes and urban poor from the streets—relatively wide open spaces in dense urban neighborhoods. Vigilantes responded with attacks on the millionaire motorists who raced through working class neighborhoods. Drivers were stoned and, in at least one case in Germany, beheaded by piano wire strung across the street.

Before the automobile, there was the bicycle. The early bike culture looked a lot like the car culture. It appealed especially to young men in rut, and the races drew crowds. When they raced along public roads—as youngsters will do—they earned the name "scorchers." A speeding bicycle does not sound all that scary until you realize that, into the 1880s, the rider coming at you sat as high up as a Cossack. Because no one had yet invented the bike chain, the pedals on early bicycles were attached directly to the hub of the front wheel. As physics tells us, with direct-drive pedals, mechanical advantage—and hence speed—increases with the diameter of the wheel. In the quest for higher speeds, racers would try ever larger wheels. As physics also tells us, when you sit atop a five-foot-diameter wheel, it is both easy and painful to fall off. The rider who hit a hole in the road, or a good-sized stone, would take a header. As it would be for Marinetti and the automobile, this danger was a good part of the attraction.

With the invention of the bike chain in 1885, cyclists came down to earth. Now, sensible women and even children could ride bikes. Millions flooded the roads and by the 1890s there was a full-on bicycle craze. As with automobiles later on, bicycles elicited a bit of moral panic. It was the bicycle as facilitator of women's liberation, manifest in its impact on fashion, that really caused consternation. Victorian-era costumes made it difficult for the fairer sex to pedal the modern bike—as anyone who has gotten a skirt or pant leg caught in a bike chain can imagine. Bloomers were one solution, although they—Gasp!—revealed the ankles. Facing off against the moralists, advocates of women's lib celebrated the way the bicycle was modernizing women's place in society. Bicycles also gave rise to the road trip, an outing we usually ascribe to the automobile.

It is impossible to guess what millions of such road trips meant to their riders. Literary evidence nevertheless offers some tantalizing insight. Two of the best artistic representations of the bicycle tour come not from the United States but England and France. Nevertheless, such works found readers here as well. In H. G. Wells's *The Wheels of Chance: A Bicycling Idyll* (1896), our hero Mr. Hoopdriver sets off on a bicycle tour holiday. Along the way, the store clerk meets a coquettish cyclist, a "Young Lady in Grey" who bites her lower lip and says things "very prettily." The two kiss across the chasm of class and fall deeply in love. Perhaps Wells's story inspired Maurice Leblanc's French cycling novel, *Voici des ailes*, two years later. Leblanc had a Gallic rather than a Protestant sensibility, so his cycling tour ends with loosed corsets, bared breasts, and swapped husbands. Remember your etymology: *automobile* is a French word, as is *chauffeur*.

These characters used their bicycles to make an escape, evading society's confines by wandering the countryside guided only by whim and fancy. Herein lies one answer to the question of why the IC car won out over the electric vehicle and steamer. The automobile would be expected to facilitate the same sort of freedom as the bicycle—only more so.* Automobile innovator Hiram Maxim concluded, "The bicycle had created a new demand which it was beyond the ability of the railroad to satisfy. [It] directed men's minds to the possibilities of long-distance travel over the ordinary highway."

---

* Some recent scholarship has framed such stories and escapades—particularly in the automobile context—not as examples of freedom and pleasure but as opportunities for sexual violence. Passage of the Mann, or White-Slave Traffic, Act of 1910, supports this idea. The act made it a crime to transport women across state lines for "immoral purposes." Such transport was facilitated by the automobile. See Katherine J. Parkin, *Women at the Wheel: A Century of Buying, Driving, and Fixing Cars* (Philadelphia: University of Pennsylvania Press, 2017).

Although both electrics and steamers outnumbered internal-combustion cars at the turn of the century, by 1917, only 50,000 electrics were registered compared to 3.5 million IC cars. Steamers were all but gone. There is little to be gained in considering gasoline cars as "better" than electrics or steamers in any objective sense. Goldfish can't fly and pigeons can't swim. That doesn't make one better than the other. Gasoline cars were, however, the best at realizing the vision of what some segments of American society wanted the automobile to be.* Steam engines did not need gear boxes and ran quietly compared to gasoline cars. They offered the mechanically minded plenty of whirligigs and dials to play with. I won't discuss steamers much further, to the disappointment of steampunk cosplay fans everywhere, I'm sure. They are not on the table today as a possible alternative to the IC engine. Electrics are.

The qualities and range of the electric vehicle (EV) of 1899 served the needs of daily transportation quite well. The electric delivery wagon was far better than the horse-drawn kind, if only because it occupied half the space. The powerful torque of the electric motor allowed the electric wagon to carry a heavy load and the weight of the batteries mattered less. Private electric automobiles were also ideal for the city. They accelerated quickly and, quite unlike gasoline cars of the day, stopped easily as well.

The most common technical complaint against the battery-powered electric vehicle—then as now—is that it lacks range. Elihu Thomson, one of the founders of General Electric, tried to develop

---

* Precise language for comparing these three technologies becomes complicated. Both steamers and IC engines ran on a variety of hydrocarbon fuels. Properly, the steamer should be called an "external combustion" engine. Similarly, the electric vehicle runs on energy produced by a chemical reaction taking place inside a battery. The original source of the energy to create that chemical reaction came—remotely—from the steam or IC engine used to charge it. In that sense, all three run on the energy in the chemical bonds created by plankton millions of years ago. For the IC engine, I like the term sometimes offered in the early days: "hydrocarbon explosion engine."

an EV but said, "It's like a calf. If you move it, you have to take the cow along too." But faulting an electric for inadequate range only makes sense in reference to an IC car. In other words, how much range is enough depends upon the purpose of an automobile. According to historian Rudi Volti, "In the first years of the century, 98 percent of all car trips covered fewer than 60 miles." A standard EV range was about 40 miles on a charge, though some claimed 70 and a Detroit Electric claimed a record 241 miles on a single charge in 1914. Cities might also have provided charging infrastructure. The *New York Times* noted an "electrant" at the auto show the following year, "Which is designed to supply electricity as a hydrant supplies water." A quarter in the slot would dispense enough juice for twenty-five miles of travel. "It is expected that these automatic devices will be installed in suburban villages and places on the main lines of travel." That expectation was never met, but the idea highlights the electric's need for a commitment to infrastructure.

Low speed was the other complaint, although EVs held land speed records (for every form of motive power) in the early days. A French and a Belgian racer traded the land speed record back and forth during 1898 and 1899 with speeds in the neighborhood of 60 miles an hour. In 1902, Walter Baker set a record of 102 mph in his Baker Torpedo. Baker would have set many more records but he had a tendency to crash. As a practical matter, however, electrics could not hope to sustain such speeds for very long. Nevertheless, in an urban environment, raw speed is no measure of a machine's ability to cover distance. This was true in congested cities a century ago, and it's true today. In 1908 the owner of a Studebaker electric, with a top speed of 17 mph, challenged the owner of a 40 horsepower IC car to a race through Philadelphia. She proposed a practical contest, including stops to simulate a typical day of shopping and social calls. In the congestion of city traffic, and without having to crank start her machine after every stop, she won by ten minutes. The speed complaint was thus a complaint not about practical application in the city but about thrills. Elihu Thomson, who used the poetic metaphor of cows and calves, concluded that the EV was inferior because "It's too tame."

So, the electric was a perfectly viable automobile for city traffic, superior to the gas car in many ways. Yet it provided neither the thrill and danger that rescued Vanderbilt from his ennui nor the romance of the open road and escapism of the bicycle. A 1902 report on "The Problem of the Automobile" in *Electrical World and Engineer* pointed out that the EV would never afford the freedom of the bicycle or gasoline car. Even if charging points or battery-swapping stations were available in the hinterland, the writer concluded, "One does not wish to limit his country tour to lines of travel along which he can strike charging facilities . . . [one] wants to have a certain liberty of action which a journey fully prearranged cannot give." Had the EV won out against the IC car in those early days, our patterns of life would now be entirely different. Indeed, had this period of random technological mutation selected for the electric, the social history of America would be unrecognizable. The EV struggles in the marketplace today because it is a pigeon being asked to swim like a goldfish. We live in the world the IC automobile made. That world is not conducive to mass transit or even walking. It is little wonder that the EV, too, struggles to compete on the IC's terms.

For all its practical advantages and its ability to fulfill the desire for freedom, speed, power, and violence, the IC car lacked the electric's cultural weight. At the dawn of the automobile age, Americans saw electricity as futuristic, magical, and progressive. According to historian David Nye's study of the social and cultural impact of electricity at the turn of the last century, "Anything electric was saturated with energy, and the nation came to admire 'live wires,' 'human dynamos,' and 'electrifying performances.' " Street lighting and amusement parks opened up the night for entertainment. Electric elevators made skyscrapers possible. Neon "violet ray" tubes could cure any number of ailments at home. From any mail order house you could buy an electric hairbrush to cure dandruff or electromagnetic clothing that would invigorate the body. The Chicago World's

Fair of 1893 featured 100,000 light bulbs. Not to be outdone, New York's theater district shone so brightly that it earned the nickname "The Great White Way." Thomas Edison was known as the "Wizard of Menlo Park" for his New Jersey laboratory that invented all manner of electrical devices, including the incandescent lightbulb. He created the first electric utility when his Jumbo dynamo began spinning at the Pearl Street Station in 1882.

Even those who had the background to understand and even invent electric technologies could not help but be enraptured by it. Henry Adams, great grandson of president John Adams, had a spiritual epiphany on coming face to face with a Jumbo dynamo at the Paris Exhibition of 1900. In "The Dynamo and the Virgin," he writes: "The dynamo became a symbol of infinity . . . he began to feel the forty-foot dynamos as a moral force, much as the early Christians felt the Cross." (Adams wrote in the third person.) Like Henry Adams, a young clockmaker from Neuchâtel, Switzerland, named Hermann Lemp had an epiphany, though of a more secular kind. He came face to face with Jumbo at the first International Exhibition of Electricity at the Palais d'Industrie in Paris. "Jumbo, with its hundreds of incandescent lamps, and the completeness of the accessories, decided me to sail for America," he reported. On arrival, he walked into the Wizard's offices, carrying with him the differential galvanometer he had made, just for the fun of it. Lemp went on to work with Elihu Thomson and secured more than two hundred patents on everything from x-ray machines to diesel-electric locomotives. It was Lemp who built the automotive calf Thomson rejected.

The EV would have been a natural extension of the existing system of urban mass transportation. Aside from walking, most city dwellers had few transportation options besides the trolley—or streetcar. Electrification of the trolley lines had transformed the city, expanding its reach and inverting its geography. In so doing, trolleys helped create the market for automobiles. Into the 1850s, the American city had remained the merchant's walking city. Poor and rich lived side by side, though in different conditions. As waves of migrants arrived from Eastern and Southern Europe, they squeezed into dense neighborhoods and filled the city to overflowing. Here was a problem that electrification could solve. By adding overhead wires and electric motors to horse-drawn trolleys (and subtracting the horses) these early forms of mass transit could travel faster and farther, and carry more people. As urban historian Sam Bass Warner showed in his seminal transportation history of Boston, the "streetcar suburbs" began to develop even before electrification. But, electricity supercharged the growth of the metropolis and the inversion of its class dynamics. The working class, with less stable employment, used crosstown lines to navigate the city as they often changed jobs. The wealthiest, who had stable jobs, could travel far out on the longest lines where new houses and quarter acre lots gave them a respite from the industrial city. "Patterns of development followed little logic beyond the availability of dry land and the enterprise of speculators, builders, and trolley companies," writes Robert Wiebe in his social history of the era. In fact, many streetcar companies were actually real estate developers, profiting from the rising price of the land their trains served.

The city became the metropolis and its middle-class citizens began to commute. It was a short step from there off the increasingly crowded streetcar and into the driver's seat.[*]

In this context, Albert A. Pope got into the electric car business. He was by far the nation's leading bicycle manufacturer and is supposed to have said about the IC car, "You can't get people to sit over an explosion." Ironically, executives at Pope Manufacturing chose an engineer with a penchant for explosions to head up the company's new "Motor Carriage Department." Hiram Percy Maxim, whose father had invented the machine gun, graduated from MIT and was in the grenade business before being hired by Pope. When Maxim

---

[*] The word "commuter" is an early twentieth-century invention. Streetcar companies commuted the ticket price if you bought a weekly pass, just as parole boards commuted sentences.

proudly showed off his prototype IC car, his boss said, "Well then, Maxim, let me tell you something. We are on the wrong track. No one will buy a carriage that has to have all that greasy machinery in it." He figured it might be a fun toy for mechanically inclined young men, but not a useful machine for the average buyer. Pope went on to become a leading manufacturer of electric cars under the Columbia brand name. He was wrong: plenty of people were willing to sit over an explosion. Many were also willing, even eager, to put up with greasy machinery.

The market for electric cars was limited in part by their relatively high initial cost. So, Pope fell in with the Electric Vehicle Company, which had a different business model in mind: Mobility as a Service (MaaS). Customers could buy a car from them, or lease one, rent one, or pay by the mile for a ride. The potential profits were much greater than selling a vehicle outright. The EVC would capture every drop of potential revenue from their vehicle assets by running them continually. The economics of electric vehicles have not changed. As they transition to electric cars, and as they develop driverless technology, the world's automakers are reviving the EVC's MaaS business model. "We're a mobility company," they say.

Henry Morris and Pedro Salom had launched the Electric Vehicle Company in Philadelphia with a $10,000 capitalization in 1896. The pair had developed the Electrobat with a layout similar to the horse-drawn hansom safety cabs of London and a range of twenty-five miles in city traffic. Passengers sat inside a comfortable cabin while the driver sat in the open to the rear. The Electrobats were large, heavy, refined machines. The cars would be stored at central stations where a highly automated system would swap out a depleted battery pack in seventy-five seconds. Then, the Electric Storage Battery Company bought the Morris and Salom startup even before it had made a sale. Capitalization increased thirtyfold to $300,000. Beginning in Philadelphia and expanding quickly to New York, the new Electric Vehicle Company became a raging success. Cars were rented out so often and for such long intervals that few were available as taxicabs.

As of January 1899, fifty-five cabs were in fleet service and forty more were leased to customers under a long-term service contract. According to *Horseless Age,* "Many aristocratic people . . . are so enthusiastic that they declare they will not bring their horses to the city another winter, but will leave them at their country places." From there things went mad. The EVC ordered 2,000, 8,000, wait! 12,000 new cars. These would include hansom cabs, landaus, and coupes. A giant EV holding company would open branches in every state and territory in the union. There would be a "worldwide network of branch EVCs," wrote the press. The EVC planned a paper value of $200 million.

The expansion plans made sense. The EVC business model worked. According to historian David Kirsch, the company was likely profitable on its own. But the shareholders of the holding company under which it operated may have had more to gain from rapid expansion than the bottom line. The modern parallels are so perfect as to be almost scary. Uber, for example, has been expanding rapidly but not making money. Still, it has a market capitalization as high as Detroit automakers, companies which actually return profits to shareholders.

Another facet of the EVC business was the need for monopoly. The company had to monopolize the electric cab business in order to have a critical mass of vehicles. Only then could riders count on being able to get an EVC cab when they wanted one. Again, the same is more or less true today: ride hailing services need to achieve nearly monopolistic scale to survive. Unless they reach a critical mass of drivers (or driverless cars), they cannot serve customers. App-enabled flexibility reduces the tendency toward total monopoly as drivers can effectively operate for two ride-hailing services—think Uber and Lyft—simultaneously.

Monopoly was a dirty word in the app-less 1890s. President Teddy Roosevelt, elected in 1901, became known as the "trust buster." E. P. Ingersoll, owner of the motor journal *Horseless Age,* attacked the EVC as a trust in his every editorial. Ingersoll battered the electric battery as well. "The history of storage battery traction is strewn with wrecks and failures," he wrote. The battery electric would not work "until the laws of the universe are superseded." He warned against those who would "force" electrics on a "credulous world." With Ingersoll's constant attacks, the EVC became known as the "Lead Cab Trust," according to Gijs Mom, the leading historian of the rise and fall of the electric car in this period. Mom concludes that Ingersoll's technical complaints overshadow his real enemy: monopoly. Ingersoll believed the EVC trust would prevent the dawn of a utopian Horseless Age based on the internal-combustion motor.

A *New York Herald* investigation late in 1899 revealed that the EVC had secured a loan fraudulently. The scandal sent EVC stock plummeting from $30 to 75 cents a share. In 1900, *Horseless Age* cancelled all EVC ads and then named and shamed the "floater(s) of watered stock companies." In 1901 the EVC began to collapse. Chicago liquidated in the early spring. Boston folded two months later. Whatever the technical demerits against the battery electric, commentators at the time noted that "the dismal failure of public electric automobiles in several cities tended to give the motive power a black eye irrespective of its real merits." In other words, the business failed the machine rather than the other way around.

As horseless buggies like the Curved Dash Oldsmobile evolved into automobiles, EVs evolved into drawing rooms. By the time Henry Ford's wife, Clara, started driving her 1914 Detroit Electric, the technology was highly refined. At a time when gasoline cars like the Model T were open to the elements, Clara sat in a cozy drawing room with seating for three, surrounded by a greenhouse of glass. Mounted crystal vases held flowers. Deeply tufted upholstery covered the chairs. The feminine, luxury appointments denote this as a "woman's car." The car's top speed of twenty-five miles an hour was deemed more than enough for the fairer sex.

As we enter our own automotive revolution, it pays to keep in mind the gendered nature of the car culture and the transformative role both electrification and the end of driving will have on it. As they lost out to IC cars, EV makers began appealing especially to women. That marketing of EVs to women evinces not a biological imperative but the perpetual construction of the driver's seat as a prerogative of masculinity. Drivers took command of their gasoline cars from the exalted captain's chair, gripping the steering wheel and reaching for various levers and knobs by hand and foot. Clara Ford sat in the rear of her Detroit Electric, more of a hostess than a driver. She had a single bar, push-pull tiller to steer and a second that engaged reverse. Her luncheon companion would nestle in beside her and a third lady, perhaps being dropped off at the dressmaker's, sat opposite, facing the rear. With the controls folded away—as they were for easy entry and egress—the Detroit Electric looks for all the world like an autonomous mobile parlor.

Now the auto shows are replete with such interior design studies with steering wheels that fold into the dashboard. The Mercedes-Benz "Luxury in Motion" concept features swiveling white leather seats and wooden floors; Yanfeng's XiM7 interior switches into "meeting mode" with chairs that slide and turn. The intervening century of change is there. The tufts are gone from the upholstery and there are no flower vases. Add these back and Clara Ford would feel right at home.

Before most Americans have ever seen a driverless car, expectations have developed around it. The original automobile was likewise freighted with expectation. It would provide the freedom of the open road—the road trip—and with it the fantasy that women would loosen their corsets. Men would demonstrate their masculinity through mastery of grease, gears, and gasoline. Autoists of both sexes would don the fearsome steampunk look of goggles and gauntlets. The internal-combustion car that had to be coaxed and muscled to life, with its lubes and explosions and thrusting pistons, that would be the car for men. The IC car that would roar and thunder, not slip silently by on electrons, the IC car that would inhale great gulps of atmosphere and exhale noxious smoke. That would be America's car.

Chapter 2

THE CAR FOR PEOPLE WHO HAVE NONE

Several men helped Ford build his first car in 1896, but Norman Rockwell, and Ford himself, advanced the myth of a lone genius and his devoted wife.

THE ELECTRIC VEHICLE COMPANY, HAVING FAILED IN ITS BID to monopolize the Mobility as a Service business, had one more trick up its sleeve: the Selden patent. When it first formed in 1899, the company acquired patents not only on electric automobiles but also for the very idea of the hydrocarbon explosion automobile. The pioneers of gasoline automobiles, men such as Karl Benz and brothers Charles and Frank Duryea, apparently never dreamed they could secure so broad a patent. A little-known patent attorney from Rochester, New York, however, dreamed big.

In 1879, George B. Selden filed an application for "a safe, simple, and cheap road-locomotive light in weight, easy to control, and possessed of sufficient power to overcome any ordinary inclination." Although he filed the patent nearly a decade before the Benz Patent-Motorwagen went on sale, the patent office did not issue it until late 1895. That delay was by Selden's design. He was waiting for the automobile market to heat up. Selden was an okay amateur inventor, but one farsighted patent attorney. History unfairly records him as a patent troll. But, neither he nor the rest of the EVC crowd lived under a bridge.

The Seldenites started to monetize their patent in 1900 by suing the nation's leading automaker, Alexander Winton. After two years of litigation, Winton threw in the towel, prompting industry leaders Olds, Packard, Pope, and twenty-three others to settle as well. The automakers recognized the validity of the patent and agreed to pay a 1.25 percent royalty with one-fifth going to George Selden and two-fifths to the EVC. The balance would go to the newly formed Association of Licensed Automobile Manufacturers, made up of the patent automakers themselves. The ALAM chose its own members and operated as a trade association. It also created staggering new efficiencies by standardizing small parts. It's hard to believe, but automakers used slightly different sizes for things like nuts and bolts. For example, a single parts supplier had to produce 800 different lock washers, using 800 different dies; standardization brought that number down to sixteen. Today, the nonprofit Society of Automotive Engineers (SAE) oversees standardization.

Were they the pure patent trolls conventional wisdom believes them to be, they would have willingly admitted any automaker and collected their royalty. But the ALAM rejected applications from dubious firms lest they undermine the association's brand. Among those turned away was a middle-aged tinkerer who had already failed twice in the automobile business, angering his investors and partners in the process. His newly formed company had dim prospects and barely enough capital to get going. His crazy long-range business plan to disrupt the world looked doomed to fail. Rather than sell into the highly profitable market of wealthy city folk rushing to buy cars, he planned to sell cars in the tens of millions to hayseeds and yokels who obviously could not afford them. His product would be the Model T and his name was Henry Ford.

Henry paid a visit to Fred Smith, head of Oldsmobile and then president of the ALAM in 1903, just as Henry was forming the Ford Motor Company. Would the association look favorably on his application? It would not, Smith replied. Ford Motor was merely an assembler of parts manufactured by others and in any case Ford had already gone bankrupt twice. But, as his company grew, the ALAM demanded a royalty. Ford's investors urged him to settle. Smith met with Ford and his trusted lieutenant James Couzens. Couzens shouted, "Selden can take his patent and go to hell with it!" Smith replied, "The Selden Crowd can put you out of business—and will." Ford, who had been sitting with his chair tilted against the wall like a naughty school boy—as was his wont—jumped up and scowled, "Let them try it." They did.

We need to examine Ford's life, his company, and his car in some detail if we are to appreciate how the shape of American automobility developed in the critical years between 1908 and 1927. The ALAM and Ford Motor Company represent different paths to mass automobility. Under the ALAM, automobility would have diffused steadily outward from the paved cities and downward from the wealthy to the middle class. Instead, mass motorization exploded quickly as rural folks adopted the Model T in greater numbers than their big-city compatriots. To most Americans Ford was a benevolent authoritarian—compared often to Mussolini—who bestowed mobility on the common man. In other words, the Model T was not simply the product of American capitalism but of a particular vision of our motorized future. To understand American automobility, we have to come to terms with the personality of Henry Ford.

*   *   *   *

HAD SIGMUND FREUD sat down with Karl Marx over pastries in a Viennese coffeehouse collective to discuss Freud's new patient, Marx would have ejaculated, "Oh that Ford is a theoretical nightmare! He owns the means to produce machines that annihilate space with time yet he denounces the fetishization of capital and his fellow capitalists."

"Ah, you must understand his relationship with his mother, with his father. You must analyze his childhood," Freud would reply.

Henry Ford was born in 1863, on a Dearborn, Michigan, farm far removed from the raging Civil War. "I never had any particular love for the farm," Ford told an interviewer in 1923. "It was the mother on the farm I loved." Henry's mother had died in childbirth when the boy was twelve years old.

"His was the love of a boy frozen in time," Freud would explain, then add triumphantly, "Of course it was the father who had gotten her pregnant. Sex and death together, you see."

According to Henry, "There was too much hard hand labour [*sic*] on our own and all other farms of the time." He tried to develop soy milk because he considered the dairy cow an inefficient machine. There was no romance in milking her twice a day.

His mother delighted in Henry's tinkering, reinforcing his obsessive fascination with machinery. When a new toy came into the house, the family had to keep it away from Henry lest he dismantle it. His first encounter with a traction engine on the road had him leaping from the family wagon and peppering the engineer with questions. Henry got his first pocket watch as a gift shortly after that encounter. He immediately took it apart.

The pocket watch, his mother's death, and the road engine encounter, all occurred the same momentous year. Suddenly, he was accountable only to his father, William, who did not share his wife's enthusiasm for the boy's tinkering. "My father was not entirely in sympathy with my bent toward mechanics," Ford wrote. When Henry took up fixing watches as a hobby, William took him to task for doing the work without pay. Rather than quit, Henry fixed watches by stealth, slipping out of the house to deliver them. The senior Ford fully expected his eldest son to continue the family business. A well-regarded fixture in the community, William served as a church deacon, member of the school board, and justice of the peace. His own pioneer parents had chopped down the trees and killed off the bears to bust Michigan sod in the 1830s. He and his brothers had inherited this land and made prosperous farms of it. But Henry hated the farm.

At age sixteen, he ran away from the Dearborn farm to the manufacturing center of Detroit, letting his five younger siblings carry on with the 4:00 a.m. milkings. Later, in a last-ditch effort to bring him back to the land, the elder Ford gave Henry forty acres of timber with the proviso that he give up "being a machinist." The idea was for Henry to clear the land for his own farm. "I agreed in a provisional way," Ford wrote, as if he said yes with his fingers crossed behind his back. Henry built a small cottage so he could marry Clara Bryant in 1888, which union produced one son, Edsel. As soon as he was done clearing and selling off the timber, however, he moved the family to a rental in Detroit.

Henry took a job tending steam engines at an electrical plant. He also landed a side gig getting paid by a jeweler for the watch repairs he had been doing gratis. At one point, by his own estimation, he had some three hundred watches on hand. Engines remained his true passion. On Christmas Eve, 1893, Henry brought his first experimental engine into Clara's kitchen. It consisted of a cylinder made from gas pipe, a gear to open the intake and exhaust valves, a homemade piston, and a flywheel taken from a lathe. He taught Clara how to splash gasoline into the cylinder and operate the valves (it had neither a carburetor nor a camshaft). He plugged it into a wall outlet for spark and spun the flywheel. The houselights flickered as it came to life.

Three years later, Henry, now forty-three, produced an experimental vehicle dubbed the Quadricycle. It featured four wheels, tiller steering, and a motor Henry had built based on one described

by E. J. Pennington in *American Machinist*. When he had it running, Henry had a mind to drive proudly out to Dearborn to show
old dad. Clara squeezed in beside him and held their two-year-old
son on her lap. Ford had affixed a doorbell to the front of the little car. Witnesses report that Ford would "clang the gong" to chase
pedestrians off the street. Henry's sister recalled a "sense of bewil-
derment" at riding in her first horseless carriage. William Ford, however, refused the offer of a ride. He stood and stared. "I could see
that old Mr. Ford was ashamed of a grown-up man like Henry fuss-
ing over a little thing like a quadricycle," a friend of the Ford family
recalled. Resigned, Ford drove Clara and baby Edsel back to Detroit.

After reciting this biography to Marx, Freud would explain all
about Oedipus and the theory of displacement. To the automobile
magnate, anyone trying to dictate to him was dad incarnate. That
meant William Ford, George Selden, Fred Smith and the ALAM;
it meant organized labor, it meant investors, New York financiers,
and, to his mind, the rest of the Jews.

Then Marx would make Freud pick up the check.

* * * *

ABSENT DIAGNOSIS AND treatment for oppositional defiance dis-
order, and fixated on mechanical contraptions, Henry Ford went off
the deep end. He quit a good job with the Detroit Edison Company
in 1899 to turn his full attention to inventing automobiles. Clara—
he called his wife "The Believer"—supported him. But it was a bold,
or reckless, move for the father of a preschooler with little money to
spare. He eventually found William Murphy, a friend of his father,
who assembled some money to start a car company. Henry was not
pleased. "A group of men of speculative turn of mind organized, as
soon as I left the electric company, the Detroit Automobile Company
to exploit my car," Ford claimed later. The DAC struggled on for a
few years, selling at most a couple of dozen vehicles. Ford's design
wasn't bad, though plenty of other firms were already selling better
cars. The company built a delivery wagon, an easier proposition than

building a car. Delivery of the delivery wagon took far longer than expected, though it appears to have delivered mail packages reliably when it was finally delivered. The shareholders were still hoping to make money and began insisting that Ford actually build some cars to sell. You know, Henry, like an Oldsmobile or something. People seem to like that. Ford, however, resisted their picayune goals as he continued to refine his universal automobile. The company ended with a whimper.

Having left a steady job at Detroit Edison for the ill-fated DAC, Ford went even farther out on a limb when that company failed. Neighbors began to consider him a full-on nut job. He took what little money he had saved and set about building a racer with faith that winning races would attract capital. Clara and Edsel moved in with seventy-five-year-old William Ford to economize. (Imagine that conversation. No doubt Clara negotiated the terms.) Always lean, Ford shed still more weight. In 1901, he challenged Alexander Winton, not only a major manufacturer and an early signatory to the ALAM agreement, but also the fastest driver in the country.

Detroiters turned out enthusiastically for a day of races. A city judge ordered court adjourned at midday so everyone could attend. Several cars were signed up for the final race of the day, the Sweepstakes, with a $1,000 purse. Only three came to the line, however, and only two got off. The Ford had trouble keeping up with Winton, especially in the turns. Winton had a quarter-mile lead when his engine faltered. The long shot Ford took the checkered flag. Clara wrote to a friend: "The people went wild. One man threw his hat up and when it came down he stamped on it, he was so excited. Another man had to hit his wife on the head to keep her from going off the handle. She stood up in her seat and screamed, 'I'd bet Fifty dollars on Ford if I had it.'"

After the win over Winton, Murphy called the old gang back together to create the Henry Ford Company out of the ashes of the DAC. But instead of converting racing prowess into sales, Ford went after more prize money. Once again, he treated his backers with contempt. As he wrote to his brother early in 1902, "My company will kick about me following racing but they will get the Advertising and I expect to make $ where I can't make ¢s at Manufacturing."

Ford's company kicked quite a bit. The frustrated Murphy brought in Henry Martyn Leland. With a twinkle in his eye, frameless glasses, and bushy Vandyke beard, Leland looked every bit the world-renowned engineer that he was. His pedigree stretched back to the beginning of American mass production and interchangeable parts at the Springfield Armory. By the time Leland set up shop to supply Detroit's growing auto industry, his machines could build anything out of metal more perfectly than anyone else in the world. His parts were accurate down to 0.25 microns—1/300th the thickness of a human hair. Leland had supplied engines for the Curved Dash Olds. His perfectionist machining boosted that engine's horsepower by about 25 percent. Had Ford reconciled himself to the support of the éminence grise—two decades Ford's senior—the Henry Ford Company might have survived. But Ford was a "cut and try" man, unable to read blueprints, according to some who worked with him. Much of the actual design and construction of his cars—from his first Quadricycle to the Sweepstakes racer—had been done by friends and colleagues. Leland was just the kind of mentor Henry Ford needed. Instead, he again blamed his investors: "[The] company was not a vehicle for realizing my ideas but merely a moneymaking concern—that did not make much money." Despite Ford's assessment, Murphy and the other investors made plenty of money once they took "Henry Ford" off the marquee and renamed the company "Cadillac." Leland's precision built the premier American luxury brand. From John McCain's "Cadillac Health Plans" to the singer Lorde's line about "driving Cadillacs in our dreams" the name still connotes luxury and quality. (Ford got his revenge in 1922 when he bought the struggling Lincoln Motor Company from Leland.)

Having quit his own company, again, Ford went back to the races. The car that won the Sweepstakes race against Alexander Winton in 1901 was a buggy that topped out around forty-five miles an hour. His next car, just a year later, was a fearsome machine that shot flames out the side exhausts. It would compete in the five-mile Manufacturer's Cup, "the event of the day, of the meet and probably of the season—for it brought out prominently a new winner in the 'unlimited class,'" reported the *Automobile and Motor Review*. Again it pitted Alexander Winton, commanding his own "Bullet," against the Ford, driven by America's first celebrity racer, Barney Oldfield. The fearless Oldfield had never actually raced a car. His celebrity came from bicycle racing. To appreciate how insane Oldfield was, you have to see the car—christened the 999—on display at The Henry Ford Museum. The engine sucked in five gallons of air twelve times a second and traveled at more than ninety miles an hour. It had no body, steering wheel, transmission, or brakes. Oldfield sat in a gondola-style chair, comfortable in a drawing room but hardly comforting at ninety. He steered by gripping either side of a flat iron bar attached to a vertical pipe. The open crankcase sprayed oil everywhere. When it was over, Oldfield had set a track record. The crowd "awoke in pandemonium and over the fence went Detroiters in bunches to lift the new speed merchant from his seat with outstretched arms and an abundance of enthusiasm."

Victory attracted a new backer. The high-flying coal magnate Alexander Y. Malcomson funded Ford's return to the car business. Malcomson installed his trusted aide James Couzens to keep tabs on the idiot-savant tinkerer. The Ford Motor Company incorporated with barely enough capital to stay afloat. Horace and John Dodge (yes, those Dodges) agreed to build pretty much the entire car for a share in the company. FMC would assemble Dodge parts into Ford cars. Their entanglement would end badly in 1916.

True to form, Ford was soon tussling with his backers. Henry's five investors, as well as the Dodge brothers, wanted him to build the luxury, six-cylinder Model K. But Ford wanted to dump the K in favor of a single model, the popular Model N. The highly praised N, a beta version of the Model T, sold like hotcakes. Nevertheless, at about $2,800—more than five times the retail price of the

Model N—even the lackluster sales of the Model K accounted for most of the company's profits. Henry outmaneuvered Malcomson until the latter had no choice but to sell out his share. Just in time for the Panic of 1907, Henry gained complete operational control of the Ford Motor Company. Malcomson's accountant and fellow investor James Couzens endured Ford's wrath until 1915. Without him, Ford's bookkeepers were said to have been reduced to weighing stacks of invoices to estimate the company's financial position.

By the time the first Tin Lizzie rolled off the assembly line on October 1, 1908, Henry Ford was forty-five. He was on his third car company, and that company was on its seventh model.

The Model T weighed in at just 1,200 pounds with a twenty-horsepower, 177-cubic-inch engine, a 100-inch wheelbase, and room for five in its most popular, four-door configuration. This Touring version sold for $850. The nearest competition came from Overland, Buick, and Oldsmobile. There were cheaper cars, more powerful cars, and more reliable cars, but none at once as cheap, pound-for-pound powerful, and reliable as the Ford. David Buick had the best seller when the T debuted, with a better designed, comparably sized engine and a shorter wheel base of 92 inches. But at 1,500 pounds and $1,250 for the five-passenger model, it was both significantly heavier and more expensive. Oldsmobile's Model 20 offered basically the same package and price as the Buick but with a hefty curb weight of 2,100 pounds.

Ford himself embodied lightness as a virtue. In every picture he appears to have lost weight since buying the suit on his back. While Wall Street bankers dined on fatty meats, Ford literally ate weed sandwiches. Being light, Henry's car could be propelled by a smaller engine. The smaller engine created less torque, which could be handled by a lighter drivetrain and running gear. Vanadium steel, a strong new alloy, allowed lighter parts. Ford made the frame so exceedingly light, in fact, that it flexed and moved with the ruts and craters of the typical rural road. In the title words of the hit song from 1915, "The little Ford rambled right along."

Bending and twisting puts a lot of stress on the engine, gearbox, and driveshaft. To solve that problem, the Model T used only three motor mounts with a gimbaled mounting at the front. Now the frame could twist all it wanted while the motor swung like a sailor in a hammock. As a bonus, the Lizzie was one mount lighter, one mount cheaper! Similarly, Ford considered the usual scheme of using four leaf springs—one at each wheel—extravagant. Instead, the Model T used a horse-and-buggy suspension with transverse springs. The setup made the tall-wheeled T bouncier and tipsier than rivals, but added to its off-road prowess. As a bonus, the Lizzie was two springs lighter, two springs cheaper! Ford cast the entire motor as a single block, which made it stronger and lighter. Its removable cylinder head improved serviceability. Fuel trickled down from a tank under the driver's seat—saving the weight and expense of a fuel pump. Spider Huff, who had designed the ignition for Ford's first car, fitted magnets onto the flywheel to create a magneto. Not only did the magnets generate spark, they worked like the paddles on a riverboat to lift oil from the pan and splash it all over the inside of the engine. The magneto, flywheel, and oil "pump" functions were thus consolidated into one component on a Model T. The rather inefficient thermosiphon principle cooled the motor (more or less): water heated by the explosions in the engine set up a slow-moving current that flowed through the radiator for cooling and then back to the engine. The principle powers the Gulf Stream, so it would be good enough for Ford. Other cars had brakes at the wheels (Panhard et Levassor debuted a popular setup in 1891). A single transmission brake was good enough for Henry. By World War I, most manufacturers had moved on to modern three- and four-speed gearboxes. Ford stuck with two speeds until the end.

To operate the Model T's gears, the driver must confront three foot pedals, none of which is the gas. The gas "pedal" is a stalk behind the steering wheel that looks for all the world like a modern turn signal lever. The pedal to the right squeezes cotton bands around the transmission to set gears in motion and apply the transmission brake. The middle pedal engages reverse, and the leftmost pedal activates both low and high gears. Most people learned to drive on a Ford, so they had no reason to think this setup bizarre. In fact, the transmission was especially forgiving of novice drivers. If you're too young to remember the death-knell of grinding the gears of a manual transmission, you can replicate the sound by dropping a spoon into a garbage disposal. But the cotton bands made for cottony-smooth shifts.

In some ways, the Model T was an open-source car. Ford obviously had a negative view of patent law and never enforced his patents. Better brakes, better wheels, better bumpers, a Ford could use them all, and all were for sale on the aftermarket. Entrepreneurs offered more than 5,000 accessories, including anti-rattlers for the spindle joints, anti-rattlers for the doors, and anti-rattlers for the fenders. Ford Motor itself offered few upgrades. The factory introduced an electric starter option in 1919 for an additional $75, a significant premium. Or you could buy a $10 aftermarket one. For the low price of one dollar, The Hot Spot Generator Company would sell you a gadget to light a fire inside the engine compartment below the intake manifold. The idea was to warm up the air going into the motor to ease starting. Farmers completed the same operation for free with a gas-soaked corn cob. Several makes of auxiliary transmission were available. These sliding-gear (read "grindable") transmissions picked up where the planetary transmission left off to give a greater torque and speed range. With the addition of studded steel wheels the Lizzie so equipped could plow the land. Virgil White invented a kit to add a second rear axle, tracks, and front skis to a Tin Lizzie. About 20,000 of these snowcat kits were sold. Buyers who wanted to go camping without roughing it could bolt on the Lamsteed Kampkar body (built by Anheuser-Busch) and get a half-century jump start on the VW Microbus. Even without such extras, farmers used their Model Ts as utility vehicles. One photograph depicts an enterprising farmer pulling a two-ton load of hay to market. The stack reaches twenty-five feet in the air and drapes over the car until it brushes the ground. The rear axle used as a power take-off (by jacking up the back end), Fords sawed wood, churned butter, and threshed grain. At least one owner used his Ford to power a clothes washer with tremulously disastrous results.

People found plenty of uses for their Model Ts beyond the farm. They took to the road to see America, staying in tourist camps and camping willy-nilly in the National Parks. Just getting out and joy-riding meant a cool breeze on a hot evening. Saturday shopping in town became a thing for farmers. The Sunday drive entered the lexicon and enforced a new kind of family togetherness. The car also let young people roam free from the watchful eyes of parents.

*   *   *   *

THE FIRST FULL YEAR of Model T production, 1909, coincided with Ford's first court loss to the Seldenites. Sales totaled $9 million, which put him on the hook for roughly $110,000 in royalties. Ford appealed, recognizing that he could come out a big winner even in defeat. Ford advertising and an eager press had succeeded in painting the ALAM as a predatory monopoly in a distinctly anti-monopoly political climate. Henry hadn't just jabbed a finger at the ALAM's Fred Smith in private. He had repeatedly vilified the ALAM in public. Spite and marketing found common cause.

Back in 1903, at the same time Smith and Ford were meeting, the ALAM was running announcements describing the twenty-six-member manufacturers as "pioneers in this industry [who] have commercialized the gasolene [sic] vehicle," which was true. They would sue anyone who built, bought, or sold an unlicensed car, they announced. Ford Motor ads replied, "We are the pioneers of the gasoline automobile. Our Mr. Ford made the first gasoline automobile in Detroit, and the third in the United States." None of which was true. Dim was the hope for compromise between two sides unable even to agree on the spelling of gasol(i/e)ne. Henry Ford publicly taunted the "trust." He would give them "$1,000 if they would advertise his business by commencing suit against him." If the Seldenites thought that was just braggadocio rather than proof that Ford would resist settling, they had no insight into Henry's defiant and reckless character. Sigmund Freud did not answer their calls. So the taunts continued until Ford got what he asked for.

Ford spent the next six years paying lawyers. Seeing the patent validated in 1909, more companies joined the ALAM, swelling it to seventy-two members. Ford alone appealed the verdict. It wasn't quite the O.J. trial, but it garnered enormous press. Ford pledged $12 million to indemnify anyone who bought his cars. "Get a Ford and enjoy it. We'll attend to the tom toms," he advertised. Finally, after 14,000 pages of testimony, complex arguments about the technical history of gasoline engines, and a comical demonstration of a patent Selden motorcar that failed to run, the outcome of the widely reported trial was announced in 1911. Ford prevailed.

"The suit became one of the four or five foundation stones upon which Ford's reputation was built," according to David Lewis's exhaustive history of Ford's public image. He became front page news, "lauded on all sides as a giant-killer, as a symbol of revolt against monopoly, and as a magnificent individualist." "All men with red blood" should applaud him, editorialized the *Detroit Free Press*. At the manufacturers' banquet during the New York Auto Show, just days after the final verdict, the general manager of the ALAM and even George Selden himself joked with Ford about the trial. The *New York Times* called it a "Love Feast."

Ford's next court battle, in 1916, pitted him against his earliest backers, Horace and John Dodge. Henry planned to build a new industrial complex on the River Rouge just a few miles from his boyhood home. It would dwarf the existing Highland Park factory, itself a huge plant in its prime, taking raw materials in its great maw at one end and disgorging standard-issue machines at the other. Ford kept enormous amounts of cash in reserve to build the River Rouge complex. Meanwhile, he kept cutting Model T prices. Ford had announced a price cut because he did not believe in earning "awful profits," he told the media. It made no business sense: he was already building Tin Lizzies as fast as he could sell them; by a rough estimate the price cut left $40 million of potential profit on the table.

The Dodges still owned 10 percent of the company, a legacy of their role as FMC's original supplier—manufacturers, really, of its first cars. Ford's price cuts and monomaniacal pursuit of vertical integration and manufacturing scale for its own sake came right out of their pockets. They especially needed cash to expand their own highly successful car company. They entered the market in 1915 and maintained their status as a top-five producer for more than a decade. The all-steel, mid-market Dodge was a step up from the Model T. They wanted their fair share of dividends. That's why in 1917, the day after his son Edsel's wedding, the Dodge brothers sued. The court enjoined Ford, halting construction at the Rouge while it adjudicated disposition of $39 million in dividends.

Victory for the Dodge brothers hinged on Ford's claim that he was not in it for the money but to make the world a better place. The Dodge lawyer asked Ford, under oath, about the purpose of the highly profitable Ford Motor Company. Here is the transcript:

> PLAINTIFF'S LAWYER: No, I will ask you again, do you still think that those profits were "awful profits?"
>
> FORD: Well, I guess I do, yes.
>
> PLAINTIFF'S LAWYER: And for that reason you were not satisfied to continue to make such awful profits?
>
> FORD: We don't seem to be able to keep the profits down.
>
> PLAINTIFF'S LAWYER: Are you trying to keep them down? What is the Ford Motor Company organized for except profits, will you tell me, Mr. Ford?
>
> FORD: Organized to do as much good as we can, everywhere, for everybody concerned.

This time Ford lost even on appeal. The decision was easy. The judge did not have to weigh claims to dividends or evaluate corporate strategy. He simply noted that the purpose of a corporation was to make money, not bestow cars upon the masses.

The Dodges got their millions, but Ford kept up the fight in public. He convinced a gullible press that he would quit Ford Motor to start yet another company to build a better car at half the price. The seven company stockholders saw their investments suddenly at risk. Uncharacteristically, Ford borrowed $75 million to buy them out. It had cost him a fortune, but he emerged in complete control of the company that bore his name.

Ford found himself in dire straits when the economy tanked in 1920. He needed cash. He pressed his dealers to buy more inventory and sell more parts. He reduced staff and consolidated departments. The company collected and sold off anything not nailed down: lamps, tables, files, typewriters. "We literally took out a trainload of desks and furniture and sold them!" he boasted. Every pencil sharpener was sold. The public offered donations.

Surviving the 1920 depression was yet one more win. He had beaten William Ford, Henry Leland, and the Seldenites. He had outwitted Malcomson and the Dodges. He had won the hearts and minds of the working man. Ford's stature grew with each victory. He won and kept on winning. He proved to the world, and to himself, that with an unbending will alone, Henry Ford made all things possible.

Writing in 1926, the great British editor and essayist J. L. Garvin argued that the Model T Ford would resolve the battle between capital and labor, would rescue capitalism from itself. The "exceptional personality as in the case of Henry Ford is more important than ever," Garvin wrote, "for progressive efficiency of production on the capitalist side and for promoting payment, welfare work, and other encouraging conditions." That's what so confounded Karl Marx. Ford was not playing by the rules of the capitalism game. If not a capitalist exactly, what was he? Henry Ford (and I mean this in the nicest possible way) was a totalitarian dictator and demagogue.

Again, the point is not to psychoanalyze Ford, or contemplate the nature of capitalism. I'll leave that to Siggy and Karl. The point is to understand that Ford created a deep connection between automobility and the American creed. Ford's demagoguery aligned a segment of the American car culture with a strand of agrarian Populism that will have no place in the robot car future.

Huge swaths of America embraced Ford as their own Mussolini. "Mussolini of Industry," a radio personality said of Ford after visiting the great man in Dearborn. "Probably Henry Ford would resent being called a despot—even a beneficent despot," wrote Waldemar Kaempffert. The onetime director of Chicago's Museum of Science and Industry was at once awestruck and critical in his 1926 profile of Ford: "[H]e is an industrial Fascist—the Mussolini of Highland Park." Not only did Ford rule the Detroit-area boom town, his factories spread through Europe and his agents were "in every part of the world." Ford himself told Kaempffert, "There is too much tradition in all human activity. . . . If it stands in the way of real progress, it must be broken down." To me, Ford sounds here rather like F. T. Marinetti, the Italian Futurist who, as we saw, celebrated the cleansing fire of the car crash. To Ford biographer Allan Nevins, Henry "was talking like Mussolini" in this instance. A worldwide YMCA poll ranked Ford second behind Mussolini as the greatest living man in the world. Not to be outdone, America's police chiefs took their own poll and voted Ford ahead of Mussolini. Ford extended greetings to Joseph Stalin. Stalin wrote back, "May God preserve him." Adolf Hitler (in 1922, when he was still a mere white supremacist rabble-rouser with his own uniformed militia) decorated his office wall with a large picture of Ford. The table in the outer office displayed German translations of the Flivver King's books. "If you ask one of Hitler's underlings of the reason of [sic] Ford's popularity in these circles he will smile knowingly but say nothing," the *New York Times* reported. "Hitler Acclaimed by 200,000 in Fete" read the headline set next to "Henry Ford Getting High Honor from German Government" on his seventy-fifth birthday in 1938. There was a three-column image of Henry smiling with the Germans as they draped him with a sash and pinned him with the Grand Cross of the German Eagle from Hitler's Reich. Jewish groups organized a boycott, but in fairness, Karl Kapp, the German consul, had traveled all the way from Cleveland to Detroit to confer the medal. Besides, Charles Lindbergh got one. Two months later came *Kristallnacht*.

Ford had no compunction about endorsing the Nazis in 1938 because he had been carrying their water since 1923. Over the course of two years, his newspaper, the *Dearborn Independent*, published *The International Jew*. The preface to the collected editorials began:

"Not only does the Jewish Question touch those matters that are of common knowledge, such as financial and commercial control, usurpation of political power, monopoly of necessities, and auto-cratic direction of the very news that the American people read; but it reaches into cultural regions and so touches the very heart of American life."

Ford Motor sent copies to all of its dealers. Model T customers found *The Protocols of the Elders of Zion* in the back seat when they got home. A leader of the American Jewish community described Ford in 1925 as a "multi-millionaire prodigally pouring his wealth into the crucible of hate." A defamation lawsuit eventually forced Ford to quit it and issue a public apology.

My uncle, an erstwhile rabbi, once described anti-Semitism to me as "hating the Jews more than absolutely necessary." Nativism and anti-Semitism were certainly endemic in the 1920s when support for the Ku Klux Klan was at its height. (Thirty thousand hooded Klansmen marched on Washington in 1925.) So all we need to do with Ford is figure out why he made such a federal case of it. Even his most dogged biographers—apologists and critics alike—cannot explain more than a baseline anti-Semitism. I conclude that his extra helping of Jew hating arose from his belief that Jews had "financial and commercial control" of America. Ford's Jews were Shakespearean Shylocks and the international bankers dragging us into war. They were cosmopolitan and greedy. Ford's opposite views on the "Negro Question" support this analysis. Ford described racial harmony, based on his own experience sawing lumber on the land his father had given him, as "the colored man [sawing] at one end of the log and the white man at the other." He was on close terms with the African-American scientist George Washington Carver. The pair experimented with, among other things, edible weeds. (Ford served his weed sandwiches at meetings, to no one's delight.) Ford also developed relationships with black ministers in Detroit and hired black workers at three to five times the rate of his competitors.

Twice a week or more during the 1920s, the newspapers would report on Henry's doings, his latest pronouncements on war, politics, the economy, education, the inefficiency of the farm, and a good diet. According to newspaperman and future Republican senator from Michigan Arthur Vanderbilt, "Ford had to his credit 'more erratic interviews, more dubious quotations, more blandly boasted ignorance of American history, more political nonsense and more dangerous propaganda than any other dependable citizen that we have known.'" He was an ardent isolationist who believed that nefarious war profiteers (and Jews) were agitating to draw America into Europe's Great War. His views were unchanged as a member of the America First Committee in the lead-up to World War II. Certainly these views were shared by many members of what might best be called "Ford's base." Whether they hated the Jews more than absolutely necessary or not, the Prairie Populists who owned more than half of the Model T's made, were well aware of the frugal farm boy's world view. They feted him in any case.

It would be comical to describe the Model T as an anti-Semitic machine. But in its day, and certainly since its passing, leading writers have reflected on the Model T as the machine for "real Americans," and in this they echo the ideology of Ford himself.

The most often referenced, poetic, and complete panegyric is found in a 1936 *New Yorker* essay and subsequent book. The title says it all: "Farewell, My Lovely!" The author was E. B. White, he of the motherly spiders, talking pigs, and elements of writing style. "It was the miracle God had wrought," White wrote.

Now, I'm not alone in offering a eulogy to an old car (don't get me started on the Saab again). There are engines I miss (stay tuned), but reveries of a transmission? The only ones I've found are to that cotton-banded contraption on the Model T. White sang of the tranny in his essay. He is worth quoting at length:

> The Model T was distinguished from all other makes of cars by the fact that its transmission was of a type known as planetary—which was half metaphysics, half sheer friction. Engineers accepted the word "planetary" in its epicyclic sense, but I was always conscious that it also meant "wandering," "erratic." Because of the peculiar nature of this planetary element, there was always, in a Model T, a certain dull rapport between engine and wheels, and even when the car was in a state known as neutral, it trembled with a deep imperative and tended to inch forward. There was never a moment when the bands were not faintly egging the machine on. In this respect it was like a horse, rolling the bit on its tongue, and country people brought to it the same technique they used with draft animals.

White admitted that the transmission brake did not work, forcing the driver to engage reverse just to stop. It could also fail to find neutral, in which case you could be run over while standing at the radiator to crank the car. But for E. B. White, that was a good thing. "I can still feel my old Ford nuzzling me at the curb, as though looking for an apple in my pocket," he wrote.

White's equine metaphor reflects the image of the Model T as of the heartland in contrast to the Olds, Buick, Packard, and many other higher-priced cars suited to the cities. "As a vehicle, it was hard working, commonplace, heroic," White remembered in 1936, "and it often seemed to transmit those qualities to the persons who rode in it."

White was raised in a New York City suburb, so his equine metaphors are likely more literary than personal. Historian Reynold Wik, raised on a Dakota farm, speaks from direct rural heartland experience. His Model T serves as a defiant rejoinder to literary elites like White. He describes Ford as a folk hero to "the lowly—the farmers, the working men, and the people in the small towns of the nation." Wik counts himself as one of the lowly, having been inspired to pore over the tens of thousands of letters at the Henry Ford Archives by his own experience with a 1920 Model T. (These were the basis of his monograph, *Henry Ford and Grass-roots America.*) They wrote letters to Mr. Ford, "in candid prose, because the common man was too busy to concern himself with literary expression. Few farm hands could shock grain all day in the blazing sun and then spend the evenings writing in the style of William Shakespeare or Thomas Jefferson."

In contrast to these paeans to the Model T, for Sinclair Lewis the "universal car" marks the lower bound of automobile citizenship. When Lewis published *Babbitt*, a satire of suburban life, in 1922, the Model T granted access to motorized society, but only just. Ford sold 1.3 million Model Ts. That same year, however, General Motors sold 460,000 vehicles, all of them superior to the Model T in styling and comfort. The Model T might still be the more practical car for the rutted roads and self-sufficiency of the hinterland, but in the protagonist George Babbitt's suburban milieu, to own a Model T was to cling to the bottom rung of the middle-class ladder. Lewis opens with "a limousine of long sleek hood and noiseless engine" crossing a concrete bridge followed by poor, middle-aged George Babbitt being awakened by the "familiar and irritating rattle of someone cranking a Ford: snap-ah-ah, snap-ah-ah, snap-ah-ah." Babbitt knew from Model T woes:

> Himself a pious motorist, Babbitt cranked with the unseen driver, with him waited through taut hours for the roar of the starting engine, with him agonized as the roar ceased and again began . . . a sound infuriating and inescapable. Not till the rising

voice of the motor told him that the Ford was moving was he released from the panting tension.

White and Wik depict the Model T as the heroic embodiment of rural life. In contrast, Lewis portrays it as a trial to be endured for the sake of automobility.

Without digressing into the resurgent celebration of being uneducated and even willfully ignorant, it is worth again highlighting the enduring presence of the Populist Model T. Although the terms "flyover country" and "coastal elite" have supplanted Flivver-era descriptors, the divide is still very much with us. The Model T's spiritual descendants are the Ford F-Series pickups. In choosing them, buyers choose America. Like the Model T, these body-on-frame vehicles defy change and modernization. Let the Europhiles in Boston drive their Swedish Volvos and the Los Angeles elites have their holier-than-thou Teslas; let New Yorkers rely on ride hailing and Mobility-as-a-Service. We F150 drivers will stick to a rugged American vehicle at home in the heartland, where space and gas are plentiful. The Model T was the best-selling vehicle of its day; Ford's F-series pickups have been the best-selling vehicle in the United States for the last three decades. Pickups from GM and Fiat Chrysler hold the number-two and number-three spots, respectively. The American pickup too transmits E. B. White's "hard-working, commonplace, heroic" qualities to its drivers.

Henry Ford's monomaniacal, dictatorial, and simpleminded approach to running a car company created the original category killer, a juggernaut that swept all other low-priced cars off the field. He built cars in staggering volumes though seemed unmoved by the staggering profits that resulted. The Model T's uniqueness in design and quality has long been remarked upon and treated with wonder and awe. Here at the dawn of the second automobile revolution, attention must be paid as well to the Flivver's wellspring. It arose in contradistinction to the American automobile as intended by the ALAM and as reimagined by today's driverless car prophets.

Yet the personality and the style that had made Ford and his car such a phenomenon proved his undoing. Ford fibbed when he claimed to have told his sales force, "A customer can have any color he wants so long as it is black." But the line speaks truth. At first, orders came in so fast that a waiting list grew. But when customer tastes changed, and the rest of the industry adapted to that change, Ford drove his Model T into the ground.

Millions continued to worship Henry Ford. He was their hero because he had given them a car when they had none. But sales and production peaked in 1923, by which time he had cut prices down below $300 to maintain volume. The Model T was a conveyance plain and simple, demonstrating, if anything, its owner's indifference to fashion. Unfortunately for Ford, fashionable car buyers soon became very different indeed.

Chapter 3

GM'S SLOAN:
We're Not in Kansas Anymore

Movie star Clara Bow posing with her 1927 Cadillac LaSalle Roadster, the semi-custom car that some could afford and to which all could reasonably aspire.

THE CRUSH OF CAR FANS AT THE 1923 NATIONAL AUTOMOBILE Show forced the event's operators to close the doors for half an hour each evening to let the crowds thin out. Inside the Grand Central Palace, visitors saw 350 car models from seventy-nine manufacturers on the main floor and 336 accessories exhibits upstairs. Of these, one little Chevy was the main attraction. "The Long-Heralded General Motors Small Air-Cooled Chassis Exhibited," thrilled the *New York Times* on opening day in January. It was a technological tour de force, the brainchild of one of the industry's most celebrated engineers, Charlie "Boss" Kettering. It would be the "next Model

T," cheaper, yet more powerful and up to date than the old Ford. Buyers would swarm to the dealership to swap Lizzies for GM's lightweight, elegantly simple, robust, and low-priced Chevrolet.

Air cooling has a lot to recommend it. A conventional automobile motor relies on water circulating through the engine block and out to a radiator to maintain the proper operating temperature. Relying instead only on air flowing over the cylinder heads eliminates weight and complexity. "Parts left off weigh nothing, cost nothing, and don't cause service problems," Kettering is supposed to have said. In 1902, the Franklin Automobile Company had introduced a high-end air-cooled model and went on to enjoy modest success. Ferdinand Porsche, an engineer's engineer like Kettering, used only air-cooled motors for generations of Porsches and Volkswagens for these very reasons. The small motors that power chainsaws, lawn mowers, and snowblowers are still air cooled. These engines typically employ cast-iron cylinder heads with integral fins to increase surface area and dissipate heat. But iron conducts heat poorly, so for Kettering's larger motor, cast-iron fins would not suffice. He decided instead to weld copper fins to the iron cylinder head because copper conducts heat with ten times the efficiency of iron. Further, Kettering designed a radically new air-flow system and fin shape. His 1922 patent depicts a single band of copper encircling each cylinder head like the petals of a daisy. A squirrel-cage blower (which looks like a waterwheel) pulls air up through the copper petals and out through louvers in the hood. GM dubbed it the Copper-Cooled engine.

Welding the two dissimilar metals together presented a monumental engineering challenge because iron and copper expand at different rates. But the Boss was up to the task. After graduating with a degree in electrical engineering, the Ohio native had gone straight to work for National Cash Register. He electrified the till and racked up twenty-three patents in five years. Then, he invented the first workable electric starter—widely considered by historians to be among the most significant technological achievements in the history of the American automobile. Some suggest it finally killed the electric car. Others, that it made the gasoline automobile more palatable to women. Henry Leland's 1912 Cadillacs were the first models fitted with Kettering's starter, and Kettering soon grew rich selling starters to every automaker. His Dayton Engineering Laboratories (known as Delco) also created the first electric headlights, a huge improvement over gas lamps. A lightweight, air-cooled car for Chevrolet would outshine any of those, he believed. "It is the greatest thing that has ever been produced in the automobile world," Kettering declared.

Enthralled by Kettering's vision, GM president Pierre DuPont planned production of 1,000 Copper-Cooled cars in February, with a target of 50,000 cars a month by October. Instead, by the end of May, the magical motor was dead.

Customers complained of burning oil, worn cylinders, loss of power, and broken fan belts. The engines ran so hot that the fuel charge inside combusted spontaneously. The rest of the car didn't perform much better. Axles and clutches broke. Out of 759 cars built, a third were scrapped at the factory. GM voluntarily (such a quaint notion) recalled the 100 cars that had actually made it into consumers' hands. The testing had revealed serious flaws in the engine's design and manufacture. It also revealed a serious flaw in the design of General Motors as a corporation. Still believing in his design despite the test results, Kettering blamed the manufacturing engineers and plant managers. They resented being given direction from the head office, according to Kettering, and sabotaged his efforts. The engineers at Chevrolet, as well as the Oakland car division, which also ran tests, blamed Kettering's design. Kettering threatened to quit General Motors. The man at the top, Pierre DuPont, could exercise little authority to intervene because Delco, Chevrolet, and Oakland were in an important sense independent companies. A sequence of consolidations begun in 1916 had landed Kettering the title of GM President of Research, but he remained largely unconstrained as the Boss at Delco. GM bought Oakland in 1909. Chevrolet only joined in 1917.* Thus, what GM required was not better technology but better management. It needed a manager who could integrate many formerly independent companies and balance the egos and interests involved.

GM's founder was many things. A manager he was not. In 1908, two weeks before the first Model T rolled out of Ford's Piquette Avenue Plant, William Crapo Durant started GM. Billy—even when his net worth was pegged at $120 million, no one called him Mr. Durant—was the fruit of an unlikely union. His mother traced her family tree to the *Mayflower* and came from a long line of leading lights. His maternal grandfather, Henry Crapo, was elected mayor of leafy Flint, Michigan, in 1860. Five years later, the voters sent him to the governor's mansion. Billy's father was an unambitious bank clerk who quit working altogether as soon has he married into money. He also drank too much and was "imbued with a mania for stock speculation." Billy inherited an abstemious lifestyle and work ethic from his mother. His impetuous nature and susceptibility to stock mania came from Dad. Just six months shy of high school graduation he suddenly dropped out to look for work. A charming firecracker of a man at five foot eight with a winning smile and bright eyes always alert to the next big deal, Durant didn't much like the job he was given at the family lumber yard. He was not meant for humping lumber. So, he took a second job with a druggist and had a side hustle selling patent medicine. Literally a snake oil salesman, he traveled the countryside putting on medicine shows. From patent medicine, he moved on to selling cigars, water, gas, and insurance. Whatever it was, he could sell it. Next he started selling carriages designed by Dallas Dort (who just happened to be Henry Ford's grade school classmate). The two-wheeled, horse-drawn sulky built of ash and hickory wowed Durant. With its rubine red paint job, it was a one-horsepower Mazda Miata. Durant took the wagon to the

* Technically, Chevrolet bought the much larger General Motors.

Wisconsin State Fair and returned to Flint with 600 orders. That was in 1886. By the end of the century, the Durant-Dort Carriage Company was selling some 100,000 carriages a year.

The snake oil and carriage salesman decided to get into the car business next. Flint-based Buick Motors had a great product and lousy finances. David Dunbar Buick's valve-in-head engine was way ahead of its time. It was more efficient and powerful than the side-valve engines then common. The company was capitalized at $75,000, but in September 1904 it owed $75,000 to three banks. David Buick himself had $11,000 in debt. The consummate salesman signed on to the all but insolvent company as chairman on November 1. He immediately increased the company's market capitalization to $500,000 and by 1908 had created a booming business. Durant then became an M&A specialist, Millikenesque king of the leveraged buyout. Bankers at J. P. Morgan, fresh from rescuing the American economy from the Panic of 1907, saw money to be made consolidating and rationalizing the overpopulated auto industry. Durant promised he could do just that.

The bankers' attempt to organize the major players with Durant fell apart, partly because Ford, enemy of finance capital, demanded cash on the barrel head. Henry also objected that consolidation tended to increase prices. Ford, Durant said, "was in favor of keeping prices down to the lowest possible point, giving to the multitude the benefit of cheap transportation." At this point, Henry was deep into his battle against the Seldenites and their Association of Licensed Automobile Manufacturers. Surely he saw in Durant another attempt to monopolize the industry. As for Durant, he had secured a license with the ALAM but, apparently, failed to pay his dues. He squabbled over details with the Seldenites, but never objected to the organization in principle. After all, Durant too was trying to consolidate the industry.* In any event, the bank of Mor-

---

* The ALAM began legal action against Durant two weeks after he founded GM, but the dispute was quickly settled. Oldsmobile and Buick were already members of the ALAM, but Buick owed back royalties.

gan eventually balked when they suspected Durant of playing fast and loose with Buick stock. Durant was not deterred. On September 10, 1908, he incorporated General Motors as a holding company (the name was spur of the moment as the lawyers discovered "International Motors" had already been taken). He soon had a crowded ark of twenty-nine companies, including Buick, Olds, Oakland (later renamed Pontiac), and Cadillac. He'd lay money on any company with a patent he liked. Cartercar had a transmission made of paper that he thought might catch on. It didn't. He bought the Champion Ignition Company because he thought Albert Champion had a good idea for a new kind of spark plug. He did. In 1909, he again tried to buy Ford Motor, but Henry again demanded actual cash. Cash wasn't really Durant's thing. Had someone told him about credit default swaps he might have fainted from joy.

Billy quickly realized the ark was leaking. Buick's profits were strong, but not strong enough to keep GM afloat. Oldsmobile had great brand recognition but an outdated product. The company's "Curved Dash" buggy was by far the best-selling vehicle in the United States in its prime. Olds moved 5,000 units in 1904. The waltz hit, "In My Merry Oldsmobile" kept the name alive: "Come away with me, Lucille/ In my merry Oldsmobile/ Down the road of life we'll fly/ Automobubbling, you and I." Not until the Beach Boys sang "Little Deuce Coupe" would a car song get such play. Durant needed a new model, but developing one takes time and a large capital investment. He had neither. So, he drove a Buick Model 10 down to the Olds factory:

> Arriving at the plant, I had the body placed on two ordinary saw horses and asked the plant manager if there was a crosscut saw. When it was produced, I asked to have the body cut lengthwise from front to rear and crosswise in the center from side to side (bodies at the time were made of wood), giving me an opportunity to widen and lengthen the body, changing the size and appearance completely. When finished, it was a handsome

creation, painted and trimmed to meet the Oldsmobile standard and priced to trade at $1,200 ($200 more than the Model 10). This gave the Oldsmobile dealers a very handsome small car without interfering in any way with the Buick Model 10. A happy solution to the problem—placing the Oldsmobile Division of General Motors immediately on a profitable basis.

Thus Durant created the appearance of difference between two models from two separate brands that were nearly identical. Still, the Buick in Oldsmobile clothing was not enough to save him.

Two years into his grand project, Durant was out of cash. A group of bankers floated the company a loan on the condition that Durant surrender control to them. Durant was "ignominiously cast out" of GM by "hard-faced bankers at a rate of interest which would have made Shylock crimson with shame." That, according to Henry Ford's sympathetic biographers Nevins and Hill, who make no mention of the bankers' horns. The bankers set about polishing GM, fixing the accounting and setting the company to rights.

It was about this time, in 1914, that the DuPonts began investing in GM. The DuPont family had made its fortune selling explosives. The American Civil War built the business, and it boomed during the Great War. (When Henry Ford denounced the " 'money lenders' whose financial interests caused wars," the DuPonts' ears must have burned.) Seeing the threat of peace on the horizon, Pierre DuPont looked for another business to keep up dividend payments to the rest of the clan. He saw in GM a new outlet for his chemical business. Cars need paint and varnish—chemical coatings. He also believed that when the bankers exited GM in 1915, its stock price would jump. He scored big on that bet. Over time, DuPont ended up owning about a third of GM. In 1928, GM stock accounted for $29 million of the $41 million DuPont earned. (The tight alliance continued until it was broken up under antitrust laws in 1959.)

Meanwhile, the ever-optimistic Durant had started yet another car company. He tapped race car driver and mechanic Louis Chevrolet to produce a car for him to sell. Chevrolet's light car sold well, well enough to put money in Durant's pocket. He immediately plotted his return and found traders willing to exchange each share of their GM stock for five shares of Chevy. In other words, he diluted Chevy's stock and leveraged it into a hostile takeover of GM. (Hostile is the technical term. Durant did not have a hostile bone in his body.) After a proxy fight, Durant returned as GM president in 1916 and "the big show was on again," as his lieutenant put it. In short order he merged Chevrolet and GM, bought Kettering's Dayton Labs, along with the nation's largest body builder, Fisher, and Frigidaire, the appliance maker, among others. He was doing what the Seldenites had done, though by enticing investors rather than wielding the club of a patent. He was consolidating and rationalizing the industry.

The DuPonts did not realize that, as president, Durant had been betting his personal holdings of GM stock, on margin, at the Wall Street casino. When stock prices collapsed during the 1920 recession, it began to appear that Durant couldn't cover his losses. The nobles got nervous. DuPont and his entourage marched into Durant's outer office. "We waited patiently, for several hours, interrupted only by lunch time," wrote one of the wealthiest men in the world, describing the scene to his brother, Irénée. In the inner office, Durant was stalling until he could figure out how much money—and how much debt—he actually had. When he finally gave an audience he had only a few penciled notes of his position. The account was vague but seemed to indicate over $20 million in uncovered debt. "We told him that his position differed so entirely from that represented to us . . . that it was impossible for us to sit in a meeting with him . . . unless he agreed to make a complete statement," Pierre wrote placidly to Irénée. "He did not agree to this point and we left the room."

Billy was too big to fail. Had he started a fire sale of GM stock, the DuPont money would have gone up in flames too. So, the DuPonts did for Durant what the rest of us did for General Motors in 2008: they bailed him out. The GM board sent Durant packing after his five years back in charge and put Pierre DuPont at the helm. Billy tried to relive his Chevrolet glory by creating a new conglomerate, but only his exuberance survived that venture. He would file for bankruptcy in 1936. In the end, he owned a small lunch counter and bowling alley in the shadow of the Buick plant in Flint. At the time of his death, without a penny in capital, Durant planned to build fifty bowling centers across the country. His nephew told reporters, "He no longer can bear the thought of an automobile." For all his stock watering, though, Durant had created a stable of companies that dominated the automobile market and defined the American automobile for the rest of the century.

Pierre DuPont had modernized the management of E. I. du Pont de Nemours and Company, the family business, and the Durant episode demonstrated his level-headed financial acumen. He was more excitable, however, when it came to automotive engineering. He registered a childlike enthusiasm for the Copper-Cooled car in a letter to Boss Kettering: "Now that we are at the point of planning production of the new cars I am beginning to feel like a small boy when the long expected circus posters begin to appear on the fences, and to wonder how each part of the circus is to appear and what act I will like best." As the auto show reception demonstrated, the two swept the press and the public up in their vision. DuPont and Kettering persisted despite the clear evidence that the visionary engine might kill GM. The motor head and his fan boy would have to be reined in.

Fortunately for everyone involved, Durant's acquisition of the Hyatt Roller Bearing Company during his 1916 shopping spree included one Alfred Pritchard Sloan, Jr. Sloan turned out to be a management genius and the most important CEO in GM's history. He was everything that Durant was not. Tall, quiet, and urbane, Sloan had matriculated MIT just as the Panic of 1893 hit. Coxey's Army marched on Washington and William Jennings Bryan preached against the "Cross of Gold." Primal fear of unemployment chased Sloan through the curriculum and he graduated the youngest in his class in 1895. Later that year, he joined Hyatt as a draftsman. The company had good products, a diverse and large body of customers, but was being mismanaged into the ground. Dad lent him some money so that Alfred and a partner could buy out the company's owner and turn it around. Durant later paid $13.5 million for Hyatt, making the Sloans millionaires overnight. True to form, Billy paid out mostly in GM stock. Alfred P. Sloan, Jr., then saved Durant's company from Billy himself.

Sloan had misgivings about Durant's seat-of-the-pants management style as early as 1918. So, he drew up an "Organizational Study" to give some order to the chaos. He dutifully took the fruit of his labors to the boss. Durant reacted enthusiastically, took a copy to study, and then promptly forgot about the whole thing.

That decided Sloan to jump ship before Durant could run GM back onto the rocks. In the summer of 1920, he took a month's leave. Sloan, an elegant figure from his high-neck collars to the spats on his ankles, did what conflicted millionaires do: he ordered himself a Rolls Royce and made the crossing to England to collect it. He and his wife would tour the Continent searching for Sloan's soul. It's sadly indicative of the genre that the biographies of the Great Men of the Auto Industry contain bare mention of women. Yet even by this standard Mrs. Irene Sloan remains invisible. Alfred Sloan, a private man, was even more protective of his wife's privacy. The details are few. Irene Jackson hailed from Roxbury, Massachusetts, and married Alfred when he was twenty-three. The couple had no children. Sloan was so devastated by her death in 1956, after fifty-eight years of marriage, that he immediately resigned the GM presidency. How Irene felt about Alfred's career crisis and the European trip is a mystery. Whatever those conversations involved, the Sloans never took delivery of the Rolls and never made the tour. An Atlantic crossing took about five days in the 1920s, which apparently was long enough for Sloan to make up his mind. They returned immediately to the United States. Alfred would stick with GM out of a sense of duty to the company and to his family's fortune that it contained.

Sloan found Pierre DuPont a more attentive audience for his cherished Organizational Study. DuPont responded as favorably as

Durant had, but DuPont followed through. By this time, the postwar recession had thrown the company into dire straits. "In short," Sloan said, "there was just about as much crisis, inside and outside, as you could wish for if you liked that sort of thing." After Durant's ouster, DuPont remained in charge because it was his money. But he relied heavily on Sloan and made him chief executive on May 10, 1923. "I exercised power with discretion," Sloan said. "I got better results by selling my ideas than by telling people what to do." Where Ford had ruled by fiat, Sloan operated by consensus. Committees would draw up rules to be ratified by other committees and boards. Sloan appealed to GM's corporate commandments and encouraged managers to live by them. Conflicts would be adjudicated in reference to those rules. Soon after Sloan took the reins, the Copper-Cooled Chevrolet would severely test that strategy.

It was just the kind of conflict Sloan's rules were meant to manage. Many years distant from designing roller bearings, Sloan was in no position to challenge either Kettering or the division heads on engineering grounds. In fact, he heaped praise upon the Boss and begged him to stay on board (Kettering did). Sloan simply pointed to the strategic business plan he had developed and that the executive committee had ratified. The Copper-Cooled Chevy did not fit into that plan. GM had ignored "commercial-mindedness . . . to pursue an engineering dream," Sloan said.

Mopping up afterwards, Sloan had a moment of clarity. GM did not exist to make the Copper-Cooled Chevy; GM did not even exist to make cars. GM existed to make money. Sloan formed a committee and the committee wrote down Sloan's first commandment: "The primary object of the corporation, therefore, we declared was to make money, not just to make cars." The company considered. Customers hardly cared whether their engines were wet or dry, they concluded. The company decided. It would cut the engineer's balky contraption loose and wring profits from the existing Chevy. Even if it wasn't altogether new, its development was paid for. Perhaps a bit of color was all Chevrolet really needed.

The star of the 1923 National Auto Show had been an engine. For 1925, it was a paint. Until then, mass market cars came only in black, which was no drawback because, as anyone who has viewed the films of the era knows, everything in those days was black and white. Organizers moved the show out of Manhattan anticipating a larger throng than the crowds of 1923. Stepping into the vastness of the Bronx Armory, a visitor must have felt like a girl in a gingham dress swept off the Kansas prairie and dropped into a world of color. Sloan and DuPont—who, again, had bought into GM in part to become a paint supplier—developed "Duco," a quick-drying color paint. It blew car buyers away. "It has not been possible to give the public lasting colors, lasting two-tone effects because blues, light greens and maroons faded too soon," the *New York Times* reported from the show. "The public has been patiently using cars finished in black, dark green, and dark blue." In fact, Henry Ford's "any color so long as it is black" comment notwithstanding, the first Model Ts came only in red, green, or gray. High-volume production, however, demanded fast drying and only black paint dried fast. Black became standard across the mass market until Duco. "Now we may expect lighter colors, more colors and more combinations to give a touch of individuality to the car," the reporter continued. Recall E. B. White's description of the Model T as "hard-working, commonplace, heroic." "It often seemed to transmit those qualities to the persons who rode in it," he adjudged. Duco painted cars bestowed the opposite: individuality, luxury, and distinction. GM offered the Oakland in "True Blue" and the Oldsmobile Touring car in a "two-tone Duco finish, moleskin gray above molding and Russian brown below, scarlet striping." Color was also a strategy to add more car gals to the army of car guys. "There is much at the Automobile Salon at the Hotel Commodore to interest the woman motor enthusiast, especially the color effects, which are new and daring," a reporter described this small luxury show. Bright, subdued interiors with "more elaborateness in details" were now matched with bright exteriors. By 1927, all of the mass market automakers could buy DuPont paint and give women what they wanted too. Asked to comment on the National Automobile Show, "the artist Captain H. Ledyard Towle" described the show as a "Blaze of Beauty." He added: "The use of lacquer gives the manufacturer an opportunity to try out an extraordinary number of color schemes. The result is that the present show represents the high water mark in color harmony."*

Model T customers too had color options for 1925. Lizzie got an optional nickel-plated radiator, on a "streamlined" hood, and new choices of pinstripes. Buyers could choose Duco paint schemes such as "Highland Green, or Fawn Gray both with Cream Stripe," or "Royal Maroon with Vermilion Stripe." Even a Populist farmer might be enticed. Henry had become, if not a slave, at least an indentured servant to fashion.

Seeing the popularity of color, Sloan extended the strategy. He put styling the body and painting with color first, relegating engineering innovation to the back seat. What GM needed therefore was a Kettering of styling, a man with vision and the determination to see it through. That man was Harley Earl.

Lawrence P. Fisher, of Fisher Body, which Durant had bought in 1916, discovered Earl on a tour of Cadillac dealers in California. (Into the 1990s GM rocker panels still sported an embossed plaque with an elegant blue coach and the words, "Body by Fisher.") Hollywood's A-list were trusting Earl, barely more than thirty, to design custom bodies worthy of the red carpet. What really impressed Fisher was the young designer's methods for creating them. Earl used clay models that he could shape quickly and that would take

---

* In fact, Towle was no disinterested artist. He was the lead colorist for DuPont. That color palette was his. Towle was a camoufleur during World War I, and he worked with GM designer Harley Earl during World War II on camouflage. Towle described his Duco color schemes as "reverse camouflage." See: Elspeth H. Brown, Catherine Gudis, and Marina Moskowitz, *Cultures of Commerce: Representation and American Business Culture, 1877–1960* (New York: Springer, 2006), pp. 27–28, and Regina Lee Blaszczyk, *The Color Revolution* (Cambridge, MA: MIT Press, 2012).

supple curves more readily than the standard wooden mockup. The medium also favored Earl's penchant for rounding off corners and melding individual design elements into a pleasing whole.

Fisher brought Earl to Detroit and set him to work creating a new car for Cadillac. Earl took as his inspiration the Hispano-Suiza, a luxury machine powered by that company's massive aircraft engines. They say beauty is in the eye of the beholder; it is not. It's in the Hispano-Suiza. Automotive historian Ralph Stein describes the spirit of the car, the feeling Earl set out to capture:

> Had you been a gay young Continental in the feverish Twenties, a dashing blade who found it absolutely necessary to transport himself and his blond of the moment from Maxim's in Paris to the gaming tables of Monte Carlo, there would have been only one eminently correct machine for the journey—a Hispano Suiza.

I've had Stein's *The Treasury of the Automobile* since I was a wee lad. The tulip-wood-bodied Hispano-Suiza stretches across two pages of the slim silver volume. I stared at it for hours. I'm staring at it now. The hood takes up the entire forward half of the car. In the *Treasury* image (reprinted from *Esquire*) the owner is at the wheel—because it's a driver's car—while his uniformed chauffeur sits in the distant rear as if in a dinghy towed behind the boss's yacht. It parades slowly down a palm-lined boulevard before an ornate colonial palace. Every car in this luxury class had a custom-built body, made to order. Earl would give the public a semi-custom Hispano-Suiza, a car that some could afford and to which all could reasonably aspire.

Earl's offering, the LaSalle, fulfilled Fisher and Sloan's vision of a stylized car. It came in a range of models—LaSalle was an entire Cadillac sub-brand—but Earl himself, hat set at precisely the right kilter, posed in a two-seat convertible. As on the Hispano-Suiza, the hood takes up the front half. Earl emphasized that proportion by painting the hood one color and the rest of the body another. The wire wheels are relatively small. This lowers the car and emphasizes the elegant fender line. The spare tire rests half hidden in a scooped-out section of the front fender so as not to break the hood line. With the LaSalle, Earl began a career that would define the look and feel of the American automobile for half a century.

LaSalle was such a success that Sloan made Earl head of a new and powerful "Art and Color Section." Remembering the conflicts between Kettering and the GM divisions that helped torpedo the Copper-Cooled Chevy, Sloan told Earl, "Harley, I think you had better work just for me for a while till I see how they take you." Sloan's backing became legendary. According to Bill Mitchell, who worked under Earl and later succeeded him, "He had a button in his office that I inherited where he'd punch Sloan. If he'd had a meeting with somebody who was stubborn, he'd get Sloan and he'd say, 'Alfred,' you know his voice would change, 'how are you Alfred? Well, fine. You know the son-of-bitch Klingler, I want you to fix him.'" No one else called Mr. Sloan "Alfred."

The La Salle, which, poetically, debuted in the year of the Model T's final demise, represented a fundamental shift from an American automobile that drafted people into the motorized army to the American automobile that made each driver feel unique. Each GM brand would mark the driver's place on the socioeconomic ladder. Buyers would climb though fine gradations from the lower-middle-class Chevrolet, through the Olds, and then the Buick, to the upper-middle-class Cadillac. Oakland/Pontiac was always a tough fit. It sort of slotted in between Chevy but was more of a sporty half brother to the others. Even if buyers became brand loyal—"We're a Buick family," "Jimmy's a Pontiac guy"—there was always next year's model. "The change in the new model should be so novel and attractive," Sloan said, "as to create demand for the new value and, so to speak, create a certain amount of dissatisfaction with past models as compared with the new one." The strategy introduced planned obsolescence into the car market. "Automobile design is not . . . pure fashion," Sloan said, "but it is not too much to say that

the 'laws' of Paris dressmakers have come to be a factor in the automobile industry—and woe to the company which ignores them."

By definition, as soon as you drive your car off the dealer's lot, it
ceases to be new (and has the steep market depreciation to prove it).
Travel around the block and you will come upon them again, the
virgin cars, with only three miles on the odometer, looking brighter
and better than your own. A Model T Ford, you bought once and
for all. Instead, GM had you buying again and again. For customers,
that meant taking on debt. Banks were slow to warm to car loans,
so automakers themselves offered financing. Even today, customers
trade in their old models and roll over their car loans. Trade-ins and
car loans mean buying perpetually. The automobile has thus became
a everlasting aspiration, material without being real.

In addition to a new form of buying, Sloanism (as it has become
known) required adopting a new form of manufacturing. Fordism's
highest volume and lowest price strategy demanded highly special-
ized machine tools that could be operated by any idiot. Under Sloanism, flexible machine tools could be reconfigured periodically by a
skilled machinist yet still be operated by an unskilled worker—the
man who, according to Ford, wanted a job in which he did not have
to think. Also, flexible machine tools had a residual value that spe-
cialized tools could not match. A small investment in worker skill
and a careful look at depreciation tables returned huge profits. Ford
never mastered that kind of sophisticated bottom-line calculation.

Of course, the stylized, Sloanist American automobile still carried drivers and passengers from point A to point B. In other words,
it added a new layer of consumerism to the transportation function
of the Model T. It is this duality—the American automobile as both
a transportation machine and a consumer product to be desired,
owned, and enjoyed as a driver—that will make it so difficult for
the driverless car to dislodge. It may well be possible to find a better transportation machine, an automated pod, perhaps. How such
a machine would fulfill the American automobile's second purpose
remains to be seen.

Again, the American pickup truck offers a case in point. Into the 1990s, the pickup was a low-priced utilitarian vehicle, a modern Model T. Drivers put up with poor handling, slow acceleration, and a lack of the convenience and comfort options found on automobiles. They gave up the back seat. Today, pickups are no-compromise vehicles with comfortable seating for five, powerful engines, and better handling. What were once modern-day Model Ts—simple, rugged, easy to repair—are now Model T simulacra. But they now trade in the emotional appeal of conservative, rural values, Henry Ford values, rather than their substance. The men who buy them are no more immune to the dictates of fashion than the customers of Paris dressmakers. Men don't go in for petticoats, of course, so their fashion statements are advertised on patriotic (or jingoistic) NFL and NASCAR telecasts as rugged machines for building America.

Sloan's insistence on profit over all, and his reliance on consensus rather than fiat, had a dark side. GM never demonstrated much in the way of social responsibility. Obviously putting profits first had this effect. But there was more to it in Sloan's case. He all but dissolved himself into the company. Whereas Ford called his wife Clara "The Believer," Sloan dedicated his book to Irene as his "Partner in the Enterprise." People have a conscience; bureaucracies do not. GM's attacks on safety and environmental legislation, and its periodic scandals, have a long history that began with the adoption of laminated safety glass during the 1920s.

The transition to closed cars meant more glass, and more deadly shards. In fact, some buyers resisted enclosed cars because of the glass hazard. Safety glass had been invented in 1906 in England and (beginning in 1923) was marketed under the trade name Triplex. It consisted of a sheet of celluloid (a plastic) sandwiched between two sheets of plate glass, which strengthened the glass and kept it intact. As with four-wheel brakes and other safety features, Detroit lagged behind the Europeans. Triplex entered the US market in 1926. Ford adopted it almost immediately. A test driver, Harold Hicks, went through the windshield of a prototype Model A, the Model T's successor. "The two Fords [Henry and Edsel], looking at the wreck of that car, decided right then and there that we must have laminated glass in the windshield," according to Hicks.

GM was fully aware of the benefits of safety glass. Its Yellow Cab division had ordered safety glass for the partitions between the passenger and the driver. But GM resisted using safety glass at first and then introduced it as a selling point. Cadillac got safety glass all around for the 1929 model year. "Protect yourself and your family with Crystal-Clear Non-Shatterable Security-Plate Glass," headlined one ad. Eventually this luxury feature would work its way down the GM product line, but profits could be maximized by selling it at the highest end first. Giving safety glass to all brands at once would violate Sloan's first commandment and Sloanism itself. "The way things stand now with our volume increasing at a decelerated rate," Sloan wrote, "I feel that such a position [of adding shatterproof glass] can do no other than to materially offset our profits." The urging continued until finally, in 1934, several states prepared to require it by law. Sloan still resisted, telling a meeting of the National Automobile Chamber of Commerce that "compulsory use of safety glass in cars was very costly and meant many millions of dollars of expense to buyers of cars." Sloan next called for a delay until all states could agree on a deadline.

The story of safety glass is one of GM's resistance to outside pressures and of using even safety to distinguish its makes from one another. The story of leaded gasoline is one of the company's architects actively pursuing a product known to be dangerous: lead.

Lead is highly toxic. Children exposed to lead suffer decreased muscle and bone growth, and develop learning disabilities and behavior problems. High levels of lead can cause seizures, unconsciousness, and death. Adults can also develop maladies such as high blood pressure, memory and concentration problems, and muscle and joint pain. These facts make it a poor candidate for burning inside an engine and exhausting into the air we breathe. The toxicity of lead had been known for at least a century in the period around 1920 when GM researchers decided it was, in fact, the perfect candidate for burning inside an engine and exhausting into the air we breathe. It solved the irksome problem of engine knock. And, while it was neither the only nor the best antiknock compound, it was the gasoline additive that best served the interests of GM and DuPont.

From the beginning, internal-combustion engines had a troublesome tendency to make a knocking, or pinging sound, especially under heavy load, such as when going up a hill. After the fuel-air mix enters the engine cylinder, the rising piston compresses it. The fuel charge is then ignited, greatly expanding its volume and thereby pushing back down on the piston. The more it is compressed, the more violently and powerfully that explosion occurs. That's a good thing because it gives you more power and efficiency out of a given amount of fuel. Too much compression, however, and the explosion happens so quickly and with so much force that it smacks hard against the piston. Engine parts take a beating and much useful work is lost. Fuel research took on a new urgency in the 1920s because experts began predicting that the gasoline supply would be used up in twenty to thirty years. That posed an existential threat to GM and oil companies such as Standard Oil. Kettering realized that greater compression would allow engines to become far more efficient—fifty miles per gallon was suggested. Ethyl alcohol—bio-fuel in modern parlance—would eventually be needed, Kettering believed, but would demand enormous amounts of farmland. Meanwhile, high compression gasoline could serve as a bridge fuel. Kettering and his assistant Thomas Midgley experimented with dozens of additives before identifying tetraethyl lead as a suitable solution. It is not entirely clear why Kettering and Midgley began to argue around 1923 that tetraethyl lead—which Kettering had renamed "Ethyl" to keep GM's research secret—was the only option. They had discussed iron carbonyl with German chemists who considered it an effective and far less toxic antiknock additive. The Europeans adopted that.

GM opened an experimental production line in 1923, which was shut down in 1924 when two workers died. These deaths in April were not reported, but when another worker died in October (at a second plant), the newspapers took notice. The New Jersey medical examiner found that a "mysterious gas" at the plant was causing insanity. The following day another worker died and forty more were hospitalized. The Public Health Service held hearings and warned of lead poisoning but did not have the authority to do much about it. The development of Ethyl, at the time still a closely guarded trade secret, had become big news and a big problem for GM. A number of prominent scientists wrote directly to the researchers to warn of toxicity. But GM moved forward toward commercialization.

Sloan had become "gravely concerned about the poison hazard" following the first deaths. It is hard to know what actually worried Sloan. Was it worker health or the potential public relations fiasco? It is hard to know because Sloan ordered all of his records destroyed upon his death. Writing in 1963, Sloan said that when Midgley did his research, "Of course he did not yet appreciate . . . the toxicity . . . problems." In fact, Midgley had taken a leave in 1922 and gone to Miami to recover from lead poisoning.* Midgley and his colleagues knew the lead hazard well. But they also knew it could be highly profitable. Midgley calculated that supplying Ethyl to just 20 percent of the gasoline market would net about $40 million a year for GM and its partners. He was way off. Heavily marketed Ethyl became such a huge hit that it knocked competing antiknock compounds out of the market. It achieved 90 percent market share.

The predicted energy crisis passed, as they always seem to do. This has been a recurring pattern in the history of the American automobile. The price of gasoline spikes. One side proposes reducing the amount of gasoline used (through conservation, better engines,

---

* Midgley died at fifty-five in a bizarre accident that might have been related to lead poisoning. He developed paralysis and so designed a harness to help him get out of bed. One day he became entangled in the contraption and died of strangulation.

or alternative fuels). The other side says, "Drill, baby, drill." The other side always wins. Lead additive did not end the energy crisis of the 1920s. Instead, new geological tools revealed huge new oil fields. New refining techniques extracted more and better gasoline out of every barrel of oil. The octane rating—a measure of gasoline's anti-knock properties—improved. GM did not use higher compression engines to double gas mileage as promised. Instead, GM (and Ford and Chrysler) used them to produce more power. The gas stations advertised Ethyl, the toxic killer with the name of a kindly old aunt, as a magical product: "Try just one tankful of Ethyl, just for the sheer fun it will put into your driving. Feel the fun of having the back of your seat nudge you forward . . . hear the fun of hushed, obedient power. . . ." Poison or not, GM loved lead, as did a public hopped up on Ethyl.

Behind all of Sloanism, indeed behind the entire car culture of the 1920s, sat envy. During the Roaring Twenties, even as most incomes grew, income inequality grew more. It reached a point not seen until, well, now. No matter how shiny the new Chevrolet, it paled in comparison to a Cadillac. Pretty as it was, a Cadillac was still a poor man's Hispano-Suiza. Then there were those who could not even swing the new Chevy. They were left with a broken down old Ford.

F. Scott Fitzgerald makes this automotive desire central to the plot of *The Great Gatsby*. Fitzgerald was a car guy. "When I was a boy, I dreamed that I sat always at the wheel of a magnificent Stutz," he recorded in his notebooks, "a Stutz as low as a snake and as red as an Indiana barn." (Jay Leno describes his Stutz as the equivalent of a Camaro or a Mustang "back in the day" and "one of the sexiest cars of the period.") Fitzgerald did own a Stutz Bearcat for a time. He ended up, however, driving a second-hand Ford. A "dust-covered wreck of a Ford crouched in a dim corner" represents that same thing for cuckolded mechanic George Wilson in *Gatsby*. He'd like to sell it, but even if he does, there's little profit to be had. Tom Buchanan has promised to sell him an expensive coupe that Wilson might turn over for a profit. Sadly, Buchanan only dangles the coupe as cover for his trysts with Mrs. Wilson. Pathetic George Wilson will take his revenge, with a gun.

Like Wilson, Americans struggled to get hold of the cars GM dangled before them. Buying a Model T once and for all was one thing, but trading in an old car to buy a new car every few model years took some doing. By 1923, nearly 80 percent of buyers took out a loan to purchase their cars. As the market for cars grew soft, more and easier credit was extended.

Durant had built GM on a pile of credit. His success was spectacular until his debts caught up with him. The same was true of the automobile economy writ large. Loans were repaid. Prosperity reigned. Until it didn't.

Chapter 4

AUTOMOTIVE ANXIETY DURING THE GREAT DEPRESSION

REACTOGRAPH MACHINE

Dr. Lowell Sinn Selling, director of Detroit's Traffic Court Psychopathic Clinic, tests the reactions of a traffic scofflaw in his battle against "insanity at the wheel."

"WHEN MR. AND MRS. MIDDLE AMERICA SAT DOWN ON their front porch to read, in their small town far from the Madison Avenue crowd," explained John Heidenry in his biography of Lila and DeWitt Wallace and the American literary institution they created, "the magazine that brought a smile to their faces was the *Reader's Digest.*" With 1.5 million subscribers, it was the most widely circulated magazine of the day. The *Digest*, of course, collected articles from other publications and shortened them down to be read by porch light. But after listening to a tow truck driver tell stories of the wrecks he had collected, DeWitt Wallace decided to take a chance on original storytelling. He wanted something that would cut through the background noise of accident statistics and "drive carefully" pabulum. He hired J. C. Furnas to report on the kind of grisly scenes he'd learned of during his ride in the wrecker. For the August 1935 issue, Furnas came back with "—And Sudden Death," a shockingly graphic description of motor vehicle bloodshed.

"Like the gruesome spectacle of a bad automobile accident itself, the realistic details of this article will nauseate some readers," an editorial warning began. "Those who find themselves thus affected at the outset are cautioned against reading the article in its entirety, since there is no letdown in the author's outspoken treatment of sickening facts." Who could *not* read ahead after that introduction? Furnas rails against the dry statistics of the safety propagandists. Even their posters are too tame. They dare not relate the full picture, which should be a motion-picture complete with sound effects, he says. The movie would show:

> the slack expression on the face of a man, drugged with shock, staring at the twist in his broken leg, the insane crumpled effect of a child's body after its bones are crushed inward, a realistic portrait of an hysterical woman with her screaming mouth opening a hole in the bloody drip that fills her eyes and runs off her chin . . . the raw ends of bones protruding through flesh in compound fractures, and the dark red, oozing-surfaces where clothes and skin flayed off at once.

His message: "You're gambling a few seconds against this kind of blood and agony and sudden death." Furnas was not unaware of the designed-in dangers of the American automobile. He notes the "lethal array of gleaming metal knobs and edges and glass inside the car." He quite properly describes the steering column as a spear aimed at the driver's liver, spleen, and abdomen. The best possible outcome, he adds, is to be "thrown out as the doors spring open." Individual moral failure and disregard for one's fellow man were the article's themes, not the designed-in dangers of automobiles or roads. Furnas delivered a jeremiad to every careless driver. He took his title from the Anglican *Book of Common Prayer*: "Good Lord, deliver us. From lightning and tempest; from earthquake, fire, and flood; from plague, pestilence, and famine; from battle and murder, and from sudden death."

Eight million reprints of the story were ordered and sent out to some 8,000 corporations. General Electric provided it to every stockholder. Judges handed it to traffic offenders in court and had them copy it out word for word. The state of Wyoming issued it with license plates. Tollbooth operators gave copies to Manhattan commuters. Newspapers began to adopt the title and the tone when they reported on crashes. A syndicated cartoon and movie short also appeared based on the piece. Arthur A. Ballantine, one time under-secretary of the treasury, published "After 'Sudden Death,'" a call for automobile liability insurance reform. When Furnas died in 2001 (at the age of ninety-five), the article formed the centerpiece of his obituary. More than one safety expert of a certain age pointed to the article as a factor in their career.

There is no evidence that the "Sudden Death" media storm caused drivers to exercise more caution or choose safer or less speedy cars. Bigger, higher compression motors could propel a sedan at ninety miles an hour or more, and they sold. In fact, generations of high school driver education students were later subjected to the very thing Furnas wished they would be: motion-pictures complete with sound effects. Studies conducted since the 1970s have shown they don't make teens safer drivers. Furnas did, however, crystallize a generalized anxiety around the car culture. I don't mean to suggest that concerns about automobile safety were insincere, only that such concerns are endemic. As we have seen, automobile violence— "Privileged Sports" running down children—had been there from the beginning. Newspapers periodically editorialized and depicted the Grim Reaper at the wheel, mowing down pedestrians. The National Safety Council, which began as an industrial safety organization and grew to lead the traffic safety movement as a quasi-public agency in the United States in the 1950s, not only publicized the annual death toll—which Furnas did not think provided enough of a jolt—but produced propaganda posters depicting grim scenes. Historians who sift the media looking for hand-wringing over automobile violence will find it in every era. Death and the automobile have always gone together.

My focus here is on the particularities of this angst and the historical specificity of the solutions in the Depression era. For example, today's traffic safety experts decry drunk, distracted, and lead-footed drivers. The only thing left is to eliminate these bad drivers with smart driverless cars that reduce accidents by a factor of ten or more. The safety conversation in the 1960s depicted the automobile itself as an unsafe and therefore defective product. To err is human, but it should not be a death sentence. In the 1930s, the safety conversation took place within the context of a severe economic depression. Laissez-faire capitalism caused chaotic boom-and-bust cycles of great prosperity followed by misery and hunger. The Depression brought forward radical ideas—some more palatable than others. Father Coughlin on the radio called for nationalization of industry and wannabe dictator Huey "Kingfish" Long in Louisiana called for limits on wealth accumulation. Francis Townsend proposed a guaranteed income for people over sixty years of age. Upton Sinclair ran for California governor in 1934 with a plan to "End Poverty in California" through progressive taxation and works programs. The free market had failed and something else had to take its place. Franklin Roosevelt's New Deal program grew the federal government and centralized authority to rein in the forces of capital and save capitalism from itself.

The road too would have to be reined in. J. C. Furnas called on drivers themselves to use the manners and sense that seemed to exist before the automobile—or at least before the Model T passed from the scene. But that solution was backward looking. Despite his more graphic depiction, traffic safety efforts had appealed to manners and morals since the beginning. It had become clear by the 1930s, however, that such entreaties did not work. Drivers could not be expected to police themselves.

Increasingly, traffic had become seen as an engineering problem. The earliest traffic engineers were not engineers at all; they were municipal managers, men who kept the sewers from backing up, the lights on, and the streets clean. Their field was governing. Civil engineers began to replace municipal managers by the 1930s. To them, traffic was less a problem of proper governance than a problem of fluid dynamics: smoothly flowing traffic became their ideal. Forensic psychiatrists and industrial psychologists also tried to solve the traffic problem by identifying high-risk, or "accident-prone" drivers. Some bad drivers were educable, according to the theories of Freudian psychology, but others were simply ill suited to the speed and dangers of the automotive age. In the name of traffic safety, they began identifying and fixing or removing inferior types from the road. Imbeciles, idiots, the feeble minded, mental defectives, and morons (all clinical terms in those days) would have their licenses stripped. The poor, immigrants, and African Americans, they found, might also have to be removed. Call it automotive eugenics, the same American science behind compulsory sterilization, which was upheld by the Supreme Court in 1927 "for the protection and health" of society. Road society deserved nothing less.*

Also, the automobile had generated the economic activity, shaped governance, and defined progress itself. So, it is no surprise that Depression-era anxieties about the nature of capitalism, governance, and progress itself affected the evolution of automobility. During the 1920s boom, car factories consumed a quarter of the nation's

---

* It is important to understand that the American eugenics movement was in the mainstream of scientific thought in the United States until after World War II. Although we might look back and assess the field as pseudoscientific, that is not how it was regarded at the time.

machine tools, three quarters of its plate glass, 80 percent of its rubber, and 90 percent of its petroleum products. In 1926, automakers sold $3 billion worth of cars and Americans traveled 141 billion miles. By 1929, there was one car for every 4.5 persons in the country. The whole country could go a-motoring all at once. Governments spent $2.24 billion on roadbuilding and collected $849 million in motor vehicle taxes. Roadbuilding in turn encouraged new home construction, new schools, and the expansion and relocation of businesses. Automobile services, from gas pumps and garages to motels and tourist camps, all contributed to economic activity. Historian Thomas C. Cochran concluded that the economic impact of the automobile on the economy of the 1920s is unknowable. "No one has or perhaps can reliably estimate the vast size of capital invested in reshaping society to fit the automobile."

As long as that immeasurable expansion continued, it was easy to ignore those in the industry who were warning about market saturation as early as 1925. New drivers accounted for three out of every four cars sold in 1913 but only one in four by 1927. Also, income inequality had worsened during the 1920s, narrowing the market breadth that had supported mass motorization. Despite the boom, the lower 93 percent of the nonfarm workforce had actually seen their disposable income fall during the second half of the decade. So, automakers and their dealers had to sustain themselves on replacement sales. Even those got harder to come by as cars got incrementally better and more durable. The number of cars over eight years old increased by 50 percent between 1929 and 1931. So, they juiced the market with easy credit.

Along with everything else, the automobile revolutionized consumer lending and the culture of indebtedness. "Until automobiles came off the assembly lines by the millions, there was no other object of universal use so costly as to require a scheme for time payments," wrote historian Daniel Boorstin. Alfred Sloan understood early that extending credit to buyers would not only facilitate sales but create an ancillary profit stream. He had gotten involved in the car loan business in 1915, even before joining GM. At the time, many sober bankers still considered automobiling a frivolous luxury or even a passing fad, and therefore unworthy of credit. In 1919, Sloan created the General Motors Acceptance Corporation to extend loans to GM customers. By 1923 nearly 80 percent of the 3.5 million cars sold were bought on time. By 1925 there were more than 1,700 finance companies. To keep moving the metal, dealers lowered payments and extended loan terms from twelve out to eighteen and twenty-four months. They extended credit to bad risks—subprime loans in the modern idiom. When the loans went bad, those 1,700 finance companies ended up repossessing and then dumping used cars on the market, further suppressing prices and undercutting new car sales.

Henry Ford's pronouncements against debt and bankers notwithstanding, even Ford Motor got into the business of "buying on time"—as consumer loans were then known. Edsel Ford set up the Union Guardian Trust as a holding company to buy stock in twenty-five Michigan banks in order to facilitate car loans. When many of those loans were not repaid, the teetering mountain of debt collapsed. The holding company took to shifting money from one account to another and one bank to the next just ahead of monthly financial reports. It was a madcap financial farce. They told state regulators one thing and shareholders another. In 1932, the company reported an income of $1,316,952 before issuing a small correction. By "$1.3 million profit," they really meant "a $1.8 million loss." The federal response could only be called corrupt. President Herbert Hoover tried to prop up the Michigan banks with a loan from the government's Reconstruction Finance Corporation, even though Union Guardian had no collateral. Hoover was determined to go ahead, in violation of the rules, until then Senator James Couzens—the same man who had split with Ford in 1915—threatened to denounce the loan from the Senate floor. Hoover then asked Henry Ford to cover the loan with $50 million of his personal fortune. Ford said he would not risk his own money "to keep Jim Couzens from making a speech."

Repossessions, bank collapses, and market saturation clobbered the industry and the market for new cars, but not Americans' desire to own and drive them. New car sales fell by 75 percent, from 4.5 to 1.1 million between 1929 and 1932. Yet car registrations fell by only 10 percent. Historian James Flink considered the case of Muncie, Indiana, more closely. New car sales there had collapsed, but gasoline sales held relatively steady between 1925 and 1935, and the number of cars per capita rose slightly. Flink chose Muncie because the town was the subject of the famous "Middletown" studies by sociologists Robert and Helen Lynd. On their first visit to Middletown (as they called Muncie) in 1925, the pair saw that automobility had rewoven the fabric of society. On their return, they found the car's impact undiminished: "If the word 'auto' was writ large across Middletown's life in 1925, this was even more apparent in 1935, despite six years of Depression," they wrote. Residents held on to their automobiles when they could barely afford to keep them in good repair or even fill their tanks with gas. The automobile had become a necessity as much as a marker of success. They "cling to it as they cling to self respect," the Lynds reported.

"Cling" is the operative word because, without the means to buy a new car, the old jalopy had to hang on. The same is true today for those who have yet to recover from the Great Recession or have long been on the wrong side of the inequality equation. Periodic surveys show that a third or more of families don't have savings enough to pay $500 for an unexpected car repair. Along with the anxiety are the indignities. There is the key fob that no longer works, so your passenger has to stand in the rain waiting for you to unlock; the electric window that struggles to close, and the broken cup holder that dumps your coffee at every sharp turn. The grinding noise from the brakes is ignored to the point where filling the gas tank more than halfway becomes an exercise in hope. To drive a Saturn (a defunct GM brand) that was built in Spring Hill, Tennessee, twenty-five years ago is to live in constant fear of being stranded at the side of the road.

As John Steinbeck described in *The Grapes of Wrath*, things were little different during the Depression. "Along Route 66, . . . the men driving the trucks and the overloaded cars listened apprehensively. How far between towns? It is a terror between towns," Steinbeck wrote. Tom Joad's apprehension fills his senses as the family's Hudson labored on toward the promise of greener pastures. The migrant drivers feel with their feet on the floorboards and the palms of their hands on the gearshifts. They learn the difference between rattling tappets (noisy but not harmful) and a thudding so low and faint that it is felt more than heard (could be oil starvation). A broken fan belt, a blown tire, or a catastrophic radiator leak may strand them. The Joads travel 2,000 miles to California, worrying every mile.

* * * *

THE ANXIETY ON THE road was matched by anxiety in the auto plants. In an earlier era, workers looked to their companies for largess. Business was booming in the teens and most of the twenties, so much so that a worker unhappy at one plant could easily find work at another. In fact, in 1914, Henry Ford faced such high turnover that he famously announced a "Five Dollar Day." He would double worker salaries, he said, to help out the common man. As usual, the realities did not quite measure up to the press releases, but workers cheered Henry and flocked to Ford's factories. Ford announced he would do the same again when the Depression hit, but he could not maintain such largess—or single-handed control of workers' fates. He had reopened his factories in 1927 to build the new Model A. But in the spring of 1932, he again had shut down to retool for a new model and again laid off his workers. On a frigid spring day that year, thousands marched from Detroit to Ford's River Rouge colossus in Dearborn. They were met with tear gas, fire hoses, and bullets. With the "Ford Hunger March," the era of welfare capitalism in the automobile industry ended and the age of industrial unionism began in earnest.

Unionization drives by the politically radical Industrial Workers of the World (the Wobblies) attracted attention as early as 1909, but gained little traction with auto workers. Also, skilled craftsmen had joined guilds and unions since the nineteenth century. But industrial unionism—organized by industry rather than by the nature of the job—only began in earnest during the Depression. In November 1936, GM workers began a series of "sit-down strikes" to win recognition of the newly formed United Auto Workers. A crowd of 150,000 supporters gathered in downtown Detroit. Workers struck GM plants around the country, but the real action was in Flint, the General's birthplace. Alfred Sloan complained that workers were ungrateful and that the union had committed "terrible acts of violence" and finally "seized our properties" to achieve its ends. But he got little sympathy from the Congress or FDR's secretary of labor, Frances Perkins. (Sloan hated her with a passion.) On January 11, Flint police tried to stop food from being delivered to the plant and a battle broke out. Strikers threw nuts and bolts and milk bottles at the police. Police fired riot guns and tear gas, but failed to dislodge the strikers. Michigan governor Frank Murphy called out 4,000 national guardsmen, who set up gun emplacements, fixed bayonets, and surrounded the plant. But he refused to have them attack the workers. After six weeks, GM capitulated. The UAW then organized Chrysler after strikes at nine plants in 1937.

In May, UAW leaders were awaiting a shift change during which they would leaflet workers. A photograph captures the small group standing on an overpass, smiling, as they are approached by Harry Bennett, Ford's pugilistic head of security, and his enforcers. In the next shot, they are being beaten. Despite Bennett's efforts to confiscate film, one photographer was able to sneak his out. The "Battle of the Overpass" turned the tide in favor of labor. But Ford held fast, even through ten days of strikes in 1941. In the end, it was Clara's threat to divorce him if the conflict continued that changed Henry's mind.

*   *   *   *

THROUGH COLLECTIVE ACTION, labor gained some control over their working conditions. Calls for safe driving, collective action— up to and including the Furnas article—were not working on the road. Some spoke of "automobile rabies," others, "motor madness." Somehow, it seemed, otherwise sensible people went crazy behind the wheel. While the workers were taking control from below, traffic safety in the 1930s would demand control from above.

Miller McClintock earned a PhD in municipal management from Harvard's Department of Government and published *Street Traffic Control* in 1925. It became the standard work for training in the field. Supported by Paul Hoffman, president of Studebaker, McClintock established the Bureau of Street Traffic Research at Harvard.* He directed transportation studies for major cities, including Boston, Chicago, Cleveland, Kansas City, Los Angeles, San Francisco, and Washington. Sometimes he enlisted Boy Scouts to stand on street corners and count cars. McClintock worked hard to distinguish himself as a professional technocrat who applied scientific principles to the street traffic problem. "The opinions of casual observers have often been helpful . . ." he wrote in *Street Traffic Control*, "but more frequently plans and methods based upon such information in assisting a city with its street problems have been found useless or worse than useless."

The amateur he had in mind was William Phelps Eno, scion of a wealthy New York City real estate family. Eno attributed his almost unnatural love of traffic control to a childhood trauma: his mother and he had become trapped in a "blockade" of traffic on Broadway in 1865. Only about a dozen carriages were caught up in the jam, but the seven-year-old Eno saw that no one had a plan for untangling the mess. He vowed to bring order out of the street traffic chaos. In 1909, he convinced New York City's police commissioner to institute the nation's first comprehensive set of traffic regulations. His

---

* As a matter of convenience for McClintock, the bureau was initially created at UCLA.

favorite tool was the gyratory (the traffic circle, rotary, or round-about, depending on your local dialect), around which traffic would flow smoothly, like water in a stream. He railed against the "block system" of traffic lights and perpendicular intersections. "Vehicles accumulate behind the block and rush through in a mass when the block is raised instead of filtering through continuously," he com-plained. In 1921, he created the Eno Foundation for Highway Traffic Regulation with *Ex chao ordo*—order from chaos—as its motto. Eno subsequently endowed a program at Yale and offered a scholar-ship to students who would study the gyratory.

McClintock agreed that Eno's beloved gyratory was suited to large, open spaces. But, on congested streets, "it has been attempted in various cities, but that in practically all cases it has been discarded after a thorough trial." Also, it had "one very serious disadvantage." Pedestrians cannot cross unless traffic stops. For city traffic, there-fore, McClintock promoted the block system to accommodate the automobile to the city and give pedestrians a fighting chance.

In 1936, Harvard president James Conant and dean of engineer-ing Harald Westergaard started pushing McClintock and the BSTR out. Traffic "engineering" should be taught by engineers, they said, not by some guy in the university's Department of Government. McClintock's data collection by Boy Scout and subsequent analyses did not pass muster with the engineers. He immediately severed his ties and joined the program underwritten by Eno at Yale but left in 1942 and never looked back. He became president of the Mutual Broadcasting System, was executive director of the Advertising Council, a board member of Muzak (the elevator music people), and produced educational films.

Before the Ivy League intrigue, McClintock had already secured his status as the nation's celebrity traffic engineer. That there even was such a creature speaks to public enthusiasm for anyone who could help solve the "traffic problem" and, in so doing, restore prosperity.

It's hard to know what to do with a tale of sexually charged traffic lights. H. L. Mencken, the caustic critic of American culture, considered traffic engineering worthy of a short story in his middle-brow magazine. In 1933, Samuel Grafton wrote "The Traffic Engineer" for Mencken's *The American Mercury.* The story opens with our hero admiring the new "triple light installation at Dead Man's Corner." The cop on the beat steps up and salutes. "They cuss when they got to wait out a triple light, but nobody is going to be killed here anymore," he says. But our hero has gotten crosswise with a corrupt city councilman whose brother-in-law sells an inferior brand of traffic light. His job in jeopardy, the traffic engineer takes time to contemplate his life's work:

> He ran his hand caressingly over the mound [of reports]. As he stood there he saw through the window a lithe young girl of slim waist and high breast, crossing the street, attractive even though high-heeled short-vamp shoes made her feet look like the hooves of a dainty little horse. I may have saved her life by some of my lights, thought the traffic engineer. . . . It's possible. He felt like a knight taking a solemn oath on a sacred scroll as he stood there with his hand on the pile of reports.

Grafton's story may have been satirical, but it is hard to tell because nonfiction portrayals of the traffic safety establishment sound to the modern ear just as comical.

Consider traffic policing. Franklin Kreml taught courses with McClintock at the BSTR and later founded an institute at Northwestern University devoted to traffic policing. He promised to reduce traffic crashes by "selective enforcement" of laws, focusing on those drivers and those violations most likely to cause a crash. He used bogus statistics as evidence that his schemes worked brilliantly. The press presented him as a heroic traffic cop fighting traffic crime. Tales of the Evanston Accident Investigation (AI) squad, worthy of the era's radio crime dramas, began to appear in popular magazines. Writing for *Atlantic Monthly,* one author enthused,

> A new kind of detective has begun to unravel a comparatively new kind of crime in the United States. . . . Small boys will hold him in awe and weary men of affairs will regale themselves by reading of his sleuthing. . . . His prey includes storekeepers, dentists, clerks, housewives—the kind of people most of us are. The crimes in which he specializes are those which involve violations of the traffic laws.

When the AI squad came upon an intersection accident and got conflicting accounts, they pulled out their special AI-squad camera, their special AI-squad lights, their special AI-squad brake testers, and their special AI-squad typewriter of the type that small boys held in awe. Each driver blames the other, but the detectives are not fooled. "When you put your brakes on you were traveling not less than 30 miles an hour," the AI cop tells the dissembling driver. "My instruments tell me that from the length of your skid mark and the condition of your brakes." No matter, the guilty driver is so impressed by the "power and intelligence of the police" that he pleads guilty and pays a $25 fine. Perhaps this propaganda worked. Based on Gallup and other pollsters, support for stricter enforcement was overwhelming. Of course drivers favored stricter enforcement of *other* drivers.

The traffic engineers and traffic police remain as critical elements of traffic safety and they are still considered apolitical experts—technocrats. In other words, whatever their fledgling errors, we still believe in the underlying premise of stoplights, one-way streets, and deterrent policing of the rules of the road. Another breed of traffic safety expert has not fared so well: the traffic psychotechnologist.

Industrial psychologists and forensic psychiatrists were out to combat "Insanity at the Wheel," according to the title of a *Scientific American* cover story from 1939. The subject of the article was Lowell Sinn Selling, director of the Traffic Court Psychopathic Clinic for Detroit's municipal court. Selling's lieutenant, Alan Canty, had no graduate degree, so he gave himself the title of "traffic Psychotech-nologist." The clinicians used the tools of Freudian analysis to iden-tify and weed out bad drivers before they could cause serious harm.

Drivers were sent to the clinic if a judge or even someone at the DMV thought they might be a bad risk. In his article, "The Ortho-psychiatry of the Young Traffic Offender," Selling described the nine-teen psychophysical tests that "patients" underwent. At the end of a five-hour ordeal, the psychiatrist would write up a diagnosis and recommendation for the court. Some lost their licenses while others were let off. Remarkably, although nearly every patient received up to a dozen diagnoses of mental deficiency, there is almost no correlation between driving history (traffic infractions, recidivism, or accidents) and the recommended punishment. Instead, punishments correlate strongly with diagnoses which in turn correlate with race, ethnic-ity, gender, and sexual proclivities. Clinicians concluded that African Americans were often "primitive," "feeble minded," and therefore "poor risks" as drivers. So, they were twice as likely as whites to lose a license after a clinic visit. Gender bias is revealed in the fact that women were rarely sent to the clinic. Those few who were examined got to keep their licenses more often than men. Nearly everyone over sixty-five was labeled "senile."

Selling and his colleagues come out even worse when you see the qualitative data. I've reviewed thousands of these medical records, and here are two of my favorites. "This is an unpleasant dark haired Jewish boy with thick lips and a long nose." Of the Roman Catho-lic son of a Syrian immigrant, "a swarthy individual who is not too pleasant looking."

As the Motor City, Detroit judges believed they should take a leading role. But the Recorder's Court Traffic Clinic was not alone. Similar clinics operated in Chicago, Baltimore, and other major cit-ies. In addition, the Harvard Traffic Bureau established fifteen "field clinics" to educate drivers and evaluate their fitness for the task. "These clinics have tested several hundred thousand persons and have visited nearly every state," according to the BSTR's psychologist Harry R. DeSilva.

Tellingly, DeSilva's report on "accident repeaters" in the *Journal of Psychology* saw fit to record immigration status and parentage. Using "199 volunteers" and "56 repeaters," the latter presumably coerced into the study, DeSilva found, "Of the repeater group, 21.5 per cent reported foreign birth, a figure approximately 13 per cent higher than shown by the volunteers." Russians, he found, were the worst.

Getting bad-risk drivers off the road would not only save lives, it would help save democracy. As automobility exploded, American courts did not have the bandwidth to cope with all of the violations and all of the disputes arising from crashes. In 1932, a writer for *American Magazine* embarked on an 8,000-mile survey of traffic courts in twenty-one states:

> I found, throughout the nation ample justification for a growing bitterness among our millions of motor car owners who have come to resent and ridicule an outrageous system of traffic law enforcement which violates almost every American principle of justice and equality.

Other commentators referred to "tribal justice" and called out both ticket fixing and small-town speed traps. Expert opinion supported such press accounts. "What [motorists] see and hear—and sometimes smell—in these courts does not tend to create respect for law," noted the Chief Justice of New Jersey. Here the justice highlights a serious side to the way the average citizen experiences traffic jurisprudence. The most likely interaction between most middle class people and the cops in daily life is mediated through the automobile. The traffic stop—then as now — thereby shapes public attitudes toward policing. Today, we spend little time in traffic court. The cost in time taken to go to court is so much higher than the cost of a ticket, that the traffic officer has become judge, jury, and executioner as soon as they write the ticket. In the 1930s, however, a court appearance was common. "Our kind of government cannot exist long once respect for the law is destroyed," the chief justice warned.

Underlying this threat to democracy was the sheer volume of traffic court cases. A 1930 study of 431 cities found that about 40 percent of the arraignments in lower courts were for traffic violations alone. The volume of cases was, in turn, a function of the chosen solution to the traffic safety problem: deterrence policing of driver behavior. Just as the city was remade to fit the automobile in the postwar era, jurisprudence was reformed to facilitate automobility. Today, a parallel system of administrative justice, mostly adjudicated by insurance company claims adjusters or a cop on the scene, has freed up the courts. Even that administrative system will become redundant in the age of the driverless car.

Historians have tried to explain Eno as a "car owning millionaire," and dismissed Kreml and McClintock as shills because of their industry funding. The evidence does not support those accusations. McClintock, for example, argued against such perks as free parking. "After all," he wrote, "the ability of a transportation vehicle to bear terminal charges at both ends of the run is not a very severe test of its utility." Eno loved horses, became obsessed with traffic before there were cars, and never drove.

The point, however, is not whether they were champions of automobilists or pedestrians. It is that the traffic engineering, traffic policing, and traffic psychotechnology of this period were interlocking brands of sophistry. Lowell Sinn Selling's admixture of racial science and Freudian psychology, his offensive pseudoscience, was unleashed by the claim that neutering "poor-risk" drivers, reducing them to mere passengers and pedestrians, could advance road hygiene. It rested atop the claim that traffic police were conducting themselves in a just and scientific manner rather than, for example, harassing black people for driving. The traffic engineer's light presupposed Fred the cop, the state's instrument of deterrence and force. An unbroken chain connects the traffic light to the red-light runner to the police stop to the day spent in an overwhelmed court to the final promise that the traffic psychiatrist could excise bad drivers before they could kill again. To the algorithm wizards and their disciples, we are all of us sinners, all bad drivers, so we all must go.

* * * *

FURNAS'S FAMOUS *Reader's Digest* article was often paired with a Grant Wood painting, *Death on the Ridge Road*. Although each was created without the other in mind, both appeared in 1935, and the two were reprinted and adapted together.

Wood presents to the viewer a rural landscape that has been distorted by odd angles and disjointed shapes; the pieces don't quite fit together. Even the light confuses, the rolling hills at once bright and in shadow. It takes a moment to orient yourself. Then your eye follows the barbed wire and the power lines to the hilltop. Now the scene resolves around a red juggernaut of death rising over the ridge. The freeze frame of machines in motion suggests a narrative. The trucker must be racing to market to get the best price for his product. The sinewy, up-to-date, deluxe model is too powerful and fast to be hobbled by the ambling yokel in the Model A. It sweeps past a puttering Ford as it races up the hill and around a bend. The crash will be head on. The trucker alone stands any chance for survival. The chauffeur, everyone, surely everyone in the luxury car, will die in an instant or bleed out in the wreckage.

We cannot see inside any of the vehicles, but one can imagine the pair from Wood's "American Gothic," subscribers to the *Reader's Digest*, driving the sedate Model A. *Death on the Ridge Road* is really about that couple, easing along in their mild-mannered car over the same route they have been traveling since they got their first Model T. They are not innocent of the metropolitans and their inhuman speed. After all, their grown children still come home from the city once a year. But here on the ridge road, the high-speed, urban culture has suddenly, violently invaded their quiet lives, their "simple, elemental existence," as the artist described it. Wood, an Iowa native, was a proudly Midwestern painter. He rejected the abstract modern art he had seen in Europe, responding with a style art historians call Regionalism.

Furnas and Wood go together because they share a wistfulness for the slower, simpler times when people set on the front porch and knew their *Book of Common Prayer* hymnals by heart. Wood criticized Depression-era automobility with its darting metropolitan limos and hurtling red cubes of commerce entirely unsuited to the curving, cresting, two-lane highways endemic to the American heartland. A Furnas reader might swear off speeding, certainly speeding along winding country roads. On the other hand, a Wood viewer might reasonably come to the exact opposite conclusion: the rural road with its blind curves and steep hills was unfit for modern motor traffic. Fast cars weren't the problem; in fact we needed to produce more of them to put union members back to work and supercharge the consumer economy. Heavy trucks and impatient drivers weren't the problem either. Installing traffic lights, enforcing the rules of the road, and eliminating bad drivers might reduce the death toll. But there could be no *Death on the Ridge Road* at all if the ridge on the road were eliminated. Why not put a wider, flatter, straighter, faster road in its place? Why not build roads to put people back to work, improve safety, and, best of all, expand mobility? That is exactly what we did.

Chapter 5

THE HIDDEN HISTORY OF THE SUPERHIGHWAYS THAT TRANSFORMED AMERICA

GM's Futurama exhibit at the 1939 World's Fair drew 25 million visitors. From plush seats on a "magic carry-go-round" visitors gazed down on the world of 1960, a superhighway utopia.

FEDERAL GUIDELINES FOR THE INTERSTATE HIGHWAY SYStem allow only a gentle incline of six feet for every hundred feet of horizontal roadway. Interstates must have at least two lanes in each direction and opposing traffic must be physically separated. Changes in direction are accomplished with banked curves that outsmart centrifugal force and are gentle enough to allow full visibility as drivers ease through them. Such superhighways allow no possibility of a *Death on the Ridge Road* because there are no ridges, no blind curves, and no need to challenge oncoming traffic to pass Ma and Pa Kettle. In effect, engineers designed the IHS to compensate for the driver's worst behaviors and the nuts behind the wheel who had been slowing down the continued rise of automobility.

We associate the Interstates with the postwar era of booming babies, conspicuous consumption, and backyard barbecues. In 1956, Congress passed the National Interstate and Defense Highways Act (formally known as the Federal-Aid Highway Act of 1956) and construction began. For many Americans, it was a time of renewed prosperity and peace following a dark age of economic deprivation and war. The civil rights movement was gathering steam and the US automobile industry stood astride the world. Under President Dwight D. Eisenhower—for whom the system is now named—corporate Republicans were in ascendance. Popular historians and commentators usually only tell us what the Interstates *did*. They facilitated white flight, urban decay, and geographic segregation by race. They favored the automobile over mass transit and created a deadened landscape of sprawl. They provided for the national defense in the shadow of the hydrogen bomb and brought distant cities and natural wonders within reach. To understand what the Interstates *are*, however, we need to start at the beginning. The Interstates are not the product of Republican free-market ideology but of its opposite: statist central planning by Washington. Rather than a celebration of individual, automotive freedom, superhighways are a form of concrete commuter rail. The Interstates are safety, they are urban renewal, and they are a monument to hope for a better future. We will continue to get everything precisely backwards as long as we start only with the birth of the Interstates in the prosperous 1950s and the presidency of Dwight Eisenhower. To put things right, we must go back to the moment of conception during the Great Depression and the presidency of Franklin Delano Roosevelt.

FDR summoned Bureau of Public Roads head Thomas MacDonald to the White House in 1937. The president had a US map pinned to the wall and on it he drew three east-west and three north-south routes. He asked for plans to create a "self-liquidating" highway network—one that would pay for itself. After two years of study, MacDonald delivered *Toll Roads and Free Roads,* his superhighway blueprint, to FDR and the Congress. The federal government had opened the Office of Road Inquiry to study rural roads in 1893. But the first coast-to-coast route, the Lincoln Highway, was a private affair in 1913. The feds only began funding roadbuilding with the first Federal Aid Road Act of 1916. At the time, crossing the country by automobile was still a daredevil's adventure. In 1940, the Pennsylvania Turnpike, later designated Interstate 76, opened as the nation's first superhighway. But World War II diverted resources from highway building, and it would take until 1956 for the many stakeholders to wrangle out a funding mechanism to build the Interstates.

The rationales for building the system changed little from conception to fruition. The highways would provide jobs, eliminate crashes, renew the cities, and all around be just lovely. When he received the *Toll Roads* report, FDR immediately seized on it as a job-creating public works program. MacDonald, who led the nation's roadbuilding agencies from 1919 until 1953, believed strongly that the highway network—like Hitler's *Autobahn*—would be critical to national defense. Paul G. Hoffman of Studebaker and Miller McClintock, the nation's celebrity traffic engineer, had long advocated for highway building on the basis of safety. Two years before *Toll Roads and Free Roads*, a parallel federal report, *Our Cities: Their Role in the National Economy*, had already been put before the president. It noted that the "outmoded street system" had produced "blighted areas and slums, premature land subdivisions, and jerry-built potential slums." Modernist planners would use interregional highways as a tool for clearing "slums" and renewing the cities they cut up and encircled. The Interstates would serve all of these rationales and more. The public demonstrated enormous enthusiasm for superhighways when they thronged GM's Highways and Horizons exhibit at the 1939 World's Fair. Millions of visitors got a glimpse of 1960, the future that superhighways would unleash. The roads would be so wide, fast, and capable of handling so much traffic, that they would remake the world.

More prosaically, the American Automobile Association, commercial truckers, the construction trades, the Portland Cement Association, and even state governments—all thought highways were a good idea. And they all wanted someone else to pay for them.

By 1956, the reputation of auto executives had been thoroughly rehabilitated from the days when Henry Ford shuttered his plants and Alfred Sloan faced off against the sit-down strikers who had "stolen company property." FDR and the New Deal were out; big business and free enterprise were in. No one summed it up better than General Motors CEO "Engine" Charlie Wilson. Ike had nominated Wilson to serve as secretary of defense in 1953. At his confirmation hearing, a senator asked Wilson if he might face a conflict between his interest as a stockholder and champion of GM and his interest serving the US Government. "I cannot conceive of one," Wilson replied, "because for years I thought what was good for our country was good for General Motors, and vice versa." Again, if we see the Interstate Highway System as the product of the tail-fin era, we get things backwards. The pendulum had indeed swung away from central planning, labor unionism, and the Great Depression. The Interstates, however, were a throwback. To build them was to celebrate not the freedom and self-determination of the automobile but the power of the state to limit freedom for the greater good.

George Will got the Interstates backwards in his critique of the Obama administration's efforts to invest billions of dollars in high-speed rail infrastructure. In a piece in *Newsweek* in 2011, Will mansplained that "liberals love trains" because they hate freedom:

To progressives, the best thing about railroads is that people riding them are not in automobiles, which are subversive of the deference on which Progressivism depends. Automobiles go hither and yon, wherever and whenever the driver desires, without timetables. Automobiles encourage people to think they—unsupervised, untutored, and unscripted—are masters of their fates. The automobile encourages people in delusions of adequacy, which make them resistant to government by experts who know what choices people should make.

When the average person or innocent commentator misinterprets the political and sociological impact of the Interstates, she or he should be educated. When a Pulitzer Prize–winning pundit with a PhD in politics and a resume that includes six years as editor of the *National Review* misrepresents the Interstates to present a pernicious interpretation of the American automobile and American politics, he should be derided. The goal of such representations is to beggar mass transit by defining it as un-American and socialistic in contradistinction to the great American automotive freedom machine. How dare anyone challenge my love of country or car because I want to ride a superfast train from Boston to Washington?

In fact, the Interstate Highway System was by any measure the largest government project in American history and it was neither a blueprint for nor an exemplification of American freedom. The federal government put up $116 billion of the $129 billion that it cost to build the system over the course of four decades. Government experts laid out the system's 41,000 miles of highways with design speeds of fifty to seventy miles an hour, and established ever increasing standards for the comfort and safety of drivers. Government planners decided where to put the 1.6 billion metric tons of rock, sand, cement, and asphalt in the system. In the process, they scripted and supervised people's movements, choosing where they could alight and escape. To do all of this they razed entire districts of homes and shops using eminent domain to condemn and take privately held land. They succeeded in producing the most fantastically expensive and obdurate system of transportation in history. During the Roosevelt administration, Progressive experts were ready to do whatever it took to restore prosperity and build a future that reflected their values.

Whether or not Progressivism depends on "deference," it does have an abiding faith in the ability of rational analysis, science, and engineering, to reduce the hazards of modern life. Food and housing safety, environmental conservation (not to be confused with preservation), and even market efficiency can be improved by rational, expert control. The efficiency expert Herbert Hoover was a Progressive and Progressives celebrated the automobile as a cleaner, safer alternative to the horse. But automobiles did indeed go hither and yon and parked wherever they pleased. At first, automobile roads did not exist. Again, the Model T's off-road prowess was a great virtue because outside of town even the roads were off-road. Automobilists wanted to go faster and more comfortably, however, so governments improved on dirt roads with crushed stone and pavement. Still, hither and yoning traffic was crashing with deadly frequency on ridges, at intersections, and on two-lane highways.

Studebaker's Paul G. Hoffman translated MacDonald's plans for lay readers in his 1939 book, *Seven Roads to Safety*. He explained that engineers have eliminated left turns. "The safe way to make a left turn is to keep going to the right. That's the basis of the 'clover leaf.'" "Intruders" must be "excluded" with access limited to "infrequent, carefully planned places of entry." Just as passengers cannot jump on a liberal's train while it is in motion, drivers can only enter the freeway at dedicated stations—on/off ramps—for safety's sake. Superhighways could "eliminate 98 percent of highway accidents," according to "Dr. Miller McClintock; We could build highways so nearly accident-proof that drivers would have to be very ingenious to cause them!"

Land to build cloverleafs and accident-proof highways could be taken by eminent domain. But one plan to pay for such expensive highways depended upon expropriating an additional tens of thousands of square miles of private property and depositing it in government accounts. Thomas MacDonald knew how to engineer fast, safe roads, and figure out where to put them. He was an "engineer's engineer." The *Washington Post* described him in 1934 as "Blue-eyed, canny, he hugs his desk but gets enthusiastic over the open spaces. Likes to pound rocks, hunt for road sites and breathe ozone." He also engineered ways to pay for them. He had titled his 132-page landmark report *Toll Roads and Free Roads* with the funding question in mind. The real title should have been "No Toll Roads" because MacDonald had already concluded that tolls would be inadequate and counterproductive. He came to this conclusion honestly. His studies showed that sparsely traveled sections of the network could not generate enough traffic for tolls to cover construction costs. He also argued that the cost and disruptions of collecting tolls diminished their usefulness. Long queues might encourage drivers to choose alternate, toll-free routes and thereby undermine the whole project. Building and staffing tollbooths, not to mention stocking them with chocolate chip toll house cookies, costs money.

No one should doubt that had MacDonald and the Bureau of Public Roads come down on the side of tolls, the face of the nation would look entirely different. With a toll, the driver pays for driving by the mile. Without a toll, the marginal cost of driving—of going that extra mile or extra hundred miles—is a small fraction of the total cost of car ownership. In essence, the more miles you drive, the cheaper every mile becomes. The most revolutionary yet unexamined aspect of the driverless car business model as it is now emerging is that it will charge riders by the mile.

In lieu of tolls, or the increased gas taxes opposed by truckers, motorists, and the states, MacDonald proposed a Federal Land Authority for "excess-taking" of a right of way. The idea was for the government to take by eminent domain a wide swath of land—far wider than needed for the actual road. The road would raise the value of that land, which the government could then sell at a profit.

As if by magic, the road would pay for itself. FDR loved the idea. Parsimonious legislators would have no reason to object.

To build support for his excess-taking scheme, Roosevelt held a "no black tie—very informal" stag dinner at the White House with Norman Bel Geddes as the guest of honor. Bel Geddes had created GM's Futurama, which was proving to be the most popular exhibit at the 1939 New York World's Fair. It was a visionary plan not just for new highways but for the exciting future that such highways would bring into being. A scale model of the Futurama exhibit (itself an enormous mock-up of the "World of 1960") was set up in the West Hall of the White House. Guests would see what dreams may come from excess-taking. Roosevelt would use MacDonald's Federal Land Authority to take land for roads and anything else he could think of. Had FDR read *Toll Roads and Free Roads*, Appendix C, "Excess Condemnation for Purpose of Recoupment," he might have realized that the Supreme Court had already nixed the idea. MacDonald did offer some thoughts on the "possibility and legal status" of excess-taking in that appendix. The excess-taking plan never reached the court. Sadly, despite the dinner party, senators and congressmen wouldn't get on board. Until the day he died, FDR regretted not offering an open bar at his very informal, no-black-tie stag dinner.

Taking an extra wide swath of land would also have increased the highway's usefulness as a tool of urban renewal. Looking at the origins and destinations of urban traffic, MacDonald's researchers had found that most drivers wanted to "leapfrog" from their leafy suburbs over their old urban neighborhoods (those places they had escaped when they had enough money) to get to the central business district. The report found:

> The former homes of the transferred population have descended by stages to lower and lower income groups, and some of them have now run the entire gamut. Almost untenable, occupied by the humblest citizens, they fringe the business district, and form the city's slums—a blight near its very core! Each year a few of

these once prouder tenements, weakened by want of repair, tumble into piles of brick, not infrequently taking a human life in their fall. Each year a few of them make way for parking lots—unsightly indexes to needed facilities of higher dignity!

Highways would cut the Hooverville rot from the city like a surgeon's knife. By the time the bulldozers actually got to work on urban Interstates in the 1960s, such "urban renewal" had become controversial to say the least. One man's slum turned out to be another's vibrant African-American or immigrant neighborhood.

The Depression-era hope for highways has become part of the driverless car dream. Enthusiasts claim that the always in motion robot cars will eliminate the need for parking lots. Such eyesores could then be redeveloped for "facilities of higher dignity." As history shows, however, parking lots were built not to serve a demand for cars but as a last resort to derive income from unprofitable land.

Using roads to weed the urban fabric has a long history. Baron Haussmann's wide radial avenues cleared out the clutter and disease of Paris beginning in 1853; traffic circulation was at the center of Daniel Burnham's improvement plan for Chicago in 1909; Le Corbusier, Frank Lloyd Wright, and Norman Bel Geddes all drew visionary, modernist plans that used roads to cleanse the city. Perhaps intentionally, their sketches have buildings and roads, but often no people. Superhighways, along with urban "superblocks," would raise such plans to staggering new heights. They would kill the city to save it.

Of course, the statist New Dealers had passed from the scene by 1956, when funding for the IHS was finally sorted out and work began in earnest. Still, central planning and encouraging automobility was necessary to defend the nation in the Cold War. The role of the direct military rationale for building the Interstates, however, can be difficult to characterize. The system's great origin story, as good as any told by a Silicon Valley unicorn, doesn't help. Once upon a time, mobilization for World War I had been slowed by clogged rail lines. In 1919, after the war, a convoy of army trucks embarked on a combination victory tour and cross-country trek. The "truck train" followed the Lincoln Highway. A young lieutenant colonel named Dwight David Eisenhower took part. His report concluded that driving heavy trucks across the country was impossible without better roads. Therefore, Ike built the freeways and the rest is history. In 1991, the official name of the IHS was changed to the "Dwight D. Eisenhower System of Interstate and Defense Highways."* Wartime evacuation served as another rationale for highway building. Annual "Operation Alert" civil defense drills during Ike's presidency practiced evacuating cities by highway to dodge the Soviet atomic bombs. The president evacuated to a tent city outside Washington. Peace advocates decried these as propaganda exercises, given the absurdity of outrunning a hydrogen bomb in heavy traffic. In any case, adding "defense" to any bill during the Cold War aided passage. The "National Defense Education Act" passed in 1958.

The Pentagon still includes virtually the entire IHS in something scarily called STRAHNET (not to be confused with SKYNET, the artificially intelligent neural net that became self-aware and set off Armageddon in the *Terminator* films). STRAHNET defines the Interstates as key to the "logistical ability to rapidly move troops to the theater." In any case, the statism and central planning of the New Deal go hand in hand with military planning for national defense. The network was always conceived of and built to serve civilian needs first and foremost.

In the end, a federal gas tax was enacted to support a highway trust fund in 1956. States, which had resisted an underfunded federal mandate, went happily along with the new math: the feds would pick up 90 percent of the construction costs. The Portland Cement Association, the truckers, the automobile companies, the AAA,

---

* Keep a lookout for small commemorative signs standing in odd places along the Interstates. They have five stars in a circle with the words "Eisenhower Interstate System" on them.

and Ike could all declare victory. Ribbon cuttings and ceremonial ground breakings became routine, and more than one state claims to have built the first mile of Interstate. These highways are so massive, inert, and commonplace, that they have become part of the landscape. It is as if they have always been here.

American studies professor Cotton Seiler casts a fresh eye over that landscape when he explains:

> The Interstate Highway System was an attempt to affirm and reproduce the practices associated with the individualistic "American character," at a time [the 1950s] in which anxieties about that character's decline enabled the performance of an idealized political subjectivity. . . .

Seiler writes for an academic audience steeped in European social theorists. But he correctly identifies a strain of cultural analysis that tries to make sense of driving the Interstate as both rehearsing American ideals of freedom and submitting to governmental control. When the exit ramps lead only to crawling surface streets and Howard Johnson's has the concession for every rest stop, you are trapped on a concrete rail line of the central government's making. Sometimes critics fail to balance those negatives against the comfort of familiarity and the luxury of commanding your own private rail car at breathtaking speeds of seventy—or eighty—miles an hour.

Today, the Interstates account for just 1.2 percent of all road mileage but a quarter of the total vehicle miles traveled. How you feel about the Interstate Highway System likely depends on the amount of traffic congestion you face on your commute. Always remember that you're not stuck *in* traffic; you *are* traffic. You, and all of those drivers around you, have chosen the highway over surface streets or underfunded, mismanaged, and crumbling mass transit systems. We'll return later to the life course of the Interstates, to the racism and anti-urbanism of their building. For now, I want to admit that they are monumental and at times intentionally beautiful creations. Engineers prefer straight lines, but sometimes add curves to give drivers the perfect view of the city skyline or inspiration as they pass below mountains and over rivers. The highwaymen took good care of their customers, the drivers. Highways razed city neighborhoods and have scarred the land. Still, they are twice as safe as surface streets and can be stunningly beautiful to drive on a supercharged road trip. They remind us, for better or worse, what it is to be an American.

PART TWO

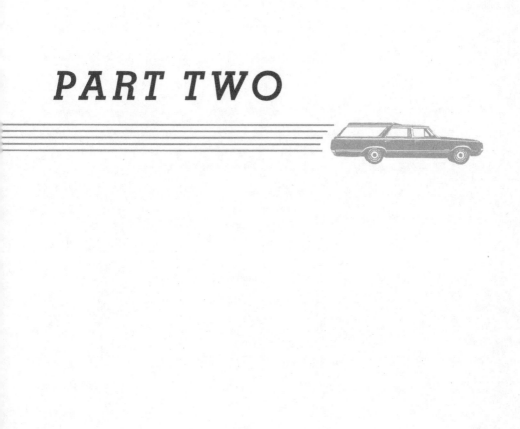

Chapter 6

MIDCENTURY FLYING CARS

The American Main Street "is rich in contentment and well-being. It bustles with hearty and
wholesome activity. And as you know firsthand, it
revolves very largely around the family car."

WHILE *TOLL ROADS AND FREE ROADS* SAT ON PRESIDENT
Roosevelt's desk awaiting funding and well before the attack
on Pearl Harbor, the president enlisted Detroit in the war effort.
Ford Motor Company developed and built trucks with the Cana-
dian Department of National Defence in 1939 and began putting

out military equipment from its British subsidiary the same year. It held $1 billion in defense contracts by 1941. FDR contemplated nationalizing Ford Motor Company to ensure that its erratic leader would continue to serve the war effort. Chevrolet signed a contract with the government to produce high-explosive shells in April 1940. A month later FDR appointed GM president William Knudsen to run the National Advisory Defense Committee. For all the interest in wily generals, and the grit of the Greatest Generation, it was America's industrial might—what Roosevelt had in 1940 declared "democracy's arsenal"—that defeated imperial Japan and the European fascists. Japanese generals knew they had lost when they failed at Pearl Harbor to deliver a knockout blow to the American navy. Japan could never outproduce the United States. Ferdinand Porsche, Hitler's car designer, had visited Detroit in the 1930s with other industrialists. When war broke out, they too considered Germany's cause lost. The Germans had a better tank, the Japanese, a better fighter plane. But neither could match the US for sheer numbers. The Rust Belt (before it rusted) would win the total war. The automobile sector had already proven itself the font of incalculable economic activity. In the 1920s and 1930s, the American economy rose and fell on the industry's fortunes. During the war, it became the nation's main line of defense.

The car culture merged with patriotism ten weeks after America entered the war. On February 22, 1942, automobile production ceased (beware anyone selling a 1943 Chrysler). Ford, General Motors, and Chrysler converted all of their factories to build planes and tanks and trucks and guns and artillery. They were joined by Nash, Studebaker, Packard, Willys, and the others, as well as parts makers and suppliers. Organized labor contributed by signing a "no strike" pledge for the duration (although there were wildcat strikes). Car sales should have boomed when the war plants started hiring. Sadly, workers ended up with money in their pockets but no cars to buy. Some buyers had already made down payments, but they never got their cars.

To make matters worse, the government began rationing gasoline and discouraging driving. Actually, there was plenty of gasoline—the United States led the world in production—but not enough tires. The Allies had lost their rubber connection when Japan captured the plantations of Malay (Malaysia) from the British in 1942. Fully 90 percent of American rubber came from the region's trees. The US responded with a crash research program to create synthetic rubber, but this took time and meanwhile army trucks needed tires too. So, to save on tires, gasoline rationing began December 1, 1942. Also, a "Victory Speed" limit of thirty-five miles an hour was enacted and drivers were encouraged to join "car-sharing clubs."

The Office of Defense Transportation (ODT) calculated that the average car ran 9,600 miles a year but that only 5,400 of those miles were for "necessary" transportation. Picnics and visits to grandma were "unnecessary"; church services qualified as necessary. With the expectation that car pools could reduce that figure a bit more, everyone got three gallons a week, good for 100 miles, or 5,250 miles a year (The average American driver today drives over 15,000 miles annually and needs four or five gallons to travel 100 miles.) Every car got a ration. Nonessential workers affixed an "A" sticker to their windshields, entitling them to their three gallons per week. War workers got twice that amount with "B" stickers. The one percent—including 219 members of Congress—got special "X" stamps for all the gasoline their limos might need.

Government enlisted the support of radio and movie producers. Jack Benny, whose Sunday night radio program was the most popular show on the air during the war, regularly built gas rationing into his plot lines. Bugs Bunny did his part at the movies. The rascally rabbit nearly plummets to his death aboard a plane afflicted with "gremlins." As only a cartoon plane can, it screeches to a halt inches above the ground because it has run out of gas. His life saved, Bugs breaks the fourth wall and cracks, "You know how it is with those A cards."

The ODT also printed posters, and magazine and newspaper advertisements. "Is that trip really necessary?" they asked. Dr. Seuss stacked workers seven rows high in an old sedan over the slogan, "Help win the war. Squeeze in one more." Mickey Mouse, Donald Duck, Goofy, and friends piled in together: "Share your car. It's patriotic." Alongside the cheerful posters hung the maudlin. A worried mother pleads, "Won't you give my boy a chance to get home?" "Don't travel unless your trip helps win the war," the poster advises. For the unmoved, the government offered the ominous. An angry Uncle Sam peers down godlike, warning, "Fill those empty seats. Car sharing is a must." The most famous poster featured an invisible Hitler. "When you ride ALONE you ride with Hitler!" it warned. We can see him but the driver doesn't even notice! If that didn't make Americans carpool, no HOV lanes ever will.

Did Americans do their patriotic duty? Car travel fell by nearly half between 1941 and 1943 and the amount of gas put into the tanks of passenger cars fell by a third. These figures are even more remarkable considered against a booming wartime economy that otherwise would have goosed gasoline sales. Americans took far more trips by mass transit—despite crowded trains and poor service (don't you know there's a war on?). Mass transit accounted for only 15 percent of trips prior to the war but nearly half during wartime. People turned to bicycles, although to buy a new bike required proof that you needed one to commute to a job in war production. The government then designed and produced hundreds of thousands of simplified but sharp-looking "Victory Bikes," complete with a "V" painted on each fender.

Yet a black market in gasoline thrived. Ration coupons were counterfeited and people siphoned gasoline from pipelines. Newspapers reported car owners claiming their passenger cars were trucks to get more rations. Postwar researchers estimated that about 10 percent of gas sales occurred on this black market. As they had during the Great Depression, wartime Americans clung to their automobiles. Certainly, many Americans, no matter how patriotic, were willing to risk sanction, to cheat, or to steal for a few extra miles behind the wheel.

With no actual cars to sell and unable to promote the joys of motoring, advertisements portrayed war work as patriotic evidence of high quality. "Top grade motor cars make top grade defense," said Chrysler. Ford showed its tanks rolling from one victory to the next; all Willys had to do was paint pictures of its Jeeps in combat.

As victory appeared more assured, Detroit added hints of dreamy things to come. They promoted the automobile as the centerpiece of the postwar world. For its "My tomorrow campaign," Nash featured soldiers daydreaming of home. "Nash will help contribute the jobs, the opportunities, the futures which will insure the strong, vital, and growing America all of us owe to those who have fought to preserve it." Notice that no cars get mentioned in this Nash ad. Chrysler chose the theme "Imagination and Performance" for its campaign of 1945. "Imagination set our engineers wondering how trucks could be built to run under water," the ad explained. Obviously they figured it out because, look, right there, a Chrysler-built truck is plowing through the waves! For its Dodge brand, Chrysler offered only a question. "What's Dodge Going to do?" the ad asked. The DeSoto line had the company president talking to the reader. "When you drive it, you'll get a brand-new idea of tomorrow's kind of driving." There will be "Tip-Toe" hydraulic shifting and "Safe-Stop [Power] Brakes." He dreams of coming to our house and giving us a drive, but the only picture in the ad is his smiling face. Frazer said, "There's a new kind of car a-coming," but wouldn't say, or show, what it a-was. "There's a Ford in your future," was a classic teaser campaign with a crystal ball theme carried over from before the war. But now there were no cars in the ball. "Whoosh! and you're out in front!" The new Ford would be so fast the fortune teller couldn't keep up.

Indeed, what is Dodge going to do after the war? What will the Future Ford look like? What is that new kind of car a-coming? Chances were, it would fly.

Midcentury images of flying cars now populate the internet as a form of retro-futurism—guileless predictions of far-out things to come. A 1951 *Popular Mechanics* cover showed a middle manager in a trench coat and hat backing his personal "helicopter coupe" into his garage as a neighbor's copter banks off into the sky. On one level, the techno-optimism behind the everyman's flying car remains unchanged. On another, today's flying cars are something altogether different. The wartime and postwar flying car would be an American automobile—affordable, easy to operate, and a vehicle of newfound freedom—only better. Ownership would indicate middle-class achievement. Flying cars are back in the news, brought to us by the same people promising driverless cars. In fact, they plan pilotless flying machines. Google cofounder Larry Page has bankrolled the secretive Zee Aero, which seems to involve Sebastian Thrun, godfather of the modern driverless car. Elon Musk announced the Tesla Model F. (F for flying, get it?) Uber has published a 100-page business plan for flying autonomous taxicabs. The company expects a launch date of 2025. Geely, the giant Chinese automaker and owner of Volvo, bought Boston-based Terrafugia, maker of "the world's first practical flying car," in 2017. The European Union's legacy aerospace quasi-governmental corporation, Airbus, which builds a 460-seat plane with a half-billion-dollar sticker price, has been testing the A^3 driverless urban air mobility machine, with production slated to begin in 2020. Tellingly, Airbus is selling a solution not for the masses or the wide-open spaces but for "Techies in Silicon Valley" who "invent high-tech products every day." "However," the Airbus website continues, "they still do not have a solution for . . . rush hour. Commuting from Silicon Valley to San Francisco every morning takes an hour and a half . . . the Airbus solution: a flying car." If you live near where Airbus has its research hangar in eastern Oregon, stay at home with toddlers, or have the kind of job that has you on the highway at 4:00 a.m., you don't really need help from Airbus, Geely, Uber, or Tesla.

I suspect that the same tech-bro billionaires who stare up at the sky from the comfort of their air loungers floating in a swimming pool filled to overflowing with venture capital were sitting on the couch with a bowl of Cap'n Crunch when they first encountered a flying car.* The Jetsons car runs on dish soap, stops on a dime, and is topped with a glass bubble. The only noise it makes is a pleasant bubbling whoosh. It rises vertically, hovers in place, and glides through the air, swinging gracefully along to the music as the opening credits roll. Little Elroy gets his own mini flying car and descends to school as if on a water slide. Mom takes her escape pod to the shopping center, and daughter Judy to high school. This flying car swimming along through gentle curves on a wide-open airway depicts the utopian future the tech bros will grant us all. But on closer examination, the Jetsons' flying car inhabits a dystopian future full of present-day problems made worse by flying. When George gets stuck in three-dimensional heavy traffic, he's boxed in from in front and behind as well as from above and below. He suffers road rage behind a flighty "woman driver" who blocks the road. Jane, his wife, runs into a stop sign during her driving lesson, because, you see, she's a woman driver too. Also, *The Jetsons* is a cartoon.

In contrast, midcentury Americans took their inspiration from real-life aerial drama. As soon as the Wright Brothers took off from Kitty Hawk in 1903, "America's romance with aviation" began, according to historian Joseph Corn. In the first decade, enthusiastic voices proclaimed that flying took one closer to the dome of heaven and that soon, the plane would replace the car. The flying car of the 1920s would let everyone escape the foul air of the subway, where they were "rushing like moles." Personal planes would glide out of the miasma to the clear air of an exurban idyll. In 1926, Henry Ford announced his prototype "Ford flying Flivver," which seemed to commentators a natural extension of his Model T: an airplane easy to operate, built by the millions, and one that any family could afford. The little plane made newsworthy endurance flights around the country, but still required a skilled pilot. In the 1930s, FDR's

---

* The show originally ran on Sunday nights in 1962 and 1963, but they either watched like I did on Saturday morning reruns or saw the reboot in the 1980s.

head of the Bureau of Air Commerce promoted planes as cheap, safe, and easy to fly as an automobile. He suggested saving money by replacing an expensive airplane engine with a motor from a Plymouth. He called it the "Plymacoupe." He asked aircraft makers to come up with prototypes. "The idea of a cheap, safe automobile of the air seems at last out of the dream stage," the *New York World-Telegram* reported.

The Second Word War, the first air war, quieted any doubts that the future belonged to air travel. The Japanese attempted aerial "shock and awe" at Pearl Harbor. Infantry died horrible deaths "island-hopping" across the Pacific to establish postage stamps of land on which airfields could be built. The Germans would have invaded England had they been able to establish air superiority in the year-long Battle of Britain. The Allies firebombed Dresden and Tokyo. The war brought rapid technological advances. Boeing built the pressurized B-29 Superfortress that dropped the atomic bombs Fat Man and Little Boy. It cost $3 billion to develop, about double the Manhattan project budget for the A-bomb itself. The most powerful meme from the air war was that of a mile-wide convoy of bombers blotting out the sun. Travelers passing through Union Station in Chicago could look up at a canopy of model airplanes suspended from the ceiling. Over the entrance hung an enormous, triumphant sign, "For Them, Bombs." No matter what they actually made, automakers put planes in the picture. When the war ads showed tanks, planes were flying overhead. Guns were always shooting planes out of the sky. "Buick powers the Liberator," proclaimed GM.

The air war, and the Liberator bomber in particular, had the one-time pacifist Henry Ford advertising it as well. Newspapers overflowed with superlatives when Ford Motor Company broke ground on a bomber plant near the Willow Run stream, twenty-one miles from Henry's mighty River Rouge Complex and near the town of Ypsilanti, Michigan. It was by far the largest plant under a single roof, larger than the factories of the three major aircraft makers combined. The press called it "one of the seven wonders of the world," the "most enormous room in the history of man," and "the damndest colossus." They reported planned production rates of "one per hour," "dozens a day," or, repeating Henry Ford's own boast from 1940, a thousand fighter planes a day. Willow Run would not produce mere fighters, however, but the glamorous, complex, and massive B-24 Liberator bomber, at the time the most destructive airplane in America's arsenal. No matter, several publications updated their copy to read, "1,000 B-24's a day." America intended to "fill the skies with flying battleships." Ford's reputation and the application of automobile production methods to flying machines would make those numbers possible. At the time, Consolidated Aircraft, which had designed the B-24, managed only 169 units *a year.*

The numbers never materialized. As executives at Consolidated and the other aircraft makers knew, airplanes simply cannot be mass-produced like cars. "You cannot expect blacksmiths to learn how to make watches overnight," said one aviation executive. Things were made much worse by the decision to locate the plant in Ypsilanti, far from Detroit where most workers lived. The government slapped up worker shacks near the site as fast as it could, and built the Willow Run Expressway to speed commutes. (A carpool of commuters formed the backbone of *Willow Run*, a novel written in 1943.) Ford recruited women, blacks, and workers from Appalachia for jobs he could not otherwise fill. Areas of town are still known as "Ypsitucky." Nothing much helped, but neither did it cut through the initial publicity. To this day, popular histories still describe Willow Run as a production miracle.

Jet airplanes came late to the war game, and were even more mind-blowing than big bombers. On February 28, 1945, the army announced what had until then only been rumored: a jet fighter of unheard of speed and agility. It was also revealed that the Royal Air Force had been secretly shooting down German "robot bombs" (V-2 rockets) with jet fighters since the previous August. Shortly before VJ Day, the first public flight of the American P-80 Shooting

Star took place. The fighter flew from Dayton, Ohio, to New York's La Guardia field in ninety minutes. The actual flight took only an hour but at 500 knots on a cloudy day the pilot overshot the airport and had to make a U-turn at sea. The *New York Times* reported that the Air Force guys called the new motor a "blow job." The jet age had arrived.

That was just the planes. The newly perfected helicopter would be able to take off and land on a quarter-acre lot. The US Army ordered its first helicopters in 1943 and that same year Northeast Airlines said it would begin helicopter mail deliveries and airport shuttle service after the war. The bus company Greyhound applied for a permit to fly helicopters along 53,000 miles of routes. The company even provided regulators with a model of a proposed helicopter bus. Igor Sikorsky, the leading developer of the helicopter, told Congress, "Thousands of persons will be flying helicopters when the war is over, using backyards as landing fields." In 1944, Boston's beloved Filene's department store chain tested the possibilities for helicopter delivery. A test flight from its Cambridge warehouse to its suburban Belmont branch carried, among other cargo, the latest fashion, the "helicopter dress of tomorrow." In this context, expecting suburban men in trench coats to be backing their helos into the family garage in the near future seems far less far-fetched.

Futuristic flying machines were not only the subject of wartime reporting, pulp science fiction, and matinee shorts (the Saturday morning cartoons of the day). Many Americans had experienced planes through their war work and fully expected to have a personal aircraft after the war. More than two million men and women worked in aircraft plants in 1943. They produced more than a quarter million planes. Another 2.5 million men served in the Army Air Forces. The American Historical Association (AHA) prepared a fifty-page booklet for soldiers in 1945 entitled, "Will There Be a Plane in Every Garage?" It was one of many such *G.I. Roundtable* pamphlets founded upon the conviction that citizen soldiers in a democracy should discuss the pressing topics of the day. "Is it easy to fly a helicopter?" the AHA asked. "Will the helicopter replace the automobile?" the FAQ continued. "The automobile and helicopter supplement each other very well. You can use your car in crowded congested urban areas and your helicopter for all other travel." Sober experts (read: killjoys) explained that an airplane was a creature of the military and that any future development would depend on what the government did. Wartime polls revealed that 39 percent of women planned to take flying lessons after the war and 44 percent of people in business expected to own a plane. The *Saturday Evening Post* found that 32 percent of American adults wanted a plane and 7 percent reported definite plans to buy one. In 1945, the Civil Aeronautics Administration—the agency responsible for commercial aviation and air traffic control—predicted that postwar plane production would repeat the experience of the automobile with Fordist production methods churning out up to two million private planes.

Barely a month after VJ Day, Macy's opened its new airplane department to sell the lightweight ERCO Ercoupe at a price of $2,994 (or $998 down with monthly installments). "Macy's chose Ercoupe for you. Because it's safe; and as easy to handle as your family car," the store advertised. An easy flying commute would let you live full time at your weekend house in Litchfield, Connecticut. Mandel's in Chicago and Wanamaker's of New York had Piper models for sale.

Alas, here we are eight decades on from the war and still we have no flying cars. The reasons are many. There are powerful interests to overcome: gravity for one thing, and those people making money on land cars. The Portland Cement Association, not to mention the Mob, rake it in pouring ribbons of concrete. Plenty of inventors have gotten their machines off the ground since the Wright Brothers. Traian Vuia flew his light four-wheeler in 1906, Glenn Curtiss, an aeronautical pioneer (whose name is still attached to a major aerospace contractor, Curtiss Wright) debuted his in 1917. Waldo Waterman responded to the call from the Bureau of Air Commerce for a family flyer in 1937. His "Arrowbile" was safe for an amateur to fly and could be driven on the road with its wings detached. Robert

Fulton created the Airphibian in 1946 and Moulton Taylor's Aerocar took off three years later, but neither could secure capital. In other words, they were not technical failures but, like the automobiles of the 1870s and before, solutions in search of a problem. In the near future, we may indeed get soap-powered, driverless, vertical-takeoff-and-landing machines because the "Techies in Silicon Valley" need to make it to work on time. But don't call them flying cars.

In an important sense, however, the automobiles of the 1950s were flying cars. No, they didn't take to the air, but engineers designed them to float like magic carpets along open roadways. Stylists added airplane-inspired tail fins, propellers, and jet exhaust ports. Front hoods and fenders were adorned with propeller planes, jet planes, rocket planes, and birds. At first, startups and the independents took the styling lead because the Big Three needed time to reconvert to civilian production. Studebaker, Hudson, and Nash made their plays. Shipbuilder Henry J. Kaiser gave it a go. The independents pushed the boundaries of styling and construction, adopting the lessons of aircraft manufacturing to build lighter, stronger cars. There were also would-be disrupters who presented the public with radically different automobiles.

Gary Davis introduced the Davis Divan as a 1947 model and advertised it as "Years Ahead!" The Divan used lightweight aircraft aluminum panels, had an airplane shape and airplane shock absorbers. All it needed was wings. Headlamps disappeared into the nose cone. It featured disc brakes and integrated jacks for changing a tire. *Businessweek* and *Life* published features on the pseudo flying car. *Parade*—the widely distributed newspaper insert—gave it a cover and it even earned TV time. Davis claimed to have done a survey that proved the Divan was "the car America wanted." The survey may have neglected to mention that the Divan had only three wheels. It also had only one seat, allegedly Divan-wide enough for four. (Even in the publicity shots one of the slim models had to hang an arm and shoulder out the window.) Davis hired workers, took orders from excited buyers, and sold franchise rights to dealerships.

But Davis wasn't an inventor or engineer. He was a used-car salesman who, true to the stereotype, cheated them all and wound up
in prison.

A year after the Divan, Preston Tucker introduced one of the
most stunning, radical, and storied cars in American history. The
Tucker Torpedo met with an enthusiastic reception and, for a time,
it seemed as if Tucker might be able to join the automaking club.

Among the car's enthusiastic fans was a young Francis Ford Coppola. As a boy, the now famous director waited anxiously for the
Torpedo to arrive. His father had taken him to see Preston Tucker's
"Car of Tomorrow" at a New York exhibition. "I was very excited,"
Francis recalls. Dad was an unlikely car guy. Juilliard-trained, Carmine Coppola played first flute at Radio City Music Hall and with
the Detroit Symphony. He arranged music and conducted for the
"Ford Sunday Evening Hour" radio program, which led him to a
friendship with the great man himself and his second son's middle
name. Carmine was so taken with Preston Tucker and his innovative Torpedo that he not only preordered the car but invested $5,000
(equal to $50,000 today) in the Tucker Corporation. In 1947, the car
was radical. It had *three* headlights. The "Cyclops Eye" center light
was linked to the steering wheel so drivers could see as the car cor-
nered. It also looked cool. It had disc brakes when American cars
still had drums, and a small instrument panel. Passengers would hit
a padded dash in the event of a crash. If they saw the crash coming they could dive into the foot well, a "crash compartment." The
Tucker had a large interior with a flat floor because the engine and
drive wheels sat together at the rear of the car. The design, by Alex
Tremulis, can only be described as stunning. The influence of the
1936 and 1937 "coffin hood" Cord, on which Tremulis worked, is
evident. That car too was both beautiful and innovative with hidden
headlights and front-wheel drive. The front fenders of the Tucker
carry into the door with that boomerang shape so emblematic of the
fabulous '50s. Even the colors, Silver, Maroon, and especially Waltz
Blue, are standouts.

Eight-year-old Francis kept asking, "When is the Tucker coming?" Months passed. The business plan for The Tucker Corporation was creative, to say the least. Tucker raised capital by selling franchises, cars, and even accessories. He promised to have cars ready for sale in 1948. (He renamed his first model the Tucker '48 because Torpedo sounded too much like something that sinks ships.) Francis kept pestering his father. "Finally he said it was never coming," Coppola remembers wistfully, "and that the big companies didn't want it to exist, and wouldn't let Mr. Tucker buy steel or the supplies he needed."

In June of 1948, Preston Tucker ran an open letter to the automobile industry in several newspapers. He wrote about how the government wouldn't sell him a plant to build his cars. After the war, the feds ended up owning many industrial plants. For example, although Ford built Willow Run, the government then bought the plant and leased it back to Ford Motor for the duration. The government had the power to decide which companies could and could not use them for auto production. Tucker also wrote of a powerful group that had tried to infiltrate his organization with spies and bribes. Government agents had harassed his dealers and made them subject to "Congressional Investigating Committees." In the days before Kickstarter, the way Tucker financed his operations was questionable enough to draw the interest of the Securities and Exchange Commission. Eventually, the SEC prosecuted Tucker for fraud. The agency lost in court, but succeeded in putting Tucker out of business before he could begin mass production. Or, Tucker simply folded because he was undercapitalized. Or, maybe he was a better innovator and salesman, a better dreamer, than he was a businessman.

Francis Coppola never forgot the Tucker. He wrote "a sort of Brechtian musical" with Preston Tucker, Thomas Edison, Henry Ford, Harvey Firestone, and Dale Carnegie all as characters. Thankfully, George Lucas told him to model the story on Frank Capra's *It's a Wonderful Life* instead. Coppola eventually made the film, *Tucker: The Man and His Dream,* in 1988. It is an uplifting biopic of a brilliant inventor whose dreams were crushed by Detroit's oligopoly and the US senator from Michigan who did their bidding. That was certainly how Tucker believed things went down. In any case, Carmine never recovered his money, but he also never lost faith in Tucker's dream. His son Francis owns a beautiful red one now—one of only fifty-one ever produced. He displays it on a slowly rotating turntable at the Coppola winery.

Nash, the Wisconsin-based automaker, also debuted an airplane-inspired postwar model before the Big Three caught up. The 1949 Airflyte featured a wind-tunnel design, "one clean sweep from bullet nose to tear-drop tail," that helped the big car achieve twenty-five miles per gallon. The unitized body (the type of construction used for aircraft) sat "pillowed on huge coil springs." The Airflyte's most recognizable feature is its fender skirts that shroud the front wheels. Rear fender skirts are often added to give a car a longer, lower profile. Front skirts, however, are almost unheard of because the front wheels need the freedom to swivel left and right. The Nash, with its unique aerodynamic front fender skirts, appeared to hover over the road. Also, rather than placing the instruments in the dashboard, they are clustered in a single nacelle—the Uniscope—on the steering column, part of the car's "cockpit control." The "Airliner Reclining Seats" folded flat into twin beds for use by traveling salesmen and serial philanderers. Airflyte sales averaged about 125,000 a year.

Like Nash, Hudson adopted unitized aircraft construction techniques for the post war. In 1948 the company introduced the "step down ride" (a slogan that remains well known to people of a certain age). The floor was set inside the chassis frames rather than atop them, giving the car an overall height of sixty inches (about eight inches lower than prewar cars). With a low center of gravity and aerodynamic shape, the elephantine car handled remarkably well. In its first ever new-car issue, *Consumer Reports* reported, "The Hudson Hornet's low-to-the-ground construction gives it a road hugging quality unequaled anywhere near its price class." The Fabulous Hudson Hornet racer of 1951 is beloved by a new generation thanks to the *Cars* film franchise, where old "Doc Hudson" gets to teach a cocky young racer some new tricks.

I've avoided plumbing the depths of *On the Road* so far, but we cannot leave the Hudson without noting Dean Moriarty's '49. It arrives in Virginia after carrying the Beat Poets across the country from San Francisco. "But how did you get here so fast?" Sal Paradise (Kerouac) asks.

"Ah, man, that Hudson goes!" says Dean. Forget the Divan. Sal tells us, "In the spacious Hudson we had plenty of room for all four of us to sit up front." It's even better than Detroit's best: "Dean's Hudson was low and sleek; Bull's Chevy was high and rattled." For Kerouac, the Hudson was a VW Microbus, the antiestablishment car of Cold War America. As they pull into Washington, DC, after an all-night drive, it is the day of Truman's second inauguration. "Great displays of war might were lined along Pennsylvania Avenue as we rolled by in our "battered boat," Kerouac writes. He then contrasts the gentle sea cow, the "battered boat," that carries them with these bristling war machines. Dean slows down to take in a "small ordinary lifeboat that looked pitiful and foolish." "What are these people up to?" Dean shakes his head. "Good old Harry . . . Man from Missouri, as I am . . . That must be his own boat."

For 1950, Studebaker did its own take on the airplane theme and came right out and said so. "This 'next look' in cars is a 'jet-propelled' look!" Studebaker announced. "Most people say it's a car so startling, they half expect to see it take off and fly!" In fact, most people said they half expected to see it drive off in both directions at once. Its panoramic rear window lent the car an odd symmetry. Like the Nash, Studebaker's Starlight Coupe had a bullet nose. But the company fit a jet engine intake element to that nose and set a chrome airplane in the middle of the hood.

Finally, like Preston Tucker, Henry J. Kaiser entered the automotive business as a newcomer after the war; unlike Tucker, he was an old hand at mass production and well capitalized. He had become known as the Henry Ford of shipbuilding. By his methods, Kaiser

Shipyards built Liberty ships in record time and in enormous numbers. His fleets convoyed across the North Atlantic to keep the Allies supplied and they supported island-hopping in the Pacific. Kaiser Motors enjoyed brief success when it launched its first models in 1947. The Kaisers offered some unique features, such as a hatchback design, and the company advertised engineering and safety features. They came with an airplane hood ornament too, but otherwise the styling was down to earth. As the Big Three returned to production, pricing power was lost, deficits grew, and sales sank to a few thousand by 1954. "We expected to toss fifty million dollars into the automobile pond, but we didn't expect it to disappear without a ripple," Kaiser commented on his failure.

None of the independents survived the 1950s, not independently in any case. Kaiser merged with Willys, Nash with Hudson (to become American Motors Corporation), and Studebaker hooked up with Packard. Even in concert, they could not compete. "Despite the postwar seller's market for cars, not one new firm was able to get off the ground," historian James Flink concludes. "Closure of entry into the American automobile industry was now complete." The automobile industry had become what economists call a "joint-profit-maximizing oligopoly." GM owned half the market, Ford, 27 percent, and Chrysler, 17 percent. That left 6 percent of the market to be shared by every other company, including imports. GM could easily have garnered an even larger share of the market, but Alfred Sloan was wary of GM being labeled a monopoly and broken up. Some, like Carmine Coppola, saw collusion between Detroit and Washington. Certainly the government had helped enrich GM, Ford, and Chrysler with war contracts and Roosevelt had put GM president William Knudsen in charge of his defense committee. "Engine" Charlie Wilson ran GM during the war and served as Eisenhower's secretary of defense afterward.

Control of the market also gave the Big Three the power to define the look and feel of the American automobile. Engineering innovation of the type done by Hudson and Nash went against Sloanist principles. Sadly, industrial oligopoly ensured that neither Hudson, nor Studebaker, nor Kaiser, nor Tucker, nor Nash would shape the future. Instead, the postwar styling crown would end up going with the most establishment of car companies. Ford won with a Shoebox.

The '49 Ford was not as beautiful or radical as the cars from the independents, more of a shoebox than a space ship. But it was a clean break from the prewar cars. Again, the first models coming out of the Big Three used the same dies as the last prewar models. So, the 1941 Ford was the 1946 Ford. The prow of the typical prewar car widened as it moved aft to an upright windshield and tall cabin. Fenders were so low as to be mostly hidden from the driver's view. In profile they still followed the line that had defined cars since the 1910s: a French curve down to the flat running board and then a semicircular fender at the rear. In most sedans the trunk was invisible. The rear window was hardly more than a porthole.

In 1949, Ford claimed to have "The World's Newest Car." It was the first car from Detroit that had what was generally termed the "new look." The body spreads across the full width—from wheel to wheel and beyond—creating more room inside. It was like enclosing a sun porch to expand the family room. The Ford featured "Sofa-wide seats" five feet across. Presaging our girthier age, it promised "Ample room for six BIG people." With the fenders brought up to the hood line, the driver saw a bigger car out the windshield. The C pillar (the vertical support at the rear corner of the roof) is thin. The rear fenders were similarly integrated and a small crease somehow makes all the difference. The perfect soupçon of chrome in all the right places matters too: a thin line around the front window frame, a side molding neither too high nor too low, and a horizontal grille—a stunning break from the grilles of the past. The key feature of that grille is a minimalist airplane coming right at you. A center circle is held between horizontal bars, wings that stretch the width of the car. It is framed from above by a chrome arch and below by a sleek chrome bumper.

Other than the grille, it's hard to agree with the ad men that the

'49 Ford had "eye holding beauty." (Interestingly, the Kaiser had a somewhat similar shape but retains too much of the prewar feel. The C pillars are heavy and the front still has a prow.) In any case, far more Fords were being built, so Ford led the way with the key elements that would define the American sedan for nearly two generations. And, with it, the Big Three could put innovations such as the monocoque body and wind-tunnel testing—both standard today—back on the shelf.

During this time when it had lost the styling lead, GM didn't simply advertise its own cars; it advertised automobility itself. The company's "Key to a Richer Life" ad of 1950 depicted "Main Street, U.S.A.," thick with slow moving traffic. "It is unlike any other Main Street anywhere else in the world. It is rich in contentment and well-being. It bustles with hearty and wholesome activity. And as you see and know firsthand, it revolves very largely around the family car." The Budd Company was only an automotive supplier, but it joined in: "The American miracle makes it possible for almost anyone who wants one to own a car, and has provided him highways and service facilities to make its use enriching." An extended family gathers around the table, beneath the autumn leaves, while their cars look on like loyal sled dogs. Thanks to the automobile, "Grandma is no longer a legendary, distant person, glimpsed only on elaborately prepared occasions. The automobile gives the family wider horizons, and at the same time closer, almost casually arranged contact." These ads solidified the connection between patriotism and automobility initiated during the war.

Sacrifice—reduced consumption—had been the order of the day in World War II. The government cut off the supply of new cars and told drivers to limit their travel. Now it was buying: new televisions and kitchen appliances to fill up ranch homes with wide patios on which to grill American beef served with fabulously ruffled potato chips integrated to work with sour cream and onion dip. If ruffled potato chips didn't win the enemy over to the American way of life, our bejeweled sedans would. The American automobile in the 1950s shouted that the American way was better, better than communism, better than totalitarianism, better than the ways of the peasant nations.

To the modern eye, the '49 Ford is a sedate and sensible sedan, hardly the image of a flying car. It takes a bit of historical imagination to see that airplane grille the way buyers saw it in 1948, when the '49s hit the showrooms. It takes no imagination at all to see the flying glory of the mid-1950s Chevys. For '55, Chevy offered a "New Look, New Life, New Everything." The baby fat of the '49 Ford was gone. A single plane defined the hood and fully integrated fenders now. One long low line, with no separation between hood and fenders, defines the profile. Designers also wrapped the windshield glass around the side pushing the front roof pillars back. GM called this the "Panoramic" windshield and it gave the driver the same Cinema-Scope view then featured at the movies. The trunk and rear fenders got the same treatment, affording through the rear glass an equally breathtaking view of the car itself. Chrome had blossomed all over, from the hub caps to the frenched headlights and along the tail fins.

Those tail fins too were an airplane feature. GM designers got a look at the Army Air Corps' P-38 Lightning in 1941. The advanced fighter was still under wraps at the time. It was like two planes glued together with the pilot set on the wing between them. Harley Earl looked at the twin fuselages, a vertical stabilizer, or fin, at the rear of each one and immediately thought how it would look on a car. He put small bumps on the rear fenders of the 1948 Cadillac, essentially a flourish on a prewar design. But by the mid-1950s, those bumps had grown into full-fledged flying-car fins.

Consumption was the name of the game in the 1950s, a reward for winning the war and a way to prevent another Great Depression. These midcentury machines with their sofa-wide seats, wraparound windshields, and dazzling silver accents demanded to be consumed even as they themselves consumed the world. Their high-compression Firepower (Chrysler), Turbo-Fire (Chevrolet), and Rocket (Oldsmobile) engines hopped up on high-test Ethyl, swallowed the landscape, sucked down gasoline, set fresh air afire and breathed out smoke. They also burned rubber. The driver could summon all of that power with the faintest twitch of an ankle.

Exterior and interior styling matched to tip-toe acceleration, one-finger steering, and soft suspensions gave the illusion of flight—especially on the newly laid Interstates. Techies believe that in a few years twenty-first-century flying machines will get them out of traffic. Their machines will be electric, efficient, and self-piloting. The only thing they won't be is flying cars.

Chapter 7

FOREIGN INVADERS FROM *SPUTNIK* TO THE BUG

"We got a lot of publicity—all of it bad," Ben Pon said of his first attempt to sell Volkswagen Beetles to Americans in 1949.

I N 1957, A TITANIUM SPHERE POLISHED BRIGHT AS CHROME with four spindly legs sent out chirps from its orbit high above the Earth. It was the sound of a Soviet tractor far out in front in the race to space, announcing to Americans that they had been caught floating aimlessly along wrapped in Detroit's automotive confections while the Russians were moving ahead technologically.

The casual reader of automotive history considers the 1950s short-hand for gorgeous chrome and glorious tail fins. The 1957 Chevy

Bel Air stood—just stood, mind you, as a work of sculpture even before it took off—as all that American consumer society and freedom had to offer. In retrospect, it was the pride before the fall. And it all started with *Sputnik*.

The chirp heard round the world called critics of our car culture out of the woodwork. These enemies, foreign and domestic, began to question whether our automotive truths were truly self-evident. The leaders of Democracy's Arsenal had always advertised themselves as standing at the cutting edge of science and technology, proof of American superiority. *Sputnik* said, maybe not. Fifth Columnists—enemies from within—joined the attack. Physicians' groups took time out from changing their minds about cigarettes to lobby for safer vehicle designs. Apostates attacked Interstate culture. The highways and their rest stops had homogenized the wonder out of the road trip. If you lived in Los Angeles, you didn't have to hear those criticisms to realize that the auto age had problems. You could taste the smog. Sloanism itself was called to account by the onetime governor of Michigan. He asked Americans why they had forsaken the sensible age of the Model T.

Auto enthusiasts of the 1920s could reasonably describe the Model T as a liberator, but in the face of criticism, and the very tactile evidence of the 1950s, automotive liberation theology needed significant propping up. People had to be reminded to believe in the car as a freedom machine, despite accumulating evidence to the contrary. With racial tensions on the rise, outside enemies were apparently winning the Manichean struggle, and aesthetes ridiculing the American automobile, Detroit stood firm, knowing that people would always want cars to drive.

"Our national self-esteem has recently received some rude shocks," Adlai Stevenson told the United Parents Association in April 1958. *Sputnik* showed how far behind we had fallen. Stevenson, governor of Illinois and the egghead wing of the Democratic party's two-time presidential candidate, blamed driver's ed. The Russians were learning science, technology, engineering, and math (STEM in modern lingo). The American schools taught a "curriculum chaotic and cluttered with distractions" that overburdened teachers with "indiscriminate responsibilities." Driver's ed was one of those distractions. "I taught my three boys to drive a car. I think they can do as much for my grandsons—and let their high school teachers concentrate on some things that are more important, or at least harder to teach." Stevenson was not alone. Critic Inez Robb lumped driver's ed in with "finger painting, self-expression, folk dancing, life guidance, basket weaving . . . lampshade making and cheer-leading."

In fact, driver's education spread rapidly in the Cold War as part of a broader cultural emphasis on conformity. It had first entered the curriculum in 1936, supported by the National Safety Council, the American Automobile Association, and the insurance industry. They were aligned with progressive educators who believed schools should teach life skills as much as academics. By the 1950s, it was taught in the majority of public high schools. Children learned to see driving as a higher form of citizenship, one reached by obeying the law, promoting social harmony, and buying car insurance.

Adlai Stevenson might well have been able to teach his grandsons how to operate an automobile, but it took a professional educator to teach driving as a form of social control at a moment when young people were said to be exhibiting antisocial behaviors. Even as the automobile became easier and easier to operate, the driver's education curriculum grew more elaborate and the driver's ed textbooks, thicker. An English professor, Edward Tenney, wrote an extended attack on driver education, *Highway Jungle*. We had been spending millions on a course that had no impact on its putative purpose of highway safety, he said. It was instead a social hygiene course, teaching morality and consumerism in the guise of education. As Stevenson suggested, actually training a kid to drive was fairly easy.

The deadly mix of adolescence and automobiles figured prominently in the pantheon of Cold War anxiety. Children had been abandoned during the war, the theory went, because fathers were away and mothers went to work. Television in the 1950s then came between these feral children and their parents.* Tenney took his title from the film *Blackboard Jungle*, a fictionalized expose on juvenile delinquency in a vocational high school. *Dragnet*, a popular police procedural on both radio and television, dipped into the juvenile delinquency well many times. "The Big Rod" offers the true story of a hit-and-run teenage driver ("the names have been changed to protect the innocent"). Sergeant Friday catches the kid, but before he's hauled off to jail he's treated to a sermon by Friday (Jack Webb):

> I'm getting fed up with you kids roaming the streets in those death traps of yours. I don't care about you. You want to wrap yourself around a post, go ahead . . . but don't you take somebody else with you. You threw a ton and a half of metal at a 120 pound woman and then you ran away and left her in the gutter to die.

The delinquent asks how much time he'll serve. "I don't know, but it won't be enough," says Friday. *This Is Your FBI,* a police procedural even more heavy-handed than *Dragnet*, featured commentary by J. Edgar Hoover himself, the bureau's imperial director. "Juvenile delinquency, always a major problem, has recently become entwined with one of America's most serious crimes: auto theft," he warned. The plot involves a mother who cannot be bothered to look after her daughter. The teen gets caught up with a band of car thieves. She's about to be murdered when the G-men burst in, saving the day.

The advanced automobile of the 1950s added a strange new twist to the perennial alarm of cultural conservatives over the freewheeling nature of the automobile. The old complaints of reckless boys in cars and the girls who lust after them getting up to no good in the back seat remained. The postwar car, however, with its power

---

* There are periodic panics about juvenile delinquency, in the 1920s and 1980s for example. It is difficult to correlate these with any actual statistics on crime. See James Gilbert, *A Cycle of Outrage: America's Reaction to the Juvenile Delinquent in the 1950s* (New York: Oxford University Press, 1988).

steering, power brakes, and automatic transmissions, was so easy to operate that it also emasculated men and made kids soft (snowflakes, to use the modern term). Given how fat and happy American youth had become, it was no wonder that the Russians had beat us into space. What's wrong with kids today? They never learned to double-clutch a three-on-the-tree standard transmission.

Public school driver's ed sat at the center of this cultural context. At least a million teenagers were carrying around their driver's ed textbooks when *Sputnik* flew. (How many pages they actually read remains an open question for future historians.) A million more would take the course before the 1957–58 academic year ended. Supporters argued that the threat of sudden death behind the wheel would "vitalize" classroom learning as war had for an earlier generation. Kids liked driver's ed class, they said, because they got to use the "Aetna [Casualty Insurance] Drivotrainer," a driving simulator. Students also got to watch what became known as "hamburger on the highway" movies. These films showed real-life footage of crashes with the intent of scaring kids straight. Mostly they provided the titillating thrill and blood and guts of a horror movie. The geometry teacher didn't show movies. Walter Cutter, the head of the New York University Center for Safety Education, said it was science class— "the science of staying alive." He also invoked the Soviet threat:

> What we can or cannot do about controlling atomic weapons remains to be seen. It would compound that possible tragedy, if, while awaiting some uncertain future Armageddon, we did not use our intelligence and national determination to save the lives that we can save now.

Readers of the AAA's textbook, *Sportsmanlike Driving*, got an even more ominous warning in the form of a mushroom cloud on the opening page: "Whether power comes from atomic fission or gasoline combustion, man must be in control." Students also learned that America had become wholly and happily dependent upon the

automobile. The AAA told kids that buying a car, prudently insur-
ing it, and driving economically were not only vital to the "driver's
personal pocketbook, but to the future welfare of this country and
the whole world."

New drivers would also have to submit to police. Significantly,
the only time most white middle-class Americans find themselves
on the wrong end of the law is when they are pulled over. (African-
American men might reasonably argue that police already consider
them on the wrong end of the law, which is *why* they get pulled
over.) Cold War driving educators who didn't assign *Sportsmanlike
Driving* chose *Man and the Motor Car,* published by the insurance
industry, instead. It explains the importance of obedience: "The
work of traffic policemen is to protect highway users. Cooperate
with them. The life they save may be your own."* A few pages later,
a cartoon depicts a monstrous cop with overlong arms hoisting a
"Violator" car and a "Pedestrian who fails to cooperate." The violator seems safe inside his car, but the copper holds the poor pedestrian by one arm as if threatening to drop him unless he swears off
jaywalking. Society is Gulliver standing astride a Lilliputian highway in another illustration, plucking little cars from the road. "As
society awakens, those who do not 'play the game' will be removed
from the highway."

* * * *

JUVENILE DELINQUENCY, real and imagined, and its relationship to
the car culture only becomes clear on consideration. The smog problem was obvious to anyone who cared to look, or breathe. Framing
the American automobile as a source of pollution and a despoiler of
nature in the 1950s inverted previous thinking about even IC cars
and the environment. The early automobile and motor truck were

---

* The safety slogan, "The life you save may be your own" was so pervasive
during the 1950s that Flannery O'Connor took it as a title for her 1955 short
story about a man who swindles an old woman out of her car.

rightly lauded for cleaning up the city. An urban horse dropped thirty to forty pounds of manure a day on the city streets; cars dropped none. Neighbors welcomed the transformation of smelly, hay-filled firetrap horse stables into garages and horse-drawn carriages into motorcars.

Also, the automobile of the 1920s helped Americans discover the National Parks. Some admitted that the automobile might foul parkland air, but even they concluded that, on balance, letting the cars in to the parks was a good idea. Stephen Mather, the founding director of the National Park Service, promoted the automobile as a democratizing agent. Before the automobile, tourists were beholden to the railroads and fancy hotels. Only the very rich could afford to enjoy the magnificence of nature that the parks presented. Mather was a confirmed nature lover, generous donor to the parks, and friend of naturalist John Muir. He used his salesman's skills to lobby officials to fund the parks and attract visitors. (A master of publicity, Mather branded borax as "20 Mule Team Borax" and saw sales take off. He went on to become a borax millionaire.) More tourists would mean more support for wilderness protection, he reasoned. One only needs to see the awesome wilderness in person to become a tireless advocate. Mather worked with the nascent car industry to encourage car camping and had a highway built to connect all the western parks in a grand loop.

Even John Muir did not worry much about the effect of allowing cars into the parks. In 1912 Muir reported on a National Parks conference at which "comparatively little of importance was considered." One question sucked up all the oxygen: whether automobiles should be allowed to enter Yosemite. Muir wrote in a letter to the American Alpine Club:

A prodigious lot of gaseous commercial eloquence was spent upon it by auto-club delegates from near and far. All signs indicate automobile victory, and doubtless, under certain precautionary restrictions, these useful, progressive, blunt-nosed mechanical beetles will hereafter be allowed to puff their way into all the parks and mingle their gas-breath with the breath of the pines and waterfalls, and, from the mountaineer's standpoint, with but little harm or good.

By 1918, seven times more visitors at the park came by automobile than by train. They set up camp in any meadow as they pleased, pitching a tent beside the car or simply draping a tarp. The more dedicated might have added Lamsteed Kampkar bodies to their Model Ts. In 1920, one million people visited the national parks, a record. Two million paid a visit in 1925.

Fellow naturalist and best-selling essayist John Burroughs was more alarmed than Muir about the automobile. He wrote a series of articles decrying the "befouling incursions of the automobile" upon nature. Henry Ford, himself an avid birder and fan of Burroughs, responded to the articles with the gift of a Model T. Burroughs turned out to be a speed freak (by Model T standards) and drove rather recklessly. Not unlike those rural folk who decried the "devil wagons," he was anti-auto until he got a car of his own. As a new driver, Burroughs came to agree with Ford and Mather's view that the automobile's role in getting people out into God's country outshone its pollution. Ford, Burroughs, Thomas Edison, and Harvey Firestone (the tire magnate) subsequently went on a series of highly publicized glamping trips in a convoy of up to fifty cars. "The Four Vagabonds," as they called themselves, traveled with a specially built cook wagon complete with an oven and icebox. Like millions of other itinerant vacationers, The Four Vagabonds were saving the wild places by visiting them in their motorcars.

Thus, although people were aware of the air pollution hazards and the threat to nature the automobile might pose, on balance in the 1920s they considered motorization a positive development. But by the 1950s, the effects of all this glamping had become clear. Or rather, unclear. On July 14, 1955, President Eisenhower signed the Air Pollution Control Act to begin gathering scientific data on the problem of air pollution, still focused mostly on industrial emissions. As if to prove the law's necessity, smog besieged Los Angeles for two straight days that September. The *Los Angeles Times* reported, "The densest smog on record grayed Los Angeles for hours yesterday, threatening closure of industry and curtailment of traffic as ozone concentrations came within a shade of reaching the second alert stage for the first time." With the results of the studies in, the Clean Air Act of 1963 began regulating air quality and in 1965 the act was amended to limit tailpipe emissions. Meanwhile, California was out ahead. Finding that "the emission of pollutants from motor vehicles is a major contributor to air pollution in many portions of the state," the legislature had passed the California Motor Vehicle Pollution Control Law in 1960. It required vehicle manufacturers to install devices to limit smog-causing emissions.

After pulling Sloan's memo on how to delay safety glass out of their files, auto executives claimed not to have the technology to meet the new regulations. They did; indeed, any idiot with a bit of copper pipe or a garden hose did. Much of the pollution came from emissions that did not pass through the tailpipe but slipped past the rings sealing the pistons and the cylinder walls and down into the crankcase at the bottom of the engine. The crank spins rapidly, bathed in oil inside that case. Engineers had long ago figured out that when air and unburned gasoline leaked into the crankcase, the lubricating oil got sudsy and failed to lubricate properly. So, they poked a hole in the crankcase and installed a tube—the down-draft tube—to draw off those gases. This solution, in turn, created the problem that had long bedeviled the horse-drawn carriage: noxious emissions vented in front of the driver. In the 1930s, Studebaker ran a copper tube from the crankcase to the intake manifold so as to recombust the fumes. In the 1940s, Cadillac also added copper tubes. By giving the gasoline a second chance to combust and then exit the tailpipe, these engineers had reduced air pollution even without intending to. The simple technology, called positive crankcase ventilation (PCV) is now standard. (Suggest to your mechanic, "Could the PCV valve be clogged?" That won't solve the problem of the car running rough, but it will establish your bona fides well enough that you won't get the runaround.)

As late as 1959, Detroit continued to plead ignorance, claiming they had no such magic valves and no copper tubes. Then, as the mandate deadline neared, the Automobile Manufacturers Association made a surprise, stunning, blockbuster announcement: an industry scientist had fortuitously located a PCV valve among the dust bunnies under a lab bench. Americans had put their faith in the automobile industry. Detroit had put the nation on wheels, spread prosperity, and built democracy's arsenal. Now they were whining, displaying a can't do attitude. They had fallen far from the days of Model Ts and victorious war machines. Industry has since followed a standard playbook every time new pollution control, safety, or fuel economy mandates are passed. They whine, they plead, they delay. Or, as has been the case in the recent attempts to meet diesel emissions standards, they cheat.

Positive crankcase ventilation involved no moving parts and had little effect on engine performance. But for the 1966 model year, California cars would have to be fitted with additional exhaust treatment technologies. The automakers said they did not have the technology. So, regulators approved four aftermarket devices, including three catalytic converters and an afterburner (an open flame that simply burned in the exhaust stream). The automakers said they couldn't possibly install these devices on their cars. Their bluff again called, they announced that they had found their own solutions buried in a disused file cabinet in a back closet off the very same lab! These involved tuning the ignition and carburetor so that the engine ran lean—more air, less gasoline in the fuel charge. Engines sputtered and stalled. "Here's your problem," the local mechanic would discover (having shown you that your PCV was fine). "Your carb's too lean and your ignition timing is off." A quick tune-up and you would be back on the road with a smooth-running car that polluted fully as much as the old unadulterated one.

Even if the engine did not run rough, the mandated emissions control technology sapped power and made cars harder to work on and harder to operate. Suddenly there were all kinds of tubes and hoses running around the engine compartment, any one of which could leak and cause trouble. The owner's manual section on "how to start the car" became an elaborate decision tree of "if/then" statements and logical loops that barely made sense. The gas pedal had to be depressed halfway, all the way, all the way and then released, or not at all depending on the state of the engine and the ambient temperature. The engine computer manages these things now, but in California in the 1970s, the driver was supposed to do it.

Because we associate environmentalism with the 1970s (a decade that began with Earth Day), the fact that Ike signed the Air Pollution Control Act in 1955—a year before he signed off on the Interstates—may come as something of a surprise. Other facets of the car culture have a similar timeline. The Big Three, for the first time in their history, began switching to a front-wheel-drive architecture and "downsizing" its large cars in the late 1970s. Car buffs refer to the Me Decade as the "malaise era" of automobile styling, quality, and fun (the term, as we shall see, is associated with Jimmy Carter). On closer examination, however, the first wave of gloom came at the very height of the tail-fin era, the car culture's putative golden age.

*   *   *   *

THE SHARP RECESSION of 1958 on the heels of *Sputnik* further challenged American pride and faith in automobile induced prosperity. Postwar car sales had boomed since 1953, when the end of the Korean War released productive capacity in the same way, though on a smaller scale, as had reconversion after World War II. Car sales climbed from 5.8 million to 7.5 million units between 1953 and 1955. The good times didn't last long. Sales slumped down through 1957 before falling off a cliff. Americans bought about a third fewer cars in 1958 than they had in 1957; that amounted to little more than half as many cars as at the 1955 peak. The mid '50s, when the most iconic cars of the tail-fin era appeared, began to look like a 1920s bubble.

Consulting his beloved spreadsheets in the face of the slump, Alfred Sloan found that they affirmed his faith in the "car for every purse and purpose" philosophy. He saw an "upsurge in demand for the so-called compact or economy car" and concluded that buyers wanted yet more variety and choice. In the past, GM had met the American lust for novelty by adding new types of vehicles. Station wagons, hardtops, and "personal cars" from each of the many different GM brands multiplied, even though, like Billy Durant's Olds in Buick clothing of 1908, they were mostly identical beneath the surface. Now the company would offer even more choices for engines, colors, interiors, and accessories.* There is some truth to Sloan's conclusion. Customers often added accessories and upgrades to the base models. Yet what the spreadsheets could not capture—or what Sloan as the living embodiment of General Motors would never be able to see—is that many buyers wanted more than the appearance of choice that the limitless options sheets offered. They opted to escape the walled garden of the American automobile and find cars built to a different set of automotive values. They wanted, and got, a new kind of car culture: between 1955 and 1959, the dollar value of imports sold in the United States multiplied nearly elevenfold.

Outside economists looked at the same data Sloan was seeing and concluded that the tail-fin era had gone awry. Raymond "Steve" Saulnier was the chairman of President Eisenhower's Council of Economic Advisers and later served as anti-Keynesian adviser to both Richard Nixon and Barry Goldwater. A budget hawk who had voted for Herbert Hoover, Saulnier was known as "Dr. No" for his adherence to balancing budgets. He did not like increasing spending, or in a way that now seems quaint, cutting taxes just for fun. Saul-

---

* Not only could buyers upgrade accessories and appointments, they also had their pick of engines, transmissions, and even such esoteric specifications as rear axle ratios. As the number of combinations grew exponentially, factories, distributors, and dealers had trouble keeping up.

nier explained the drop in car sales as a "leading shock" to the economy, a cause of recession rather than an effect. Buyers' incomes had
not dried up, but "auto dealers' showrooms were shunned by vast
numbers of Americans." The sober economist then put on his car-
critic hat. Economic conditions certainly played a role in the boom-
and-bust car sales cycle. "But," he continued:

> It would be a mistake to ignore . . . the effect of changes in auto-
> mobile styling in this period. For reasons you must not ask me to
> explain, the American people rushed to the dealers' showrooms
> to buy the multicolored cars with wraparound windshields and
> modest tail fins that became available in the fall of 1954. Their
> enthusiasm reached an unprecedented pitch in 1955. It continued
> in 1956 and in 1957, too, but by that time the cars had evolved
> in design to an unbelievable length, width and weight. And the
> modest little tail fins of the 1955 model had become very large
> indeed, and to me, and I believe to a great many others, were by
> this time not very attractive at all.

John Keats went much further than Saulnier in his aesthetic critique. Keats is best known for *The Crack in the Picture Window*, a
sarcastic look at suburbia. But in 1958 he produced two more books,
Schools Without Scholars and the best-selling *The Insolent Chariots*. In the former, he joined others in attacking the life-adjustment
school behind driver's ed. In the latter, no facet of the American automobile escaped his rapier wit: disingenuous advertising,
crooked dealerships, choking smog, traffic clogged cities, road trips
dulled by the monotony of motel chains along the Interstates. He
mocked the customers themselves. "Detroit does not produce cars
for reasonable people like thee and me," he joked, "but for that vast
section of the American public that presumably has something radically wrong with it." He told automotive history as a love affair—
with the car playing the female lead. The American was a hayseed
with an "adolescent tightening in the groin," when he met the Model

T. But she had trapped him into matrimony and grown "sow-fat." No wonder, he wrote, that the American driver had found another mistress. The European car was "petite," and "gay," and "promised prestige." "America's marriage to the American automobile is now at an end," he announced. Besides being sexist, he was off by at least sixty years.

"Cars do not swim. Why do we give them fins?" Keats asked. Harley Earl's invocation of American military ingenuity and prowess, the tail fin, seemed an embarrassment after the launch of *Sputnik*. The '59 Cadillac, like all American models designed a few years before it bowed, had fins complete with rocket exhaust taillights. Earl's onetime student Virgil Exner had gone even bigger with tail fins over at Chrysler. In 1955, he debuted the company's "Forward Look" designs that carried a clean line from bow to stern. Where the Cadillac fins look bolted to the body—as if Earl had rushed into the design studio days before retirement and lambasted the sculptors until they agreed to add them—Exner created an integrated whole. The Caddy, even with its rockets, looked earthbound. In contrast, befitting Chrysler's reputation for engineering, Exner's 300-D appeared eager to fly into space. Despite his artistic accomplishment, however, the stylist made a fool of himself by claiming, in a speech to the Society of Automotive Engineers, that tail fins function to maintain stability, helping the car track straight in a crosswind.

As for Ford, the company seemed completely out of touch. Its cars, from the lowliest Ford sedan to the fanciest Lincoln, looked as if the designers hadn't bothered to carve the blocks of clay in the studio before taping on a bit of chrome. As if to prove how little they understood about their buyers in the 1950s, the company decided to create an entirely new line of Fords for the 1958 model year. Ford Motor conducted surveys and psychological research to determine the precise design and even the name for the car that would lure people away from Pontiac and Buick showrooms. They spent millions on a striptease campaign that tantalizingly showed a bit of bumper to get customers excited about "E-Day." The head of the Marketing Research Department enlisted the help of poet Marianne Moore to come up with a name. Among those she offered: "*Andante con Moto*," "*Pluma Piluma*," and "Utopian Turtletop." Management promptly shipped the head of the Marketing Research Department off to the Coast Guard. His replacement politely told Moore that her services were no longer needed. After considering 6,000 names they had chosen one with "an air of gaiety and zest," he wrote in a personal letter to the poet. "At least, that's what we keep saying. Our name, dear Miss Moore, is—Edsel." Poor Edsel. It was to be his father's final insult.

The name quickly became a synonym for colossal flop. (Kids today know nothing of their automotive pasts. Say to them, "New Coke was the Edsel of soft drinks." They stare in blank ignorance.) People flocked to the Ford showrooms for E-Day in September 1957. They confronted a not very exciting new car that looked like a dull old Ford, worse even. Everyone agreed that the grille was ugly, but how ugly was it? It was so ugly, some called it a toilet seat. Others saw a horse collar, or, my favorite, a Plymouth sucking on a lemon. The interiors were a hodgepodge with a horizontal speedometer and automatic transmission buttons set inside the steering wheel. And they worked as badly as they looked. The Edsel was so pathetic that the otherwise merciless John Keats felt sorry for Ford Motor. The clamor for sensible cars in the "post-*Sputnik* winter of 1958" did not exist in 1948, when the leadership began thinking about the Edsel. "The mood of 1948 was generally orgiastic," he said. David Wallace, the Ford executive in charge of planning the Edsel, also blamed *Sputnik*:

> I don't think we know the depths of the psychological effect that that first orbiting had on all of us. Somebody had beaten us to an important gain in technology, and immediately people started writing articles about how crummy Detroit products were . . . The American people . . . put themselves on a self-imposed austerity program. Not buying Edsels was their hair shirt.

Two years after it was introduced, Ford wrote off a $300-million loss and killed the Edsel.

While Ford was going wrong in 1958, American Motors was going right under an unlikely leader. George W. Romney's ascendance from political refugee to governor of the great state of Michigan is an only-in-America tale. George's polygamist parents had fled to Mexico ahead of the law and angry mobs. George W. was born in a Mormon colony in Chihuahua shortly before Pancho Villa and the Mexican Revolution chased the family back across the border to the United States. They became refugees in El Paso, Texas. Romney recalled learning the value of logic at an early age. "Mex!" his kindergarten peers would taunt him. Rather than protest his whiteness directly or stand up for the brown man, he applied a Vulcan's logic. "Look, if a kitten were born in a garage," he asked, "would that make it an automobile?" Romney's impeccable debating skills and his impressive turn at biographical foreshadowing overawed the little racists. They desisted. Further foreshadowing came in the 1930s when George W. conducted studies for the Automobile Manufacturers Association. His research showed that people were beginning to use their cars for workaday errands. The sober Romney saw in that result a return to more sensible transportation. At least those were the stories he told *Time* magazine when he graced its cover in 1959.

George Mason, the visionary leader of Nash Motors, is responsible for Romney's automotive career. With an engineering degree from the University of Michigan, Mason had risen to be the head of production for Chrysler by the age of thirty-five. Mason hired Romney to stage the Automobile Golden Jubilee in 1946, two weeks of marketing events in Detroit. Then, as Mason's assistant, Romney learned the business from the ground up. Like the other independent automakers, Nash had struggled to survive the thirties and found itself back at the precipice when the Big Three started turning out postwar models. Rather than challenge them head on, Mason focused the company on the Nash Rambler, a small, sensible, economical car introduced in 1951. He was wise enough not to call it "small," the kiss of death for an American automobile. So he invented a new category, the "compact car." Nash also developed and had produced under contract with Austin of England the Nash Metropolitan. It is just the cutest little thing on four wheels, a cartoon version of a full-sized Nash with barely more than two seats but posed as a Detroit dream boat with two-tone paint, plenty of chrome, and styling cues implying road-hugging weight. Sales averaged only about 8,000 units a year for the decade it was on sale.

The independents would have to achieve manufacturing scale to survive. To do so, Mason tried to create a single life raft into which all of the remaining independent automakers could jump. Following in the footsteps of Billy Durant, he tried to merge Nash, Studebaker, Hudson, and Packard into an integrated concern that would offer a car for every purse and purpose. This grand vision never came to pass. Instead, Studebaker merged with Packard, leaving Nash and Hudson to go home together under the unobjectionable name American Motors Corporation. Unfortunately, almost as soon as the ink dried on the merger, Mason died suddenly at the age of sixty-three. Romney had two years of junior college under his belt and a career of lobbying the government on behalf of industry when he woke up one morning in 1954 to find himself in charge of AMC. After six short months under the watch of an automotive visionary and trained engineer, AMC would have a handsome PR man at the helm.

Romney was no George Mason. At AMC his best idea seems to have been pulling out the old tooling for the 1951 Nash Rambler, updating the sheet metal, and selling it as "new" in 1958. He then did what he did best, public relations. Romney loudly derided the monstrosities other companies were building. Instead, he said, Americans should be sensible, stoic even, and buy a small car. He traveled some 70,000 miles around the country in 1958, driving his Rambler and making speeches to dealers, to women's clubs, to anyone who would listen. Romney had a toy triceratops that he would stand on his lectern. The triceratops had died out because his grille had gotten too flashy, his body too big, he explained. Detroit's big sedans would soon go the way of the dinosaurs. "Ladies," he would scold the women of the clubs, "why do you drive such big cars? You don't need a monster to go to the drugstore for a package of hairpins. Think of the gas bills!"

Romney's plan worked briefly. Sales climbed. Then, a year after the reintroduction of the Rambler, the Big Three hit the market with their own compact cars. They soon put AMC back in its place as an also-ran. But by then George W. had made the cover of *Time*, and he had political ambitions. He was elected governor of Michigan in 1963, which is what must have inspired his son Mitten to become governor of Massachusetts. In 1968, George W. would found the family business of running unsuccessfully for president.

The Rambler was not the only challenger to the ethos of the longer-lower-wider American automobile in the 1950s. Our allies from Britain invaded first with the Hillman Minx, the Jaguar XK120 and the stunning Austin-Healey 100-4. (I gasped involuntarily at my first sight of that car.) The open two-seat MG, also from England, was the number-one-selling import of 1953. With a fender line out of the 1920s, the MG was the car for drivers who fancied themselves Bertie Wooster. Number two on the list, the Minx, aimed at the mainstream. It was a scaled-down version of the American sedan, good on gas mileage and attractive enough, if not beautiful. Owners liked the car and reported 27 mpg in the city and 32 on the open road, double what they could expect from an American sedan. On the other hand, the same *Popular Mechanics* poll on gas mileage found that early adopters wanted bigger engines and more room, and they complained of being pushed around on the road by big cars. One owner said, "I find that even old ladies in big Caddies will try to outdrag me at lights." If they tried, they succeeded: the Minx did a 33.3-second quarter mile, according to the magazine's test; the typical Caddy accomplished that feat in twenty seconds. Also, parts had to be ordered from England, stranding owners for weeks when they needed repairs. Dealerships were undercapitalized while back at the factory they blamed American drivers rather than British craftsmanship for the car's faults. The British continued to succeed with sports cars but the little Minx sunk their prospects in the broader market.

The Italians arrived in 1956 with the teensy-weensy Fiat. In 1958, Japan sold 287 Toyopets, a mash-up of a Pokémon and a house pet, that couldn't reach Interstate speeds. Detroit at first ignored the imports—they were tiny and a tiny fraction of the market—and then responded by importing cars from their own European subsidiaries. Buick dealers got the Opel Rekord from GM's German subsidiary. It looked like a tchotchke Chevrolet, an aspirational representation of American abundance to display on the mantelpiece. Ford drew on its British models, and Chrysler from the French Simca. These so-called captive imports, with familiar American names and dealership networks behind them, began squishing the foreigners. Unfortunately, one little bug slipped through.

The first German KdF-Wagen, or "Strength Through Joy" car, arrived from Wolfsburg in January 1949. The man from Volkswagenwerk held a news conference on board the freighter. "We got a lot of publicity—all of it bad," Ben Pon recalled. He told the gathered press that VW stood for "Victory Wagon." They wrote down, "Hitler's car." An image captures Pon buttonholing a potential customer as the ship's crane hoisted it onto the dock. No dealer would carry it. Too soon. It didn't help that Pon's guttural Dutch sounded German to American ears. The Dutchman had to hawk his demonstrator in order to pay his hotel bill before retreating to Germany. Over the next few years, VW worked with a New York importer but only managed to sell a few thousand cars before 1953. By then, Americans were ready to let bygones be bygones. The company built a new network of distributors and dealerships intent on being sure that, unlike the British and the Italians, but like Henry Ford, they would be able to service the cars they sold. With a solid dealer network in place and a factory that took care of its customers, sales of the Volkswagen Beetle began to grow.

It was an odd little car with a rounded hood and body, distinct front and rear fenders, and a windshield that stood nearly vertical, interrupting any pretense to aerodynamic efficiency. Its headlights called to mind the large dewy eyes of an infant. The rounded body seemed plump with baby fat. While American cars floated over the highways like magic carpets, the orbicular Bug plodded along. That look remained fundamentally unchanged from the first car the Fuhrer demoed in 1938 to the final car to come off the last Brazilian production line in 2003.* It featured an air-cooled engine that, unlike the disastrous Copper-Cooled Chevrolet, was small enough to dissipate heat readily from its cast-iron cylinder head. As on the Tucker Torpedo, that engine sat in the rear, thereby eliminating the space-stealing driveshaft and improving serviceability. In a pinch, the rear end could be jacked up and the engine dropped out for a roadside repair. Ferdinand Porsche described his design philosophy as a "fundamentally new approach . . . to turn 'normal vehicles' existing hitherto in to 'people's cars.'" That claim, of course, recalls the Model T of the first automobile revolution. Like Henry's Ford, the Beetle was the brainchild of a notorious Jew hater, Adolf Hitler. It was built with slave labor during the war. Recall too that Ford had a good deal of trouble getting capital to support his plans for a small, lightweight, cheap car for the people. Capital wanted nothing to do with the Beetle either. Although they came to regret their choice, the many companies and individuals invited to invest in the Beetle saw no profit in it. It was kept alive during the war by the National Socialists and resurrected by the American occupation forces afterwards. Heinz Nordoff, VW's Alfred Sloan, would barter Beetles to secure coal and steel for the plant. The idea was not to sell cars per se, but to put men to work, to give them purpose in the rubble. In his company mission statement, Nordoff included a goal that echoed the rhetoric, if not the reality, behind Ford's five-dollar day: "To build up an enterprise which belongs to its workers more than any other

---

* The car's Art Deco shape has such enduring appeal that VW introduced the New Beetle in 1998, and then a second generation that hewed even more closely to the original, although neither has anything to do with the original under the skin.

industrial concern in the world." It is hard to imagine such a statement coming out of Detroit in the 1950s.

Sales of 980 units in the United States in 1953 ballooned to 420,000 a year and 4.4 percent of the market by 1966. Some 18 million VW Beetles eventually sold, outpacing the Model T's record of 15 million.

For all its ingenuity and appeal, the Bug did not compare well to the compact American automobiles of 1959. It was cramped, underpowered, dangerous in crosswinds, cold in winter, and noisy year-round. The car was positively deadly in a crash. Owners boasted that their Bugs offered fun, almost sporty, handling and good road feel compared to a Brobdingnagian Buick. Real Americans know that "handling" is a euphemism for the lack of power steering and "road feel" means "bumpy ride." Yet to a certain, and growing, minority of Americans even those drawbacks had appeal. To drive a Bug was to reject the car that capitalism built in favor of the socialist machine, the people's car.

Volkswagen turned its inability to keep up with the annual model change into a Clio-award-winning critique of American car culture. One print ad didn't even show the car, only a caption: "No point showing the '62 Volkswagen. It still looks the same." The implicit rejection of Sloan's annual model change again recalled the timeless Model T. While Detroit was taking low-angle photos to make its bigger-is-better sedans look as imposing as possible, VW presented a distant shot of a tiny Bug over the caption, "Think Small."

The Big Three counterattacked with domestic compact models that were bigger and more American than the Bug and their own captive imports. In 1959, Chevy presented the Corvair, followed in 1960 by Chrysler's Dodge Dart/Plymouth Valiant twins and Ford's Falcon, and in 1961, the Chevy II. It is a sign of Detroit group think and sophisticated industrial espionage operations that these cars debuted within days of each other. Chrysler had even planned to call its car "Falcon" but Ford politely called dibs. They were great cars in their own way. More comfortable to ride and drive than the imports and cheaper and less absurd than the big boats. The Dart and Valiant would stay in production an astounding sixteen years before being downsized during the bicentennial. Four years after introducing the Falcon, Ford would lop a bit off the back to create one of the most iconic cars of all time: the Mustang. The new lineup did its job. More than 880,000 were built in 1960. Imports fell from 614,000 in 1960 to 339,000 in 1961. Romney's Rambler was vanquished as well.

Of these, none was more daring than the Chevrolet Corvair. It would be the American Beetle right down to its rear engine cooled by the wind. Aluminum heads kept the weight down. The trunk had actual room for stuff and it was better looking than a Bug, most agreed. To my eye the rear deck and overhang are too long for a truly sporty profile. The shallow slope of the rear glass bleeds any sense of forward motion, let alone speed. The car looks better as a convertible, its odd greenhouse removed. Plenty of buyers in the 1960s disagreed with my assessment, though, which is all that matters. There was a version to take on every variety of Volkswagen on the market. Why not trade in that VW pickup for a Corvair Rampside? The Corvan was a better-looking version of the VW panel van. A Greenbrier will take you camping as well as a Westphalia Bus. A Corvair station wagon competed against the VW Squareback. The Ultra Van company even produced an RV using the Corvair drivetrain, one-upping the VW. None of these alt-Corvairs did terribly well. For example, 13,262 pickups were built the year they were introduced, but sales the following year fell to 4,471 and 851 by 1964.

One flavor of Corvair, however, gained traction in the marketplace. The sporty Monza outsold the standard Corvair sedan three to one. In other words, although GM had set out to make a Detroit Beetle, Americans wouldn't cooperate. Instead, they confirmed what GM executives had known all along: Americans wanted cars that looked good. They wanted cars that made them look good.

Thus, the shock of *Sputnik* had worn off a few short years later and the status quo ante was restored. Detroit had beaten back most of the imports and the Beetle still had a relatively small market share. Even John Keats and his fellow aesthetes would have to be impressed with how Detroit responded to complaints about gaudy chrome and frivolous tail fins. GM designers let their tail fins go flaccid, flopping over into a batwing shape that faded year by year. Ford had never quite embraced the tail fin, but even Virgil Exner's shrank rapidly after 1959 and by the early 1960s, tail fins were gone altogether. Chrome was shed. Although still longer, lower, and wider, the squared off shapes looked lighter and crisper, befitting the era of JFK, the Beatles, and skinny ties. The attack on Detroit, however, had only just begun.

Whereas Keats treated the chromed boats with biting comedy, a lean young Ivy League lawyer who would take on Detroit in the 1960s was dead serious. Chevrolet's innovative Corvair was his first victim.

Chapter 8

THE AUTOMOTIVE WOMB

Ralph Nader called the Corvair "unsafe at any speed" because of its tendency to flip over. In a sharp turn the car would trip over its own tires.

STRANGE AS YOUR FIRST RIDE IN A DRIVERLESS CAR MAY feel, a driver who fell asleep in her '59 Pontiac Safari station wagon would feel just as strange if she woke up behind the wheel of a 2018 Toyota Highlander—the modern mom-mobile. Even if waking up after a sixty-year nap didn't disorient her, the inside of the car would. The keyless "on" button might seem another 1950s-style selling feature like the push-button automatic transmissions of the period. The television screens would get a smile. This is the future, after all.

Actually operating the Highlander would not be much different from commanding the Safari: the horn, the brake pedal, the steering wheel, and so forth are all in the same places and operate the same way. But she would have trouble seeing through the steeply slanted windshield and past the massive, sturdy pillars holding up the roof and housing the airbags. "How am I supposed to see the cross traffic?" The high seat backs designed to prevent whiplash might induce claustrophobia. Once she'd figured out the lap and shoulder belts, she might notice the airbag warning on the sun visor, "DEATH or SERIOUS INJURY can occur." She'd have to unbuckle, then shift her three-year-old into the back seat where he would sit caterwauling that he had done nothing wrong to deserve the demotion. Again behind the wheel, she'd be afraid to back out of the driveway. The rear-view mirror would be useless because those safety seat backs block the view out the rear window. Anyway, the dictates of aerodynamics and styling have shrunk the rear window to a tiny, 1930s-era porthole. So, she'd try the side mirror. "Objects in mirror are closer than they appear," our Rip Van Winkle driver would read, wondering how *much* closer. She might give up on the mirrors and windows altogether and turn her attention to the screen in the dash with its unobstructed view of the outside world. Better still, she might close her eyes, wish it were 1959 again, and let the car drive itself.

Ms. Van Winkle's difficulties arise from a singular safety solution: the crashworthy car. The American automobile has become a wandering womb protecting a fetal driver. In the event of even a minor crash, much of the car crumples like tinfoil to absorb the blow. The vehicle sacrifices itself to save its occupants. Inside, the lap and shoulder belt lessens the chance of a "second collision" between the passenger and the inside of the vehicle. If there is a second collision, the steering wheel and dashboard are fully padded and free of sharp corners. A pair of white pillows inflates explosively—in milliseconds—to nestle the frightened riders. An air-filled crinoline curtain explodes from the roof edge, to envelope the scene, not for modesty but for protection in a side-impact crash.

All of these features have their origin in the Motor Vehicle Safety Act signed into law September 9, 1966. The law decreed that no new car could be sold unless it had safety features devised and required by the federal government. The agency that became the National Highway Traffic Safety Administration (NHTSA) issued its first thirteen Federal Motor Vehicle Safety Standards (FMVSS) within six months. Of these, none has saved more lives than standard 208, which requires seat belts and "passive restraints," or airbags. With the 1968 model year, every new car became a joint venture between Detroit and Washington.

Although 35,000 to 40,000 people manage to die in car wrecks each year, it has become pretty hard to do so inside the modern automotive womb. As long as you buckle up, stay sober, get enough sleep, and don't speed, you have more things to worry about than a fatal crash. If you're a typical driver, and have been at it more than a few years, the womb may already have saved you from serious injury or death. The crashworthy car concept has been highly effective. Yet, there are many ways to skin a cat and many ways to keep it alive. Therefore, as I have done with the invention of the automobile, and will do with the advent of the driverless car, I want to ask why this particular way of keeping us safe was chosen and how that choice has shaped the American automobile. And we should ask why it happened when it did.

The idea behind the crashworthy car emerged first among physicians examining airplane and car crashes. (Safety experts no longer speak of "accidents" as the word implies an incident that could not be prevented.) They came at the problem from the experience of treating serious injuries. Had they had expertise in crash causation, driver's education, or engineering, they surely would have proposed solutions in those realms. Also, they did not think in terms of protecting those outside the vehicle, which would be silly in the case of airplanes but a blind spot when it came to cars. Rather than focus on avoiding crashes, they looked specifically at how the human body responds when crashes do happen.

Segments of the automobile industry had shown interest in crashworthiness as early as the 1930s, but by the 1950s, when politicians were finally attending to the task of requiring safer cars, General Motors in particular had switched to antagonism and foot-dragging. So, physicians alone may not have been able to effect change. But joined by legislators and tenacious product-liability lawyers, they were able to force the industry's hand. Through tort law—the same sort of civil suits used to get toys that choke children off the market— they sued automakers on behalf of crash victims. In the past, an American automobile was defective only if it were ugly—like the 1929 "pregnant" Buick or the 1958 Edsel—or if the wheels fell off. By the 1960s, however, safety advocates defined the American automobile as a defective product because of its designed-in dangers.

Torts and federal rulemaking have proved to be blunt instruments that have led in some cases to missteps and overreach. Today, government cannot keep up. NHTSA has surrendered leadership in the area of crash testing to a private foundation, the Insurance Institute for Highway Safety. Of course, regulations might not be necessary had the automobile industry taken a proactive approach to safety. Nevertheless, the politicization of automobile safety has shaped the car culture. Rather than noble heroes, many in the automobile industry as well as many enthusiastic consumers of car culture considered the safety advocates, alongside the air quality regulators, enemies of America.

The underlying theory that the inside of the car could use some padding became obvious as soon as the closed car arrived on the market in the 1920s. The "second collision," the one between the passenger and the inside of the car, featured prominently in the gruesome and popular story told by J. C. Furnas in 1935. Again, his *Reader's Digest* article made quite clear that car interiors were loaded with lethal knobs and shrapnel. The innocent looking steering column he revealed to be a harpoon aimed at the driver's heart.

Even as Furnas worked through drafts of his jeremiad for the *Reader's Digest*, a Detroit plastic surgeon was installing soft dashboard padding (which he later patented) and seat belts inside his own car. Dr. Claire Straith made a living patching up the faces of people disfigured by chrome knobs and sharp edges. "It's a slaughter," he said. He launched a crusade. He gave slide presentations to automotive engineers showing the damage inflicted by chromed knobs and thin steering wheels. He met separately with Walter Chrysler, Studebaker's safety-minded Paul Hoffman, and the iconoclast Preston Tucker. "[Straith] described with unfailing accuracy the styling of the gash marks on each face," a Tucker designer recalled, "and compared them to the offending styling objects such as the radio grille of a particular car or the heater knob." All were convinced to design safer interiors. Tucker designers, working after World War II, even wanted to add seat belts but were overruled. "The Tucker sales department maintained that the presence of safety belts would imply that the automobile was dangerous," one stylist recalled. Their survey of airline flight attendants indicated that passengers did not like them.

By the 1950s, even the modest prewar safety improvements were lost to annual model changes. So, our time-traveling friend might have felt relieved to get herself and her boy back into the familiarity of the 1959 Pontiac—relieved until, that is, she crashed. In what today would be considered a minor collision, the unbelted driver's head would meet a horn ring as thin as a cookie cutter. If she somehow dodged the horn ring slicer, she might have ended up smashing her head against the plastic ornament at the wheel's center, permanently branding **PONTIAC** into her forehead. The padded dashboard, introduced as an option in 1956, might have helped protect her son a bit if he had been allowed to stay in the front seat, although it only covered the sharp edge and top of the dash. Because he was shorter than the average adult male, he would most likely would strike below it, instead hitting the jet-exhaust styled A/C duct, or the steel glove box door.

While interior designs had moved in the wrong direction, Straith's safety crusade of the 1930s spread to other physicians by the 1950s. Dr. John Stapp had conducted crash research for the Air Force beginning in 1947. He quietly extended his studies from airplanes to cars, even though he was supposed to stick to flying machines. He used chimps and black bears—anesthetized, at least—in crashes to see what happened. Pathologist and engineer Hugh DeHaven also came to the field of automobile crashworthiness from his experience with airplanes. He gained support from automakers by gently telling them their products were being unfairly criticized for causing injuries and deaths. He began work with the Indiana State Police to collect data on fatal and injury crashes. Such data had never been collected in a systematic way.

Thus encouraged by medical pioneers, the Society of Automotive Engineers set up a committee to develop standards for seat belts in 1955 and held what became an annual meeting. The Automotive Crash Research Field Demonstration and Conference included not only dry research papers but real live car crash tests. (Try that, American Political Science Association!) Also in 1955, the Committee on Trauma of the American College of Surgeons publicly called on Detroit to "stress occupant safety as a basic factor in automobile design." Covering the story, the college's journal editors wrote, "Anywhere from 70 to 90 percent of these [38,000 annual deaths] need never have occurred if the most rudimentary provisions had been made for the control of deceleration, that is, the safety belt as used in [commercial airliners]." The American Medical Association formally asked President Eisenhower to lobby for a congressional committee to "approve and regulate standards of automobile construction." Ike passed the request to his friend and chairman of the President's Committee for Traffic Safety, GM president Harlow H. Curtice.

Insurance companies also joined the crashworthiness crusade. Liberty Mutual Insurance worked with the Cornell Aeronautical Laboratory to design a pair of "Survival Cars" to show what was possible. The interior of the first (now on display at The Henry Ford museum) looks like the inside of a B-movie Venusians' spaceship crossed with a padded cell. With a strong structure and lap belts (notably not three-point shoulder belts), the car could in theory let occupants survive a crash at fifty miles an hour, they found. When presented with the results in 1961, GM president John Gordon described it as a "fine job of dramatizing the need for auto safety. But we wonder if the American people will accept these features." Liberty and Cornell then tried adding safety features to an existing model, but got no further in convincing GM. In 1959, leading insurers set up the Insurance Institute for Highway Safety to fund research. The IIHS changed its mission in 1968 to conduct research directly. Its first set of tests involved bumpers.

Meanwhile, Ford took the idea of the second collision seriously. Influenced by Hugh DeHaven, the company introduced its "Lifeguard Design" for the 1956 model year. The package included padded sun visors, a padded dash, stronger door locks, and seat belts. It was pushed through by Ford's Robert McNamara, one of the "Whiz Kid" statisticians hired in 1946 to bring order to the bureaucratic and fiscal chaos old Henry had created. He served briefly as Ford Motor Company president in 1960 before leaving to botch the Vietnam War as secretary of defense. The optional padded dash had not figured prominently in GM advertising whereas safety was a key pitch for the '56 Ford. Sales of the Ford suffered until "safety" was removed from the ads. Its lackluster reception led executives throughout the industry to conclude, "safety doesn't sell." It became an article of faith.

Like the cigarette makers at the time, the auto industry was not budging. But the medical profession finally gained an ear in Congress. A surgeon harangued Senator Paul Douglas of Illinois to take up the cause; Kenneth Roberts, Democratic congressman from Alabama, was able to achieve quiet passage of a law to require safety features on the government's own vehicle fleets. (He came to the issue after a car crash during his honeymoon: the wedding china, still carefully wrapped, emerged intact.) That same year, freshman senator and former Connecticut governor Abraham Ribicoff took on the issue. Ribicoff chaired something called the Committee on Government Operations Subcommittee on Executive Reorganization—a position as awesomely powerful as it sounds. A few twists of fate, however, turned the little-known senator's even less known committee into the stage for a great legislative drama. By the time the curtain fell, the star of the show was not Ribicoff, but a fellow Nutmegger who sat behind the senator and fed him questions: Ralph Nader.

Ralph Nader wrote *Unsafe at Any Speed: The Designed-In Dangers of the American Automobile* in 1965. It became a best seller and transformed American car culture. Nader is properly known as a crusader for auto safety. Nevertheless, his indictment of the industry went far beyond the complaints of others, far beyond the call for seat belts, padded interiors, and crashworthy cars. It was a product-liability brief at base, aimed at the automobile writ large. Had the umbrella industry been selling umbrellas that melted in the rain, Nader would have written a similar brief, though perhaps without the same moral outrage.

Nader's *Unsafe at Any Speed* prosecutes every corner of the American automobile industry, from the engineers and stylists to the "traffic safety establishment." Beginning in the 1920s and accelerating with the industry's response to J. C. Furnas's —*And Sudden Death*, "engineering, education, and enforcement"—the three E's—had defined crash prevention efforts. "Most accidents are in the class of driver fault; driver fault is in the class of violated traffic laws; therefore, observance of traffic laws by drivers would eliminate most accidents," he wrote, explaining the existing framework. Engineering referred only to engineering better roads. A chapter on the "Power to Pollute" describes how the industry knew that automobiles produced harmful exhausts in the 1920s but ignored that knowledge. But apparently most readers never got past the first chapter, "The Sporty Corvair: The One-Car Accident." *Unsafe* has gone down in history as the book that killed the Corvair.

Although the sporty Monza version became the best seller, the Corvair was intended as a cheap and basic car, a rear-engined, air-cooled American Beetle. As a rear-engined car, the Corvair had a heavier tail than nose that made for quick and sporty handling. Like all rear-engined cars, however, this rear-weight bias causes it to oversteer—to drive itself into an ever tighter spiral until it rolls over. Front-engined cars are safer because they understeer: when you try to turn too sharply, the car just won't do it. It plows ahead. The Corvair also used a swing axle rear suspension, again like the Beetle. The rear wheels would tuck under the body and lose their grip, exacerbating oversteer to the point where the car flipped over. Even a soft shoulder or good pothole could upend the car, Nader said. The Corvair was a defective product.

Wrongful-death lawsuits began in 1961. At least some of these suits were dismissed, settled, or won by GM. Discovery revealed, however, that Chevy engineers knew of the axle design defect (Nader's word) when the car was on the drawing board. But the company did not want to spend the short money needed to correct the problem. In fact, owners could buy "Camber Compensators" for under twenty dollars on the aftermarket. But only hard-core car guys who wanted "spirited handling" would even know about such upgrades.

By the spring of 1965, Nader had missed his first manuscript deadline for *Unsafe* and Ribicoff was getting nowhere. Auto executives ignored the hearings before the Subcommittee on Executive Reorganization. So, Ribicoff invited them to testify. The men from Detroit felt confident as they waded through the congressional snooze fest. As the questions grew more pointed, however, with Nader supplying some of them, the hearings became DC's hottest ticket. When Nader himself testified, the television cameras showed up. The television cameras, in turn, drew the interest of Senator Robert Kennedy, who drew yet more interest because he was Robert Kennedy.

Senator Kennedy's artful balancing of grandstanding and inquisition became the headline. Most famously, he asked GM president James Roche how much the company spent on safety research. About 1.25 million, Roche answered. Then, Kennedy forced Roche to tell him how much profit GM made. As a smart prosecutor, Kennedy already knew the answer; it was a matter of public record.

Roche tried to wiggle out but finally allowed that the company had earned $1.7 billion. Kennedy had scored his point by forcing the GM president to admit that the company spent less than one percent of its profits on safety research. During the next day's testimony, Kennedy mocked Chrysler executives who shrugged when asked how much they spent on safety. "Will the people from Chrysler Corporation just raise their hands?" Kennedy asked. With a half-dozen executives with hands raised in attendance, the senator feigned shock and dismay.

Then the bombshell: Nader announced that private investigators were questioning his friends, tailing him, and harassing him by phone. The dicks worked for GM. The stories were as sensational as they were comical. One private eye said he found himself "tumbling into investigators all over the place." Two men trailed Nader onto a plane in Philadelphia, but he managed to give them the slip when the plane landed in DC. Two other investigators followed a *Washington Post* reporter after mistaking him for Nader. The Capitol police intervened. Nader was propositioned twice by "attractive young women in their 20s" (he was thirty-two at the time). While leafing through car magazines in a drug store, a woman approached with the most bizarre pickup line of all time: Would he like to participate in a "foreign affairs discussion" at her apartment? Nader said he declined the offer, but did not indicate whether he chose to purchase a car magazine. Then the investigators made the mistake of calling on Nader's law school buddy, Frederick Condon. At his home in New Hampshire, Condon received the detective and took meticulous notes of their meeting. The detective asked about Nader's political beliefs and whether his ancestry—his parents had immigrated from Lebanon and Nader spoke Arabic—made him anti-Semitic. Why wasn't he married? "Are you asking me if he is a homosexual?" Condon replied.

"I've seen him on TV and he certainly doesn't look like . . ." said the detective, his implication clear. "But we have to be sure."

Condon told a reporter that none of these areas were the investigator's main concern. He mostly wanted to hear about Nader's driving record. He asked three or four times if Nader had a license and whether he had ever been seen driving a car. Testifying before a Michigan state senate committee, a chief engineer at Chevrolet similarly attacked Nader as un-American. Nader did not own a car, he said. "I don't even know if he has a license." Gay or not, communist or not, anti-Semitic or not, meant little compared to the most damning charge of all: Nader did not drive. For the record, Nader had not owned a car since selling his 1949 Studebaker but as of March 1966, his Connecticut driver's license was still valid.

GM first called the accusations of surveillance absurd. Then the company claimed they were part of a routine investigation related to Corvair litigation. One operative, by way of denial, bragged, "If we were checking up on Nader he'd never know about it." Then Ribicoff called James Roche before his committee and demanded an answer. Roche publicly apologized, but the damage to the company's reputation was done. The political intrigue put Nader's book, which had gotten off to a slow start, onto the best-seller list for thirteen weeks. He sued GM for $26 million but settled for $425,000 (about $3.2 million in today's dollars). GM's involuntary largess funded Nader's Center for Auto Safety, among other public interest groups. He hired young law students who became known as "Nader's Raiders" for their legal attacks on corporate America.

Ribicoff and others had been making slow, halting progress toward regulation. The dramatic hearings and the harassment of Nader, however, tipped the scales. As was the case with the fight against air pollution, Detroit's unwillingness to take responsibility undermined its exalted place in American culture and politics and made immediate passage of safety legislation inevitable. Even LBJ agreed. On September 9, 1966, in a Rose Garden ceremony, President Johnson signed the twin National Traffic and Motor Vehicle Safety Act and Highway Safety Act into law, creating the agency that became known as NHTSA. The *New York Times* ran a front-page photo of Johnson and Nader shaking hands after the signing.

Through Nader's efforts, and the inadvertent help of GM's Inspectors Clouseau, hundreds of thousands of lives have been saved; tens of millions have avoided injury. But for Nader's detractors, the story does not end there. Some of the critics fall into the "usual suspects" category. Henry Ford II said the safety regulations could wreck the economy. "We'll have to close down," he warned. "I think that, if these critics who don't really know anything about the safety of an automobile will get out of our way, we can go ahead with our job," Ford said. "We have to make safer cars." He mocked Nader saying that if he really knew so much about automobile suspensions, Ford would hire him as an engineer. Michigan governor George Romney reminded people that the automakers had pulled the country out of past depressions.

The legendary *Car and Driver* columnist Brock Yates routinely referred to Nader as the head "safety Nazi." "Nader could not even drive a car," Yates repeated the automotive blood libel. The outpouring of honorifics upon Yates's death in 2016 demonstrated his status as an unreconstructed hero to readers of the car mags. To Yates, the "gauleiters" were one with the environmentalists. Just as safety improvements took the fun out of driving and the style out of cars, pollution control technologies sapped engines of power. Twenty years before George Will would announce that liberals love trains, Yates observed that "those who believe in social engineering . . . see automobiles as a tool of potential anarchy. . . . A population riding obediently on carefully scheduled trains or buses makes for order," he wrote in *The Decline and Fall of the American Automobile Industry* in 1983.

Like Nader, Yates had ample contempt for Detroit's products of the time, noting that they were "slaves to inertia," able to move in a straight line but not stop or change direction without complaining. In his view, crashes could be avoided by improving handling. Instead, "They wanted Detroit to build automobiles that were invulnerable: four-wheel padded cells in which witless drivers could bash into each other without fear of injury."

Although we should expect nothing less than denunciation from industry and driving enthusiasts, many liberals despise Nader, considering him an egomaniacal spoiler in the 2000 presidential election. I can only assume that Malcolm Gladwell was still deeply depressed about *Bush v. Gore* when he penned "Wrong Turn: How the Fight to Make America's Highways Safer Went Off Course" for the *New Yorker*. Gladwell focused his attack on the distinction between active and passive safety solutions for occupant protection.

In the realm of occupant protection, seat belts are considered active safety devices: the occupant must take action, must buckle up, to gain protection. Airbags are passive safety devices: they protect drivers and passengers without them taking any action at all. In what has become a liberal talking point, automobile safety in the United States has lagged behind countries because NHTSA failed to ask, insist, or force people to take the simple action of buckling their seat belts. Australia, Canada, and most European countries enacted Mandatory Use Laws (MULs) in the 1970s. Belt use immediately jumped from about 10 percent in those countries to 50 percent after passage of MULs. With education and enforcement, rates continued to rise to over 90 percent. There is no federal law in the United States, but New York became the first state to pass an MUL in 1984 with all states but New Hampshire having them in place by 1996. Rates that had been as low as 5 percent now average 90 percent (Georgia is highest at 97 percent; New Hampshire, lowest at 70 percent). Gladwell admits that the post-1966 changes to automobiles have saved tens of thousands of lives but they could have saved 160,000 more over the same period with MULs. He even had Nader admitting as much when he quotes the safety advocate's surprise at the high levels of seat belt use we have achieved in the United States. Gladwell's most biting conclusion is this: "Nader was never the kind of activist who had great faith in the people whose lives he was trying to protect."

Gladwell tells a story of religious devotion to a false god, the airbag. NHTSA's first administrator, the epidemiologist William Haddon, became wedded to the airbag. Haddon told the industry in 1968 that airbags should be "the highest priority that the industry and the government . . . should have." Daniel Moynihan "falls under his spell," according to Gladwell; lawyers are his "biggest disciples," and Nader was a "devotee" who wrote an "homage to the Haddon philosophy." They're not Yates's "safety Nazis," just cult members. The actual airbag story is far more interesting, involving secret Oval Office tapes, suppressed consumer surveys, and accusations of car dealers trying *not* to sell customers on airbags.

Haddon's background in public health directed him to a remedy that did not "require any active contribution on the part of the user." As he told a Congressional committee in 1967, "This is the approach . . . which has been used in public health going back 50 and 100 years with such programs as pasteurization of milk, chlorination of water supplies, and so forth." Yet Nader attacked Haddon for holding confidential meetings with industry. William Stieglitz, the safety agency's chief engineer, resigned in protest over Haddon's deference to industry; he called the first safety standards "totally inadequate." Within two years, Haddon quit the agency to head up the newly reformed IIHS.

Also, Haddon was not alone in promoting the passive airbag solution. It was John Volpe, a liberal Republican appointed secretary of transportation by Richard Nixon, who first approved a rule requiring an "Inflatable Occupant Restraint System" in 1969. Furthermore, General Motors thought they were a good idea. GM told regulators in 1970 that it intended to install voluntarily one million airbags for the 1974 model year and as standard equipment on all of its cars by the following year.

Precisely what GM was up to with this announcement remains a question of some debate. The company had been investigating airbags since the 1950s and had developed workable devices. In 1973, the announced million shrank to 150,000, and in the end GM only sold about ten thousand. According to a *Wall Street Journal* cover story from the era, "The company and its dealers actively discouraged sales." On the other hand, *Automotive News* reported, "Big Ad Budget Fails to Sell Bags." GM's own survey results showed that customers wanted the bags and would pay a fairly high price for them. But, the results were suppressed until 1979. GM blamed NHTSA for not coming up with a clear standard and quit offering airbags for 1977.

Meanwhile, on April 27, 1971, Ford Motor Company president Lee Iacocca and CEO Henry Ford II met with President Nixon in the Oval Office to lobby against the airbag standard. They intended to file suit against it the following Monday in federal court.* "[My] views are, are, are frankly," Nixon began, "whether it's the environment or pollution or Naderism or consumerism, are extremely pro-business." But, he understood that the opposition forces were on the rise. "They're enemies of the system. . . . I am for the system," the president affirmed. Tricky Dick then took a cup of tea and settled in to listen.

Ford warned the president that safety and emissions requirements would add up to $800 to the price of the average car and raise the price of a Pinto by 50 percent. Ford proposed a seatbelt interlock: the car would not start until the driver buckled up. Everyone in the room agreed that soon an unchecked NHTSA wouldn't let them build cars anymore. "Look around," said Nixon, "and, uh, and, and, baby, baby bug-buggies."

Nixon sent John Ehrlichman to tell Volpe "to stop those [airbag] regulations, to make sure that they didn't go into effect." The airbag standard was delayed. Instead, for the 1974 model year, NHTSA adopted Ford's interlock system. (Not surprisingly, seat belt manufacturers also pushed interlocks.) The technology amounted to

---

* A transcript of the taped conversation was released by the National Archives under a court order arising from a civil suit against General Motors involving a fatal crash in 2004.

a switch: inserting the tongue into the buckle closed an electrical circuit. Perhaps on purpose the interlocks worked horribly. Safety minded as my parents were, they mostly left the front belts permanently buckled and tucked away. Drivers wrote their congressmen. Congressmen, knowing how to win votes, responded with no fewer than six different bills. These resulted in Public Law 93-492, signed October 27, 1974, which says that NHTSA cannot require "any continuous buzzer designed to indicate that safety belts are not in use, or any safety belt interlock system." To this day, it is illegal for a buzzer to sound for more than eight seconds. That's democracy in action.

The interlock disaster might also be a better explanation for the failure to pass mandatory seat-belt laws than Nader's elitism, Gladwell's explanation. When safety belt use rates finally began to rise after the late 1980s it was as a direct result of NHTSA's passive-restraint requirements. Safety advocates successfully sued Ronald Reagan's industry-friendly administration when it tried to eliminate the airbag rule. So Transportation Secretary Elizabeth Dole cut a deal with automakers: if they could convince enough states to pass mandatory seat belt laws (MULs), she would delay the airbag requirement. Yet the public was not necessarily on board. When New York State took up the first MUL in the country in 1984, "The mail was, I think, 18,000-to-1 against it," according to Governor Mario Cuomo. Further, many state legislatures voted for MULs with slim majorities. New York's lower house passed the bill 82–60.

*   *   *   *

ALTHOUGH I COUNT NADER among my heroes, he is not perfect. Nader's choice of the Chevrolet Corvair as the poster child for the designed-in dangers of the American automobile was unfortunate. The Corvair was the General's most innovative car in forty years, the first air-cooled car since the 1923 Copper-Cooled Chevy, and the company's first rear-engined car ever. "Adverse litigation" hurt Corvair sales in 1966, according to GM head Roche. Sales were off 70 percent year over year in early May. The Beetle had the same basic design and the same flaws. Had he instead made the Beetle the main character of *Unsafe at Any Speed*, the political struggle for auto safety might have taken a different course. After all, the Volkswagen was the car of the hippies, the college professors, the divorcees, who rejected Detroit's longer, lower, wider ethos. The bookish lawyer and son of Lebanese immigrants might have been hailed as a national hero by the public and even (sotto voce) by Detroit executives had he squashed the Bug.

In fact, Nader attacked the Beetle in Senate hearings. "I think it is hard to find a more dangerous car than the Volkswagen," he testified.* Also, Nader's organization, the Center for Auto Safety, published *Small—On Safety: The Designed-In Dangers of the Volkswagen* in 1972. I have seen no horror movie as scary as slow-motion VW Beetle crash footage. The car does nothing to protect occupants in a front-end barrier test; T-boned by an American sedan, it folds in half.

Although murdering the Corvair is reason enough for some to decry Nader, what irks me is the five-mile-per-hour bumper. NHTSA adopted a bumper standard for 1973 that forced automakers to replace stylish bumpers with spring-loaded battering rams covered in black rubber. Gone were the gorgeous "Dagmar" bumpers of the 1950s and the slim chrome bands of the 1960s. The "safety" bumper on the tiny '73 Fiat has enough room for a flight of espressos. Impalas were fitted with what can only be described as surplus cop-car pushers. The 1975 BMW 2002 looks like the Mona Lisa wearing braces.

In fact, the five-mile-per-hour bumper had nothing to do with safety. The Insurance Institute for Highway Safety had called for the standard because insurers were paying very high claims for low-speed, parking-lot-type crashes. So, it convinced NHTSA to require a bumper that would withstand a five-mile-per-hour crash without

* After the hearings, Nader did find a car he liked even less: the Czech Tatra. Ferdinand Porsche derived the Beetle from the Tatra.

damage. Nader himself told talk show host Dick Cavett during a 1969 television interview that the current bumper "at best, protects itself." He then described the high cost to consumers of low-speed crashes. The only trouble was, NHTSA didn't have the authority to promulgate regulations for the purpose of lowering insurance premiums. So, regulators came up with a workaround: FMVSS 215 requires that front bumpers protect "safety related equipment" such as brake and signal lights in a low-speed crash. Lee Iacocca of Ford saw right through the bumper ruse and told the president so during their confidential chat. "Mr. President," he said, "they [the regulators at NHTSA] don't like this bumper craze that's going on, led by the insurance lobby of the United States . . . because they realize that the more we concentrate on property damage, the less we may be concentrating on saving life and limb, which was the intent of the act." The Reagan administration was able to repeal the standard by using a cost-benefit analysis. It showed that savings on repairs were more than offset by the fuel economy penalty imposed by the heavier bumpers.

Ugly bumpers may be a small thing, but there is a larger point to be made about the duplicitous use of safety. Under the banner of safety, the first safety establishment gave us everything from the pre-textual traffic stop to driver's education. Nader had said plainly that he wanted better bumpers to protect consumers' pocketbooks. And the insurance industry wanted to protect its bottom line. But the promise of safety has enormous political power. That's why safety is the ultimate excuse for the driverless car.

Far more important than ugly rubber baby-buggy bumpers, the automotive womb does nothing to protect vulnerable road users such as cyclists and pedestrians. In that same 1969 Dick Cavett interview Nader casually said there is nothing we can do with cars to protect pedestrians. Yet inventors had demonstrated various vehicle-based solutions to protect pedestrians as early as the 1920s. There was the "Man Catcher," a net that would catch the stricken pedestrian. Trains were fitted with cowcatchers, that mustache on the front of old locomotives used to knock obstacles off the track. Some tried an automotive version. As with the pre-1890s automobile and crashworthiness, these inventions may not have been perfect. Yet certainly sit nearer the kooky end of the inventive spectrum. More scientific research on vehicle design for pedestrian protection began in 1971, about the time of Nader's comments. European Union rules now dictate that the front of a new car must hit the pedestrian low, on the legs, thereby tripping her up onto the hood rather than down onto the hard pavement. The hood must be higher than before and include a crumple zone, a feat accomplished by creating a void between the top of the engine and the hood. Volvo has introduced under-hood airbags that further enhance pedestrian safety. As has often been the case, the United States is finally catching up. Nader did not think anything could be done about pedestrians because he simply did not think about pedestrians. Pedestrians, qua pedestrians, were not automobile consumers of defective products. The Corvair didn't necessarily run over more people than the average car.

Despite these missteps, Nader and his allies in the federal government were able to achieve something no one else had. Claire Straith had experienced some success when he met with enlightened executives at Chrysler, Studebaker, and Tucker. His success did not spread or last. After years of cajoling, physicians' groups were unable to affect much change. Nader, however, succeeded by using the raw power of the courts and the federal government to force an obstinate industry to do the right thing.

Spend some time in an old car, a 1959 Pontiac Safari station wagon, say. The seat belts, if they had been ordered, probably slipped down between the bench seat and the bench back. Pulling away from the curb unbuckled, you may feel naked. But once you're comfortable, you'll notice how easy it is to see out that wraparound windshield. The A pillars, thick posts on your new car, have been pulled back, out of your line of sight. The cabin feels spacious, more like a living room than a cockpit. Without seat belts or airbags, you'll want to slow down and drive courteously. The life you save may be your own.

Chapter 9

THE ENERGY CRISIS ENDS THE AQUARIAN AGE

Americans waited in gas lines to fill their cars, and evidently their lawn mowers, during the energy crisis of the 1970s.

WE WERE RUNNING OUT OF CLEAN WATER AND BALD eagles. The rivers were too polluted to swim in, let alone to eat fish from. Acid rain was killing trees. In 1969, the Cuyahoga River caught fire (as it periodically did). That same year a huge oil slick coated Southern California when a rig blew out in the waters off Santa Barbara. Such catastrophes helped rally Americans to the environmental cause. Twenty million people celebrated the inaugural Earth Day in April 1970 and eight months later the Environmental Protection Agency opened its doors. In 1972, the Club of Rome published *The Limits to Growth*, a widely read study predicting that environmental degradation would limit future progress. The same year, NASA published a stunning photo of the Earth as a full disk fully illuminated by the sun. The image of a small blue marble against the blackness of space conveyed the message that the shared resources of our planet had limits. Woodsy Owl was everywhere in school, on trash bins, and on television exhorting, "Give a hoot, don't pollute."

Between Saturday morning cartoons, one of our favorite ads would appear. An Indian Chief comes into focus paddling his birch-bark canoe. He emerges from a vernal watercourse into the shadow of a city with its smokestacks and oil refineries. Trash laps at the bow. "Some people have a deep, abiding respect for the natural beauty that was once this country," the narrator intones. The focus changes and we see that the noble savage is standing at the edge of a busy highway. A passenger casually hurls garbage out of a moving Chevrolet. Garbage lands at feet of Native American Chief. Chief cries. It may sound corny, but not when you realize that Neil Young was on the radio that year singing, "Look at Mother Nature on the run / in the nineteen seventies." Joni Mitchell also had a hit with "Big Yellow Taxi." She sang against DDT and cutting down trees. And she concluded with that enduring line, "They paved paradise and put up a parking lot." It wasn't corny when Earth tones were in fashion.

What I will call the Aquarians challenged the Establishment on many fronts, including attacking the sacred American automobile. A slew of anti-car books hit the shelves: *Road to Ruin* (1969), *Superhighway—Superhoax* (1970), *Autokind vs. Mankind* (1971), *Dead End* (1972), *The Immoral Machine* (1972), and *Paradise Lost: The Decline of the Auto Industrial Age* (1973). John Jerome, editor of *Car and Driver* and onetime Chevrolet copywriter, put it plainly in *The Death of the Automobile* (1972). "The premise of this book is that the automobile must go," he wrote. By comparison, the early criticisms were nibbling around the edges. *Highway Homicide* (1966) and *Safety Last: An Indictment of the Auto Industry* (1966) extended Nader's brief on safety. *Highway Robbery* (1966) was about crooked mechanics and tricky car dealerships. Ronald Weiers (*Licensed to Kill*, 1968) attacked the American driver. Unlike Ralph Nader and these authors, the Aquarian vanguard wrote not to fix the American automobile but to declare and hasten its inevitable demise.

In this context, the energy crisis that began in 1973 should have set the Aquarians on the path toward final victory: the end of oil would kill off the American automobile and save us from ourselves. As I kid, I was happy imagining that by the twenty-first century we'd travel in bubble pods powered by, well, I didn't get that far. But the opposite happened. It would take time, but rather than presaging a golden post-automotive age, the gas crisis unleashed a counterattack. The automobile privilege and the American way of life would be defended, not surrendered. Beginning in 1980, the oil men took charge. They set quotas to limit small imports, encouraged the rise of large pickup trucks and SUVs, and projected American power outward to gather the world's oil and put it in our tanks.

Like the Aquarians, today's prophets of the new mobility believe the automobile has reached the end of the road. They too are convinced that—within twenty years or so—we'll be traveling in bubble pods, this time autonomous and electrically powered. Yet they revel in laissez-faire capitalism and find salvation in free-market economics, quite in contrast to Aquarians such as E. F. Schumacher. His seminal 1973 book, *Small Is Beautiful: Economics As If People Mattered*, expounded on the mismatch between standard economics on the one hand and environmental sustainability and human happiness on the other. Labor saving and capital investment to achieve efficiencies of scale—in a word, Fordism—produced machines that immiserated workers and, especially, citizens of the developing world. An "appropriate technology" should improve the human condition. Traditional economics gives us automobiles; Schumacher's economics gives us small, beautiful bicycles. Bikes travel faster and carry loads more comfortably than walking. Yet they are more affordable, healthful, environmentally friendly, and easily maintained than

big, ugly automobiles. The appropriate technology concept also figured prominently in the *Whole Earth Catalog* (1968–1972), which
Steve Jobs once called Google in book form. The catalog's origina-
tor, Stewart Brand, took his title from NASA's blue marble image
and his motivation from a desire to protect the earth.* It combined
practical how-to's with the history and philosophy of technology to
empower individuals and give them the tools to "shape [their] own
environment."

Like Schumacher, Kenneth Schneider challenged the logic of
industrial development and progress. He took this challenge directly
to the automobile in *Autokind vs. Mankind: An Analysis of Tyranny, a Proposal for Rebellion, a Plan for Reconstruction*. Schneider was a city planner with a degree from Berkeley and published in
Traffic Quarterly, the journal founded by William Phelps Eno, the
father of traffic engineering. He had been at it since the end of World
War II but somewhere along the way he experienced an epiphany
about his work as a planner: "In retrospect, I apparently put in more
time for General Motors as a city planner than for the municipal
organizations that paid me." Something more was needed: "The special pragmatic responses to the automobile's problems—the emissions control gimmicks, the safety crusades, and even the twelve-lane
freeways—serve automobility more than they do the people in the
end." They had, by polishing off the sharp edges of automobility,
allowed it to expand with devastating consequences. The same must
be said of autonomy and electrification: they alleviate some of the
symptoms of automobility but do not cure the disease. Automobiles,
however powered and however guided, occupy too much space and
use too much energy to move about. As Schneider put it, "A man
sized community cannot take cars."

Ronald Buel, the author of *Dead End*, also viewed the automo-

---

* In 1966, Brand began a publicity campaign to pressure NASA to provide
such a "whole Earth" image. Although the first cover featured the whole
earth, not until 1972 was he able to use the actual photo.

bile from an urban planning perspective. He tackled race and had a chapter entitled, "Social Justice and the Auto." He noted at the time that only 40 percent of black families had automobiles.* John Keats had no such sensibility in 1958: urban problems caused by the automobile mostly meant a lack of parking.

Buel also reviewed a proposal to reduce racial and economic inequality by handing out Volkswagens to the poor. Subsidies would "allow extension of private ownership of autos to the poor or to provide for auto-renting or organized car pooling." VWs could be purchased in bulk and then "rented out to the poor for seven or eight cents per passenger mile." He notes parenthetically that used American cars "still in good shape" could fit the bill as well. The Bugs would cost less to operate than mass transit and be as flexible as a universal taxicab system. It would be nothing less than a government-funded version of Uber. These plans never got off the ground, evidenced by the fact that there are no coin-op Beetles listed for sale in *Hemmings Motor News* or on eBay. Buel himself ultimately rejects the plan because, like Schneider, he believes even socialistic, countercultural Beetles would only further entrench automobility along with the "gross effects that our entire culture obtains from the automobile." Again, that is precisely what emissions technology and safety standards have done, and what electrification and autonomy will do: round off the edges to save automobility from itself.

As defenders of the city, Schneider and Buel might be expected to lobby for the end of the automobile. Shockingly, however, the Aquarian critique came even from the belly of the pro-auto beast: *Car and Driver*. John Jerome excoriates the car in *The Death of the Automobile*: automobiles kill almost sixty thousand and injure four million more each year, they pollute the environment more than any other industrial source, and "gobble natural resources like cocktail

---

* Nationwide, that number today is 76 percent for black households, which is still far lower than whites at 95 percent. Whites own two, three, and four cars at double the rate of black households. Latinos fall about in the middle in all categories.

peanuts." They destroy cities, make mass transit impossible, "spread squalor on the land," and jam up the courts. Cars "exacerbate our unsolved problems of poverty and race." Deep into his critique, he admits, "Oh, how I love cars, have loved cars." He writes not only of driving but auto repair: "I have also enjoyed quiet hours delving mechanical automotive innards, petting my technological triumph of the moment." He can only conjure a vague melancholy for the loss of his automotive intimates when balanced against the harm. The car has given him joy and a livelihood, yet he cheers its inevitable demise. His predictions of the transportation future have proved eerily prescient. He crystal balls ride hailing and electric cars. He expects crashworthiness—still inchoate and resented by many at the time—to become a selling point for Detroit. He considers the possibility, now come to pass, that the rest of the world will adopt American transportation patterns and thus become dependent on the automobile. Salesmen will laud, "Snow tires for the Himalayas! Antifreeze for Antarctica!" He describes scientists' doomsday scenarios: a "greenhouse" effect [quotes in the original], exhaust that blots out the sun, thereby freezing the globe, fuel combustion that consumes a quarter of the world's oxygen. "In the unlikely event that the directly automobile-related crises evaporate to allow unlimited growth, we'll run out of fossil fuels to combust," he concludes. Fortunately, smog "made us see, finally, that the automobile is the enemy" and roused us to "phase the automobile out of our economy and our lives."

If Jerome's post-automobile future vision had much impact on the car mags of the era, I have not been able to discern it. But the anti-auto campaign extended well beyond the library shelf. Ron Buel started his political life in the 1970s when he cofounded an organization to stop the construction of the Mount Hood Freeway in Portland, Oregon. Portland officials had invited Robert Moses, New York's master builder, to lay out a postwar infrastructure plan in 1943. (The economic engine of Henry J. Kaiser's Liberty shipyards had turned the city into a boom town.) Along with schools, parks, and a new city center, Moses proposed a highway network to encircle the city (a beltway). Local officials later amended and modified the plan to include freeways that would cut across the city center. In 1970, Neil Goldschmidt ran for city council on a platform of stopping the Mount Hood Freeway and using the money to build a light rail system. Buel joined his staff. When Buel wrote *Dead End* in 1972, the (ultimately successful) fight was in full swing and in 1976, the federal government agreed to shift the money from the freeway to the light rail system.*

Portland was not alone. Cities across the country used federal housing money to erase "slums" and build in their place modernist towers like Cabrini-Green in Chicago and Pruitt-Igoe in St. Louis. With the long rural segments of Interstates completed, and beltways to skirt urban areas in place, planners set about connecting the Interstate System to the city centers in the 1960s. Poor, predominantly African-American communities were cut off and plowed under by these urban freeways. Interstate 95 cuts right through the heart of the mostly black city of Camden, New Jersey. Farther south, local officials routed it through historically black Jackson Ward in Richmond, Virginia, and the Overtown neighborhood of Miami. According to the historian Raymond Mohl, "One massive expressway interchange took up twenty square blocks of densely settled land and destroyed the housing of about 10,000 people. By the end of the 1960s, Overtown had become an urban wasteland dominated by the physical presence of the expressway." Highways cut through black communities in New Orleans, Birmingham, Montgomery, and Columbia. I-75 razed Cincinnati's mostly black West End. A militant civil rights group in 1967 handed out flyers reading, "No more white highways through black bedrooms." Boston's elevated Central Artery lay atop Italian and Chinese immigrant neighborhoods.

The freeway routes certainly followed paths where land was

---

* Neil Goldschmidt went on to serve as Portland's mayor, secretary of transportation under Jimmy Carter, and then governor of Oregon.

cheapest and ever since Thomas MacDonald wrote *Toll Roads and Free Roads* in 1939 planners had thought razing parts of the city was a good idea. But the evidence is clear: local elites used routing decisions to reconfigure cities according to an ideology of white superiority and segregation.

As Mohl chronicles, freeway plans were challenged nearly everywhere. The "Freeway Revolts" began in San Francisco in 1959. During the 1960s, activists stopped or altered construction plans in cities including Philadelphia, Cleveland, Detroit, Baltimore, Miami, New Orleans, Chicago, Kansas City, Charlotte, North Carolina, and Elizabeth, New Jersey. In Baltimore, the Movement Against Destruction prevented the demolition of 28,000 housing units and the building of inner-city expressways. MAD joined with Washington, DC's Emergency Committee on the Transportation Crisis, which produced a "Freeway Fighter's Primer" in 1971. It described tactics for a "guerilla war" against highways. In the context of the late 1960s and 1970s, the revolts against the highways were of a piece with a larger set of criticisms of, even attacks against, what the automobile had done to America. The Freeway Revolts, Mohl concludes, are an overlooked piece of the antiestablishment 1960s. I would go further and say that the entire mood of the 1960s and early 1970s can be well understood through an automotive lens.

The national cultural phenomenon of grassroots protest against the highways has been overshadowed by the dramatic tale of Robert Moses and the "sacking of New York." Moses presided over several interlocking transportation, planning, and housing authorities, giving him enormous power and leeway. The singular urban planner once offered a tweet-worthy lesson on building highways: "When you operate in an overbuilt metropolis you have to hack your way with a meat axe." It's not *quite* as bad as it sounds. He knew that the key to completing big projects was to move quickly before property owners along the route could object and organize. Moreover, Moses was far from alone. His plans followed those of Bureau of Public Roads chief Thomas MacDonald: use highways to excise the city's "blight at its very core." His earliest highway schemes were completed well before the era of the highway revolts. In the 1920s, he built the Northern State and the Southern State parkways on Long Island. The Southern State would carry families from the city to Jones Beach—a blue-collar Hamptons. He built the Henry Hudson Parkway and Brooklyn-Battery Tunnel to take traffic to the elevated West Side Highway along Manhattan. In the 1930s, he almost single-handedly pushed through the Triborough Bridge complex, a project that had been stalled by the onset of the Great Depression. Using money from the 1949 Federal Housing Act, he engaged in an aggressive program of slum clearance. Neighborhoods were razed to make way for modernist "superblocks," tall residential towers set in a park, just as Norman Bel Geddes had imagined. Stuyvesant Town, built to replace the city's Gas House District, was his earliest example.

Imperious, uninterested in the thousands of families his projects displaced and the devastating financial and health effects his highways had on the people who lived along them, Moses remains an unsympathetic figure. Most famously, his elevated Cross Bronx and Bruckner expressways slashed across the Bronx. They met up with the New England Thruway and Hutchinson River Parkway at the Bruckner Interchange, first proposed by Moses in 1951. When it was finally opened after twenty years of opposition and construction, the *New York Times* called it a "$68-million spaghetti like confluence of steel and concrete in the East Bronx." The space beneath is not fit for humans, unless they stay in their cars.

The meat axe was finally stayed by angry Villagers who opposed Moses's decision to raze their Village and fly cars over lower Manhattan. The great builder's trouble began with a plan to clear fourteen blocks of "blighted slums" in Greenwich Village, home to, among others, one Mrs. Jane Jacobs. Jacobs had been a critic of modernist urban planning in general and Robert Moses in particular for years. She stood up against Moses to try to block Lincoln Center (to no avail) and battled to save the beautiful Beaux-Arts Pennsylvania Station (another tragic loss). She was not a planner but an architecture critic and writer for *Fortune* magazine. "Revitalization" projects, she found, did more harm than good by disrupting the bottom-up, natural organization of neighborhoods. William H. Whyte, author of *The Organization Man* and a fellow neo-urbanist, was her editor and champion at *Fortune*. He published her seminal 1958 article, "Downtown is for People," which led the Rockefeller Foundation to fund Jacobs' *The Death and Life of Great American Cities*, one of the most influential planning books of all time.

As chair of the Committee to Save the West Village, she led a grassroots campaign, the main purpose of which seemed to be getting thrown out of planning meetings. Eight months of community organizing paid off, however, when the group defeated plans to put a road through Washington Square Park.

A year later, Jacobs stood up against the Lower Manhattan Expressway—LOMEX. Moses had the plan drafted in 1941, but not until the 1960s did it begin to move forward. The idea was to connect New Jersey and Long Island along the Canal Street corridor, razing the SoHo neighborhood in the process. The buildings in the erstwhile manufacturing district had literally become shells of their former selves. The immigrant neighborhoods of Little Italy and parts of Chinatown would have to go as well. From the Holland Tunnel to the west, the route would have split at a spaghetti interchange halfway across Manhattan. One branch sent traffic out to the Williamsburg Bridge, a second to the Manhattan Bridge, and a third flushed it down onto the surface streets of the former slums. At some points it swelled to ten lanes. Project architect Paul Rudolph built models of towering high-rises with the look of prickly concrete pine trees along and astride the highway. There would be monorails.

"Just who does this high priest Moses think he is?" asked Louis DeSalvio, the local assemblyman. "Moses is convinced he is a junior god." By the end of 1963, the plan was dead.

The character of Moses as principal villain in the destruction of New York arises almost entirely from a single, monumental 1974 history of urban renewal and highway building in New York. Robert Caro spent the early 1970s researching and writing his 1,344-page biography of Moses: *The Power Broker: Robert Moses and the Fall of New York*. It won the 1975 Pulitzer Prize in biography. In Caro's telling, the highwayman had "sacked" New York, leaving the city in ruins. Moses drove the Cross Bronx Expressway like a spear through the thriving heart of a Jewish neighborhood almost out of spite. A better route existed just to the south. He served not the people who lived pedestrian lives in New York City but those who lived in the automobile suburbs of New Jersey and Long Island. But Caro's biography of Moses and its reception is as much a product of the Aquarian Age as it is an authoritative account of Moses's life. Caro invests in one man the power to destroy the nation's largest city. But Moses had millions of people on his side. Unionized construction workers, also known as hard hats, real estate developers, and people who simply hated the traffic when they drove from New Jersey to Long Island were on his side, and against Jacobs, in the 1960s. Even the city's liberal elite embraced the housing, hospital complexes, and cultural centers that he championed. When Caro was writing, the New York City subway cars wore graffiti livery and my mother told me to put my money in my shoe when walking the streets of the fallen city. Pornography, prostitution, and drugs dominated Forty-Second Street—a blight at the city's very core! In 1975, Gerald Ford told a bankrupt New York, according to the *Daily News*, "Drop Dead."

As for Jacobs, her thesis was that the city should remain organically diverse. Modernist planners sterilized the city and treated it like a giant playset with toy homes, businesses, and Matchbox cars. She undeniably rescued Lower Manhattan from a horrific fate. Nevertheless, she failed to appreciate what the radical Aquarians did: the degree to which the evolution of transportation technology and the imperatives of capitalism determined urban form. For example, New York began as America's premier entrepôt in the age of sail, owing to its excellent harbor and access to the hinterland provided by the

Hudson River. After World War II, changes in shipping technology pulled that economic activity to the large open spaces of the Jersey shoreline. The city's abandoned waterfront has been turned—by a combination of private and public monies—into amenities for the gentrified residents, many of whom live in high-priced loft apartments carved out of the abandoned shipping warehouses. Jacobs left Greenwich Village, and then left this world, well before the riverfront was overrun by Airbnb tourists wheeling carry-ons past empty storefronts and luxury chains that were once bodegas before the rents rocketed up. Surely the woman who felled the mighty Moses would have something new to teach us about the death and life of Manhattan.

For his part, as much as Moses was driven by his outsized ego, he was hardly alone in favoring highway-enabled suburbanization and even "sprawl." Ron Buel and Neil Goldschmidt knew that without a mass transit system connected to the suburbs, the city would be entirely abandoned or overrun with motorcars. Swamped by tourists, New York (and Portland, indeed every city) would become living history museums depicting the American city in the age of sail or the age of steam.

Anti-highway Aquarians thought mass transit was cool. In 1970, funding under the Urban Mass Transportation Act was increased from a few hundred million to $12 billion. Along with money for capital improvements and new city-wide transit systems the feds supported operating expenses and demonstration projects. The analog to GM's Futurama exhibit in this anti-auto age may be the Walt Disney World Monorail, which opened in 1971 as the "public transport of the future." I must have been about six or seven when I rode it and it blew my little mind.

In 1975, the Motor City itself got into the act by building an overhead monorail, the People Mover. The narrow concrete monorail bed of the People Mover hardly casts a shadow. But construction of the automated system—80 percent funded by the feds—was plagued by structural failures and cost overruns. By the time it finally opened in 1987, the city around it had been boarded up and emptied of people. It moves only about 4,000 people a day. I rode it in a circle a few times while doing archival research in the early 1990s. The People Mover is driverless, so I was literally the only person on board.*

The pathetic People Mover's triumphant doppelganger carries 15,000 passengers a day, without drivers, on demand, in Morgantown, West Virginia. The West Virginia University Personal Rapid Transit System is another federal mass transit experiment dating to 1975. It has seventy-one cars, each built on a Dodge truck chassis with seating for eight and standing room for another dozen. They operate autonomously, without rails, mono or otherwise. Instead, the cars sniff out electronics in the concrete road bed. These control speed, switching, station stops, and collision avoidance.

Riders summon the rubber-tired cars by selecting a destination and the car takes them right there, without making other stops. That bears repeating: unlike subways or streetcars, every PRT journey is a dedicated, nonstop trip. In other words, West Virginia University has been operating driverless cars for over thirty years. They have logged 22 million miles to date.

In 1976, Washington, DC, opened the first leg of its Metro and I'll never forget my first ride. Buying the tickets required much checking of lighted maps, reading of LED messages, sliding of bills, and pushing of buttons. Then a *2001: A Space Odyssey* monolith stuck out its tongue and there was much cheering and many pats on the back for a job well done. We removed the paper tongue and stuck it in another monolith, causing two large yellow pizza slices to part and grant us admission. The future would have no tokens or turnstiles, and the stations would be clean and quiet. Lights glowed at the platform to build anticipation like an overture. Then, a silver train from the future shot out of the tunnel and drew to a halt before us. Forty

---

* The idea behind the monorail is to combine the lost cost of an overhead rapid transit system with the unobtrusiveness of a subway. The single thin track did not blot out the sun or generate the noise of old elevated systems.

years ago even the psht-woosh of the opening doors and the hum of the electric motors sounded like tomorrow. Having ridden New York's graffiti-festooned trains many times, I expected lurching and heeling. Instead, it was magic-carpet smooth. At the end of the ride, we took an escalator so long you'd have thought it led to the pearly gates. Almost as good, we magically rose onto the nation's sunlit front lawn, the Washington Mall.

Portland opened its light rail system in 1985, and Los Angeles opened the first leg of its 106-mile system in 1990. (These too were planned in the Aquarian early 1970s.) In recent years, these systems have proven their worth, carrying ever more passengers. But, investment has not followed. BART and the DC Metro are a mess. (Boston and New York are in similar shambolic states, in my estimation.) Monorails and ticket monoliths don't figure in the current vision of the future. Instead, cities will be reborn by autonomous, individualized vehicles operating on public roads. Nothing about the nature of time and space has changed since the days when Kenneth Schneider observed that city streets don't have the capacity to accommodate such machines efficiently. What has changed, however, in the intervening years, is America's flagging will to invest in the kind of energy and space efficient, comfortable, convenient, and environmentally friendly public transit that we imagined in the Aquarian Age. Our will was crushed on the Day of Atonement, 1973.

* * * *

ON OCTOBER 6, 1973, Egypt and Syria simultaneously attacked Israeli forces, setting off the Yom Kippur War (also called the October War). The Egyptian army crossed the Suez Canal and invaded the Sinai. Syrian forces attacked the Golan. Three tense days later, the Israelis had repelled the attacks and reached the outskirts of Damascus and the city of Suez in Egypt. The Soviets supplied Egypt and Syria; the United States gave weapons to the Israelis. More importantly, the Arab nations unleashed a new weapon of war: oil. Cutting off production, the Middle-Eastern members of the Organization of

Petroleum Exporting Countries (OPEC), began an embargo against the United States to punish it for resupplying Israel during the fighting. Although the geopolitics of the Yom Kippur War are enough to explain the timing of the embargo, they do not tell the whole story.

Western energy companies had taken control of Middle-Eastern oil supplies in the lead up to World War I. Egypt, Syria, and other oil producers in the region pushed back against the Anglo-American oil giants. But they had no leverage until oil supplies became tighter. Between 1960 and 1972, world oil demand increased from 19 million barrels a day to 44 million barrels per day. Yet American oil production was not keeping pace, and by 1973, imports made up one third of the oil consumed in the United States. Americans were driving more and bigger cars. Equipment installed to meet clean air regulations had reduced the fuel efficiency of our automobiles by a further 15 percent. Meanwhile, the Europeans were developing the auto habit, and Japan was importing more oil as it industrialized. Power generators were also switching to oil as an environmentally friendly fuel, friendlier than coal anyway. Analysts had been warning for years that America needed both to conserve oil and to find more.

The efforts to drill more wells domestically had been held up by environmental concerns. Nixon had halted drilling off the coast of Southern California after the Santa Barbara oil spill of 1969. The geologists had said Alaska had oodles of oil, but a decade of exploration yielded nothing but dry wells. Then, in 1967, came a gusher. The field contained an estimated 10 billion barrels. Ecstatic oil men bought enough pipe for an 800-mile-long line from Alaska's North Slope to the port of Valdez. They hauled their Caterpillar yellow backhoes, graders, bulldozers, and dump trucks up to Alaska. Their equipment sat rusting while the oil companies fought Alaskan Natives, fishermen, and activists who had succeeded in winning an injunction against the pipeline on environmental grounds.

The State Department's chief energy expert, James Akins, had since at least 1970 been calling for conservation measures to combat overreliance on Middle East oil. In April, five months before the embargo, he implored the administration to raise the gas tax, shift power production to coal, and increase funding for synthetic fuel research. Nixon's top domestic adviser, John Ehrlichman, responded without irony, "Conservation is not the Republican ethic." On November 12, barely three weeks into the embargo, Congress passed special legislation to end the litigation and push construction of the Trans-Alaska Pipeline through, environmental concerns be damned. (It would take four more years for the oil to start flowing.) A week later, Nixon gave a speech: the government would reduce gasoline supplies to ensure that people would have heating oil for the winter; he banned Sunday gasoline sales; flying would be curtailed to save on jet fuel; there would be no Christmas lights. Even the White House tree would be dimmer. There would be no more lighted advertisements other than those announcing a business. A neon sign reading "Joe's Coffee Shop" was okay, but no energy could be spared for "The best coffee in town!" Each restriction affronted American freedom and independence. But they paled in comparison to the final insult: a national fifty-five-mile-per-hour speed limit. The next day, the Chicago *Tribune* ran a full banner headline, "Nixon orders oil rationing." The *New York Times* reported, "White House Lifts Ban on Women in Pants." The lowered thermostat in the briefing room demanded such bold action.

Within two months, the world price of oil had jumped from $2.90 a barrel to $11.65.

The Yom Kippur War, the energy crisis, and the government's response put an end to any Aquarian dreams. A *Time* magazine cover soon after the war featured the Exxon Tiger as Atlas struggling to hold up the world while a Saudi sheik pulls its tail and a politician tries to tame it with a whip and a chair. Inside, Caterpillar, the manufacturer of the kind of construction equipment idled in Alaska, laid out the anti-Aquarian view in an ad, "There are no simple solutions. Only intelligent choices." We see an integrated classroom full of kids in their sweaters earnestly crowded around a teacher. Moms made them wear sweaters, as moms will do when the school thermostat has also been lowered per government edict. "Will the energy shortage last forever?" the kids want to know. "It all depends on what we do," soothes the teacher, who is wearing a lovely cable knit. It might help a bit to "lower our thermostats, drive slower, join a car pool or ride the bus." The folks at Caterpillar say that "exotic energy sources" like geothermal, wind, solar, and tidal power are too far away. Instead, "We need to develop petroleum sources like shale and off-shore wells. And we need to research petroleum alternatives." The alternative in question is coal. There's five hundred years' worth under the United States alone. By that time, we'll be able to develop "atomic, solar, hydrogen, and other non-conventional energy sources." A Caterpillar dump truck designed for a mine sells in the neighborhood of $5 million.

During the crisis, all that mattered was getting gas. With a ban on Sunday buying, people filled up on Saturday. A station owner complained that a woman bought 11 cents worth of gas to top up her tank for the weekend. The owner of a Miami Amoco station said, "These people are like animals foraging for food." Motorists trolled for open stations that still had gas and then sat in line for hours, ironically burning huge amounts of fuel in the process. People siphoned gas from parked cars, prompting people with parked cars to buy locking gas caps. Individual states and individual stations set a limit on how much gas could be bought. The highways emptied out. There were calls for full-on rationing of the World War II variety but neither the president nor Congress wanted to take the political risk. As a Long Island man told a reporter, "You know how I feel about the environmental situation? If we're all going to hell, we might as well drive there."

Automobile manufacturers were caught short on compacts and subcompacts. They rushed to convert big-car assembly lines to small-car production at a cost estimated to be half a billion (1974) dollars. GM and Chrysler shut down eighteen assembly plants that were making full-sized cars. They laid off thousands of workers. A used Pinto (28 mph city/40 mpg highway) sold at auction for about the same price as an Impala (10 mpg city/14 mpg highway).

Meanwhile, oil profits soared. Exxon had trouble explaining a 19.2 percent jump, Standard Oil of Indiana, a 75 percent rise, and Gulf, a 139 percent increase in fourth-quarter earnings year on year. Texaco began an ad campaign to answer "7 of your energy questions." Aren't you price gouging? "Not true! All product price increases by Texaco are in full compliance with the Cost of Living Council regulations." (That there was such a thing as federal COLA rules reminds us how differently the nation approached problems fifty years ago.)

"Q: What about all these tankers that we keep hearing about anchored off the coast waiting for prices to go up?" They're only waiting to unload. Polls found that three out of four Americans believed the crisis was "not a real shortage." Drivers were simply angry. They needed a hero, someone to lead the charge against the A-rabs, and the bumbling Nixon administration. They found that hero in the person of the independent, long-haul trucker.

On December 3, 1973, the House of Representatives passed the fifty-five-mile-per-hour speed limit—the first national speed limit since the rubber rationing of World War II. Two days later, the blockades began. Eight hundred tractor trailers idled on Interstate 80 near Blakeslee, Pennsylvania. Police reported truckers causing a fifteen-mile backup at the other end of the highway. A convoy of 1,400 trucks stopped traffic at the Delaware Memorial Bridge. It took only fifty trucks to create a two-and-a-half-mile backup on I-70 in Ohio. In all, there were blockades in five states. These actions were spontaneous, arranged at truck stops and over Citizen Band radios. They were flash mobs before the term was coined. Perhaps realizing that major traffic jams were not good for public relations, the truckers followed up with a two-day work stoppage in mid-December. There were thirty-five reports of gunfire aimed at truckers who did not honor the shutdown. An unoccupied truck was bombed in Arkansas. The government's response was inadequate at best. So, the truckers parked their rigs again at the end of January, proving that the economy could not function without its truckers. The shootings resumed. A Michigan driver was wounded and driver Claudie Nix was killed. Without tanker trucks on the road, gas supplies became even more uncertain. Factories were idled for want of parts. Retailers could not restock shelves. An estimated 100,000 workers were laid off for lack of deliveries, including 18,000 in the auto industry. Consumers began hoarding goods. National Guard troops escorted truck convoys to protect working drivers. McDonald's had to airlift hamburger patties to the Midwest.

Although referred to in some reports as "strikes," these were not union organized or even employee-led work stoppages. The participants were owner-operators, men who owned and drove their own rigs. In fact, the powerful Teamsters union disavowed the work actions. So, this was not a battle between capital and labor but between small businessmen and the combined forces of organized labor, large shippers, and the large fleet owners, and government regulators in Washington. Finally, after eleven days of rolling protests, the work stoppages petered out. The Nixon administration had approved a surcharge of 6 percent on shipments to offset the price of fuel and agreed to prioritize diesel supplies.

The distinction between a union strike and the trucker protest needs a second mention. Although they were small businessmen, capitalists, the owner-operators, no matter how economists defined them, wore the same blue collars as their fellow drivers who were paid by the mile. America's truckers, the cowboys who drove the big rigs of the American Highway, earned widespread admiration. Drivers and news consumers saw them standing up for their rights. The battle was inescapable, even at the movies.

"In watching television and going to the movies, you might get the impression that the human dramas of today happen only to affluent people, people who live in and near the cities. You might say, the so-called sophisticates." Arnold Jeffers of KXIW is reporting to you live from a truck stop in Phoenix. "During the recent truckers strike, I talked to some people the media seems to have overlooked." These are "real people" who live "real dramas." (Descendants, no doubt, of the Model T owners Reynold described as too tired from the harvest to write Shakespearean or Jeffersonian prose.) Our man on the scene turns to Bud Brown, an owner-operator, for a trucker-on-the-street interview. Brown schools the reporter on life as an independent, the bank loans, the gun in the cab, and how the shippers control the business. "Just how far would you go to protect your rig, and your profession?" asks Jeffers with the gun in mind. "You never know till you're put to the test." Fade to black. "Columbia Pictures Presents."

White Line Fever (1975) capitalized on the truckers' strikes and reinforced the narrative of Big Oil and Washington against the small businessman. Carrol Jo Hummer (Jan Michael Vincent) is a soldier returned from the war to marry his sweetheart, buy a rig, and drive his way into the middle class. The syndicate tries to corrupt him with slot machines and cigarettes to smuggle. But Carrol Jo decides to take them on instead. Our hero fights back, first with his fists, then tough talk and a shotgun, because you never know how far you will go. Murderously far, apparently. Carrol Jo learns that the syndicate itself is just an arm of a giant corporation, Glass House. The violence escalates. Bad guys are thrown under trucks, good guys are murdered and their homes torched. Carrol Jo launches his truck into the Glass House sign. It's a really big sign. His Quixotic gesture rallies the "real people" to his cause. As he is wheeled out of the hospital to a welcoming crowd, our newsman from KXIW returns to report that all of Arizona's truckers are on strike in solidarity.

Columbia Pictures teamed up with Ford Motor Company to tour the country promoting the film at Ford dealerships. Six thousand dealers participated. Along with the prologue at the truck stop, the promotion locates the film squarely in the context of the truckers' strikes. True patriots should always rebel violently against an entirely corrupt system that won't let an honest man own a truck, or fuel one up.

At the start of the decade, the Aquarians were ascendant, making progress on their program to save the planet. They won battles against new highways and succeeded in renewing mass transit. Then OPEC unleashed the oil weapon—conspiring with Big Oil, many believed. The Aquarians had seen the enemy and it was us. The Reaganauts looked instead at the enemies of America, the Saudi sheikhs and even the Aquarians themselves. In 1975, in the run-up to his unsuccessful '76 presidential campaign, Ronald Reagan called it "politically inspired scarcity." To understand the origins of the so-called Reagan Democrats, look no further than the fifty-five-mile-an-hour speed limit.

Sometimes we think children don't know what's going on. Their experience of the grown-up world around them is, well, childlike. For me, the opposite is true. I have never wavered from my love of both the organic city and the natural world as landscapes that uplift the soul. Those who fight for them are on the side of the angels. I wish I had a magic wand with which to turn concrete sprawl back into verdant woodland and wetlands for paddling a birch bark canoe. As childlike as I remain, I'm also childish. I drive our minivan or my old truck rather than my wife's vintage BMW because, frankly, I cannot be trusted with the latter's sportiness. So I count myself among the Aquarians, still desperate to recover Eden, but enjoying my automotive apple. Please, don't make me drive fifty-five. If you're too young to have been forced to drive fifty-five on an open freeway, give it a try. You'll grow as impatient as a rider waiting at the monorail station for an overdue train.

Chapter 10

BANDS OF CITIZENS TAKE ON DICKY, JERRY, AND JIMMY

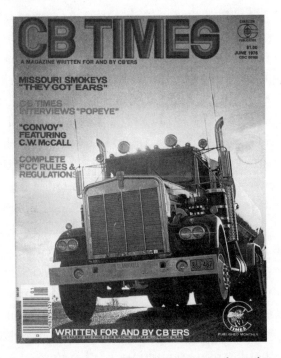

Protesting truckers used CB radios to resist the tightening noose of regulation. The public joined with them because no one, it seemed, could stand to drive 55.

O URS HAD CHROME KNOBS. WE BOUGHT IT AT THE ANNUAL Purim Bazaar White Elephant Sale. It sat mounted on the tunnel below the dash. The mic hung in a bracket above so you could grab it with authority. I had a subscription to *Mad* where I'd learned the lingo: 10-20 for location, 10-27 for change channels, and "Breaker 1-9," was like clearing your throat to get some attention. A magnet held the antenna to the roof of the station wagon. As soon as it was installed I dialed Steve, my only friend in middle school (and a transactional one at that). I told him to sit in the driveway and await my transmission. "What's your 20?" I asked, because "Where are you?" was civilian talk. I knew full well that his 20 was inside his mom's Buick Electra parked out in front of his house. I told him to "10-27 to channel 5." We signed off with "10-4 Good Buddy," and then I went inside to answer the phone. Steve was calling to discuss our chat. We didn't get the CB to chat though. We needed it to listen for big-rig drivers reporting "bear traps." When the warnings came in, even an otherwise law-abiding citizen like my father could slow down in time to avoid a speeding ticket.

Each year of late, on or about October fourth, an article on the "CB radio craze" of the 1970s will pop up in my feed. "The Citizens Band radio was the original social network" or, "the Facebook of the 1970s," writes some journo who has never said "Breaker 1-9" without irony. The analogy is good as far as it goes. Hiding behind a radio mic made it easier to ignore societal restraints and shyness. There was no pornography, but there was a lot of lascivious chatter. There is a critical difference, however, between the CB and Facebook as social networks: social networking in the 1970s was unmediated; we weren't consumers, selling ourselves for the privilege of access. There was no platform, no Facebook, no money to be made connecting us. We were just a band of citizens behind the wheel, sharing, and connecting. Furthermore, the CB culture had a particular, anti-government political bent. Millions operated with blatant disregard for Federal Communications Commission regulations and they used their CBs to avoid law enforcement on the highway. The truckers had demonstrated the value of the CB as a tool of resistance against the tightening noose of regulation aimed at cleaning the air, reducing road casualties, and ensuring energy security. Politicians heard the voice of America on the CB and responded.

During his campaign for reelection in 1976, Gerald Ford faced a serious primary challenge from Ronald Reagan. So, Ford deployed the First Mama. At campaign stops and from her motorcade, First Mama, better known as first lady Betty Ford, chatted breezily with truckers and other motorists for the press. She had a base station at the White House, but complained that her son kept it in his room. *National CB Trucker News* complained that she didn't introduce herself by her call sign (KUY 9532), and that political campaigning by CB was against the rules. The FCC demurred. But the CB turned her into a valuable campaign asset. When the president expressed worry about his chances in Texas, his wife replied, "Dear, I've got the truck driver vote for you." Not to be outdone, Jimmy Carter took to the airwaves to campaign as well. "[He] may have even given a couple of 'First Mama's' to all his CB listeners," the papers reported from the trail in Ohio. As president, Carter officially celebrated the twentieth anniversary of the CB radio in 1978. He declared:

> While CB is primarily for emergency use, the nonemergency channels bring enjoyment and companionship to millions of Americans, including my own family. In recognition of the fine service provided by Citizens Band radio, I join with CB organizations across the country in celebrating "10-4 Day," October 4, 1978.

I don't expect a president to declare a Facebook Day anytime soon.

The 27-megahertz frequency, or "CB," band was supposed to facilitate business activity, not dirty talk and speeding. As World War II drew to a close, the Federal Communications Commission— which regulates the nation's airwaves—opened up a portion of the radio spectrum for a "Citizens Radio Service . . . to provide a means of transmitting the substantive and useful messages . . . of private citizens for business or personal activities." The broadcast range would be limited to about five or ten miles in most circumstances. With an FCC license, a small business could dispatch service people by radio and travelers could request assistance. The commission warned against using a CB for "amateur-type or 'rag-chewing' activities." By law you had to identify yourself when initiating a broadcast and when signing off with your FCC-issued call sign. Further, using your CB in connection with any unlawful activity was verboten. If you violated these rules, the FCC would revoke your license and kick you off the air. By 1975, the FCC had issued a little more than one million licenses. Six months later, there were 10 million with another half million being added every month. CB radio sales doubled annually in the years after the gas crisis, reaching 11.3 million units and $2 billion in retail sales by 1976. Ford, GM, and Chrysler all offered CBs as a factory installed option (integrated into the AM/FM radio).

Ads for CB radio sets appeared in general audience magazines and on television during the craze. Howard Cosell said you should buy a General Electric. On television Casey Kasem, of Top 40 and *Scooby Doo* fame (he voiced Shaggy), said the Hy-Gain 9 was "outta sight." Radio Shack advertised its Realistic brand and had large displays featured prominently in its stores. In more than one ad, Mom's station wagon broke down, but the tow truck showed up in no time thanks to her CB. The Browning and President brands used the seductive female and her base station to advertise their sets (the latter featured Rene Russo). You could buy one made by Lafayette out of Syosset, New York, a Midland, from Kansas City, Missouri, or a Sony imported from Japan. There were CB-themed toys, tee shirts, and lunch boxes.

CBs were also at the movies. Hollywood modeled leading men after the long-haul, independent owner-operators who had led the trucker protests. More precisely, the movie stars were iterations of a popular cultural persona, the trucker. The stock trucker character of the CB craze wore a cowboy hat or a truck-manufacturer-branded ball cap: Kenilworth, Mack, Peterbilt, Freightliner, and the like. He spoke, while broadcasting on the CB at least, with a pan-Southern accent. He was rough, quick to righteous violence, and had a soft spot for sex workers. Most of all, he was a cowboy of the open road.

The entrepreneurial owner-operator had a special place in the trucker pantheon. You could always distinguish an owner-operator's truck on the highway by its chrome accents, extra lights, and livery. When he did make it home, this sparkling machine sat dwarfing his plain and modest house.

Although some of those characteristics made intuitive sense, there wasn't much to go on. Cultural studies of real truckers had not been done. In fact, the best picture we have of truckers generally and owner-operators in particular in the 1970s comes from a most unlikely place: research funded by the Association of American Railroads to determine why they were losing revenue to long-haul trucks. The railroads engaged Harvard Business School professor Daryl Wycoff to examine the business model of the owner-operator. One finding surprised him: "The average owner-operator makes less as an independent businessman than he would as an employee of a large truck line." His team concluded from field interviews that "perceived independence" mattered more than "income maximization" for drivers. The desire for independence was not the same as wanderlust. Most were from conservative rural areas with close family ties strained by their time on the road. These rural origins explain, according to Wycoff, the animosity toward the Teamsters union which animosity, it must be said, was reciprocal. Furthermore, independents looked at corruption in the Teamsters leadership—front page news at the time and tangled up with Watergate—and saw themselves as stuck in an entirely broken system. Thus, rather than the freedom of a vagabond, independence meant an "antipathy to rules and regulations." Although the owner-operator had no boss and did not have to join the Teamsters, state and federal regulations governed his or her work. These rules are "almost without exception, resented to a degree beyond the natural rebellion of the working man towards authority." Independence meant freedom from union rules, safety regulations, weight limits, and strictures on work hours. It meant freedom from the oppressive hand of government.

The work stoppages during the winter of 1973–1974 that gave rise to the CB craze presented Wycoff with a paradox: "unified action by a group of violently independent men." His team concluded that the protests were weakly organized and might not have happened at all were it not for the CB radio. Despite the long hours of solitude on the road, field interviews revealed truckers to be highly sociable. They "have welcomed with enthusiasm the opportunities the Citizen Band Radio gives them in communicating with other drivers." Without the CB radio, truckers could not have organized shutdowns. Broadcast pseudonyms known as CB handles became identities. For example, the shutdowns began with the independent and unpremeditated direct action of three truckers who used their powerful and massive machines to shut down I-84 in Connecticut. "Dopey Diesel, Doggy Daddy and myself, Bit Sissy, turned on the flashers, and blocked the eastbound lanes," one participant reported to *Overdrive* magazine, using CB handles instead of names. At one point during settlement talks with the US secretary of transportation, officials set up a trucker known by the handle "River Rat" behind a high-powered CB transmitter at a Coast Guard station to announce (prematurely, it turned out) the end of hostilities. These details—the role of the CB in organizing and ending the protests and the use of CB handles to identify truckers—figured in press reporting at the time.

One aspect of the trucker's life remained a bit of a mystery. According to Wycoff, the trucker as lothario with a "girl in every port" was more fantasy than reality. Truckers asked about the subject usually answered with some version of, "Who has the time?" Still, the trucker lived in an almost entirely male world. Of the 9,630 drivers in Wycoff's data base, only fifty-seven were women. Women drivers have reported harassment and discrimination in other research. Also, even today truck stops are known as sites of prostitution and human trafficking. (An organization called Truckers Against Trafficking has been enlisting drivers to combat the problem.) The monthly magazine *Overdrive* featured models, often scantily clad, on trucks. Mike Parkhurst founded *Overdrive* as the voice of the owner-operator and he was instrumental in the protest movement. His "CB Section" insert included a female model, a radio, and a sala-

cious caption. The stock female character in CB advertising and at
the movies was, like Rene Russo in the ad for the President brand, a
"honeypot" on a base station looking for thrills or customers.

* * * *

ON THE RADIO, television, and at the movies, American drivers
soaked up the CB culture. Claude Akins starred on two seasons of
Movin' On (1974–1976). Peter Fonda tried his hand at the genre with
High-Ballin' (1978), and Rip Torn and James Brolin got to drive in
Steel Cowboy (1978).

I've seen them all so you won't have to, but even I refuse to watch
television's *B.J. and the Bear* (1979–1980). It seemed to involve a
trucker and a chimp. It should not be confused with *Every Which
Way but Loose* (1978), which starred an *orangutan,* not a chimp.
Clint Eastwood costarred as the trucker.

I don't want to wallow in the semiotics of trucker pop culture,
but I do want to draw on a few films to show how pop culture con-
structed the owner-operator as a freedom fighter and how, through
the CB, we joined him.

The Great Smokey Roadblock, originally titled *The Last of the
Cowboys,* has Henry Fonda as the trucker "Elegant" John. He rises
from his death bed and steals his own truck from the repossession
yard so he can make one last run. Along the way, he beds down a
hooker with a heart of gold and then helps relocate the entire brothel
to South Carolina when the police try to shut it down. Then, the
chase is on and the story of the outlaws hits the airwaves, prompting populists to join their cause and their convoy. One ardent aco-
lyte, somehow keeping up with the 18-wheeler in an underpowered
VW Microbus, grabs his CB mic and calls out to anyone within the
sound of his voice: "These are the forces of oppression, the armies
of darkness. These are the people who gave you the 55 mile per hour
speed limit." Needless to say the titular roadblock proves utterly
ineffectual as the convoy plows through and across state lines. In the
world of trucker films, police cannot cross state lines.

Jonathan Demme's *Citizens Band* (later titled *Handle with Care*) tanked at the box office, but it uniquely explores all of the stock CB characters. There is the hero, a CBer who belongs to a Radio Emergency Associated Communication Team. (REACT was founded in 1962 as a citizens' brigade of first responders and still exists today.) There's Grandma Breaker, who monologues all day; the Red Baron, who spews Nazi hate using an oversized transmission tower; the Hustler, who reads pornography over the air; and Electra, who uses her CB for, well, CB sex. The trucker in the film, Chrome Angel, is a bigamist who has a hooker with a heart of gold, Hot Coffee, on the side. In a postcoital chat over coffee—apparently she truly *does* make a great cup of coffee—she laments:

> Right now you're my only steady left. I just don't have the business anymore. First they passed that bond issue then they moved the highway on me. Now that goll darn 55 mile limit. Nobody's got time for nothing.

The generous Chrome Angel buys her an RV to troll the highway. A quick in-and-out by the side of the road and the driver can still deliver on time, 55 be damned.

Smokey and the Bandit was the second highest-grossing movie of 1977, topped only by the original *Star Wars*. The theme song, "East Bound and Down," spent sixteen weeks on the country music charts and peaked at number two. The plot involves a bet to transport 400 cases of contraband Coors beer from Texas to Georgia in some arbitrary amount of time. Sheriff Buford T. Justice (Jackie Gleason) stands in for every hated Smokey in America. He is grandiose, incompetent, and racist. We are the Bandit (Burt Reynolds) driving a black Pontiac Trans Am T-top and running interference. Along the way, a convoy of trucks helps Bandit elude the sheriff. A brothel full of hookers with hearts of gold bed down the local police to keep them occupied. The public cheers. Sheriff Justice, however, isn't chasing the Bandit. He's chasing the woman Bandit stole from his son at the altar. The "good buddies" and "What's your 20s?" and "rocking chairs" (the middle of a convoy) fly fast and loose.

Bandit has held up as a comedy and transcended its era. *Convoy,* by contrast, transcends nothing. It remains, however, the touchstone of the genre and an illustrative period piece. Based on a four-minute-long 1975 hit song of the same name, it follows an ever-growing outlaw convoy in an epic battle against the police. As in *Bandit,* the CB figures prominently and the filmmaker expects the audience to know the lingo. "Rubber Duck" (Kris Kristofferson) and his small convoy have run afoul of the corrupt and racist Sheriff "Dirty" Lyle Wallace (Ernest Borgnine). They escape and the chase is on. Word of the small outlaw convoy goes out across the CB airwaves and it grows to be a thousand trucks long. The public lines the roads holding signs and blowing kisses. Along the way, the governor of Arizona decides that making nice with the truckers will help his campaign for reelection. He calls off the state troopers to give the truckers a rest. But the Duck is still an outlaw heading for Mexico—terra incognita, apparently, to US law enforcement. This roadblock holds and the army blows the Duck and his tanker trucker to smithereens. Jesus-like, the Duck returns from the dead and all is forgiven.

* * * *

LIKE THE GOVERNOR of Arizona from *Convoy,* Jimmy Carter declared October fourth "CB day" in 1978 in order to ride the populist radio wave. That declaration marks the midway point between two speeches Carter gave on the energy crisis. In the first, delivered in April 1977, Carter joined the puritanical wing of the Aquarian critique. He blamed Americans who were minding their own business captaining two-and-a-half-ton Chrysler Town & Country station wagons (11 mpg). We should do penance by driving one-ton Pinto wagons, 29 city/40 hwy. (Your mileage may vary.) When he delivered his second energy speech in July 1979, he had come around to the view reflected in the CB craze: it wasn't our fault; Big Oil, Big Government, and the A-rabs were trying to take away our right to drive as fast and as furiously as we wanted. He turned from an Aquarian to a Reaganaut before our eyes.

The presidential election of 1976 had been close, especially considering that Gerald Ford had pardoned Richard Nixon and that he faced a serious primary challenge from Ronald Reagan. Jimmy Carter campaigned as a Georgia peanut farmer, discounting the fact that he also had "Georgia Governor" on his resume. Still, he was definitely a Washington outsider and promised to bring a certain Jacksonian renewal to the presidency. I remember standing at the inauguration parade and hearing a murmur go through the crowd as we waited for the motorcade. "Oh my! He's walking!" people around us shouted. From my viewpoint on a lamppost I saw that indeed Jimmy and Rosalynn were walking, exuding rectitude, waving to the crowd. He flashed that famously toothy smile. No riding in a gas-guzzling limo for this morally upstanding man of the people.

Just shy of three months in office, Carter wasn't smiling anymore. On April 18, 1977, the president decided to address the nation. He came on television (which always annoyed us because he was pre-empting *Happy Days* or *Welcome Back, Kotter*, or some other worthy programming) and gave the American people an "unpleasant talk" about energy. Apparently it was a favorite subject, because he gave several such prime-time talks on energy during his four years. He sounded at first like an Aquarian, though not of the cheerful or even energetic variety. He was dour, scary, and scolding. But like the Aquarians he said we were running out of oil:

> We must not be selfish or timid if we hope to have a decent world for our children and our grandchildren. We simply must balance our demand for energy with our rapidly shrinking resources. . . . Many of [my] proposals will be unpopular. Some will cause you to put up with inconveniences and to make sacrifices. The most important thing about these proposals is that the alternative may be a national catastrophe.

Yipes! He had said that he felt the need to shock Americans out of their complacency because the gas lines of Yom Kippur, 1973, were gone and the heating oil shortages had ended with the spring thaw. No, things were not better, he insisted, despite appearances. The energy problem was worse "and will get worse every day until we act." The Earth was running dry, he said, wanly, and warned that production would peak in the 1980s even as demand continued to grow. "We have no choice about that," he concluded fatefully.

Then things got personal. Absent action, "Our cars would continue to be too large and inefficient. Three-quarters of them would continue to carry only one person—the driver—while our public transportation system continues to decline." We needed "smaller and more efficient cars and a better network of buses, trains, and public transportation." It had to come and there it was. He did say it would be unpleasant and warned at the top of the speech that he would make us put up with inconveniences. But small cars? Buses? Those were full on sacrifices, not mere inconveniences. American drivers would not stand for it.

Fortunately, the anti-conservation conservatives had an answer. The freshman congressman from Michigan, that place where they make those "too large and inefficient" cars, offered the Republican rebuttal. David Stockman, who would later introduce "trickle-down" economics as budget director for Ronald Reagan, said there was no reason to panic. He noted that at the moment of the 1973 oil embargo there was still enough proven reserves "capable of sustaining consumption for more than a quarter-century." Unlike Carter, Stockman knew that, paradoxically, oil reserves keep growing even as we use more oil.

In theory, oil is a nonrenewable resource. Economics 101 teaches that with supply finite and increasing demand, the price of a commodity should go up. Rising prices should then reduce demand—either by making us drive less or forcing us to squeeze into those high-mileage Pintos. In Econ 102, however, we learn that when the price of oil goes up the *supply* of oil goes up as well. That happens because prospectors, the global oil companies, go looking for more. Oil deemed unrecoverable at, say, $15 a barrel becomes worth recovering when the price climbs to $30 a barrel. In other words, "oil reserves" describes a fungible economic state of affairs rather than a geological reality. Unfortunately, shrinking demand also lowers the price.

It's a no-win situation for environmentalists but a win-win for SUV drivers. It also explains why electric cars struggle to gain traction in the American market. They are coming, to be sure, but not because we are running out of oil or because oil has grown dear. They are coming because governments in California, the European Union, and especially China want them to come.

"Overall, the planet's accessible natural hydrocarbon reserves readily exceed 20 trillion barrels. *This is the equivalent of five centuries of consumption at current rates*," Stockman calculated. [original emphasis] Even if we run out of oil and natural gas, there's still plenty of coal in the ground for centuries. As a Texaco engineer put it to me, "Hydrocarbons are a basic building block of the universe. We're never running out."

The world today is awash in oil. So, Stockman was right, and Carter, wrong. It may be that the former Sunday school teacher was unable to fathom the reserves of evil in the human heart. Dick Cheney, a man literally without a heart, served under Gerald Ford, both George Bushes, and in Congress for the oil-producing state of Wyoming. In 2001, amidst a neo-energy crisis drummed up to promote drilling and kick off a new round of wars, Cheney weighed in from his position as energy czar. He agreed with John Ehrlichman's comment, "Conservation is not the Republican ethic." "Conservation," Cheney said, "may be a sign of personal virtue, but it is not a sufficient basis for a sound, comprehensive energy policy." Of course by 2001 the evidence that burning oil was disrupting the climate was undeniable (although still denied by the likes of Cheney). Rather than a sound energy policy, America in 2001 needed a sound environmental policy. As for Cheney and Stockman, whatever else they got wrong, they certainly had Carter's number. Conservation, to Carter, was indeed a sign of virtue, a collective form of self-denial.

At the same time David Stockman was sharpening his prose, another oil crisis was looming. In 1979, revolutionaries led by Ayatollah Khomeini overthrew the Shah of Iran, an American proxy. Soon after, fifty-two Americans were taken hostage at the US embassy in Tehran and held for 444 days. The revolution touched off a second energy crisis, but not in the same way the Yom Kippur War had. There was no embargo. Instead, the chaos of the Iranian revolution led to a slow moving and accidental crisis. It began with strikes by Iranian oil workers. The strikes had reduced oil exports from about 4.5 million to less than a million barrels by the beginning of November 1978—while the Shah still clung to power. By Christmas, Iran had stopped exporting oil entirely and Tehran motorists had to wait in line for gas and cooking fuel. The situation got so bad that an American tanker sailed to Iran with an emergency supply of oil. In actual fact, the markets were able to absorb the mild supply shock of losing Iranian oil. Panic buying caused prices to spike nevertheless.

The second energy crisis unleashed complaints and emotions that had been contained by but not quieted since 1973. The CB craze had only fanned the flames. Even after the first energy crisis abated, the government had decided to keep the unpopular national 55 mph limit for safety's sake. Unlike the gentle encouragement of the 1950s—"The life you save may be your own"—the Department of Transportation took to issuing threats. "For two years now people have been trying to get you to slow down to 55 miles per hour," ran one radio ad. Some people don't realize that 55 is the law, "with tickets, and fines, and all the rest. I should know. I'm a police officer." "All the rest" is the kind of vague warning you get when you're tied up in a chair by a kidnapper.

The lower speed limit reduced traffic fatalities by between two and four thousand a year, according to a study by the National Research Council. Fuel and medical costs, as well as the cost to taxpayers, each fell by about two to three percent. The NRC recommended keeping the limit. Other studies showed that states had reduced enforcement and compliance by drivers was slipping by the 1980s. Anti-regulatory think tanks such as the Heritage Foundation and the Reason Foundation published studies challenging the science behind safety claims. In 1995, Congress returned the power to set speed limits to the states.

The 55-mph story shows again the politics of safety. Science can tell us how to be safe, but we as a society determine how safe is safe enough. It is worth remembering that the seatbelt interlock fiasco also happened in 1974. American drivers were so enraged by the warning buzzers and the fact that they could not start the car until they buckled up that Congress outlawed any such buzzers or seat belt interlocks.

The double nickel was an economic issue for truckers, amounting to a 13 percent decrease in miles traveled on average. The federal government, not the open market, still regulated fuel allocations and shipping prices. No one could claim, as leaders do today, that the invisible hand, a supposedly natural phenomenon that could not be controlled by man, was responsible. The feds were responsible. The feds were the object of their fury. In June, independent truck drivers replayed their script from 1973 with work stoppages, blockades, and violence. They closed down truck stops and a convoy of eighteen trucks marched on Washington. More than a hundred trucks created a thirty-mile-long backup on the Long Island Expressway. One trucker, wearing a "No Crude/No Food" tee shirt, told a reporter that writing your congressman didn't get results. "You do get somewhere with a strike, although we don't like to use that word; we prefer 'shutdown.' " The wording is important because, again, this was not a labor movement but a protest by independent small businessmen. States in the Northeast (including my home state of Maryland) instituted odd-even rationing. Our wagon (10 city/14 highway) had an even tag and I remember sitting in the back checking the other plate numbers while we waited for a turn at the pump. The price of gas was high, but not an undue economic burden, I suspect, for my family or the families in our circle. It was the sitting in line that worried my mother, the sitting in line that challenged the very promise of America. If you needed to drive, you needed gas, and if you needed gas you had to wait in line. What was this, the Soviet Union? Because we had sat in gas lines, whether in Benzes or beaters, because we had been pulled over for so-called speeding on the highway, we were together and we were with the truckers. We imitated their language, relied on their CB warnings to avoid the fuzz, and even turned, like them, to violence to demand our right to motor fuel. As the violence spread off the highways, we were with them.

*   *   *   *

IN ONE TRUCKER PROTEST during the second oil crisis, a convoy of twenty trucks arrived in Levittown, Pennsylvania, on June 23, 1979, taking up positions around the Five Corners intersection where four gas stations competed for customers. Levittown was a working-class, automobile suburb, a second iteration of the Long Island original. Levittowners joined the truckers and chanted, "No gas, my ass!" The police drew their guns. Police attacked one trucker's cab with billy clubs. He responded by driving through the police line, "sending them diving for cover." The residents of Levittown joined the violence. The townsfolk wrecked a farmers' market on the corner and smashed the watermelons. They shattered gas station windows before setting a pair of vehicles on fire and fueling the flames with tires. An Associated Press photographer captured a shirtless young man at the scene stoking the fire. In the background stands a hand painted sign reading, "More Gas Now!" The local board of commissioners declared a state of emergency after two nights of rioting that had sent 200 protesters and 44 police to the hospital. Over 200 people were arrested, though the spokesman for the local police said they could have arrested 500 if they'd had the manpower. He described the crowd as a mix of sympathetic citizens and "troublemakers." Young people were drunk on beer and stoned on marijuana, he reported. Police in riot gear along with a K-9 corps from Philadelphia eventually cleared the intersection, nightsticks swinging. The state of emergency imposed a curfew and made assembly of more than five people unlawful. A handful of protesters returned for a third night, but by then things had quieted down.

The Levittown gas riot spoke to a shared sense that the energy crises threatened more than mobility; it threatened to undo the middle class American dream. It is worth noting that Levittown had last seen riots in August 1957 when the first African-American family moved to the then all-white town.

Three weeks later, Carter changed his tone from pastoral to bellicose. On July 15, 1979, seven months after the Iranian Revolution that had sparked panic in the oil markets and at the pumps, he took to the airwaves again with a speech properly called "Energy and National Goals" but more commonly remembered as the "malaise speech." Historians consider it the most important of his presidency, and not in a good way. It was doomed before it was written. The president was in Tokyo while Levittown burned, the trucker strike wore on, and gas lines began to spread to the Midwest. The gas station operators demanded the Department of Energy lift prices or they too would strike. The State of Maryland sued the DOE for more gas. Carter's senior domestic policy adviser sent a memo to the president describing the political damage being done by the worsening energy crisis. Not the indictment of his budget director, not the surrendering of the Panama Canal, not double-digit inflation, nothing had "added so much water to our ship" as the energy crisis. After announcing his speech, Carter gave himself a ten-day extension. For those ten days he sat like Moses on the mountaintop receiving the word from advisers who shuttled out from Washington to Camp David. He then began firing his secretaries of energy, treasury, and transportation.

The speechwriting team had warned the president against delivering yet another energy speech on television. In a memo they argued, "The [people] do not want a Presidential preaching or the Administration piously saying, 'We told you so, but you didn't listen to us.' No more berating the American people for waste and selfishness." Put in automotive terms, stop telling people they should drive Pintos.

So, Carter shifted his scolding from the American people and the American automobile to the Middle-Eastern oil cartel, OPEC. He read quotes from letters he had received from the American people. "Our neck is stretched over the fence and OPEC has a knife," read one. "When we enter the moral equivalent of war, Mr. President, don't issue BB guns," another instructed. A labor leader, Carter said, "got to the heart of it:" "The real issue is freedom. We must deal with the energy problem on a war footing." Carter used the war metaphor just as freely himself. "We have the national will to win this war," and, "we are the generation that will win the war on the energy problem and in that process, rebuild the unity and confidence of America."

There was nothing wrong with guzzling gas, and we had plenty of it, if only those A-rab Muslims would lighten up and let our hostages go. (Yes, the Iranians are Persians, not Arabs, but Americans have never been great geography students.) Nevertheless, the president did call for sacrifice. It is hard to tease apart these two strands of logic, hard to understand how he at once called for sacrifice while saying no sacrifice was necessary. The argument goes like this: the OPEC-created embargo would require sacrifice. But sacrifice is a good thing. It vitalized the nation and empowered us to tackle the real problem, the crisis of confidence. In those bright postwar days when the paint on the Levittown houses was still fresh and the chrome on the Fords and Chryslers and Chevys still shone, we were confident. Gas rationing killed that confidence.

The president had already given four speeches on oil and energy; this was to be his fifth. It was long, over half an hour. For the first twenty minutes, he preached. He brushed off gas lines and inflation as mere symptoms of the underlying pathology, a "crisis of confidence." Americans had lost faith in ourselves and the future. We had become hedonists:

> In a nation that was proud of hard work, strong families, close-knit communities, and our faith in God, too many of us now tend to worship self-indulgence and consumption. Human identity is no longer defined by what one does, but by what one owns. But we've discovered that owning things and consuming things does not satisfy our longing for meaning. We've learned that piling up material goods cannot fill the emptiness of lives which have no confidence or purpose.

Carter offered a jeremiad worthy of both Increase Mather and the most tuned-in, turned-on, dropped-out Aquarian.

Yet when it finally leaves the spiritual realm, his speech shifts blame to our dependence on "foreign countries." He hits that word "foreign" with the same intonation usually associated with America First types. The nations of the OPEC cartel that had raised the price are full of "foreigners." The problem, then, is one of dependence on foreigners. We need energy independence.

At long last, he gets to the point, or points. "Point one: . . . Beginning this moment, this nation will never use more foreign oil than we did in 1977—never." In addition, the import quotas will be reinstated, a windfall profit tax will be made on oil companies, and a requirement that utility companies "cut their massive use of oil within the next decade and switch to other fuels, especially coal, our most abundant energy source." Conspicuously absent from the speech is nuclear power. The accident at the Three Mile Island nuclear plant had nearly created an American Chernobyl in March. *The China Syndrome* film depicting a meltdown came out in 1979 as well. In the summer of '79, nuclear power was off the table. So, the president called for more money for mass transit and a solar energy bank. "We will protect our environment," he said. He then said the opposite: "But when this nation critically needs a refinery or a pipeline, we will build it."

Carter had warned in his 1977 speech that the oil age could not continue. We would need "a new Saudi Arabia every three years," he had said. Now he bragged, "We have more oil in our shale alone than several Saudi Arabias." Whether the end of hydrocarbon energy would bring about a utopian or dystopian future hardly mattered. God-given hydrocarbons were ours to burn, if we could only muster the confidence to burn them. He may have been right that the nation faced a crisis of confidence, but mostly it had lost confidence in Carter. His solution of sacrifice, of abandoning materialism for the church pew was woefully out of touch. The truckers used violence and the movies of the CB era made light of that violence and lawbreaking. The rioters of Levittown used violence to assert their right to an automobile-fueled way of life. Drivers would carry their energy nationalism into the next presidential election, finding in Ronald Reagan a more authentic champion. At home we would "drill, baby, drill!" But if the Muslim nations were holding back, they would be held to account. The energy crisis violence would be projected outward, from Levittown, the gas lines, and the truck stops to the Middle East. The new administration would work with the oil men—men like Dick Cheney of Wyoming and George Bush of Texas—not to wean the nation of oil but to secure access to it. We would do it by covert action, by overt force if necessary. We would get the oil, wherever God had buried it.

Unfortunately for Detroit, they were as out of touch as Jimmy Carter. In 1960, the Big Three introduced smaller cars in response to the rising popularity of imports and the Rambler from American Motors. In the 1970s, they offered smaller cars like the Chevette, Pinto, and Dodge Colt to meet federal mandates. But these did not replace large cars so much as supplement them in the market—per Alfred Sloan's dictum, "a car for every purse and purpose." Also, these smaller versions of the American automobile had traditionally mounted engines and rear-wheel drive. In 1980, just in time for the Reagan Revolution, Detroit started building a new generation of vehicles. These had transverse engines and front-wheel drive. Rather than downsized American automobiles, the mainline sedans of the 1980s were upsized versions of the smaller, fuel-sipping cars from Germany and especially Japan. Just when America was getting its confidence back, learning to fight again after losing in Viet Nam, learning to love itself again, Detroit started producing cars that weren't cars at all, cars that no American could love.

Chapter 11

THE UN-CARS THAT NOBODY LOVED

The K-car rescued Chrysler from the brink of bankruptcy in the 1980s and underpinned the first minivan. Like most cars of the decade, it was no fun at all.

WHEN ASSAN MOTORS BOUGHT AN AMERICAN CAR PLANT IN 1986, Japanese managers didn't think American workers were up to snuff. They lacked the *kaizen* spirit of their counterparts in Japan and fell well short of volume and quality targets. But then a dynamic middle manager stepped up and goaded the Americans into doing things the Japanese way with a montage of baseball, calisthenics, and welding sparks. The Americans rallied. Quality remained poor and production, a bit short of expectations. Nevertheless, their pluck and spirit impressed the top brass from Japan, who let them keep their jobs.

That's how director Ron Howard saw the happy endgame for American car companies and UAW workers in his 1986 film, *Gung Ho*. The movie was born of the same stuff as the Vapors' '80s hit "Turning Japanese" and the murder of Vincent Chin in 1982 by a Chrysler foreman who blamed Japan for his troubles (Chin was Chinese). Auto workers in Gary, Indiana, had fun smashing a Honda for charity (a dollar for a swing of the sledge hammer, with money going to laid-off workers). Ford workers outside Chicago beat a Toyota to death for free. They hung a sign, "If you sell in America, build in America." Executives from the Big Three complained that the Japanese worked harder and were paid less than their American counterparts. They spoke of the "Asian quality gene." They blamed the UAW for saddling them with health care and retirement expenses as if they hadn't read the labor contracts before signing them.

So, they lobbied for expanded Social Security and a British style system of national health care. No, seriously, they lobbied for caps on the number of cars the Japanese would be allowed to sell in the United States. The Reagan administration did their bidding by threatening tariffs. The Japanese settled for "voluntary export restraint" caps in 1981: Japan would export no more than 1.68 million cars per annum to the United States. This figure amounted to a 7.7 percent cut from the previous year's sales. Japan spotted Detroit a few million points and kept right on winning the game. Japanese and American negotiators put the best face on the deal by saying that it merely gave US automakers breathing room to begin making the kind of smaller cars buyers wanted.

In fact, GM had begun developing "downsized" versions of its full-sized models immediately after the first gas crisis. "The handwriting was on the wall," Chevy advertised, explaining why for 1977 it had abandoned the "longer, lower, wider" ethos that had propelled GM to riches since the 1920s. The new model would be a shorter, taller, narrower sedan that would be "more efficient in its use of this earth's precious space and fuel." The new models were squared off, implying utility and making them look even smaller than they were. The designers must have run out of sculpting clay and used cardboard boxes in their stead, given the lack of curves. Harley Earl would have picked up his red phone and dialed Alfred. Sliding behind the steering wheel is supposed to feel like a vacation, not a day at the office. The '77s looked like a rack of gray flannel suits. The Impala ad featured a blueprint with nary a French curve on it. GM made clear it didn't really want to make this car, but "the handwriting was on the wall" as if the king of Babylon were about to meet his doom. We owned both pre- and post-1977 Oldsmobiles. I was not a fan of the change. The newer models had less road-hugging weight than their immediate predecessors. But this only added up to sloppier steering, bouncier suspensions, and a sense of diminished luxury.

Downsizing began amidst the happy patriotism of the Bicentennial. (I went as Thomas Jefferson for Halloween.) But even though downsizing shaved weight and made more efficient use of the interior space Detroit maintained the outdated architecture of the big, rear-drive American sedan. Even the smallest American cars—the Chevette, Ford Pinto, and AMC Gremlin, for example—remained based on the big-car architecture and ethos. They were front-engined, rear-drive things; the Gremlin was literally an AMC Hornet sedan with the trunk chopped off. With Reagan's election in 1980, however, patriotism turned dark and a neo–Cold War nationalism took hold. We would face down the Russkies and hang together against "Japan, Inc.," or, the "Yellow Peril," if you prefer. Xenophobia and bellicosity went hand in hand. It was "morning in America," said Reagan. The Soviet Union collapsed, but not the Japanese. Instead, Detroit would try to ape Japanese manufacturing and the Japanese architecture. They would switch to front wheel drive and transverse engines.*

Chrysler's celebrity CEO, Lee Iacocca, was unavoidable for comment in the early 1980s, spouting the themes of nationalism and rebirth. Iacocca had been with Ford Motor since 1946 and served as company president from 1970 until 1978, when he left to take the wheel at Chrysler. He became a hero when he pulled the company back from the edge of bankruptcy by convincing Congress to guarantee $1.5 billion in loans. The only alternative, he said, was half a million lost jobs. "Detroit's Comeback Kid," *Time* called him in 1983. He was back on the cover in 1985: "America loves listening to Lee." (Andy Warhol did the artwork.) His television persona was aggressive and defiant:

> When you've been kicked in the head like we have, you learn pretty quick to put first things first. And in the car business, product comes first and product is what brought us back to prosperity. High-mileage, front wheel drive, quality products. . . . Not bad for a company that had one foot in the grave.

Iacocca didn't need to mention who was doing the kicking, of course, because every third business story in those years was about the Rising Sun.

The American automobile had faced down competition before. When the Beetle arrived, Detroit pumped out hipper compact cars and called in models from its European farm teams. With safety and environmental regulations, Detroit, foot-dragging and fighting all the way, made changes. The Japanese invasion, however, required changing places: from leader to follower. Japan surpassed the United

---

* GM had offered the Oldsmobile Toronado, Buick Riviera, and Cadillac Eldorado as front-wheel drive luxury coupes in low volumes since the 1960s, although not for reasons of efficiency. Chrysler imported a modified version of a front-drive, transverse-engine model created by its French subsidiary, Simca, in 1977.

States as the world's leading manufacturer of autos in 1980; Japanese imports accounted for one in four cars sold in the US that year. From the perspective of the American driver, however, the most important change wrought by the Japanese was a new automotive ethos. As Robert Sobel, a professor of business history, explains in *Car Wars*, "Toyota did nothing less than oblige Detroit to accept a new concept of the position of the automobile in Western society." The Big Three could no longer dictate the kind of automobiles Americans should drive. Detroit had lost control of the automotive narrative to the Japanese.

In isolation the changes seem minor, the kinds of things most car buyers hardly considered. Taken together, however, they add up to a new relationship with the automobile and a new driving experience.

Iacocca's pitch, "high-mileage, front wheel drive, quality," could be summed up in one word, Japanese. In 1974, fortuitously timed with the oil crisis, VW and Honda began selling models with transverse-mounted (sideways) engines and front-wheel drive in the United States. By the early 1980s, Nissan, Toyota, GM, and Chrysler had all introduced new models using this layout. Ford followed in 1986.

Nevertheless, Detroit had one thing going for it: it built patriotically American cars. Iacocca was openly belligerent; Ford was upbeat. The company tag line, "The Best-Built American Cars," was either an exercise in managing expectations (Japanese cars were still better) or another reminder that Ford was the home team. To confront Japan's reputation for quality, Ford advertised its own quality assurance testing beginning in 1979. In 1981 the company's entire campaign was built around the slogan "Quality is Job 1."*

Over at GM things were a bit more complicated. Americana had long been a Chevrolet theme, most famously with the tag lines, "See the USA in your Chevrolet!" and, "Baseball, hotdogs, apple

---

* "Job 1" is the traditional term for the first car of a model to come off the assembly line.

pie, and Chevrolet." In 1983, coming out of a double-dip recession, GM asserted, "We are USA-1 and USA-1 is taking charge." "The Heartbeat of America" advertising soundtrack for 1987 added sap to the apple pie with its heartland footage. But GM was in a tricky spot under the leadership of CEO Roger Smith. A lifer with GM, he knew something was desperately wrong with the business. It is doubtful anyone could have revived the rotted organization in the 1980s, but Smith actually added rottenness. The company's market share dropped from 46 to 35 percent during his tenure while quality fell and debt mounted. He initiated many disastrous experiments, but his joint venture with Toyota succeeded. To reform its culture, and lower its costs, GM tried its own real-life version of *Gung Ho*. In 1984, GM and Toyota began a joint venture, the New United Motor Manufacturing, Inc. NUMMI established a plant in Fremont, California. The plant built Toyota Corollas and Chevrolet Novas, the same car in all but name. GM learned about the Toyota Production System, sometimes called "lean manufacturing," and "just-in-time production." GM learned how to engineer the production process itself to eliminate waste of all kinds. While GM learned Japanese secrets, Toyota gained a foothold that let it bypass "voluntary" import quotas.

Some of the less racist analyses of Japanese prowess in car-making pointed not to an "Asian quality gene" but to manufacturing efficiency. Mismanagement and poor product quality were fine when everyone was doing it. But the Japanese were not on board. Detroit and its supporters decried low-wage labor in Japan. UAW plant workers earned nearly $20 an hour while their Japanese counterparts were paid just short of $11 an hour. But that wage advantage was eaten up by the cost of shipping and tariffs. The difference was in manufacturing efficiency. In 1981, GM took eighty-three employee hours to build a small car; Nissan took only fifty-one. A Japanese plant stamped out 550 parts an hour, compared to 325 in the United States. Also, Japanese plants were more flexible, taking five minutes to change dies versus five hours in the US. From manufacturing efficiency flowed higher quality. The evidence of the Japanese cars built in the US suggested that American workers could make good cars too in the right corporate culture. It was nurture over nature. Soon every MBA student had to learn the "Toyota Way:" JIT, just-in-in time delivery of parts to the line; *kaizen*, continuous improvement; *genchi genbutsu*: go see for your damn self what the problem is. American management, however, could not learn the Japanese secret of treating workers well.

It is hard to escape history. Henry Ford had treated his immigrant workers like dunces and violently resisted unionization in 1940. Sloan complained that workers had "stolen our property" when they staged the Sitdown Strikes of 1936. On the eve of World War II, the workers won the right to bargain, but the UAW agreed to remain quiescent for the duration. When the war ended, the strikes resumed. Rather than share decision making and control of the production lines with their workers, management maintained the Fordist command-and-control culture. They paid off unhappy workers with higher benefits and wages—Henry's five-dollar day taken to extremes. This led to the rise of the blue-collar middle class, but also lowered productivity, fomented antagonistic relationships with line workers, and produced lousy cars.

The Japanese avoided these problems, not just with the Toyota Way but also by opening their American plants in the Southeastern United States, where they could escape the industrial unionism of the Midwest. Honda had held the line against the UAW since the company started building motorcycles outside of Columbus, Ohio, in 1979 (and automobiles in 1982). The union abandoned its organization drive after workers voted overwhelmingly in 1985 to maintain a nonunion shop. Nissan started building cars in Tennessee the following year, and two years after its GM joint venture began in 1984, Toyota chose Kentucky for its own plant. This is not to say that Japanese plants are a worker's paradise or that labor-management relations alone explain the steady rise of imports.

As more transplants opened in the Southeast, Michigan rusted.

Workers in the old industrial towns who faced decline with anger and depression found a champion in Michael Moore. Moore is the son of a line worker and grew up in Flint, home of Billy Durant and Buick Motor's birthplace. He briefly edited *Mother Jones* and later published his own alternative paper, *The Flint Voice*. His award-winning 1989 documentary *Roger and Me* broke attendance records at the Telluride Film Festival; it was an audience favorite at the New York, Toronto, and Vancouver film festivals. The art film crowd learned what autoworkers and their families already knew. GM (and its ilk) had utter disregard for its workforce, treating them as enemies rather than stakeholders. As GM's director of labor relations put it in 1968, "If they are interested in participative management, we are not. We have paid the damndest wages and benefits to keep the workers and the unions out of management's prerogatives."

The film's conceit was Moore's quixotic attempts to interview GM CEO Roger Smith. Moore made a fool of Smith by recording the CEO dodging repeated interview requests (they never did sit down). Along the way the tragicomic film documents the misery of Flint. GM had turned Durant's leafy town into a burned-out hellhole, Moore showed. In one of the strangest and most poignant scenes, Moore talks to a woman selling, "Rabbits or Bunnies—Pets or Meat." In the wake of 30,000 layoffs and the closing of eleven plants, Smith remained tone-deaf and unavailable for comment.

Routinely ranked among history's worst CEOs, Smith systematically destroyed the theoretical underpinnings of Sloan's "purse and purpose." From the time he took the reins in the 1920s, Sloan built GM into a colossal profit machine by maintaining a balance between the conglomerate, GM, and the individual car companies that made it up. Smith kept all of the car nameplates—Chevrolet, Pontiac, Buick, Oldsmobile, and Cadillac—but took away the reasons for their existence. There would be only two divisions, one for small cars and one for large. In place of Sloan's differentiation strategy, Smith introduced cost cutting. There would be one giant GM parts bin from which every division would draw. Moreover, low cost would trump quality and durability at every turn. GM confronted a PR nightmare when people found Buick engines under the hoods of their Cadillacs. The company had to add the following disclaimer to its ads: "Some [insert car line] are equipped with engines produced by other GM divisions, subsidiaries, or affiliated companies world-wide. See your [insert car line] dealer for details."

The Cadillac Cimarron of 1981 proved the utter stupidity of Smith's parts bin philosophy. Cadillac dealers will periodically ask for a smaller, sportier model that could entice young people into the brand because the average age of a Cadillac buyer is dead. But the resulting Cimarron was nothing more than a poorly built, overpriced Chevrolet Cavalier—totally unfit for a classy Mafioso. Although like any good mobster, it had several aliases: Pontiac J2000, Olds-mobile Firenza, and Buick Skyhawk. All featured a Japanese-style transverse mounted, front-wheel drive setup antithetical to tradi-tional Cadillac ride and handling.

While destroying the product differentiation that built GM, Smith left GM's dysfunctional corporate culture in place. Michael Moore had a hand in exposing that deeper cultural crisis as well. Moore's alternative paper, *The Flint Voice*, hired Ben Hamper as a columnist in 1981. Hamper provided uncensored, in situ coverage of the GM assembly line, depicting labor-management dysfunction and the absurd realities of line work. Through his alter ego, Rivet-head, Hamper recounted life as a "shoprat" at the GM Flint Truck and Bus Plant in the age of "quality" evangelism. He describes it as a "strange new entry into the GM vocabulary." In the salty lan-guage of the assembly line, Hamper relates, "The term itself was like some new intoxicating utterance that General Motors had pried outta the ass end of a golden goose." Ford had been content with a slogan, Chrysler, with having its CEO proselytize. Management at GM Flint decided they needed a mascot. The plan was to dress up the mascot as a large cat, the Quality Cat, aka Howie Makem, who stood five feet seven. "He wore a long red cape emblazoned with the letter Q for Quality," says Hamper. Howie toured the plant urging workers to do their best.* Hamper's co-workers resented being treated like children who could be made to work harder in school by a singing purple dinosaur, but Hamper remained bemused. One day, Howie disappeared. Hamper checked the plant. No one had seen hide or hair of him. A spare head was found in a back closet. When Moore learned of Howie Makem's disappearance, he grew distraught. He had been begging to print a Quality Cat interview in the *Voice*. In place of Howie, management decided to hand out "Quality Cat" drinking glasses if the "Quality level met such and such a figure."

Hamper relies on more than hilarity. He describes the demoralizing and tragic realities of life on the line. The work is so poorly organized that he often doubled up on a job while his coworker got drunk in the parking lot or slept at the work station. Then they would swap. Although such goldbricking might seem a fun way to spend the workday, one cannot read Hamper's book without realizing how disheartening labor so arranged could be. The Japanese famously let their workers stop the line with a pull of a string any time they saw a problem. GM took the opposite approach. When a woman, only two days on the job, knocks herself unconscious with a rivet gun, a coworker hits the stop button. She's out cold, lying under the line. When the "ties" (Hamper's sobriquet for middle management) show up, all they want to know is who the hell shut off the line.

Hamper calls Lee Iacocca "the born again pom-pom boy of Quality High who was currently splattering himself all over medialand with galvanic jabber." Buyers just wanted "a vehicle that didn't begin to disintegrate the moment it rolled off the showroom floor." So they

---

* I found the story so unbelievable that I contacted Hamper to confirm its veracity. He told me that years later he learned that the Howie costume was inhabited by the wife of one of his crew mates from the assembly line. Howie was a she.

chose "generic-looking imports that got about 500 miles per gallon and stuck together as firm as Stonehenge." In other words, they chose Japanese appliances.

*   *   *   *

I STILL SAY beauty is in the Hispano-Suiza, not the eye of the beholder. But what about beauty's absence? The cars of the 1980s were not ugly exactly. They did not offend the eye. Instead, they invited no passion at all, for or against. It was almost as if Detroit wanted to pretend it didn't make cars anymore. Cars create smog, destroy cities, foment unrest in the Middle East. Don't blame us, we don't make those things. Admittedly, the Japanese cars were no better looking, but they did not have to be. Their pitch was fuel efficiency and quality. Ford, GM, and Chrysler, in contrast, had only their looks going for them. When their looks were gone, so was their desirability.

In the 1980s GM debuted "a whole new kind of compact car," the front-wheel-drive X-body badged as the Chevy Citation, Olds Omega, and Buick Skylark. The Citation (one assumes that the naming committee had never gotten a speeding ticket) had a computer-controlled "clean burning engine," "impressive fuel economy," and all the design panache of a cereal box: pure utility from bumper to bumper. My father convinced his mother to trade in her massive old Thunderbird for an Omega. She called it a tin can. I drove it whenever I visited. She was right.

Chrysler launched its full front-drive lineup in 1981, the K-car in too many models and configurations to mention. Not only did the government guarantee the loans that were keeping Chrysler afloat, it also bought K-cars for federal fleets to support the new model. By 1983, the company had repaid its loans and returned to profitability. "Next year, we will build a small car right here in America," Iacocca boasted in 1984, "with quality that we're determined will beat the Japanese at their own game." As for the Germans, "Chrysler will build two sedans, LeBaron GTS and Dodge Lancer, that will challenge BMW, Audi, even Mercedes, for thousands less." Comical as it sounds to hear Chrysler LeBaron in the same sentence as BMW, Chrysler earned more money per car sold than GM did in 1985. The soporific K-car platform generally, and the K-minivans in particular, saved the company.

The Smithsonian has a 1986 Dodge Caravan minivan complete with fake wood paneling on display at the National Museum of American History. It is as inoffensive, tinny, and dull as the rest of the K-car lineup, but it created a new configuration that could replace both the station wagon and the full-sized van. It was essentially a compact K-car with two boxes to the sedan's three. It had a single sliding door and the rear windows did not open, but then kids don't buy cars. In any event, the government classified the neo-station wagon as a "light truck" for the purposes of federal regulations. That meant fewer safety requirements and more lenient fuel economy standards for the company as a whole. Chrysler still builds the most popular minivan in the country. On the other hand, it is now, like its Honda and Toyota competitors, a maxivan. (Ford, GM, and Nissan have abandoned the category.)

Ford was the last of the Big Three to adopt the new architecture. When it finally did in 1986, the front end had no grille! Air for the radiator snuck in under the bumper. Except it had no bumper, as far as anyone could tell. Body-colored plastic cladding disguised the bumper and blended it with the body. The Ford Taurus was a full-sized six-passenger American car with the exterior, according to some critics, of an Audi and interior features found on Volvos and Saabs. More critical critics called it a jellybean. The steering was tighter and the suspension firmer than the models it replaced, another European influence aimed at capturing young affluent professionals. Yuppies, the millennials of the Reagan era, were abandoning the American automobile for European cars. That's why Lee Iacocca had said with a straight face that he would build a Chrysler that would challenge BMW and Mercedes. That never quite happened, but sales were strong and the Taurus influenced styling much as the '49 Ford had. Ford ads played an American, nativist theme: "For Us! Now there's an American car that's exactly what we've been looking for. Taur-US!"

The change in architecture—from longitudinal-engine, body-on-frame, and rear-wheel drive to their opposites—changed the experience of driving. These are the details, again, about which most buyers are unaware, but which slowly transformed the American automobile. In 1891, French automaker Panhard et Levassor had introduced the *Système Panhard*, a longitudinally mounted engine in place of the under-seat transverse motor. To be clear, rather than the engine spinning in parallel with the rotation of the wheels, it spun perpendicular. This allowed not only larger motors but also established a new design language that turned the horseless carriage into the motorcar. The size of one's hood spoke to the size of one's engine and the power of one's car. But the transverse engine still made sense for little cars sixty years later. In 1959, British Motor Corporation debuted the Morris Mini with a transverse engine and wheels the size of dinner plates. Honda put one in its little Civic in 1972, as did VW when it replaced the Beetle with the Golf (Rabbit, in the United States) in 1974. Revving a transverse engine is like poking a hamster with a stick to speed up its exercise wheel. The car shows no outward signs of getting ready to move. A longitudinally mounted engine, especially a massive V8, torques the car on its long axis. The car paws the ground and snorts hot air, ready to charge.

Also, the magic carpet ride so prized since the 1950s was achieved with a long wheel base, too much power assist, and a lazy suspension. The front drive setup combined with a shorter wheel base, firmer tires, better steering, and suspension put an end to the magic carpet. Daniel Guillory, a poet and professor of English, described the effects of the new architecture on driving itself. "The way they corner and steer," he told the assembled at a Detroit Historical Society Conference in 1982:

assisted by front-wheel drive and lower centers of gravity, the way they absorb bumps and cling to the roadway, helped here by Macpherson Struts and air dams and spoilers, all these engineering changes add up to a new dialogue with space and distance. Cars, after all, are ways of addressing space, and the newest ones rolling off production lines are closer in feeling to the lunar shuttle in *2001* or the X-wing fighters in *Star Wars* than to any other artifacts in our culture.

Even the amount of air in the tires changes how cars address space. Going into the 1980s, manufacturers specified soft, squishy tires with perhaps twenty-five pounds of air. These helped give that luxurious magic carpet ride. By the end of the decade, tires had firmed up nearer to 35 psi and, with them, ride and handling.

Finally, no single factor determines how a car handles more than whether the engine delivers power to the front or the rear wheels. Rear-wheel drive is hands down more fun. Not only is the mass of a rear-drive car better balanced, it is also being pushed into turns and around corners rather than pulled. That makes it easier to spin out—which is fun! Admittedly, front drive is better if you want traction in the snow and safety, but it makes for an uneventful car chase.

Guillory also notes the emergence of "mathematically designed interiors," that showed a concinnity with the rectilinear exteriors. The LED display, with its chamfered block font, became the marker of a modern car. Advertisements featured computer-aided-design blueprints and workstations in front of wind tunnels. Reality underpinned the electronic aesthetic somewhat. Computerization of engine controls came to the United States in the 1980s in response to environmental regulations. Electronic ignitions and electronic fuel injection metered fuel and air more precisely, reducing pollution. Notably, Detroit lagged the imports in adopting these technologies. But LEDs had as much to do with electronic engine controls as tail fins had to do with stability in a crosswind.

The poet concludes his meditation on early 1980s automotive interiors with some still timely observations. Watching a girl play *Grand Prix* at the video arcade, he notes that "The windshield and video screen fuses into one." Guillroy's catalog of new electronic devices quaintly anticipates our smartphone era. He describes a "new world of buzzes, blips, and beeps [that] is part of a cluster of objects that have intruded themselves into the most personal crevices of our daily life, items like LCD watches and digital clocks, microwave ovens, pocket calculators. . . ."

Rather than chuckle—if only he knew what was coming!—we should take time to appreciate Guillory's sensitivity to the end of the American automobile. For him, a friend's 1950 Buick Roadmaster defines the real thing. It "mashed out the undulations of the roughest roads by dint of sheer weight. Its "balloon tires" made "wonderful sibilant noises."

By the end of the 1980s, Oldsmobile would decide that such reminiscences were unhelpful nostalgia. Beginning in 1989, it introduced the slogan, "This is not your father's Oldsmobile." The TV ads featured famous stars and their not-so-famous offspring. William Shatner and Leonard Nimoy, *Star Trek*'s Kirk and Spock, respectively, were featured. Spock beamed into the passenger seat of an Oldsmobile Silhouette driven by his daughter. Though it looked to many people like a DustBuster vacuum cleaner, the Silhouette sat at the pinnacle of 1980s futurism.* It had dent-proof plastic body skirts and did not look terribly out of place in France. But Tom Magliozzi, cohost of NPR's *Car Talk*, laughed at its most striking feature: a long-sloped windshield and resulting dashboard acreage. Anything smaller than a pizza box set atop it would slide out of reach.

✳ ✳ ✳ ✳

BY THE END OF THE DECADE, GM had come up with a way to reform its assembly lines, a response to Ben Hamper's biting depic-

---

* The Chevy Lumina APV and Pontiac Trans Sport were nearly identical, but GM made the new-generation, space travel theme central to the entire Olds line.

tion. In 1990, it introduced a new model from a separate, employee-owned company called Saturn. It would not be the old GM but "a different kind of car company." Saturn followed the Japanese south to escape the UAW, opening a plant in Tennessee. Having learned at Toyota's knee in NUMMI, managers encouraged *kaizen*, harmony, and no-haggle pricing at a newly minted dealer network. GM's president explained that Saturn would be GM's attempt to beat the Japanese at their own game. If Saturn couldn't do it, he said, it couldn't be done.

It couldn't be done. The first Saturns were indeed different: boring sedans but with dedicated engines and platforms along with plastic body panels that resisted dents. Saturn cultivated a very uncultish cult following of sensibly patriotic buyers who wanted more than anything to avoid negotiating with a greasy car salesman. Buyers would get a group hug on taking delivery and be invited back to family reunions with free hot dogs. But Saturn's quality and production efficiency never matched the Japanese, sales did not meet expectations, and within a few years of launching, the differences fell away. GM management, the only variable unchanged in the experiment, bought out the company and merged Saturn into an already bloated product line. Parts came from the same bin of cheap plastic bits used for every Chevy, Pontiac, Olds, and Cadillac. Then management decided to let its baby starve. They turned the Tennessee plant over to Chevrolet and used rebranded German Opels to replace Saturn's own models.

The Americans instead fell back on what they did well: selling big, body-on-frame vehicles with sloppy handling and antiquated suspensions. Thanks to some frozen chickens, Detroit found salvation in a new kind of American automobile that was cheap to make, easy to sell, and highly profitable. In fact, the vehicle had been there all along but inhabited a commercial niche. For the domestic automakers, the last redoubt of the American automobile wouldn't be a car at all. It would be a truck. American buyers, once again enjoying low gasoline prices in the late 1990s, found that the pickup truck and SUV had the 1950 Roadmaster's road-hugging weight.

Detroit's monster truck windfall goes back to LBJ's Chicken War of 1963. The French and Germans had slapped a tariff on frozen chickens from the United States, President Johnson slapped them back with a 25 percent tax on light-truck imports that remains on the books. The tariff hit its target, VW's Beetle-based Type 2 pickup, essentially banning it from US shores. Over the years, foreign automakers have used various strategies to get around the quota. VW began building small, high-mileage Rabbit-based pickups in Pennsylvania in the late 1970s. Subaru installed a pair of blow-molded, rear-facing seats in the bed of its diminutive BRAT pickup. In lieu of safety belts each seat had a pair of ski-pole handles. The seats were obviously deadly, but a BRAT so equipped skirted the Chicken Tax. Toyota and Nissan now build their monster trucks and SUVs, Chicken Tax free, in the United States. They are just as big, fuel-guzzling, and menacing as the domestics.

Detroit had been trying to broaden the market for trucks since the 1950s. In 1957, Ford created the Styleside, with rear fenders integrated into the bed, now the common style on most trucks. Dodge had the Sweptside in 1958—complete with tail fins. The El Camino and Ranchero were half sedan and half pickup. Little pickups from Japan got some love in the 1970s. Ford sold one designed by Mazda and GM called its rebranded Isuzu pickup the Chevy Luv. But trucks and SUVs did not really hit the big time until the 1990s with the Ford Explorer.

Ross Roberts was Ford Division general manager when he made the newly introduced Ford Explorer into a mainstream machine. He told the *Automotive News* that the Explorer was his favorite vehicle, "because of the functionality of it, the versatility of it. Besides, we make a lot of money off of those." He added that the Explorer was "an American-type vehicle" that fit well "with the sprawling of America." The Explorer's success has been such that it was able to weather the kind of storm that sank the Corvair in 1969. Explorers too had a bad tendency to flip over, especially when wearing the defective Firestone tires Ford fitted to them at the factory. The companies and NHTSA had been made aware of the problem as early as 1998. When Congress finally called them to defend themselves at hearings in 2000, Ford blamed Firestone and Firestone blamed Ford. Firestone also blamed drivers for not keeping their tires properly inflated. Eventually, Ralph Nader's advocacy group, the Center for Auto Safety, got action. The pattern was the same as it had been in the 1970s when Firestone also sold defective tires and then fought class action suits and a NHTSA recall. The Greek tragedy of the whole affair was that the Ford and Firestone families had intermarried and Harvey Firestone and Henry Ford had been two of the Four Vagabonds who went glamping every year in the forest, as we have seen.

Both the Suzuki Samurai and Isuzu Trooper SUVs faced similarly existential threats when *Consumer Reports* labeled them "Unacceptable" and "Unsafe," respectively. In 1988, *Consumers* showed the Samurai tipping over in a test designed to mimic swerving around a sudden obstacle. Sales plummeted 70 percent following the story. After putting the Isuzu through the same test for its October 1996 issue, *Consumers* said the Trooper had "a unique and extremely dangerous propensity to roll over." Both Suzuki and Isuzu sued. The outcome in both cases might best be called a draw.*

In actual fact, all SUVs tip over at twice the rate of cars. But, rather than try to kill the SUV, the government saved it. Ford agreed to fund a consumer education campaign. The result was the unintentionally hilarious and devilishly clever "Esuvee Safety Campaign." It featured a hairy, bucking buffalo that would have fit in with the

---

* The jury in the Isuzu trial found that *Consumer Reports* falsely reported that the Trooper had a unique tendency to tip over, but that *Consumers* had not acted maliciously and awarded no damages. Suzuki initially settled with *Consumers* but later sued when the magazine bragged that its testing caused Samurai sales to "dwindle away." Again, judges found no malice.

Muppets. One television ad featured "Esuvee" riding as the main event at a rodeo. Cowboys buckled their shoulder belts before the gate was opened. The tag line: "Keep it on all fours." Then, NHTSA created Federal Motor Vehicle Safety Standards for tire pressure monitoring systems and electronic stability controls. That little light on the dashboard that comes on when your tire is low is there thanks to the Ford/Firestone controversy. It's also there because, be honest, you haven't been following the manual's recommendation to check the tire pressure once a week.

The attention paid to the safety and environmental impacts of the SUV brightened the dividing line between rural and urban, progressive and laissez faire, in the car culture. Also, it resurrected questions of driver responsibility and vehicle design. After all, you *were* supposed to keep your tires properly inflated and if you couldn't drive well enough to keep your SUV on all fours, well, you really ought not drive one. Also, the rise of the SUV in the 1990s, coming as it did on the heels of the Japanese small-car invasion, suggests the American automobile resists downsizing and diminution.

The ultimate SUV villain remains the Hummer. When Arnold Schwarzenegger saw the military version, the High Mobility Multipurpose Wheeled Vehicle, the Humvee, up close, he said, "Look at those deltoids; look at those calves." The action movie star had one customized and drove it proudly around Los Angeles. He then went to AM General, which made the Pentagon monster, demanding that they produce a civilian version. He got his way and civilian Hummers rolled off the production line starting in 1992. Then, in 1999, GM bought the brand. It added a Hummer H2 and Hummer H3 to the lineup. The original had been a barely modified battle truck. The newer iterations were standard GM SUVs restyled to look militaristic. Schwarzenegger became the Republican governor of California.

The meteoric rise of giant SUVs spawned a breed of SUV haters. *High and Mighty: The Dangerous Rise of the SUV*, by Pulitzer Prize winning *New York Times* reporter Keith Bradsher, comes down firmly on the side of the haters. Bradsher argues that SUVs are categorically less safe than passenger cars because they roll over. He puts their popularity down to the diabolical work of automobile design and marketing, especially a Svengali named Clotaire Rapaille. Over several pages, we learn that the French-born medical anthropologist is the most influential psychoanalyst working for the Big Three. Rapaille relies on Jungian psychology to divide "people's reaction to a commercial product" into three levels: intellectual, emotional, and reptilian. He goes right for the Jungular. "With the detachment of a foreigner, Rapaille sees Americans as increasingly fearful of crime." Teenagers are especially, and irrationally, afraid because they play with "menacing toy action figures," watch murders on television, and play video games. Violence saturated teens want a car that says, "I want to be able to destroy. I want to be able to fight back, don't mess with me." Bradsher admits that teens don't actually buy SUVs, but youth culture is what matters. People buy SUVs because they are afraid of crime and violence.

Bradsher uses Rapaille to rehearse an explanation made since the 1930s as to why Americans make foolish purchase decisions when it comes to buying automobiles for transportation. In his review of the new models for 1936, *Consumer Reports* founder Dewey Palmer blamed Marxian false consciousness or the inability of buyers to resist the stylists' and advertisers' promotion of styling over safety. "[M]akers of cars are bringing forward as many new talking points as they think the credibility of the public will stand," he wrote. According to historian Alan Raucher, Palmer believed that "the industry exploited the average man's desire for status by providing a delusion of grandeur." John Keats extended the argument across an entire chapter, "The Ad and the Id," in *Insolent Chariots*. Of course those within the industry, indeed the public in general, conceive of car buyers as sovereign consumers free to choose from among many new and used models—free even not to buy at all.

True, SUVs are less safe than cars because they roll over. But, as any Corvair buff will tell you, much depends on the skill and attention of the driver. Also, next time I plan to be in a crash between a Beetle and a Hummer, I plan to be in the Hummer. Is it not possible, at least within the confines of consumer society, that Americans actually *want* to drive SUVs because they are all we have left of the great and true "American Automobile." Other than a forty-year-old full-sized sedan from Detroit, the SUV is the only game in town.

Not only do many Americans prefer buying large SUVs, and not only do automakers prefer selling these highly profitable vehicles, but the federal government pitches in as well. For example, the IRS tax code has a lovely handout called Section 179 depreciation, also known as the "Hummer Tax Loophole." I am not qualified to offer tax advice, but as long as you use it for business, the IRS lets you write off the cost of a vehicle as soon as you buy it—provided that it weighs more than 6,000 pounds. Even as subsidies for EVs have come under fire, the feds will subsidize your monster truck purchase. The rules have been tightened somewhat in recent years, but, as with the Chicken Tax, the Michigan congressional delegation won't let this one expire any time soon.

Fuel economy standards on SUVs are also less strict. The result is that well into the twenty-first century, the most popular vehicles on the market have fuel economy ratings nearly identical to the most popular vehicles of the 1970s. All of these giveaways to a market segment that Detroit owns and, for the most part, only Americans buy, keeps plants humming.*

In our town, every other vehicle at school drop off is an SUV, many of them the giant, body-on-frame kind. There are Suburbans, Yukons, Expeditions, and Navigators. All of them are driven by moms, I think, although I can't really see up into them from the ovoid safety of the minivan. Consider the 2018 Nissan Armada. (Nissan must have found that "Fleet of Warships" didn't focus group as well.) The Armada stands six and a half feet tall. Sedan driv-

---

* Fuel economy calculations have changed over time, but the fact remains that the large SUVs have numbers in line with the big old cars.

ers can't see into it and pedestrians can't see past it. More to the point, it is designed to strike fear and trembling into the hearts of all those foolish enough to face off against it on the highway. The front has the look of those "roo bars" used to thrash through the Australian outback. Nissan just calls it a "muscular grille." At the sides are steroidal fenders, "rugged and athletic" to muscle through traffic. And running boards. Not the running boards of old, mind you, those automotive verandas custom made for joy riding. No, these are tucked in under the body, only for use by the peerage, sharp-edged to keep out the hoi polloi. Then there's the Toyota Sequoia. "Named for the largest redwood trees in the world," Toyota explains. The sheet metal is rounded to give the impression of a muscle-bound lug stuffed into a sharkskin suit after gorging on whey powder at GNC. Even the hood is swollen. You could be run down by this thing without the driver ever knowing it. The Dodge Durango SUV is also "muscular," and the Dodge Ram 1500 pickup, "Looks as if it would win a bar fight," according to car journalist Tom Voelk's review. Its "Wagnerian engine note" is "pure cave man in its primal tone . . . it's highly recommended." Each new model year gets meaner, more aggressive, and more intimidating.

On roads crowded with giant redwood trees, fleets of warships, and battering rams, Americans are abandoning cars. Sales of pickup trucks and large SUVs continue to grow, but a new category, the crossover, has emerged to replace the old sedan and hatchback. In 2018, car sales slipped below 30 percent of the market with no end in sight. Now, instead of a full-sized, mid-sized, or even a compact, a buyer can choose the SUV look and SUV altitude. For example, Chevy's pint-sized Sonic sedan was selling well until GM introduced the Chevy Trax crossover. The two are built on the same platform and are almost identical, but sales shifted immediately and dramatically to the Trax. It's 15 percent heavier and half a foot taller than the Sonic, so the driver enjoys a higher perch. Automakers argue that buyers prefer the crossover to the low-slung sedan or hatchback because it offers more utility. I believe the desire to see and be seen also motivates buyers: behind the wheel of a sedan, you cannot see past a crossover, let alone a minivan, truck, or full-sized SUV; also, you have a better chance of being seen, and therefore spared, by Wagnerian pickups on the prowl. For automakers, crossovers mean profits. To see and be seen in a Trax, buyers pay a $5,100 premium.

Time was when "longer, lower, wider" was the mantra of automotive designers. Each new model had to occupy more acreage than its predecessor. Certainly the philosophy went too far; witness the 1973 Chrysler Imperial, with a total of nine feet stretching past its axles. Our 1975 Oldsmobile Custom Cruiser came in at nearly twenty feet overall but less than five feet tall. That voluminous wagon, with its pale blue topsides and simulated wood-grain panels, oozed domesticity. It may have been a dinosaur, but only of the vegetarian, gentle giant, brontosaurus type. The Custom Cruiser and her ilk are gone. Now you meet Tyrannosaurus Rex when you run out for a quart of milk.

Still, I try not to judge SUV drivers harshly. Caught in the cross fire of an automotive arms race, the sensible thing to do is armor up. So, now we find ourselves in a quagmire of our own making. Fortunately, like the drones flying over the battlefields of America's forever war, the driverless car is here to save us.

PART THREE

Chapter 12

FUTURE VISIONS OF ROBOT CARS

YOUR PERSONAL "FLYING CARPET" Step into it, press a button, and off you go to market, to a friend's home, or to your job. Take off and land anywhere; no parking problems. Plug in to any electric outlet for recharging. They're working on it!

MORE POWER TO YOU!

America's independent light and power companies build for your new electric living

Tomorrow's higher standard of living will put electricity to work for you in ways still unheard of!

The time isn't too far off, the experts say, when you'll wash your dishes without soap or water—ultrasonic waves will do the job. Your beds will be made at the touch of a button. The kids' homework

will be made interesting and even exciting when they are able to dial a library book, a lecture or a classroom demonstration right into your home—with sound. (Some of this is happening already.)

To enjoy all this, you'll want a lot more electric power, and the independent electric companies of America are already building

new plants and facilities to provide it. Right now these companies are building at the rate of $5,000,000,000 a year, and planning to double the nation's supply of electricity in less than 10 years.

America has always had the best electric power service in the world. The electric companies are resolved to keep it that way.

AMERICA'S INDEPENDENT ELECTRIC LIGHT AND POWER COMPANIES

Company names on request through this magazine

The electric flying car was pure sci-fi in the 1950s, but driverless car technology was real. Why has it taken six decades to develop it?

IN THE SAME WAY THAT THE AUTOMOBILE WAS AVAILABLE IN the 1860s, if not earlier, we could have embraced driverless cars in the 1990s, the 1950s, or even the 1930s, but we did not. Suddenly, however, inventors and investors are coming out of the woodwork to create driverless cars. It's 1895 all over again. To understand why now as well as how today's driverless cars differ in ideology from those of the past, we might start by talking to Google.

In the fall of 2017, sounding for all the world like a middle-school guidance counselor, Google's Waymo subsidiary launched a propaganda campaign for the driverless car, "Let's Talk Self Driving." The web banner includes the promises made since the 1930s about the self-driving car:

> Imagine climbing into the back seat of a car and just pushing a button to go. You don't have to drive at all. Your driver—the car—handles all of it, while staying constantly vigilant and seeing 360 degrees all around you. Everyone moves around safely, drunk and distracted driving become a thing of the past and we all get time back in our day.

Below the green cross endorsement of the National Safety Council, the conversation continues: "Human error is involved in 94 percent of today's crashes." Founded in 1913, the NSC became the clearinghouse for the "traffic safety establishment" that Ralph Nader denounced in *Unsafe at Any Speed*. They were the ones who advanced the "three E's" (engineering, education, and enforcement) approach to safety and coordinated the work of safety professionals in traffic policing, traffic engineering, and driver education. Signatories to the Let's Talk campaign also include the Foundation for Senior Living ("Because age shouldn't slow anyone down"), MADD ("Because we can end drunk driving"), and the Foundation for Blind Children ("Because everyone wants independence"). The three E's are gone, but the logic remains: humans are implicated in nearly all crashes, so driving requires constant, tedious vigilance. But automobility is an inherent good, so drive we must until our robot minions can take over. The tech companies may not care that they are repeating the past. To them, as to Henry Ford, "History is more or less bunk." Yet when driverless cars were proposed in the 1930s, tested in the 1950s, and proven effective in the 1990s, their proponents made the same case. You would climb in, push a button, and go. Technology would make car travel far safer and more relaxing than it had ever been.

Google's conversation prompt does, however, contain new twists. First, the tech giant wants you to imagine climbing into the *back* seat, not the front. In the 1950s, everyone wanted to be in the driver's seat or, if they could not, at least in the front row. No one would have been fooled into thinking the back seat was cool.* In Google's framing, the driver's seat is no longer exalted. You are the "Privileged Sport" from the turn of the nineteenth century, riding in luxury while your robot chauffeur toils away.

Second, the Google car works alone. It carries on board all of the smarts it needs to see "360 degrees all around you." A basic rule of robotics holds that the more constrained the environment, the less intelligent the robot itself needs to be. The robot car offers a prime example of this rule. Constrained on an Interstate Highway—without stoplights, pedestrians, cross traffic, or any of the other myriad challenges of surface streets—the driverless car needs only moderate intelligence. Embed guide wires or lay magnetic bread crumbs down the lanes of the Interstate and even a fairly dumb robot car can navigate. Add reflectors and sensors to every car on the road, and things get even easier. In other words, an excellent way to achieve the self-driving goals Google wants to rap about would be to sprinkle smarts throughout the system—the fleet of vehicles, road environment, and control infrastructure—as a whole. This integrated approach defined previous instantiations of the driverless car. In combining public infrastructure and individual vehicles, previous generations of robot car inventors followed what might be called, without too much of a stretch, a collectivist ideal. This time is different. Google and GM and all the rest

---

* The installation of dangerous front passenger airbags has softened the younger generation up. They have become accustomed to being forced to sit in the back. See Chapter 15.

are trying to deliver cars that can go anywhere, any time, on-road or off-road, without any help from the outside. These corporations prefer wicked dumb roads and wicked smart cars. They prefer cars that are rugged individualists with the self-discipline of a Randian hero. As students of the car culture, we know by now to consider technology within its historical moment. The robo-car collectivists of earlier eras believed "what was good for America was good for General Motors and vice versa." They believed that the American automobile had built the middle class, won our wars, and generated the abundant American Way of Life. Their robo-car would extend the utility and grandeur of the superhighway. (I'll say it again, the Interstate System is the largest public works project in American history.) By contrast, rugged robo-car individualists only expect government to get out of the way.

When GM began promoting the self-driving car of the future in the first half of the last century, the future it invoked was one with national purpose. The Buicks would be driverless, but that would mean little without the state-funded Interstate Highway System—itself the subject of wild public enthusiasm at the 1939 World's Fair. GM never had to ask for a conversation like Google's rap session. The General just shouted from the rooftops and the public gathered around, all ears.

The line to get into GM's Highways and Horizons pavilion at the 1939 World's Fair snaked along freeway-style on ramps and merged at the entrance. Some 28,000 people a day, 25 million over the course of the eighteen-month-long fair, waited in that line.* As a boy, even Ralph Nader stood in that line expectantly, shouting to his parents, "GM! GM! GM!" Americans needed their hope in the future rekindled as war clouds gathered in Europe and the Great Depression ground on. Four months after the exhibits opened, Hitler and Stalin conquered Poland; by the time it closed in 1940, France had fallen.

---

* The line was shorter over at Ford, where people got to ride around in the same 1939 models available at their local dealers. Meanwhile, Chrysler showed off a talking Plymouth.

Once inside, 2,150 visitors at a time took their plush seats on a "magic 'carry-go-round'" to gaze down on the world of 1960, an America remade by superhighways. The highways bring a Disney-sized amusement park within driving distance of a steel town's Bessemer furnaces. Tiny trees laden with fruit sit under individual glass domes. "Strange? Fantastic? Unbelievable? Remember, this is the world of 1960!" As the seats orbited, a narrator described a "superb one-direction highway, with its seven lanes accommodating traffic at designated speeds of 50, 75, and 100 miles an hour. . . ." Elaborate interchanges—far larger than the tiny cloverleafs of 1940—and wide grassy buffers ornamented the miniature highways.

At the fair, GM gave the public far more than a new highway network. It was a new world of unencumbered, high-speed, hyper-mobility on a gargantuan scale. Now, we could live in the open country and commute to a clean, modern city. We could cross great distances and view the wonders of nature from elegantly engineered ribbons of concrete. We could enjoy nothing short of automobile utopia.

Like current-day driverless car disciples, Futurama's visionary designer Norman Bel Geddes described driving on surface streets as a grind. Drivers are annoyed by "policemen's whistles, confusing highway signs, and irritating traffic regulations," according to *Magic Motorways,* his companion book to Futurama. "They are appalled by the daily toll of this planless, suicidal mess." ("Appalled" was probably too strong a word. More like "mildly disappointed when they thought of the daily toll at all.") None of the efforts to remove "blundering" drivers from the roads, none of the traffic fiats or safe-driving encouragements had worked. In 1940, the driver is "as bad a driver as the fellow who drove a Chalmers in 1910, and there is no expectation that by 1960 he will be different. His eyesight is no better, he reacts no faster, he doesn't think any better, he gets drunk just as easily, he is just as absent-minded," wrote Bel Geddes. He offered a plan to "Eliminate the Human Factor in Driving."

The driver of the future, Bel Geddes predicted, would also have the aid of "a traffic control tower from which efficiently trained, uniformed experts advise drivers by radio control signals when and how they may change lanes." Bel Geddes described radio beams and wires embedded in the road surface that would take over control of the car from the driver. Such systems were being used for airplanes and railroads, he argued; they would work just as well for automobiles. "In 1960 they all stay out of the ditch. It is not done by law, but through the very nature of the car and the highway. They still blunder, of course, but when they do, they are harmless." Here Bel Geddes sounds like Ralph Nader, but when Nader's drivers blundered, the cars would still crash. Owing to seat belts, airbags, and crumple zones, less harm would come from those crashes, but Bel Geddes's cars wouldn't crash. It must be noted that Bel Geddes did not dream up these ideas on his own. For example, traffic engineering expert Miller McClintock worked closely with Bel Geddes and he drew on expertise from more than a dozen transportation related organizations.

A decade and a half after Futurama closed, the hope of a world remade by superhighways remained undiminished. By 1956, concrete was being poured to fulfill that hope and two years into the Interstate era, Walt Disney broadcast "Magic Highway U.S.A." Its positivist vision took us from European conquerors, past the Conestoga wagons, to the main event: the Magic Highway. Much of this midcentury science fiction is indeed today "science fact!" Rear-view cameras, prefabricated overpasses, and air ambulances, check. The tunneling machines are not atomically powered or cartoon fast, but roads can now be run through mountains and under cities at sci-fi speeds compared to twenty years ago. In 2017, Bertha, a giant mechanical worm with her own Twitter feed, finished tunneling beneath the Seattle waterfront, burying yet another offensive elevated highway.* Pants pockets and purses now carry Disney's imag-

---

* The highway opened in 2019, replacing the double-decked Alaskan Way Viaduct. Like the highway projects associated with Robert Moses, the elevated highway cut the city off from its waterfront.

ined "synchronized scanning map." We have realized the "speed, safety, and comfort" promised for yesteryear's highways of tomorrow. Travel by road is nearly ten times safer today than it was in 1939 and twice as safe on superhighways as it is on surface streets. We also have the decentralization (now derided as sprawl) promised by the planners of the 1930s and 1950s. "Yes, more and more highways are being opened every day," says the Magic Highways narrator, "but we're still not building them fast enough."

Driverless cars would do the longest-distance, highest-speed travel on the Disneyfied highway of the future. "As father chooses the route in advance on a push-button selectric, electronics take over complete control." Father still knows best, so he sits where the driver would, but "with no driving responsibility, the family relaxes together." For longer trips, destinations are programmed in by punch card.

Such electronic control was well within the technology of the time. Vladimir Zworykin, a television pioneer who invented the first practical TV camera, worked with RCA and GM to create an electronic guideway at the General Motors proving grounds. Experiments began in 1953. "This growing number of automobiles and people killed in accidents meant something should be done," Zworykin told an interviewer in 1975:

> My idea was that control of automobiles should be done by the road. A simple cable could be embedded in the roadway. An automobile passing over that cable would indicate the vehicle's speed and location. All that you need to get information from another automobile or from traffic lights or obstacles is a reflector, like license [plates] can be made into reflectors.

By 1958, GM and RCA had completed a full-scale demonstration on the company's test track in Warren, Michigan.

The technology Zworykin described featured prominently on three GM Firebirds; part test beds, part auto show concept cars. For 1953, Harley Earl designed the first Firebird as a fighter plane complete with a Plexiglas domed cockpit. Firebird II debuted at GM's 1956 Motorama, which was a travelling show in the tradition of Futurama. The car had an "electronic brain," cameras, and sensors to sniff out Zworykin's metal strip in the roadway. A member of the uniformed "Autoway Safety Authority" would provide route guidance and make hotel reservations. Once dialed into the automated highway, the driver would push the steering yoke into the dashboard and relax. One dash screen showed engine parameters while another showed a midcentury version of a Google map. "Though the realization of such a 'dream highway' belongs in the far, far future," admitted the Motorama Firebird brochure, "it utilizes present-day knowledge and experience gained through electronic control and computation, radar and television—all now in operation." In 1958, Firebird III appeared, complete with not two but *seven* tail fins and twice as many Plexiglas bubble domes as the original (because you can never have too many tail fins and bubble domes). A single joystick controlled acceleration, braking, and steering. "Want to sit back and relax? Well then, set in the speed you want to drive and switch over to automatic guidance. Release the stick and Firebird III is on its own, receiving its commands from a wire in the road." The Firebirds also featured the engine of the future, a gas-turbine, set up for real-world beta testing. A turbine has only one moving part, making it far lighter and less prone to failure than a piston engine. Plus, it sounds like a flying car! Ford and GM each tested the concept for heavy trucks. Chrysler made plans to sell its conservatively styled (by jet car standards) Turbine Coupe. The company leased fifty of the cars to eager members of the public who reported back that they were indeed suitable for daily use. Like the Copper-Cooled Chevy of the 1920s, the simplicity of the gas turbine seduced engineers. But the Big Three saw no business case to develop it, especially with smog regulations on the horizon.

Similarly, GM and high-tech RCA had no business imperative to bring their automated driving experiments to market and government, no need to force the issue. Unlike today, nothing beat the car business of the 1950s when it came to profitability. As for improving automobile safety, no one should doubt that highway deaths served as Zworykin's personal motivation. On the other hand, it should be lost on no one that when GM promoted highways for safety at the World's Fair in 1939, at the Motorama shows of the 1950s, and again for the 1964 World's Fair, it was simultaneously undermining any efforts to make its products safer. Still, when GM and RCA conducted their tests in the 1950s, safety advocates in government and the medical community were beginning to coalesce around the solution of crashworthiness that would be adopted fully in 1966. Drivers would blunder, cars would crash, but drivers and passengers would emerge unharmed. The idea of using electronics to avoid a crash altogether did not have a seat at the safety table.

Automated vehicle research did not end with the Firebirds. The Federal Highway Administration (still called the Bureau of Public Roads at the time) picked up support for the work in the 1960s and continued to fund collaborations between academia and industry until 1980. Then, Ronald Reagan took office. In the dry but plaintive words of Petros Ioannou, a controls engineer at the USC Center for Advanced Transportation Technologies who worked in the field, "the Reagan administration introduced new policies and brought new appointees whose priorities did not include advanced research in transportation systems."

By the late 1980s, those cutbacks began to seem shortsighted. There was plenty of room for all the traffic that had been projected in 1956, but not nearly enough for the amount of traffic that actually materialized. Car travel further increased by 40 percent during the 1990s. Yet we kept driving more. Imagine how much more traffic there would be if there wasn't so damn much traffic! If government did not have the money or the space to build our way out of congestion, existing highways would have to be made more efficient. The "post-Interstate era will emphasize system performance rather than system building," said Senator Daniel Patrick Moynihan. In 1991 Congress passed and President George H. W. Bush signed the landmark Intermodal Surface Transportation Efficiency Act (ISTEA, pronounced "ice tea"). "Intermodal" was a radical word because it indicated that, for the first time, gas tax money would be diverted from highway building in order to fund public transportation.

ISTEA also required the secretary of transportation "to have the first fully automated roadway or an automated test track in operation by 1997." So, in August of 1997 a platoon of eight Buicks, traveling nose to tail with no room for error, cruised flawlessly down an intelligent stretch of the I-15 in San Diego. They sniffed out magnets set in the roadway, which guided the steering while braking and acceleration were controlled by radars and vehicle-to-vehicle radio signals. Radars also detected obstructions in the roadway and could tell the car to swerve around them. It was called "hands-off, feet-off" driving. Drivers conspicuously read the newspaper and waved both hands out the window. The Department of Transportation Intelligent Vehicle Highway System (IVHS) "Demo '97" succeeded.

The videos promoting the event have a government-produced feel and only VHS-tape resolution, but they show the technology working as advertised. A guy in a safety vest, one hand out the window, the other holding what appears to be a self-destruct button through the open sunroof, says, "This is pretty cool. I wonder what the other traffic thinks." His Pontiac then swerves around a pair of traffic barrels in the lane. "No hands!" I can't help notice that he's in a Pontiac (ad slogan, "We build excitement!") while the Buicks travel in an orderly line. Unlike the autonomous vehicles being deployed today, the cars of Demo '97 worked in concert. Today's Randian robot cars, with their smarts all on board, work alone. Also, under the ISTEA rules, any enabling equipment would have to be "backwards compatible" so they could be sold on the aftermarket and installed on existing models. The benefits of the technology could thereby accrue far more quickly than the thirty years it takes to renew the entire vehicle fleet through new car sales. That's not good for business though. The current iteration of the driverless car adheres to the Sloanist strategy. Just as GM gave "Security Plate Glass" to Cadillac owners before letting the safety feature trickle down to Chevrolet customers, GM began offering Super Cruise, its first baby step toward those Demo '97 capabilities on its Cadillac CT6 Platinum, an $85,000 sedan.

The 1997 demonstration was really a swan song for the Intelligent Vehicle Highway System. It was conducted only because the law demanded it. In fact, it does not seem to have even been that difficult. The engineers, realizing their funding would not be renewed, appear to have pulled an all-nighter to put on the Buick parade. Since then, we seem to have lost our appetite for public infrastructure spending, intelligent or otherwise. The American Society of Civil Engineers gave us a D on roads (dragging our infrastructure GPA down to a D+ overall). The whole thing just smacks of the trains and public transportation liberals love.

Furthermore, *not* building infrastructure fits well with the Randian philosophy of Silicon Valley honchos and Republican congressmen. "We don't have the money to fix potholes," said Anthony Levandowski in 2013, when he was head of Google's robot car project, "why would we invest in putting wires in the road?" (RCA's Zworykin would have an answer.) Further, bad roads are a good excuse for smart cars, as Audi made clear in a 2011 pitch. The A6 sedan, with its squinting headlights and a rapacious grille, is about to conquer a half dozen photogenic potholes:

> The roads are underfunded by $450 billion. With the right car, you may never notice. The highly intelligent new Audi A6 is here. And not a moment too soon. After all, the roads aren't getting any smarter. That's why we engineered a car that makes 2,000 decisions a second.

The pitch seems tuned to the psyche of a Russian oligarch so hostile to the commonweal that he blasts through Moscow in his Audi A6 in black on black with an imitation police siren on the roof.

We have missed the chance to get the kind of autonomous vehicle highway systems promised by Futurama, Disney, the Firebirds, and the Clinton-era Intelligent Vehicle Highway System. Today's driverless cars come not from the collectivist engineering visions of the 1930s or the Federal Highway Administration of the 1990s. They were envisioned by the war department.

*　*　*

BY 2004, the Second Gulf War was afoot. Unsafe driving had taken on a new meaning. Autonomous ground vehicles would let the Pentagon keep fighting its forever wars without having to send so many telegrams and chaplains out to the homes of fallen soldiers. Smart infrastructure, magnets under the concrete, was not on the table. Things buried in the road in Iraq tended to blow up. The military needed go-anywhere machines that could operate in traffic or off-road, in places where the rule of law held firm and in lawless war zones. "Hand-off, feet-off" driving would not be enough. "Driverless," "autonomous," "robot" cars, that was the thing. The drivers would stay back at base, safely behind the blast walls.

To develop a driverless solution, the Defense Advanced Research Projects Agency (DARPA) held its first Grand Challenge in 2004 on a 142-mile course in the California desert. Nobody finished. The top-scoring vehicle covered only 7.5 miles. So, DARPA offered a do-over the following year—and doubled the prize money. The team from Carnegie Mellon arrived with a pair of giant red Humvees (one in uniform, one in civvies) loaded for bear. The entire passenger compartment had been scooped out of the larger one and filled with a mysterious gray cube painted with the logos of Caterpillar, Intel, and something called "Boeing Phantom Works." A big Chevron oil flag adorned the rear quarter panel. The tail fin was misplaced: someone put it on the roof behind a spherical Hollywood klieg light. If it had been painted the color of sand rather than cardinal red, it could have just rolled off the battlefield from Fallujah. The menacing war machine won second place. First place went to a little blue Volkswagen named Stanley.

Stanford University's Sebastian Thrun was the biggest brain behind Stanley. He went on to found Google X, the secret lab that developed, among other projects, Google's self-driving car. He also cofounded Udacity, an online learning platform. Having taken his CS373 "Programming a Robotic Car" massive open online course on Udacity, I'd give him excellent marks on Ratemyprofessor.com. He is a gentle, patient, and delighted professor who lectures in a melodious German-inflected English. The only lame Silicon Valley thing I've heard him say is that Google Translate works really well. Befitting Thrun's persona, the lasers and cameras and antennas atop the little VW Touareg looked more suited to a Mars science rover than a battle tank.

In 2007, DARPA followed up with the Urban Challenge in which thirty-five teams competed in events on suburban streets closed to regular traffic but with an additional thirty "manned" vehicles on the road. Half of the cars were eliminated fairly quickly and MIT and Cornell had a fender bender. Neither was disqualified. "The robots were separated and allowed to resume their missions," according to DARPA, sounding more like a kindergarten teacher sending a note home than a branch of the war department. When the DARPA challenges began, the military said it planned to have one third of its land vehicles operate autonomously by 2015. Along the way it abandoned that goal, but not before passing the baton.

DARPA's rugged individualist robo-car might have remained a science experiment were it not for seismic shifts in the automobile market and the rise of ride hailing services over the last several years. In 2009, when Google set Sebastian Thrun the task of building a self-driving pod on the heels of his DARPA win, the company had no particular business model in mind. Indeed without the military's interest, the Google pod was a solution in search of a problem. But, when you have $100 billion in advertising revenue lying around, and extra space at your X Lab, why not? Now, however, environmental and safety regulations as well as increased competition and saturated markets are eroding the business model that underpins making and selling cars. Driverless ride-hailing might be a better bet. After all, investors value ride-hailing companies that lose money many times more highly than automakers who still do eke out a profit. But, those investors have also learned why ride-hailing companies are unprofitable: human drivers expect to be paid in real money. So, whether we want robot cars or not, the leaders at Uber, Lyft, Ford, and GM and the rest don't just want them. They need them.

"Companies collectively earn less than their cost of capital and most companies destroy value," finance professor Aswath Damodaran concluded after analyzing the auto business. In 2015, Fiat Chrysler chairman Sergio Marchionne delivered a now famous presentation, "Confessions of a Capital Junkie." He emphasized the very high cost of research and development—two billion euros a week across the industry—for the poor financial returns. In the last several years of his career (before his untimely death in 2018), Marchionne had been seeking a merger to spread new-vehicle development costs. Unable to find a dance partner, the Fiat CEO turned to the only profitable end of his business: large American pickups and SUVs built by Chrysler.

Marchionne's retreat into trucks highlights an ironic but little noticed consequence of the rush to autonomy. To fund the expensive transition from the legacy automotive business to the dawning age of the environmentally friendly electric, driverless car, Detroit must lean heavily on its most gas-guzzling, revanchist, and profitable segment. Ford earns an estimated $13,000 every time it sells an F150 pickup. The company reported to Wall Street that it lost out on a billion dollars in a single quarter because it could not build its pickup trucks fast enough. In a 2016 earnings report, GM said profit suffered because it had been selling too many of its cheap Cruzes, Sparks, and mid-range Malibus. Nearly all of the $12 billion in North America came from big SUVs and pickup trucks. High-end luxury models also return a solid profit, but nothing beats an SUV. That's why even Ferrari, Jaguar, and Porsche have unapologetically added SUVs to their lineups.

Worst of all are the electric cars. GM sells each all-electric Chevy

Bolt at a $9,000 loss—even after up to $10,000 in government incentives. Marchionne only half-jokingly begged people not to buy the electric Fiat 500e hatchback, saying he lost $14,000 on every one he sold. Why sell a money-losing product? The 500e, like the electric versions of the Chevy Spark, Ford Focus, Honda Fit, and Toyota RAV4, is a "compliance car." Ten states, collectively accounting for 28 percent of the new vehicle market in the United States, require an automaker to sell a certain number of these ZEVs (Zero Emissions Vehicles) or, in effect, pay a fine. In fact, the California Air Resources Board has a means tested program that gives poor people free electric cars. My middle-class friend in Oakland put down $2,000 to lease her Chevrolet Spark (a tiny hatchback). The state of California then thanked her with a gift of $2,500. The monthly lease is $85, half of what the family pays for their cell phone plan. Tesla has yet to turn a sustained profit, losing a staggering amount of money on every luxury car it sells. In fact, the company earns a good deal of money from the carbon credits other manufacturers pay so they won't have to build their own ZEVs. None of this is to say that EVs won't someday, even soon, be sold at a profit. The cost of batteries continues to fall as manufacturing scale increases. Nevertheless, it is hard to imagine EVs ever achieving the staggeringly high profit margins of pickups and SUVs.

Given this mismatch between electric vehicles and the legacy business model supporting automobility, both Fiat Chrysler, in partnership with Google, and General Motors have turned to driverless ride hailing as, if nothing else, a way to offload their EVs. Fiat Chrysler sells over 100,000 of its gasoline-powered Pacifica minivans each year, but fewer than 5,000 of the plug-in hybrid-electric version. Fortunately, Google buys in bulk: 100 in 2016, 500 in 2017, and an announced 62,000 beginning in 2018. GM uses the battery electric Bolt as its driverless test bed.

No matter how they are powered, autonomous cars remain too expensive for individual sale. Mass production and engineering investment will surely lower the costs of the technology, but right now just one piece of equipment, the Light Detection and Ranging (LIDAR) sensor, costs more than most private vehicles.

I have refrained thus far from regaling you with the wondrous tech in a self-driving car, including the binocular camera systems, the interpolation algorithms, and data-driven parameter tuning. It has not been easy to hold back. So let me at least offer brief regalement about LIDAR. When you see a picture of a robot car, or happen to run into one on the street (which you won't do, of course, because they're so darn safe), notice the coffee cans on the roof. That's the LIDAR. Inside is a spinning laser that bounces off an object and measures how long it takes for the laser light to return. The information is used to calculate distance. It works much like sonar (which uses sound waves) and radar (radio waves), technologies that date back to the early twentieth century and World War II, respectively. Those Chock Full o' Nuts cans run about $75,000 each. The race is on to cut that cost by a factor of 100 or even 1,000 by replacing the LIDAR's mechanical components with a single chip. So central to the autonomous car's future is LIDAR that Google engineer Anthony Levandowski is alleged to have stolen Google's plans for a solid-state LIDAR and, in essence, sold them to Uber for many millions of dollars.* The companies reached a settlement in which Google got $245 million of the ride-hailing giant's equity and Uber offered a "sorry, not sorry" apology. The US Patent and Trademark Office subsequently reexamined the LIDAR patent and invalidated it. Among other problems, examiners noted that the patent featured a "magic ground wire which shows current moving in two directions along a single wire." Meanwhile, John Krafcik, CEO of Google's Waymo, declared that the company's chip design had reduced the cost of LIDAR by a factor of ten. Dozens of other companies are now in the race. In the tradition of the Wizard of Menlo Park's rev-

---

* Levandowski left Google to found Otto, an autonomous vehicle software startup. Several months later, Uber bought Otto for $680 million and announced that Levandowski would head up Uber's self-driving car program. Google and Uber settled a trade-secrets lawsuit in February 2016.

olutionary battery announcements, statements to the press seem to have gotten ahead of the technology.

So, with driverless cars too expensive to sell to the public, automakers hope to follow in the footsteps of the Electric Vehicle Company and the original Mobility as a Service model. Recall that the underlying business model of the EVC was sound; it was done in by hype and capital structures.

As much as car companies want to become Mobility as a Service companies, the MaaS ride-hailing companies want to eliminate their drivers. In 2015, the Uber Advanced Technologies Center opened in Pittsburgh. To staff it, the company that takes pride in its damn-the-haters approach poached forty scientists and researchers from the Carnegie Mellon Robotics Lab, the people behind the cardinal red Hummers in the DARPA Grand Challenge. The *Wall Street Journal* reported that some scientists were offered hundreds of thousands of dollars to jump ship. It is not uncommon for computer scientists to move between academia and industry, but the suddenness of the move highlights the urgency with which Uber is chasing the robot car dream.

Uber should have a ready pool of drivers. Private cars are an underutilized asset so that the marginal cost of taking that extra trip as an Uber driver is exceedingly low. You can be your own boss and work where and when you want to, so Uber serves the underemployed who need extra cash. But how much extra cash? It depends. According to the *Washington Post*, drivers in Denver average $11.21 an hour and in Houston the wage is $8.43. Detroit drivers average $6.60/hour, which is below the minimum wage. Another estimate pegs New York City as the highest-paying market but did not offer net earnings. An MIT study found that about half of Uber drivers earn less than minimum wage.* For its part, Uber advertised that

---

* The study made headlines with its original finding of a $3.37 median wage. The researchers had made several errors, but the revised study showed that about half of drivers still made less than minimum wage. See "MIT Study That Found Low Pay for Uber Drivers to Be Revisited," Reuters, March 3, 2018, https://www.reuters.com/article/us-uber-wage-study-idUSKCN1GF0RL.

one New York City driver earned $90,000 working forty hours a week. Otherwise, it has been coy, saying only that rates vary and that these aren't wages at all because the drivers aren't employees. Driving for the number-two player, Lyft, comes out about the same, and many drivers work for both simultaneously. Turnover is higher even than it was at Ford Motor Company before the five-dollar day, with only 4 percent of drivers lasting a year.

Meanwhile, anecdotal evidence does not paint a bright picture for an Uber using human drivers. Drivers in South Australia complain about low wages. *Bloomberg* found that "When Their Shifts End, Uber Drivers Set Up Camp in Parking Lots Across the U.S." When Uber driver Fawzi Kamel happened to pick up then Uber CEO Travis Kalanick as a fare, he complained that he was going broke. The scene was captured by Kamel's security camera.

"[B]ut we have competitors. Otherwise we'd be out of business," Kalanick counters on the video, which was posted to YouTube.

"You choose to buy everybody a ride," Kamel scoffs. Things go downhill from there. Kamel tells the CEO that Uber has bankrupted him and complains that the prices keep dropping. Kalanick throws a tantrum, swears, and offers some Ayn Randian life coaching. Finally, state and local governments have begun to push back against the ride hailing juggernaut with regulations requiring driver background checks, permitting fees, and minimum wages. These will only further raise the cost of doing business.

All of the ride-hailing services will have to reconcile the fact that drivers cost too much. Alan Ponsford is a leading designer of buses—yes, buses are designed—and a consultant to the industry. He tells me that the London double-decker is the most expensive bus out there, yet the driver still accounts for 60 percent of its total operating cost. "Overhead walks on two legs," Ponsford related. A driverless double-decker bus would be a boon to London mass transit, but Americans don't do much mass transit. For now, the adventure capital money is on Uber, even if it has to make its business model work with human drivers.

When Oldsmobile, Buick, and Ford Motor started out, they assembled cars with engines, chassis, and wheels built by others. They sold those cars for cash, which enabled them to pay their suppliers sixty to ninety days later (per the terms of standard business practice). Ford was immediately profitable because he gave the public what they wanted. At present, driverless cars cost too much to build, electrification will only delay profitability, and the public still has not warmed to the idea.

My goal is not to predict the future but make sense of the past and understand the present. The fact that past autonomous vehicles—as inchoate and imperfect as today's experiments—never advanced to the point of becoming part of the transportation system suggests that neither the producers nor the consumers of the American automobile, nor American voters nor their representatives could muster the enthusiasm for the project. In the present, the profitability of the 120-year-old business model that made us a nation of drivers has eroded. It's not impossible to imagine a scenario in which fleets of robot cars, still owned and operated by the manufacturers, turn a profit that matches the stock pickers' hopes. It is also not impossible that the economics of the entire business are in fact imaginary.

Meanwhile, we will be treated to a steady stream of benevolent rhetoric about how rugged individualist robot cars will save lives, let the blind see, end the misery of driving, and make the world a better place. Perhaps, but first, let's talk about it.

Chapter 13

THINK OF THE LIVES WE'LL SAVE:
The Rhetorics of Robot Cars

"Does your car have any idea why my car pulled it over?"

Driverless cars, signified by their strange rooftop sensors, are leaving us all a bit disoriented. Do we really want them?

THE DRIVERLESS CAR HAS BY NOW BECOME SO ICONIC THAT a *New Yorker* cartoonist can signal it as a character by drawing a box camera mounted to the roof. "Does your car have any idea why my car pulled it over?" the cop shyly asks a motorist by the side of the road. We can peer up from the magazine, bemused at the disorienting pace of technological change. The driverless car stars daily in the news, in opinion columns, and the business pages. It is on the tip of everyone's tongue. The robot car will disrupt the car culture, reinvent mobility, and unleash trillions of dollars of economic activity. Best of all though, it will save 36,000 lives a year and eliminate 2.9 million injuries. Or so we are told. Those lives are lost, we hear, because we drivers are responsible for 94 percent of crashes. Eliminate the driver, eliminate most crashes, save lives. In truth, we don't really know as much as we think we do about what causes crashes. We don't really know if driverless cars are safer. We don't even seem to know quite what a driverless car is. Some people even think they can buy one today.

As early as 1912, the courts were debating whether or not the automobile constituted a "dangerous instrumentality." Most judges concluded it wasn't inherently dangerous—like a lion or a grizzly bear—but that it was dangerous enough to require regulation. That legal finding of danger opened a Pandora's box of traffic regulations and traffic policing. Ralph Nader, Edward Tenney, and others exposed the self-serving pseudoscience behind the traffic safety establishment's "three E's." In addition to the transformation of the automobile itself, we have learned a great deal since 1966 about crash causation. Yet science alone does not guide our response. For example, the law provides for severe penalties for driving while intoxicated. Yet sleep deprivation is itself a form of impaired driving and was cited as a factor in 850 deaths in 2014. (The actual number is likely much higher.) "Failure to signal" is against the rules, although perhaps "driving while black" might be a better name for the infraction. During the Montgomery bus boycott, police used the proverbial "busted taillight" to harass the "church wagons," private cars being used to replace lost mobility. African Americans have endured such treatment, but when white people faced similar harassment in the 1980s, they took the cops to the Supreme Court.

The sobriety checkpoint emerged in the Reagan Era in response to the pressure of Mothers Against Drunk Driving. Candy Lightner founded the advocacy group in 1980, after her daughter was killed by a drunk driver while walking to church. With the unimpeachable power of grieving mothers and President Ronald Reagan's personal backing, MADD forced action. The "victims" in MADD's early media campaigns were always children, their murderers, drunk drivers. (In reality, most children who die in alcohol-related crashes are being driven by the intoxicated driver.) Civil liberties lawyers challenged these sobriety checkpoints as violations of the prohibition against search and seizure. The Supreme Court agreed that a seizure (as defined in the Fourth Amendment) takes place when a driver is stopped but rejected the challenge, six to three. The horrible toll of drunk driving outweighed the minor inconvenience of being seized, the majority found. Chief Justice William Rehnquist wrote in his 1990 opinion, "Drunk drivers cause an annual death toll of over 25,000."

In 2017, Mothers Against Drunk Driving put its weight behind Waymo's #letstalkselfdriving. "There are 10,000 deaths due to drunk driving—each and every one of them 100% preventable," MADD argues on the Waymo site. "No more victims." Notice that the new figure is 60 percent lower than the one that alarmed Rehnquist. It would be lower still were it not for the fact that the threshold for drunk driving—the blood alcohol level—has been cut in half. In other words, far more drivers now count as legally intoxicated. The actual statistic kept by NHTSA, "Alcohol-Related Traffic Fatalities," includes cyclists and pedestrians under the influence. Also, it uses a lower blood alcohol threshold than the law allows. Only a pedant would bother shaving 500 or even 1,000 lives from the MADD total. The point, however, is that advocates need big numbers to support their proposed agendas—whether they be reducing the blood alcohol threshold or letting robo-cars loose on public roads. What now appears to be an alliance between MADD and Waymo should put us on notice: robot car promoters will rely on the same declaration of a crisis used to justify unwarranted search and seizures. Further, by declaring a crisis, robot car promoters can ask for a large degree of freedom—just as police did—to do as they please.

Not surprisingly, the true believers preach the driverless car gospel louder than anyone. Anthony Levandowski, the brilliant engineer who headed up driverless car projects for both Google and Uber told Burkhard Bilger of the *New Yorker,* "Once you make the car better than the driver, it's almost irresponsible to have him there." Those who might oppose his righteous crusade are either irresponsible or irrationally afraid of a robot uprising. "Every year that we delay this, more people die." Elon Musk, who seems to have inherited Henry Ford's genius for grabbing headlines, put it more combatively when he chastised the media for writing negative stories about Tesla's "Autopilot." "If, in writing some article that's negative," he told reporters, "you effectively dissuade people from using an autonomous vehicle, you're killing people." The context was negative publicity surrounding what was widely reported as the first Autopilot death. Musk grew more pugnacious when a financial journalist suggested that Tesla should have alerted investors to the "material fact that a man had died while using an auto-pilot technology that Tesla had marketed vigorously as safe and important to its customers." Musk responded: "Indeed, if anyone bothered to do the math (obviously, you did not) they would realize that of the over 1M auto deaths per year worldwide, approximately half a million people would have been saved if the Tesla autopilot was universally available. Please, take 5 mins and do the bloody math before you write an article that misleads the public."

Karl Vogt, whose driverless car startup GM bought for about $1 billion, told *Forbes* that driverless cars were his "true calling." Like Levandowski and Musk, Vogt emphasizes safety. "Part of what's driving him is the fact that some 33,000 Americans are killed by highway accidents each year, 90% of the time because of human error," *Forbes* reported.

Vogt may be rounding down: most sources reference human error as causing 94 percent of crashes, injuries, and deaths. "Today, 94 percent of traffic accidents involve driver error," said Secretary of Transportation Elaine Chao, introducing federal regulations designed to encourage further development of driverless cars. She went further in NHTSA's "Automated Driving Systems 2.0: A Vision for Safety."

"The major factor in 94 percent of all fatal crashes is human error," she wrote. Chao pulls that figure from NHTSA itself. The National Motor Vehicle Crash Causation Survey conducted between 2005 and 2007 found that in 94 percent of crashes, the "critical reason for the critical pre-crash event" should be attributed to the driver. I haven't done the bloody math, but I have read the bloody footnotes. A huge distance separates that carefully crafted phrase "critical reason for the critical pre-crash event" and the shorthand, "drivers cause 94 percent of all crashes." The study's authors took pains to highlight this fact:

> *Although the critical reason is an important part of the description of events leading up to the crash, it is not intended to be interpreted as the cause of the crash nor as the assignment of the fault to the driver, vehicle, or environment.*

The emphasis is decidedly in the original. Yet even NHTSA officials have trouble communicating the difference. I exchanged several emails and spent a half hour on the phone with a representative of the NHTSA press office who could not explain the difference between the footnote and the shorthand and must have hung up the phone and headed off to lunch thinking I was dense. I myself began to wonder. I felt headed for a lifetime of scratching "94%, 94%, 94%" in tiny letters on the worn pages of a composition book. Was I making too much of an italicized footnote? Then Daniel Blower, associate research scientist emeritus of the University of Michigan Transportation Research Institute, talked me back to sanity.

I had tracked down Dr. Blower's "Large Truck Crash Causation Study Methodological Note." The LTCC study involved intensive work by NHTSA field teams and served as the model for the National Motor Vehicle Crash Causation Survey, whence the 94 percent. "Note that the critical event is not the 'cause' of the crash," Blower told me via email. "When considered carefully, the statement that drivers cause 94 percent of crashes is not very helpful," he wrote. "The fact is that in the vehicle-driver-environment system, the driver is the last thing that can do anything to avoid the crash." In other words, no matter how poorly designed the intersection, or how inadequate it is for the increase in traffic since the day it was built, drivers navigate it every day without incident. The "did not crash" figure dwarfs the number of crashes, which implies that drivers routinely compensate for the hazard.

The 94 percent fallacy and its corollary that driverless cars will be infinitely safer has created a fascinating cottage industry around the idea of death by autonomous auto. Although calling attention to the potential for fatalities would seem to argue against their deployment, in fact the commentaries reinforce the idea that driverless cars present a revolution in auto safety. "The ethics of saving lives with autonomous cars is far murkier than you think," writes Patrick Lin, director of the Ethics + Emerging Sciences Group at California Polytechnic. Lin has tirelessly promoted driverless cars as a unique, neonatal moral actor. Lin's comments have appeared in the *Atlantic*, in *Wired*, on NPR's *All Things Considered*, and in an elaborately animated TED-Ed web video in which he narrates a philosophical thought experiment. To paraphrase: Your driverless car trails an overloaded truck on a three-lane highway. Suddenly, the trucker's load tumbles off the back. Quick as a flash, the car—let's call her Porsche—assesses the situation. She can swerve left into an SUV, swerve right into a motorcycle, or stay straight and collide with the boxes just ahead. A teraflop later, the car has taken into account who is riding in the SUV (the children are our future), whether or not the biker is wearing a helmet, and what's in the boxes. What will Porsche do? It's a cute cartoon. Lin's voiceover is at once soothing and foreboding. My question is why was Porsche tailgating a truck full of boxes in the first place?

Homicidal speculation also comes from the home of the guillotine. "Autonomous vehicles need experimental ethics," suggests Jean-François Bonnefon of the Toulouse School of Economics. "Are we ready for utilitarian cars?" Bonnefon, a research psychologist, calls for supporting research psychologists, who can determine our preparedness for Benthamite Buicks.

These questions are too juicy for anyone at the bleeding edge of business and technology to ignore. And in the contest for clicks and eyeballs, all subtlety is lost. From *Digital Trends*: "Should your self-driving car kill you to save a school bus full of kids?" "Who will a driverless car be programmed to kill?" asks a *Fast Company* headline. *Wired* has given Patrick Lin plenty of space for his opinion pieces, headlined by such warnings as, "The Robot Car of Tomorrow May Just Be Programmed to Hit You" and "Here's a Terrible Idea: Robot Cars With Adjustable Ethics Settings." But soberer outlets are riding the story too. The CBC reports, "Computers could decide who lives and dies in a driverless car crash." Even the *Cornell Journal of Law and Public Policy* came up with a horror-movie headline: "Who Lives and Who Dies? Just Let Your Car Decide."

Young programmers certainly should speculate on such things if it helps them to think outside their code. Consider the problem of a car barreling down a street when a crippled boy's crutches break. Should Porsche swerve left to avoid the kid but risk killing the driver against a utility pole? Or should it slam on the brakes and hope for the best? I imagine the coders writing something like this:

```
if (kid_in_street > 16) {
kill kid_in_street;
lp "We are sorry for your loss.";
}
else {
kill ass_in_Porsche;
lp "Serves you right, schmucko.";
}
```

These philosophical "what-ifs," whatever their benefits to coders or philosophy PhDs facing slim job prospects, actually shrink our capacity for deep thinking about the driverless car. When Google's Waymo implores #letstalkselfdriving, they welcome a sidebar about driverless cars making life-and-death choices. Such serious-minded discussions support a self-aggrandizing vision of the totalizing power of the algorithm. Let's confab about who poor little Porsche should be forced to murder. But let's ignore the better question: Why was Porsche going so damn fast in the first place?

The conviction held by Lin and others about the driverless car as a wholly new kind of moral actor can only be sustained by presenting the road environment as an apolitical, amoral engineered system. In reality, the technocratic language of highway and traffic engineering obscures an ideology.

Traffic engineering trades safety for mobility. More than one in three road deaths occur at intersections where "turning moments" and crossing traffic result in deadly "T-bone" crashes. When considering how to make an intersection safe, the engineers begin with a bias toward flow. "Does this intersection warrant any control at all?" they ask. If it rarely sees traffic, no control of any kind is warranted. If it has enough traffic, it gets a stop sign. More cars, and sometimes pedestrians warrant a stoplight. Drivers hate stoplights. Driverless car promoters employ the same balance, putting mobility first and then adding safety as conditions warrant. Some people in the public and not-for-profit sector think they have a better idea.

"At least one government has taken a radical position with regard to road safety by, in effect, removing human life from the road transport, trade-off decision-making process," noted the 2006 *Handbook of Highway Engineering.* That government was Sweden, birthplace of the three-point safety belt. Radicalism has spread to Canada, the United States, European nations, and many individual cities. New York is one of ten US cities trying to create a world in which not one life is lost to automobility. "No level of fatality on city streets is inevitable or acceptable," states the city's Vision Zero Action Plan. The approach is holistic. New York's radical privileging of life over automobility will require changes in political accountability, the culture of mobility, and road designs, proponents argue. Road speed limits will have to be lower. Actually, we already have the technology to do all of these things while we wait for the driverless car to be perfected and commercialized. Planners and engineers call it "traffic calming." It amounts to reengineering streets so that vehicles slow down to a speed where they no longer present a hazard. Again, Nader was a bit off when he described the Corvair as "unsafe at any speed." Surely it could handle twelve miles an hour.

Notice that Vision Zero is about changing the culture of mobility by framing all road users as citizens with equal rights to safety and security. It means refighting the battle over street space won by the automobile at the turn of the last century. The Naderite approach frames citizens as consumers who have a right to safe products. Inadequate door latches, twitchy suspensions, and steering columns that skewered the driver, these were typical of his targets. His radical move was to insist that the American automobile was not a demigod that had built the middle class, won the wars, and bestowed unprecedented mobility, but a consumer product like any other. On speed limits, pedestrians, and cyclists, Nader was silent. The ultimate measure of Vision Zero's success will be whether American culture changes from one that privileges driving to one that accepts the equal rights of all road users.

Changing culture is hard, but the success of the "designated driver" campaign shows it can be done. MADD brought the issue of drinking and driving to the fore, but its campaign for a punitive response—demonizing drunk drivers and encouraging checkpoints—did not work. In 1988, Jay Winsten of Harvard's Center for Health Communication began a campaign imported from Scandinavia: ask people to take turns staying sober when out on the town. The campaign succeeded in convincing Hollywood to embed designated driver messages into television shows in more than 160 episodes, including episodes of the most popular program of its day, *The Cosby Show,* and *Cheers,* a sitcom, fortuitously set in a bar. Vision Zero seeks to redefine the automobile in much the same way.

Its potential for saving lives aside, Vision Zero lacks the gee-whiz appeal of the driverless car. It arose not from wondrous, world-shifting algorithms but from the tedious reality of public meetings where everyone gets to say their piece. Although New York City's mayor Bill de Blasio endorsed Vision Zero, New York State's governor served up the city's pedestrians and cyclists as algorithmic guinea pigs. According to a statement by Cruise Automation, GM's autonomous car startup that will operate with Governor Andrew Cuomo's blessing, "New York City . . . provides new opportunities to expose our software to unusual situations." New York's pedestrians may object to being called unusual situations.

We can have safer, more hospitable streets as well as the active safety features of autonomous cars. Cars should be able to stop themselves and avoid running off the road whether or not the person inside is paying attention. They should be able to maintain a speed safe and appropriate to conditions. They should be able to see things a human driver cannot easily see such as blind spots and the area directly behind the bumper. In fact, with varying degrees of success, many of the newest cars can. The rhetoric around autonomous vehicles has gotten so heated, however, that some people think that means we have robot cars.

* * * *

"DRIVERLESS CARS MADE ME NERVOUS. Then I Tried One," wrote David Leonhardt, a regular *New York Times* columnist, about his 2017 trip in a Volvo S90. He "began laughing" at the autonomous braking. For this he was excoriated by the automotive press (those in the know). *Automotive News* was kind: "When your 'self-driving car' isn't autonomous." *The Drive* was not: "Terrified *New York Times* Columnist Confuses Volvo with Magical 'Driverless Car.'" The mortification of Leonhardt did not stop *New Yorker* staff writer and *Times* columnist James B. Stewart from describing his experience with "semiautonomous driving" when he used Tesla's "Autopilot." "Semiautonomous" is a slippery term. GM introduced the "Autronic Eye" automatic headlight control in 1952—"Biggest Advance in Night Driving Safety in 30 Years!" I wonder if buyers of the 1958 Chrysler Imperial with "Auto-Pilot" cruise control considered their cars semiautonomous. Automatic chokes, antilock brakes, radar-enhanced cruise control—none of these things were described as steps toward a future of autonomous cars when they were deployed. Where does automation end and autonomy begin?

The Society of Automotive Engineers (the legacy of the Seldenites and the ALAM) has helpfully tried to explain the situation with SAE J3016. It defines five levels of automation with such phrases as "Operational Design Domain," "Conditional Automation," and "Monitoring of Driving Environment." Level 5 is the Holy Grail, the driverless car, except that it's actually Level 6 because the whole thing starts at Level Zero. Most of us are driving zeroes. Unfortunately, government and journalists have touted the engineers' framework as if it answered all the difficult political questions around driverless cars. They tout it as if engineers were really good at explaining things to lay people.

I'm no engineer, so allow me to clarify: there are cars that help you drive, cars that pretend to drive, and cars that actually drive themselves. Radar-based help-you-drive tech has been on the market since the 1990s in the form of advanced cruise control that speeds up and slows down in sync with the car ahead. Lots of models now offer blind spot warnings and automatic emergency braking. Cars that pretend to drive can do all of this but also follow lane markers and sort of read speed limit signs with cameras and software. This sensor data can also be combined with GPS mapping. I don't count that as driving, since the kids and I built a Lego robot that could do the same thing. Anyway, here in Massachusetts, we treat lane markers as a luxury. Highway departments might as well use daffodils: the yellow and white lines appear in springtime and are long gone by the first frost. Even cars that can accelerate, brake, and "see" through cameras are miles away from the self-actualized automobile that can make its way through time and space unaided.

No matter what automakers, futurists, and journalists may proclaim, true self-driving cars remain experimental. The conversation around the relative safety of driverless cars therefore remains speculative. Already they have run red lights, sideswiped parked cars, rolled over, rear-ended street sweepers and fire trucks, and killed a woman pushing a bicycle crossing the road in Tempe, Arizona.* Safe or not, the experiments will continue. Meanwhile, people are dying because they think they bought a driverless car.

That's what happened to Josh Brown, a forty-year-old tech entrepreneur, who was convinced that his car could drive itself. "Tessy," as he called his $100,000 Model S, was equipped with the company's "Autopilot" system. Having spent the first week of May vacationing with family at Disney World, on the morning of May 7, 2016, Brown left the Winnebago and pointed Tessy toward Cedar Key, Florida.

As he crested a small rise on State Road 27A near Williston, sixty-two-year-old Frank Baressi began slowly turning his tractor trailer left across the sleepy highway. Nearly a quarter mile separated the two vehicles at this point, which according to investigators gave each driver 10.4 seconds, plenty of time, to see the other and react. The Freightliner cab had already cleared the road by the time of the crash, but the fifty-three-foot-long trailer and its load of chilled Florida blueberries still blocked both oncoming lanes.

"It was like just a big white explosion," said Terrence Mulligan, a witness. The black electric car shot out from beneath the trailer and through the white smoke as if driven by a stunt man in an action-movie trailer. Brown was clearly visible still strapped in the driver's seat as the decapitated car bounded down the roadway. Mulligan

* Elaine Herzberg was killed by an autonomous test vehicle developed by Uber and carrying a safety driver. The system did not intervene and the driver was distracted. As of this writing, the National Transportation Safety Board is still investigating the March 2018 crash.

gave chase in his powerful pickup—"I've got a Ram 5.7"—but he had trouble keeping up. The Tesla jumped a culvert, ripped through two wire fences, and broke a utility pole before disappearing into a clump of trees. It came to rest up a small embankment in someone's front yard. Another motorist started up the driveway on foot to check on Brown but he turned around before reaching the car. "You don't want to go up there," he told Mulligan.

The trailer had sheared off the roof of the car and with it the top half of Brown's skull. Fully exposed, still belted and surrounded by depleted airbags, the empty cranial cavity showed clearly.

On June 30, in an unsigned blog post entitled "A Tragic Loss," Tesla Motors announced that Autopilot was engaged at the time of the crash. NHTSA had opened an investigation the day before and Tesla Motors needed to get ahead of the story. Despite Brown's death, according to "The Tesla Team," Autopilot was still safer than "manual driving." The evidence: Autopiloted Teslas had gone 130 million miles without anyone dying. "Among all vehicles in the U.S., there is a fatality every 94 million miles. Worldwide, there is a fatality approximately every 60 million miles."

Those figures are disingenuous. Autopilot became available only with model year 2015 cars. Nearly 20 percent of cars on the road are more than fifteen years old. Older cars are less safe on average than newer cars, so looking at only 2015 models would at the very least cut Tesla's gap. If owners abided by the manual, Autopilot would have only been engaged on superhighways, which are twice as safe as surface streets. In other words, if all those miles were on the Interstates, manual driving comes out way ahead with an average of one fatality for every 200 million vehicle miles traveled. Ultimately, however, this is all a parlor game because we cannot verify the 1:130 million. Only Tesla actually knows how many miles have been covered with Autopilot engaged. As for NHTSA, the agency had to subpoena Tesla for a mere forty miles of its Autopilot data. It then had to rely on a technician from the company to download and translate that data.

The problem of data proprietorship is not easily overcome without a robust regulatory regime. Four months before the Florida crash, there was another fatal crash that may also have been Autopilot related. Gao Yaning, a twenty-three-year-old man behind the wheel of his father's Tesla, died when the car plowed into the rear of a street cleaning truck on a divided highway. The deadly crash was captured by a dashboard camera (not associated with the car's driver assist systems) and the Beijing haze gives it a post-apocalyptic quality. We see no evidence of braking or evasion before the image winks out. Media coverage in the United States was scant. A company spokeswoman said Tesla has no way of knowing whether Autopilot was engaged during the crash. "Because of the damage caused by the collision, the car was physically incapable of transmitting log data to our servers," she said. She added, "We have tried repeatedly to work with our customer to investigate the cause of the crash, but he has not provided us with any additional information that would allow us to do so." That may be true, but we don't know. The owner, Mr. Gao's father, is suing Tesla China.

Although it did not include all the data the safety officials wanted, Josh Brown's Tessy had a treasure trove. Investigators could see where it was during every moment of the trip, when it was accelerating and braking, and whether Brown had his hands on the steering wheel. (A hand on the wheel applies a tiny amount of torque, which is detected by the power steering sensors.) The Tesla also revealed that the Autopilot had been engaged on roads—including two-lane, undivided highways—that were outside of its "Operational Design Domain." But why was the car allowed to operate out of its ODD at all? The whole premise of automation is its ability to make up for human failures. Brown's failure was being blinded by the promises of the rhetorical robot car.

I must admit that Brown is a hard man for me to eulogize. I am not so heartless as to shut my eyes to the immeasurable grief of his friends and family. No one should die because they failed to read the terms of service before clicking "OK." And, he's certainly not alone: police have caught people asleep at the wheel while on Autopilot, and there have been several crashes in the US in which Autopilot has been implicated. The NTSB has yet to release reports on any of these. But Brown was a road hazard. He earned himself eight speeding tickets in six years, including one for doing sixty-four in a thirty-five zone. He posted videos on YouTube boasting of the car's autonomous capability, videos in which he chats leisurely as the car drives. One clip got more than three and a half million views after Elon Musk tweeted an endorsement. Brown had used the Autopilot for all but about four minutes of his fateful forty-one-minute trip. He had a hand on the wheel for a total of twenty-five seconds. Only by chance was he done in by a trailer full of Florida blueberries instead of T-boning a slow-moving school bus full of kids.

The police ticketed the trucker for failing to yield the right of way—which he did by definition of the rules of the road because he was making a left turn. (This crash therefore counts toward the 94 percent human-error total.) In the previous five years, seven crashes had occurred around the intersection, but it did not warrant any kind of traffic signal according to official guidelines. After a six-month investigation, NHTSA issued its report. "Sigh of Relief for Self-Driving Cars as Tesla Cleared in Probe," was *Bloomberg*'s headline. "Exonerated" figured prominently in other news stories. The typical round of news/commentary followed. "NHTSA Drops Tesla Autopilot Investigation, Highlights Technology Strengths," the *Motley Fool* said. "After probing Tesla's deadly crash, Feds say yay to self-driving," wrote Jack Stewart from *Wired*—again conflating driver-assist systems with driverless cars. Elon Musk spun the report as concluding that Autopilot was not only vindicated but also that it reduced crashes by 40 percent.

In fact, NHTSA did not "clear" self-driving cars or even driver-assist features. The agency's Office of Defects Investigation simply concluded that the car's software and hardware were working as intended when the fatal crash occurred. The system was doing its job. Recognizing a truck of blueberries across the roadway was simply not part of its job.

NHTSA offered faint praise for the owner's manual, but similarly suggested it was being asked to do a job for which, in the real world, it was ill-suited. "Although perhaps not as specific as it could be, Tesla has provided information about system limitations in the owner's manual . . . ," the agency noted. But it made clear that providing this information in the manual was not enough to meet safety obligations. As always, the best bit was buried in the footnotes: "While drivers have a responsibility to read the owner's manual . . . , the reality is that drivers do not always do so. Manufacturers therefore have a responsibility to design with the inattentive driver in mind."

President Obama's transportation secretary Anthony Foxx highlighted this footnote, but few listened. Perhaps he is now hunched over a worn composition notebook endlessly scribbling "Read the manual . . . read the manual . . . read the manual."

Tesla Motors made changes to the Autopilot system in response to the crash, including reducing the amount of time the driver is allowed to go "hands free." When the next fatal crash happened in 2018—a single car crash against a highway barrier—an official Tesla blog post defended the system and faulted the driver:

> The driver had received several visual and one audible hands-on warning earlier in the drive and the driver's hands were not detected on the wheel for six seconds prior to the collision. The driver had about five seconds and 150 meters of unobstructed view of the concrete divider with the crushed crash attenuator, but the vehicle logs show that no action was taken.

Meanwhile, German regulators demanded that Tesla stop using the "misleading term autopilot when promoting the system." The company removed the term from its Chinese website as well. Mobileye, the Israeli company (now part of Intel) that supplies vision systems for many vehicle manufacturers, broke ranks with the electric carmaker. Mobileye CEO Amnon Shashua said Tesla was "pushing the envelope in terms of safety." NHTSA concluded the same: "[Autopilot] is a driver assistance system and not a driverless system." Tesla's spokesperson responded that the company had never advertised Autopilot "as an autonomous technology or self-driving car." Those details were mostly out-shouted in the press. Tesla's "driverless car" was exonerated.

As far as most of the media was concerned, that was the end of the story. By the time the National Transportation Safety Board issued its own final report on the crash, six months after NHTSA and more than a year after the event, the news cycle had moved on. The NTSB, best known as the people who investigate airliner crashes, brings the heavy guns. Investigators pointed out the obvious: checking that drivers put their hands on the wheel every five minutes or so is not the same as making sure they are driving. Since Tessy did not actually know how to drive, in effect, no one was driving.

NTSB member Christopher Hart then issued a supplementary statement to the report that summarized both the NHTSA and NTSB findings in plain language. The owner's manual, he agreed, does warn that the system should be used "only on highways and limited access roads." Relying on the owner's manual is a bad bet, however: "It fails to consider the human reality that very few owners . . . read the manual. Some may look at it only twice a year, to reset the clock when daylight savings time begins and ends."

"Adding to the problem is the moniker, 'Autopilot,'" Hart continues, " . . . Joe and Suzy Public . . . may conclude from the name 'autopilot' that they need not pay any attention to the driving task because the autopilot is doing everything."

He closes with the plaintive cry of a defanged G-man up against the profit motive: "The potential benefits of automation on our streets and highways are truly phenomenal, but they must be pursued carefully and thoughtfully, and hopefully the automakers will inform the process with automation lessons learned from aviation and elsewhere."

From this one crash, the NTSB made new recommendations and reiterated old ones. It told NHTSA to collect data on how automated systems perform during a crash as well as how the driver and the automated system behaved for a long interval before the crash. NTSB said the law should require such data be accessible to safety investigators. Further, it made the obvious point that programmers should not let the car drive in places that their code had not anticipated. General Motors introduced its Cadillac "Super Cruise" system for 2018, its version of Tesla's Autopilot. It works only on limited-access highways and has a driver-facing camera to watch that you are "paying sufficient attention." It is too early to declare the system safe or safer than Tesla's, but GM appears to have taken a more conservative approach to the technology and the marketing.

The NTSB also reiterated a recommendation it had made before. NHTSA needs to require vehicle-to-vehicle (V2V) safety systems. Such systems do not rely on $100,000 coffee-can LIDAR systems, binocular vision cameras, or massive amounts of energy-intensive, on-board computing power. V2V is an updated version of the system Vladimir Zworykin worked on for RCA and GM in the 1950s. Every vehicle broadcasts its location and velocity. Linked to already available electronic engine controls and emergency braking systems, V2V would thereby ensure that no two vehicles could occupy the same space at the same time. The technology could be "backwards compatible" so that it could be added to existing automobiles; its benefits would accrue far more quickly than awaiting a turnover in new models. Had Baressi's trailer been fitted with a V2V radio beacon and had Tessy been fitted with a radio receiver, Brown might well be alive today. Moreover, V2V cars would be able to do something no self-driving car has ever been able to: detect vehicles that are outside its line of sight. There would be no more blind corners, no trucks parked in the way. Traffic control devices would also have such technology (known as vehicle-to-infrastructure; V2I) they could stop cars from, for example, running red lights. The Federal Communications Commission allocated the radio frequencies for such a system two decades ago. That action was part of the Intelligent Transportation Systems initiative that sent the fleet of Buicks down a San Diego freeway. NHTSA has been pushing V2V for more than twenty years. Vehicle manufacturers have been pushing back. The reasons given are the same as those against safety glass, safety belts, and airbags. It is too expensive, not ready, and not as good as technology they plan to employ some time in the future. The presidential administration that took control in 2016 has scrapped the entire project as part of its crusade against government mandates. Of course, if V2V had been mandated for the last twenty years, think of the lives we would have saved! On the other hand, there would be far less excitement about the potential for Pentagon-derived automated vehicles to transform the nature of automobility.

Two roads to safety diverge before us at this moment. Down the one to the left is Vision Zero with its refusal to sacrifice life on the altar of automobility. Along that route we find proven, collective solutions like redesigning streets for pedestrian safety and comfort. We find streets that not only *are* safer but also *feel* safer, thereby encouraging people to get out of their cars. We find V2V, a high-tech safety technology that has been on the shelf for two decades, but one that requires collective action to be effective. Sparkling on the right is the robot car brought to us by engineering luminaries such as Anthony Levandowski and business tycoons like Elon Musk. Internet giants and global automakers are on board as well, if only to hedge their bets and promote themselves as technology leaders. Down that road are better cars, more cars, and huge profits. As a nation of drivers, we should be able to choose the road on the left if we want, even if it means facing up to the embedded and twisted ethics of automobility as it exists today. For better or worse, we won't have to make that choice. At this particular fork in the road, the rhetorical robot car has already chosen for us.

Chapter 14

MY CAR HAS LEFT
FOR COLLEGE

The author's 1978 Dodge Adventurer circa 1995. It had to be euthanized when Massachusetts would not let it immigrate because it suffered from a bad case of rust.

THE SLANT SIX MAY BE THE ONLY ENGINE WITH A NATIONAL fan club. I fell in love when I first discovered it under the hood of a '78 Dodge Adventurer pickup. Engineers had designed a traditional tall, skinny, inline six-cylinder motor and then slanted it 30 degrees to one side. Eureka. The interwoven sculptures of the intake and exhaust manifolds stand prominently atop the obtuse side. The necessary warts—fuel pump, oil pump, starter, coil, and distributor— are tucked out of sight inside the acute angle. Like a limbo dancer, it could now slide under a stylishly low hood line and had a lower center of gravity than an upright six. It had more power than the inline sixes from Ford and GM of its day without the irresponsible power and thundering hoofbeats of the V8s. It loped along with the clippety-clop of an old mare. Legends abound about running the thing with maple syrup for lubricant and still seeing 400,000 miles. You could not kill a Slant Six, which made it the perfect engine to mentor me in car repair.

The Slant Six first appeared in the 1960 Plymouth Valiant and went on to power a range of Chrysler models for the next twenty-seven years. An engine being sold as new nearly three decades after its development speaks to the stagnation in American automobile technology during the first hundred years of its existence. Until the 1980s, the only significant technological innovations were the electric starter (1912) and the automatic transmission (1939). Then, everything began to change. Mechanical engine controls gave way to microchips that manage the fuel, air, and spark that every gasoline engine needs to operate. When something goes wrong, the computer logs the error, illuminates the "check engine" light, and tells the mechanic which black box to swap out. Steering, throttles, brakes, and even suspensions now rely on sensors, microchips, and computing power. All are a step toward a future in which the car joins the "internet of things," a machine persistently linked to the global neural network. As this transition accelerates, shade-tree mechanics become more and more like the laborer on Ford's assembly line, men who, as Henry put it, are better off knowing nothing at all. "Above all, [a man] wants a job in which he does not have to think," Ford proclaimed. But for us, the joy of car repair runs precisely the opposite of mindless toil: one meditates, one thinks on the unstructured data flooding in from the task literally at hand. Our knowledge is in our heads but also in our hands. Your hands won't tell you what's wrong with a faulty circuit board.

The end of car repair threatens American manhood. All we're good for now is fixing the Wi-Fi, which we pretend is more complicated than unplug, count to ten, plug back in. Electric and autonomous cars will only leave us more bereft. Yet, more than male egos are at stake. We are the canaries in the coal mine.

Even if you're a driver who would no sooner change your own oil than wipe someone else's bottom, you should beware these efforts of global automakers to quash the independent and shade-tree mechanic. It is part of a plan to complicate the concept of car ownership the way Amazon, Apple, and the other tech giants have complicated the ownership of books, music, and other media. Consider the difference between a paper book and a Kindle. You can loan your book to a friend, who can then pass it on to their friend, or you can give it to charity. Amazon generously lets you loan out an e-book— but only for fourteen days, making you more of a library than an actual friend. Apple only lets you share with your family. Automakers know a profitable business model when they see one. For example, modern cars, led by Tesla, can now be updated "over the air" via a cellular connection. In fact, Tesla gave buyers the option to buy a Model S60 and then, whenever they decided to upgrade, go on the web, click on a button, have $9,000 charged to their credit card, and about forty miles of range added to their battery pack. The batteries, and the range, were always there. The nine grand bought a software key that unlocked them. It became the world's first in-app automotive purchase. Having subsumed automobile diagnostics and repair into the machines themselves and, further, into their own global enterprises, they are turning their attention to driving. By the time you realize what has happened, we independent and shade-tree mechanics, we Sons of Liberty, won't be there to save you.

The Sons of Liberty are fighting back, though. I joined the battle in 2012 upon walking into the Salem, Massachusetts, Autozone and facing a small sign encouraging support for the Massachusetts "Right to Repair" ballot initiative. If passed, shade-tree and independent mechanics would remain free to access manufacturer diagnostic data. If defeated, data would become the exclusive purview of automakers' own dealers. It promised to be a bitter fight because dealerships depend on service profits. They actually lose money selling new cars. Our adversaries would not be the small dealerships that used to sponsor little-league teams and floats for the Fourth of July parade. We live now in the age of the mega dealers and superstores. Of the roughly 17.5 million cars sold in the United States in 2016, 3.1 million were sold by just ten dealerships. These guys don't sponsor little league; they air commercials during the World Series.

We won! It was not even close: 86 percent in favor to 14 percent against. Better still, fearing that other states would follow suit and thereby create a patchwork of new regulations, the auto industry capitulated and signed an agreement with a coalition of stakeholders to support the right to repair. The Sons of Liberty kept information free.

* * * *

UNLIKE THE TERM "car guys," which I have described as gender neutral, when I say "sons" of liberty I do mean sons. Car repair is an act of performative masculinity. Many mechanics have stories of handing Dad (or occasionally, Mom) a wrench. That's not the way it was for me. Growing up, none of my friends fixed cars and none of their dads did. It was beneath or beyond them. I don't know where my car repair impulse came from. So, I had nowhere to turn. I just plunged in and pulled the dipstick.

In the days when oil still came in cans, service stations still had service. "Filler up and check the oil," you would say to the white-suited Texaco man.

"You're down a quart, Mister," he'd announce. He'd pull a quart of Texaco Motor Oil from the rack set jauntily between the gas pumps and pierce its lid with a combination can opener and spout. He'd check your radiator, and maybe top up the water in the battery, before taking your cash or an imprint of your charge plate and handing you the carbon paper. Don't expect that level of service even at the full-serve island any more. The Texaco man was there to win hearts and minds during the price wars of the 1950s and 1960s. Texaco, Exxon (née Esso), Mobil, and the rest were looking for market share. By the time the State of Maryland allowed me to drive, the energy crisis had killed off the Texaco men. The self-service gas station would turn out to be the thin edge of the wedge that has us bagging our own groceries and making our own plane reservations. I didn't mind though.

How hard could it be to check my own oil? It wasn't like the Model T. I didn't have to crawl underneath and look for oil spilling out on my tie. I had a dipstick. I popped the hood, slid out the épée, wiped it clean, and dipped it again. Plenty of oil. I started checking the oil at every fill-up and with growing confidence. It was always fine. Then, while out one night with a friend, driving my mother's Olds Delta 88, the oil check went so smoothly I should have been suspicious. I popped the hood, checked the level, and dropped the hood. Mike and I were easing along on an empty boulevard—like that quiet moment in an Iraq war film before the IED explodes—when BAM! There was great confusion and everything went black. The hood had flipped open, caught the air, and peeled itself back, tearing open like an anchovy lid. Apparently the body work was very expensive.

Finally, one red-letter day I pulled the station wagon into a gas station. It was a quart low! I proudly stepped inside and grabbed a bottle of 10W 40. I poured it in.

"That's oil," the gas man told me.

"Uh-huh, it was low."

"You're adding it to the power steering reservoir."

He put the oil in the right place for me and told me not to worry about the power steering fluid. "It's kind of like oil," he said. It's not. He was a nice gas man.

Undeterred by my oil-checking fiascos, I was determined to learn to change my own oil. The manual for the '75 Custom Cruiser told us to change the oil every 7,500 miles, our 1999 Saab wanted fresh oil only every 10,000 miles, my colleague's new Mini, 15,000. But I grew up believing that the more frequently I had an oil change, the better chance I had of sliding through the gates of heaven. In my defense, there used to be a lot of oil change propaganda. *Eight Is Enough*'s Dick Van Patten, among other trusted television dads, told me to go to Jiffy Lube every 3,000 miles if I loved my car. Shockingly, the oil companies went right along with the 3,000-mile gambit. "Hey Mr. Toolbelt," Leah Remini (the inexplicably hot wife of the fat man-child on TV's *King of Queens*) would ask on behalf of Quaker State, "why don't you change your oil every 3,000 miles?" Women know when you lie, she warned.

I tried my first oil change while in a student ghetto. I didn't have the proper tools. I removed the drain plug with pliers, rounding it off in the process. So, I turned my oil changes over to Jiffy Lube. Already the names are disingenuous since a "lube job" refers not to an oil change but to lubrication of the chassis. The modern chassis has all the lubrication it will ever need when it leaves the factory. Yet with faith that real men changed their oil at three grand, I was going to the so-called Jiffy Lube or the Quick Lube every other month. There was the stale coffee offered with corn-based "whitener" in place of cream, the smattering of magazines with titles I'd never heard of, and the daytime TV. Things really got bad when I found myself waiting to see how Judge Judy would rule. Then the petro-sommelier would come in for the upsell. My car would do better on synthetic. One guy tried to sell me a chromed drain plug that was specially designed so that only Jiffy Lube could change my oil. Then they'd put that little odometer sticker on my windshield—current mileage plus 3,000—and charge me $29.95 ($19.95 with a coupon). I grew depressed. I resolved to try again.

At that point, I owned my own house, a set of wrenches, and proper ramps. Over time, I got better. Now I can do it effortlessly and with a minimum of mess. I can go in the house and get something else done. I drink my coffee with real cream while the last drop drips out. That little luxury makes up for the fact that the surplus value of my labor has gone negative. It actually costs more to buy the oil and filter than to have it done. A loss leader, the dealerships call it. Still, I persevere.

I hadn't advanced past the oil change by the time we moved to Southeastern Michigan, for grad school. I figured, given my proximity to Detroit, I could learn to fix cars almost by osmosis and started looking for an old car to work on. I decided I needed an old pickup. "Need" isn't quite the right word. But there is no word, at least in English, for the desire for a truck that wells up from the soul. John Jerome explained it best forty years ago in his book *Truck: On Rebuilding a Worn-Out Pickup and Other Post-Technological Adventures*. The onetime managing editor of *Car and Driver* who had declared *The Death of the Automobile* in 1972 "needed" a pickup truck to haul horseshit for his garden. "Think of all the other things we could do with it," he implores. "Oh, my, yes: a full-time working truck. All of a sudden I can't invent problems fast enough to keep up with the solutions such a truck would represent." The first problem I invented was hauling lumber to the university woodshop (otherwise easily accomplished with a roof rack on the Saab). Other solutions would surely crop up. I "needed" a truck.

In 1993, I found a 1978 Dodge D100 in Adventurer trim with a Slant Six, painted the color of autumn leaves offset with faded chrome. I bought it from a dad with crisp dress slacks and a perfect lawn. He had it in the newspaper classifieds for $1,100. I offered $900 to his wife. We settled on an even thousand. In 1978, Detroit was just getting started transforming the American pickup from a lowly workhorse to the highly profitable suburban status symbol it has become. "Built for him . . . and her," said the Adventurer brochure. "For the man who wants to move anything from cement blocks to sports gear. Plus ride and handling to ease a lady through her chores." It had the features every family needed, giving "all-around use-value for jobs, recreation, or as a second car, at moderate cost." We see Mom, just outside Swensen's because Jimmy wanted an ice cream and Mom doesn't mind a mess. She paid extra for the full vinyl seats.

Because this was before every third driver drove a truck, I looked forward to lending it heroically to friends. I would always be the answer to, "Do you know anybody with a truck?" Well, no good deed goes unpunished. The very first week, my neighbor borrowed it and ripped the door off by backing up with it open. The tree he hit had barely a scratch. He bought me a rusting junkyard door and had it painted. The paint never matched but he still had the gall to grouse that the paint job cost more than the junkyard door itself. My neighbor was an idiot. But I forgave him because what can you expect from an MBA student? My beautiful two-tone Adventurer became an ugly beast. At least now I could work on it confident that if I really screwed up, it wouldn't be a huge loss. The brakes were the first thing to go.

* * * *

I'M LYING ON A BED of gravel staring up at a rust-colored sky hanging so low I can reach out and touch it. I don't dare. Every time I shift my body so the marble shards of the driveway can dig into fresh flesh, every time I turn my elbow or cant my wrist for leverage, another bit of that sky flakes off and pirouettes down into my hair, my mouth, my eyes. I should be sore, uncomfortable, claustrophobic, bloody even. Somehow I'm not. Though come to think of it, I'm not making any progress either. Again and again I coax the steel lines into place. I reach down. My left hand finds the seven-sixteenths flare-nut wrench. It's glazed with hydraulic fluid and I struggle to grip it. I offer up the compression nut to the nipple. I twist the nut home. I do it again and again, a mantra of gentle torque. The sharp stones slowly melt beneath my shoulders. The falling rust morphs into gray snowflakes. It would appear that I spent too much time underneath the truck today. It has invaded my dreams.

I was under the truck because the brake lines had rusted through. This had occurred during our first real Dodge Adventure, a trip that took us beyond the Ann Arbor city limits. "Do you think we'll make it?" my future wife had asked. "If we don't, we don't," I replied, reassuringly. We were off to save a bunch of money on cabinets by buying seconds direct from the KraftMaid factory. "There's the entrance," Melissa pointed as it drifted by. Hmmm . . . I thought I had pressed the brake pedal soon enough. Ah well. We made a U-turn and bought the cabinets. Loading up I noticed some kind of liquid dripping from the frame rail. It was slippery and smelled like damp acorns and maple syrup. It was brake fluid.

At the dawn of the automobile age, figuring out how to stop a car took about as much ingenuity as figuring out how to make it go. The sprag, an iron bar that hung beneath the chassis on a hinge, worked like a ship's anchor. On approaching a hill, the driver released the sprag to drag along the ground. If the car started to roll backwards, it would dig into the earth. Next came brakes operated by a hand lever or foot pedal connected by rods or pulleys, or both, to bands that cinched around the transmission or the wheel hubs. These systems grew increasingly balky and were prone to failure. Hydraulic fluid provided the solution. In place of the rod or cable, hydraulic fluid flowed through a tube from the brake pedal to the brake shoes by means of a liquid inside a tube (called a brake line). The liquid easily negotiates the bends and turns in the vehicle and remains undisturbed by the bumps and twists in the road. Early systems used castor oil, which doubled as a home remedy for constipation. Modern systems, which became standard by about 1939, use a deadly combination of mineral oil and glycol. Strangely, because it causes renal failure, neurological damage, and death, brake fluid has a pleasant odor. The sweetness of the glycol and the nutty aroma of the mineral oil invite drinking the same way a precipice tempts leaping.

By 1978, NHTSA had, thankfully, forced automakers to install a dual braking system: the brake pedal pushed fluid down two separate networks of tubes so that if one failed, the other would still effect a stop . . . eventually. That's what happened to us at the Kraftmaid factory.

Doing the job involved buying new parts, acquiring new skills, and, happily, getting to buy a very special new tool. I ran out to Murray's Auto Parts, a local chain, the mascot of which looks like a cross between Animal from the Muppets and Tommy Chong. I'm sure they know their market, but he seems not to say, "Buy parts from this guy!" but, "Would you buy parts from *this* guy?" They sold lengths of brake line to splice into the existing system, and that's where the fun began. I bought a double flaring tool. I'm still not sure how a double flaring tool differs from the single flaring kind other than clearly being twice as impressive. Inside the red, blow-molded plastic case sat a swage, clamped shut by giant wing nuts. A pointy screw thingy did the work of the blacksmith's hammer. The instructions said to put one of the coin-sized dies inside the tube, clamp it in the swage, and bring the hammer down. The idea was to enlarge the end of the tube just enough so that it would capture and hold a brass fastener—much as a knot holds the end of the thread when you start a sewing project. My first three (or was it twelve?) splices leaked, with the brake lines getting slipperier each time. The job took most of a day and invaded my dreams that night.

The brake lines on my twelve-year-old F150 with 160,000 New England miles on it still look as good as new. My double flaring tool sits forlornly in its blow-molded case in a drawer, unused since the mid '90s.

After a few years of happily driving, fixing an oil pump, replacing brake pads, exhaust pipes, and the like, I faced diagnostic problem 101: engine fails to start.

A gasoline engine needs fuel, air, and spark to start. When it fails to start, one of those things is failing to show up for work. Failing to start is not the same as failing to turn over. Turning the key connects the battery circuit to Boss Kettering's electric motor and cranks the engine. As a public service, let me point out that even if your headlights and radio come on, your battery could still be too weak to crank the engine. Cranking sets everything in motion so that the engine can suck in a charge of fuel mixed with air (as the piston goes down), compress it (as the piston goes back up), explode it (when the spark plug fires) to send the piston back down, and then exhaust the exploded gas (when the piston comes back up). Suck, squeeze, bang, and blow are the four cycles of a four-cycle engine. Thus the bang, or power stroke, happens only once every fourth time the piston rises. It is the squeeze that caused the knocking that so troubled GM's Kettering.

The first diagnostic tests should ensure that you have the three ingredients necessary for combustion. The gas in the tank may not be getting to the engine because the fuel filter is clogged. Or, the fuel pump may not be doing its job of sending gas from the tank to the motor.

Air and fuel must also be mixed in the right proportions. That's the carburetor's job. The carb on the Slant Six was not much different than the one on the Model T or the Benz Patent-Motorwagen for that matter. All pull air over a fuel nozzle to atomize it and send the resulting mist into the cylinders for proper exploding. The engine needs a richer mix (less air and more fuel) on startup; at speed it needs a leaner mix (more air to fuel). Ambient temperature and humidity also have an effect. Back in the day, the driver took all of this into account and dialed in the right mix by hand. By 1978, we expected the carburetor to do the measuring and adjusting for us. So, inventors added floats, tangs, springs, cams, connecting rods, needle valves, thermostats, and adjusting screws, retaining pins, clamps, gaskets, brackets, and bushings. A carburetor parts list of eighty or a hundred items is not uncommon. A carburetor's life is not easy.

By contrast, the spark plugs have a simple job. Plugs provide a 50,000-volt bolt of Lilliputian lightning that arcs across a gap to ignite the fuel-air mixture inside the cylinders. The trick is for each plug in each cylinder to fire at just the right moment. The distributor choreographs that operation. It has a cap, which looks like what a mad scientist would use to transfer the mind of a squirrel to a chipmunk, with a nest of wires leading out to the spark plugs. Inside, a pointer rotates like the spinner for a children's board game. The rotor touches the right wire at the right moment, closing a circuit and firing the plug. All of this action happens in fractions of a second and thousands of times a minute.

The grand hyperkinetic dance of carburetors and distributors is gone. Electronic sensors and circuit boards sit motionless inside black boxes. The "check engine" light illuminates when something goes awry. That was not the case in 1978. In 1978, the check engine light was between your ears.

When the Slant Six in the '78 Dodge cranked but failed to start, I asked if it had spark, gas, and air, and that all three were showing up to work in the right combination and at the right time.

I removed a spark plug and grounded it against the engine block while Melissa cranked it. I could see the arc of Lilliputian lightning. That gave the ignition circuit a clean bill of health. I popped the distributor cap off the rotor and had a look around. There was no sign of a crack or a short. The timing could be off, but if so, the engine should still run, though roughly. In that case, I would tune it by ear just by twisting the distributor cap until the motor sounded happy. Or, I could use my timing light, a strobe set up to fire at the same time as the spark plugs. My chromed timing light doubles as a mid-60s sci-fi ray gun. It now sits in its blow-molded plastic case in the drawer next to the double flaring tool.

Next, I would check for air by removing the cover and inspecting the air filter. Air coming into the carburetor passes through a paper filter, which can get clogged by dirt, dust, or fur from a kangaroo rat that has exploded inside the engine compartment (as on the Saab's camping adventure). A clogged air filter does not normally present as a sudden inability to start, but I would have to remove it anyway to check the carburetor intake. I scanned the area for kangaroo rats, and had Melissa crank it again. No soap.

With the carburetor now visible, I could ask, was it getting gas?* There are safe ways to answer this question. I did not employ them. I chose to get a can of gas out of the garden shed and pour it directly into the engine. All it needed was a thimbleful. I did not have a thimble. So I just lifted the three-gallon can over the carburetor and slop-

---

* Yes, there was gas in the tank; I'm not an idiot. And no, I had not checked for gas in the tank until that point because I am an idiot.

pily poured in way more gas than it needed. "Crank it," I told my ever-patient future wife. The engine burbled, then gurgled. "Again." Further gurgling, and the black smoke of overly rich combustion blowing out the tailpipe. I held the carburetor's choke open. "Again." It spat gas on me like a put-off llama. Again. Finally, the dead engine had cycled through enough suck, squeeze, bang-less power strokes, and blow strokes that it finally banged and then came to life.

I let it run for a while. Shut it off and it started again. I let it sit for a while, shut it off and started it again. I went out the next morning and started it cold. The carburetor was doing its job. Problem solved.

Only it wasn't. Gas splashing was just a workaround. I tried carb cleaner, knowing it wouldn't help. It didn't. Sometimes I could pump the gas pedal like a bass drummer and get it going, but not always. I resolved to keep a can of gas in the bed and a fire extinguisher tucked under the seat. With these solutions, failure to start became but a minor annoyance. I learned to live with it, but never fully let it out of my mind.

Condition: truck starts mostly fine in the winter, occasionally hard, and sometimes not at all. Must be the cold. Starts mostly fine in the spring, occasionally hard, and sometimes not at all. Must be the Michigan damp. Starts fine in the summer, occasionally hard, and sometimes not at all. Might be the heat. As the leaves began to fall, I realized that I had run out of excuses. It had failed to start in the cold, the damp, and the heat.

Sometime during these meditative months, a soon-to-be ex-friend would ask, "Why don't you take it to a professional?" Of course that was a pinprick to my pride, but there was more to it. Failure to start happened intermittently and never when the engine was warm, so had I driven it to the mechanic, he would ask me to leave it over-night. The next day, or maybe the one after that, he would call to say it started fine so he changed my fuel pump. I couldn't pick it up till tomorrow though because it was already almost five o'clock. A week or a month later, it would fail to start again because, of course, the old fuel pump was working just fine, thank you. At this point, I might have concluded that the mechanic in question was either not competent, dishonest, or both.

Shady mechanics make for good exposé fodder for *60 Minutes* and *20/20,* and the like. In his book *Auto Mechanics,* historian Kevin L. Borg traces the mechanic's bad rep to the dawn of the automobile age and locates it in class conflict. The first professional mechanics were the chauffeurs of wealthy autoists who had to tinker with the master's car almost daily. These driver-mechanics developed a reputation for joyriding and taking kickbacks from the city garages where the cars were stored. Society magazines reported on and editorialized about what they labeled "the chauffeur problem."

In 1940, *Reader's Digest* undertook a survey of mechanics around the country to test the conventional wisdom that many mechanics are crooked. The magazine sent Roger Riis, son of the muckraking photojournalist Jacob Riis, on a forty-eight-state automobile tour to root out dishonest mechanics. He took Miss Lioy May along with him reasoning that "women, because of their more limited knowledge of mechanics, would be gypped more often and more flagrantly than men." They conducted their survey by yanking a spark-plug wire (a problem easily solved and put right in seconds) and pulling into a garage complaining of a rough engine. They reported their results in a collection of articles compiled as a book entitled *Repair Men May Gyp You.* They found that, "Three out of five garagemen overcharged, invented unnecessary work or charged for work not done, parts not needed, or parts not installed." The worst crooks would wheel out a testing cart full of dials and switches and gauges. There was the Ford Laboratory Test Set, the King Motor and Ignition Tester, and the Stromberg Motoscope, among many others. None compared to the Weidenhoff Motor Analyzer for style. Some looked like pinball machines; others, the Wizard of Oz's control panel or a midcentury juke box. Never were these used for diagnosis. "They were *always* used to buck up a crooked explanation," Riis reported. Riis generally found the small-town, one-man garage to be more honest. He quickly identified the loose wire and plugged it back in, often at no charge.

Gus Wilson could serve as Riis's platonic ideal. A gray-haired veteran mechanic who always wore a crisp uniform and pondered with a pipe in his mouth, he ran the Model Garage in an idyllic small town. The fictional Gus had automotive adventures in the pages of *Popular Science* from 1925 to 1970, solving every mechanical mystery thrown at him. The Fonz, who took television—indeed all of America—by storm in the middle 1970s represented both sides of the mechanical coin. He was raised by a single mother in humble circumstances in a rough neighborhood, according to his *Happy Days* back story. He wore greasy coveralls at work, had once run with a street gang, and rode a motorbike. But Fonzie was a hero, always fighting for good over evil and, not incidentally, scoring all "the chicks." He could start the jukebox at the malt shop with a bang of his fist and transform the Cunninghams' old DeSoto into a street racer. He was Gus in a ducktail haircut and leather jacket.

Tom and Ray Magliozzi played honest mechanics for urbane National Public Radio listeners on their *Car Talk* program. To my disappointment, but evidently to the approval of the NPR audience, the show shifted from car repair to relationship counseling. Fortunately, one can still find Ron Ananian, *The Car Doctor*, on AM radio. Ananian answers questions from shade-tree mechanics, although he closes each show with the tag line "Good Mechanics Aren't Expensive; They're Priceless!" He's certainly right. Car owners speak with devotion about their own trustworthy mechanic. The trouble for lay people is figuring out which mechanic we will get when we pull into the service bay. Will we get Gus, or will we come face to face with a double-talker and his Stromberg Motoscope? Amazon reviews and the Google algorithms haven't yet colonized this little corner of commerce, so they're no help. We rely instead on imperfect folk wisdom. "Do you know a good mechanic?" a local woman recently asked on a Facebook group dedicated to such things in our small town. The answers came in fast, furious, and contradictory. One commenter's favorite mechanic was another's crook. The only comment ignored was mine: I suggested she learn to fix it herself.

In any case, even the best mechanic struggles with a customer who arrives with vague descriptions of intermittent symptoms. Gus or the Fonz surely would have solved my carburetor troubles in a heartbeat, if only they were real.

* * * *

AFTER LIVING WITH the perplexingly intermittent failure to start around the full twelve months of the calendar, the answer came in a flash of inspiration. Thinking back over the past year, I suddenly realized that the weather didn't matter. The truck's down time did. Only after sitting parked for about a week did it exhibit symptoms. I concluded that the carburetor bowl was leaking, which explained why pouring in gas got the engine to start. In fairness to me, I had investigated that possibility earlier. But I had never seen a drip or a stain that might indicate a leak. I now realized that the leak was so slow, the fuel evaporated as quickly as it escaped, leaving no trace. I suspected a bad gasket and bought a carburetor rebuild kit.

The rebuild kit contained new cork gaskets, rubber O-rings, brass needle valves, finicky springs, and tangs for bending. There was a replacement carburetor float, which worked like a toilet bowl float to open or close the needle valve. It looked like a mouse-sized lifesaver. Rebuilding a carburetor is the open-heart surgery of car repair, a job that requires study, dexterity, and keeping track of all the parts. Precise adjustment controls the mixture of air and gasoline, which in turn regulates speed, power, and pollution. I cleaned the workbench, laid down white paper, and took the device apart, piece by delicate piece. I observed, recorded, and observed some more. I bent tangs, bent them back, bent them again. I mused about the fact that before computers the most critical of adjustments were made by the rather imprecise bending of tangs. I adjusted screws. Finally, everything was back together and back on the truck. I stomped down on the accelerator a few times and turned the key. Victory!

Five years of grad school and two as an instructor in the College of Engineering brought an end to our time in Ann Arbor and the 1978 Dodge D100 in Adventurer trim with the Slant Six engine went the way of all things. The body had so much rust that Massachusetts wouldn't let me register it when we moved there. Rust is like aggressive cancer, or entropy. You can fight it for a time, but eventually it wins. Michigan lets you drive a rust bucket because that is where they make rust buckets, and they're proud of them. Not so in Massachusetts. The bottom of the crappy MBA door had returned to dust. Melissa had put her boot through the floor pan, which I was able to patch with a piece of sheet metal ingeniously bent around a steel pipe. She worried she was getting fat, but I explained about entropy. Worst of all, the entire cab was sinking around the truck's frame like the Leaning Tower of Pisa. Four large bolts had held the cab to the frame. The bolts still held fast, but the cab's sheet metal had rusted around them until all they held was the six square inches of metal in their immediate vicinity. The guy from the charity that came to pick it up was surprised I was parting with it. It ran, after all. I explained about Massachusetts. He understood immediately.

I walked around Woods Hole bereft for over a year until one day I came upon a Slant Six in an '87 Dodge parked outside the public library. I was so thrilled I bought the entire truck. Chrysler had renamed it the Ram, a sign of the rising bellicosity of American pickup designs. It even had an alpha male ovine hood ornament standing ready to ram any vehicle that crossed its path. The seats were a cheap crushed velour in place of woven fabric and vinyl. Plastic door handles had replaced the steel chromed ones. It had only one tone, a nondescript blue. Everything about it reflected the intervening years of the Chrysler bankruptcy and the decade during which Detroit whistled in the dark. Only the Slant Six made it worthwhile.

I prophylactically replaced the distributor cap and rotor, the plug wires, the air cleaner, eventually the water pump and the oil pump. There was a leak in the exhaust manifold, so I took it off and gave it to a crooked mechanic who had a machine that could grind it perfectly flat again. The carburetor worked fine. I left it in the garage when we moved overseas, but by the time we returned there was a third kid. We needed room for another car seat. I let it go.

Now that the kids are older, I can get by with the single bench seat of my 2007 F150. It's the kind of cheap truck landscapers buy for their immigrant workers to drive. (I bought mine for three grand from a roofing company.) It's about as close as you can still get to an honest old truck in salty New England. Mine's got the traditional eight-foot bed (not the now stylish five or six), making it the only high-school-marching-band-parent pickup that can carry the marimba. Mine's got the right number of doors, two. Status trucks have four. The windows crank up and down by hand. My daughter stove in one whole side of the bed, so that's good. I'm busier these days, so the black boxes and diagnostic computers are welcome. I've done a few repairs, but they've been pretty simple, except for the rust.

Things rust apart, but they also rust together. "Rusted solid" is a recurring theme in car repair, although it is rarely spoken of. The pictures in the manual show fully intact, often pristine parts being changed out. Why in heaven's name are these people removing pristine parts? If it looks that good it's either under warranty or not broken at all. The Haynes manual's "Replacing the Power Steering Pump" sequence for the F150 describes just three steps, and number three is, "Installation is reverse of removal." Easy enough. But the steering pump I'm looking at has melted into a fist-sized ball of rust.

From rusted solid has come to me some of my most creative and spiritual car repair experiences. I've stared down at solid rust, a broken stud, a stuck bracket, in anger. Then, my body evaporates. As a two-hour job stretches to four, five, or six hours, my ears stop hearing a knock on the door or a ringing phone. My eyes focus only on the metal six inches before my face. I am unable to feel tired, hungry, or sore. The fitting and I become a world unto ourselves. The distinction between mind and body breaks down as my deductive reasoning merges with what my hands have learned over these many years of mechanical engagement. Indeed, facing down rust dissolves many of the binaries we use to organize our world.

In his classic text, *Zen and the Art of Motorcycle Maintenance: An Inquiry into Values* (1974), Robert Pirsig describes at length his experience with a rusted, frozen, stuck screw. "Stuckness shouldn't be avoided," he instructs. "An egoless acceptance of stuckness is key to an understanding of all." Categorical thinking and rational engagement with the material world created the working automobile. The shop manual applies these same ways of knowing the world to get a broken car (or motorbike) back on the road. It all works perfectly until we are faced with that stuck screw. For Pirsig, the stuck screw breaks down the dualities of Western thought, his ego disappears and he becomes one with the universe. John Jerome, too, comes to understand technology in a way that engineering blue prints and shop manuals fail to capture. "I thought of the truck as something that either works or needs fixing," Jerome observes in the final pages of *Truck*. Then he realizes: "Separating work with truck from work on truck is indulging in spurious dualities. Workshop-manual thinking. I'm going to have to learn to cut that out." In other words, an old truck is like Schrödinger's cat, both working and broken simultaneously. Matthew Crawford's 2009 best seller, *Shop Class as Soulcraft*: *An Inquiry into the Value of Work,* updates Pirsig, as his title suggests.* He finds "manual work more engaging *intellectually*." When educational policy values the "knowledge worker" over the trades, it creates a false dichotomy. The scholarly Kevin Borg also describes the mechanic's job as interstitial. It occupies a category somewhere between production and consumption. All three philosophers of technology lament the increased automation. Sadly, neither Pirsig nor Jerome survived to offer commentary on the rise of the robot car.

* * * *

I WAS CONSIDERING all of this philosophy while staring at a rainbow. Knowing that rainbows form when white light divides into its

---

* Pirsig and Crawford fix motorcycles, not cars, but I'll allow it.

component colors has never dimmed the emotional experience of seeing one. Only this rainbow is under the front of the truck. A flashlight, a closer look. The power steering system has sprung a leak. It shouldn't be that bad a job. I can buy crummy parts locally or, for a bit less even, I can buy good parts by mail. The power steering should last until they come.

"Outlying warehouse . . . expedited shipping, you should receive it. . . ." Alright, it will still last. I'll have to give my wife instructions in case it rains and the kids won't bike to school. (Then she takes the truck and I use the van for carpool.) "Don't turn the steering wheel too much," I advise. "Don't pin it."

"I never pin it," she replies, without a hint of accusation that I've insulted her. I'd almost worried she would ask what pinning it meant. Instead I'm reminded that I married well. It will last.

The rain didn't start until the afternoon, so the kids had biked in the morning. Now I'd have to pick them up and throw the bikes in the bed. It will last. The rainbows follow me home, still visible even in the fading winter light. Time to clear out space in the garage and wait for the parts.

It was simple enough by the book, three steps, installation is reverse of removal. Probably two hours, three at the outside. Until I faced down that stuck nut. Those don't scare me anymore, mostly. There's Rust Buster, a gas torch, or if worse comes to the absolute worst, a cutoff tool, a drill, and a tap and die set. This was not just any old nut though. It was a captured nut—a much larger version of the brass nuts I had used on the brake lines. Only this one is buried inside the steering rack. After removing the front wheel, I could just reach it from the wheel well, but without any room to apply enough torque to overcome the rust. There was no way in from above. If I rounded it or broke it off, I might have to replace the entire rack. Drilling and retapping was out of the question. I hit it with a ball peen, soaked it with Rust Buster, heated it with a MAPP-gas torch. The heat of the torch could not seem to overcome the mass of the casting. The treads of the captured nut were buried too deeply for the Rust Buster to reach. Now the uniquely pungent Rust Buster smell filled the garage with its citrus undertones and top notes of oil as sharp as peppermint. After it's been at work on oxidized metal for a time, its odor hints of urine. Nothing would budge this nut.

I started to get more reckless. By now I had been living inside the wheel well for the better part of two days and am considering moving in permanently. It's a life without excess baggage. The few tools neatly arranged on the garage floor constitute the sum total of my possessions. But, we're going to need the truck, so I can't stay here forever. I hit it with a bigger hammer. I aim the torch at the recalcitrance and walk away for a good quarter hour. I reach the bargaining stage of grief and begin calculating the number of right and left turns it would take to get the truck to the Pequot Filling Station. Gary, a dead ringer for Gus, has a lift and the tools to get the front axle off in a timely fashion. I leave the Rust Buster on overnight and then try heat again.

On day three of my two-hour repair job, nearing the point of final acceptance, the flames of power steering fluid lick out allowing the casting to heat up fully. I put an open-ended spanner on it and pull again. Did it move, or did I round the nut? My head's not sure, but my hands know: it moved. "Free at last! Free at last! Thank God almighty, it's free at last." I literally dance a jig. The rest was easy. Installation is reverse of removal.

By then it is Friday afternoon, so I invite Bobby Pirsig, John Jerome, and Kevin Borg over (Crawford's always too busy). Jerome, as usual, brings the beer. "Why do we do this to ourselves?" I ask. Pirsig winds up for a Chautauqua about resolving the dialectic of Western thought but thinks the better of it. Jerome itemizes his list of increasingly grandiose rationales for rebuilding an old truck: he needed a truck and a hobby, he needed to prove his mechanical acumen, he needed to lash out against creeping consumerism and government control. Seeing that he's reached the point of absurdity, he avows he will never do it again. Borg begins with a few words about the social construction of whiteness and masculinity but then the fight goes out of him. We deep thinkers should be frustrated that our tools of inquiry prove inadequate. I'm not though, perhaps the others aren't either. We are not the gearheads some imagine us to be, not unaware of the explanations Marx or Freud might offer for why we do what we do. Nevertheless, amateur car repair stands up nobly in the face of the close analysis that would dissect it into meaninglessness. Perhaps we will understand it only when it is gone forever.

Chapter 15

KIDS TODAY

Mad Mike from MTV's hit show *Pimp My Ride* shows off what kids today want more than cars: screens, screens, and more screens.

I 'M SITTING IN THE PASSENGER SEAT. "WHAT ARE YOU DOING!?" Molly asks, with genuine curiosity and a touch of that tone only teenage girls can muster. We're outside the YMCA, high atop a bluff, where I've been waiting. Molly's always the last one out of the gym, always dusted with chalk. The other girls have already found their chauffeurs, but there's Molly, slow as molasses. I worry she's limping but it's just that she keeps her team bag so loose that it bangs against her left shin. I should be used to it by now. "You're going to drive," I explain.

"I don't know how to drive." It's a soliloquy by Molly standards. Mostly we get single syllables, sometimes only a post-verbal grunt. It's six words this time. And this time there's no hint of adolescent disdain or argument. There's only bemusement at the very thought. We made her take the state-required driver's ed course over the summer because she was faffing around the house. So, she sat for the state-mandated thirty hours and followed the state-mandated curriculum, to earn a driving permit. The course has the usual stuff, don't drink and drive, how to hold the steering wheel, why you need car insurance. The only thing that seemed to matter, however, was the rules of the road. That's what's on the test for a learner's permit. So, that's what Molly learned. The odd thing is that in much of Massachusetts, as in many places, the rules of the road are not the ones written in the manual. We drive according to traffic folkways, accepted norms of behavior that are in fact technical violations. The traffic laws exist mostly so the police can pull over anyone who fits the description, it seems, and so the insurance companies know whom to bill in an accident.

The state also has parents take a two-hour class. It started with a ten-minute video sponsored by GEICO, the scared-straight video. These used to be of the "hamburger on the highway" type, which showed shattered cars and bloody bodies strewn across the pavement or hanging out of a half-opened car door. This modern one was much scarier: parents talk about their teenager, the one who died shortly after she or he got a license. I cried. Then I went home and decreed that Molly was not taking driver's ed and that Molly would not be getting a license any time soon, perhaps ever.

"I don't know how to drive," Molly had said. So I drive while she escapes through that four-inch window to Snapchat with the girlfriends she saw in the gym moments ago. On rare occasions I've taken that demon iPhone from her, but only with great difficulty. She's a gymnast, solid as a rock and possessed of an iron grip. Plus, she has sharp nails. I have to pry back her fingers one at a time.

Molly, born in 2000, is at the epicenter of our present revolution. She is the bull's eye of the target market for Uber, robo-electric cars, and Brooklyn. And she's scaring car companies to death. There has been a precipitous and steady drop in the percentage of young people getting their licenses: a drop by half for sixteen-year-olds, a third for seventeen, a quarter for eighteen, a fifth for nineteen, etc. (The figures have stayed about the same for other age groups but increased substantially among the over-seventy set.) Perhaps you've caught some of the headlines. "The End of Car Culture," declared Elisabeth Rosenthal, asking, "Has America passed peak driving?" in the *New York Times* in 2013; "Automakers Prepare for an America That's Over the Whole Car Thing" and "As habits change, cars may go way of the horse and buggy," declared her colleague Neal Boudette in 2016.

Detroit needs to figure out whether kids don't like driving, don't like shopping for cars, don't care about cars, or simply don't need cars. Michael Sivak and Brand Schoettle of the University of Michigan Transportation Research Institute have been documenting this trend for several years. They still don't have an answer. In one survey asking people under forty years of age why they did not have a license, the number-one response was "too busy." As anyone who has been turned down for a lunch date knows, "too busy" is code for "there are other people I'd rather see." By the same token, "too busy to get a license" says to the car, "I'd rather see other machines." Respondents also said that owning a car was too expensive and that they preferred other options, like getting Mom to drive them. The ability to communicate online ranked below environmental concerns as a reason to eschew driving.

Nevertheless, the researchers suggest that the internet has something to do with this slow death of the car culture. It makes intuitive sense that with the World Wide Web kids today don't need to come together in time and space the way they used to. They socialize over social marketing platforms independent of where they are. Perhaps you've witnessed, or been a part of, this bizarre scene: a group of kids gets together, turns on a movie, and flops onto the couch. They then spend the rest of the evening staring at their phones. They may look up when the slasher cuts the virgin's throat. Mostly they see each other through those four-inch screens, pausing occasionally to ask the gang to "like" their latest Instagram.

Maybe kids today have less interest in the original mobile device because they feel transported by their new mobile devices. Or it could be that they like staring at screens. I know I did—and we only had five channels, plus the two snowy ones we could pull in on UHF from Baltimore. Auto companies are finally playing "if you can't beat them join them" by adding as much Wi-Fi and as many screens as possible to their cars. My screen devotion theory is based on the fact that this trend began before the advent of the internet, as evidenced on *Pimp My Ride*.

Pimp My Ride was MTV's almost-engaging automotive reality makeover series hosted by the charismatic Xzibit, a rapper whose winsome smile betrays the smart Detroit-born Alvin Joiner behind the gangsta masquerade. The original series ran from 2004 to 2007, ending just as the first iPhone debuted.

In each episode, Xzibit does a Publisher's Clearinghouse ambush on a lucky contestant whose "ride" will be "pimped" by the Stanislavsky-trained "crew" at West Coast Customs, a twenty-first-century chop shop in the shadow of LAX. After the rebuild comes "the reveal," as reality showmen call it, in which the MTV-gen driver squeals with glee at her new personality on wheels. *Pimp* won its Sunday night time slot against basic cable, had a worldwide following, and popularized the phrase "Pimp my . . ."

Los Angeles car customizing of the type practiced on *Pimp My Ride* has a long and noble history. "Chopping" down roofs, "zeeing" frames, and "channeling" bodies brought the prewar aesthetics into the postwar age. These custom cars, or Kustoms in the language of the natives, were inscrutable to any establishment adults who might happen upon them. Tom Wolfe's classic essay on customizing, "Kandy-Kolored Tangerine-Flake Streamline Baby," reads like the field notes of a cultural anthropologist. On his visit to the Burbank "Teen Fair," Wolfe recounts, "We're out on old Easter Island, in the buried netherworld of teen-age Californians, and those objects, those cars, they have to do with the gods and the spirit and a lot of mystic stuff in the community." The scene Wolfe describes in his 1963 essay is one of mainstream Anglo-America. But the pimping of rides began with Chicanos going "low and slow."

What became known as lowriding was a uniquely Mexican-American contribution to the car culture. It extends the style of the zoot suit, a loose fitting, exaggerated form of the traditional men's suit (Cab Calloway often wore one). To young Chicano men from East L.A., the zoot suit became the standard uniform for a night on the town. In the automotive equivalent, a lowrider's ride drapes over its wheels and hangs inches from the ground. Zoot suits attracted attention, often of the wrong kind. American sailors beat ethnic Mexicans and stripped off their suits during the "Zoot Suit Riots" of 1943. Similarly, the customized cars of the barrio attracted the attention of police. California law forbids operating a vehicle with a body that hangs too low.* Ground clearance became the perfect pretext for a traffic stop. Cops kept tabs on Mexican immigrants with rulers. The lowriders responded ingeniously: they added air pumps and hydraulic systems that would raise the car with the flip of a switch. Now they could go low and slow on the boulevard but high and fast when the cops circled by.

When it began, *Pimp* seemed worthy of that heritage. In an age of irony, the show presented a sincere appreciation of cars *qua* cars, machines into which young people could pour their dreams. The series debut featured a Daihatsu Hijet microvan redone with a groovy paint job, a two-tone interior, and a ridiculous chrome spoiler. The van had a George Barris cool and stood ready for at least a very tiny pimp.† Episode Two turned a plain-Jane 1978 Cadillac into an even pimp-worthier ride. Dropping the suspension, adding flashy wheels, a candy red paint job, a row of taillight hearts, and plenty of golden

---

* The current law, passed first in 1959, states, "It is unlawful to operate any passenger vehicle . . . which has been modified from the original design so that any portion of the vehicle, other than the wheels, has less clearance from the surface of a level roadway than the clearance between the roadway and the lowermost portion of any rim of any wheel in contact with the roadway." California Vehicle Code Division 12, Chapter 1, § 24008.

† George Barris was one of the all-time great customizers. The Batmobile for the 1960s *Batman* series may be his best-known creation.

chrome, the WCC crew produced a vehicle the great pimp characters
of the era Antonio "Huggy Bear" Fargas or Max "Goldie" Julien
would have been proud to cruise.

After the Caddy, the show left cars *qua* cars behind and began
rebuilding them as suitcases for electronics: DVD players, flat-screen
monitors, and video game consoles. Screens in the dashboard, screens
in the headrests, screens in the steering wheel. Walls of screens in the
ceiling and trunk. Screens on the car's exterior. Clearly, kids today
prefer screens over cars. That's because as the screens have become
sharper, smaller, bigger, and more ubiquitous, the cars have become
more boring. Kids missed out on the fun of handling tiny Japanese
cars. They've never commanded an American dreadnought. They
know only the cars of the mushy middle.

In the 1970s and even into the 1980s, many teens and young adults
would have had handed down to them, or bought secondhand, a
heavy hunk of Detroit iron like the two-ton 1974 Chevy Impala. The
automotive womb had yet to close in, seat belts were still optional,
and a car could carry a study group's worth of sophomores or give a
randy pair room to try multiple positions. The headrests were there
for styling, not for safety; the bench-backs came up no higher than
your shoulders, about as far as a movie seat or a comfortable chair.
You could throw your arm over it for a chat. You could pull a DJ in
through the radio and party on cushy seats and snuggle with your
pals. You could enjoy the ride.

Alternatively, you might have had an old Corolla, a Civic, or
even a VW Rabbit. These were little cars, cute little cars, cute little foreign cars. The original 1973 Civic had a wheel base under 87
inches and an overall length of 140 inches. They featured the new
transverse-engine, front-wheel drive layout with firm handling and
tight suspensions. They were go-cart sized, and driving a go-cart is a
blast. Then came the un-cars that nobody loved. American cars had
shrunk and the little Japanese had grown. They converged around
a middling size that has neither go-cart handling nor road-hugging
weight. The 2019 Honda Civic rides on a 106.3-inch wheelbase and

is three and a half feet longer than the original. Soften up the ride for the American tush and you're left with a machine neither cute nor fun nor magnificent in its massive luxuriousness. The three-ton Cadillac Escalade (base price, $78,000) doesn't even do the trick. To ride in one of these modern monstrosities is about as much fun as airline travel, albeit in business class. You ride in comfort, but strangely alone. So, the kids escaped to their screens.

The Edsel fiasco notwithstanding, automakers are not stupid. They know how to sell stuff. Kids want screens? We got screens. Automotive archaeologists point out that Buick and Olds offered a touch-screen option in the 1980s, using a cathode-ray tube (CRT). It controlled the radio and displayed a fan icon that spun when you turned on the climate controls. It even had a "navigation function." Although the nav system amounted to a compass and a trip computer, the graphic exemplified the *Star Wars* aesthetic that English professor and poet Daniel Guillory described. The green grid vanishing to the horizon recalled the display on Luke Skywalker's X-wing fighter. As the host on Maryland Public Television's *MotorWeek* (a Saturday treat for me) noted, the actual physical buttons were easier to operate than the ones on the screen. Plus, he said, you have to take your eyes off the road to see the screen.

Things have only gotten worse. Tesla's Model 3 has no dashboard gauges at all and precious few buttons. Owners on the many Tesla fan sites gripe there that the car does not project the vehicle's speed onto the windshield using a "heads-up display" of the type offered by more conventional carmakers. Everything is done via a seventeen-inch touch screen set low between the seats. "A simple swipe of the interactive display opens the all glass panorama roof," says Tesla of its replacement for a sunroof switch. There are radio controls, climate controls, navigation, even a QWERTY keyboard. It's not exactly progress, but it does give the driver a "hyper-individualized experience" because it shows a picture of your car in the correct paint color.

Old-school buttons, dials, and sliders can be found by touch. Not so on a screen. They should be called "look screens." So, why do we have them? They're certainly cheaper and more flexible than having to add ever more buttons to a car's interior. Mostly, though, they are like the blue LED font of old, the style of our time. Kids love screens, but they love touch screens even more.

Touch-screen controls do double duty as video monitors. Consider the backup camera. I can attest to the value of the backup camera because I ran over my tenant for the lack of one. In my defense, I was backing my pickup into the driveway—very slowly and carefully— using my rear-view and side-view mirrors and even turning around. He was sitting down pulling weeds from a crack in the driveway. I didn't hit him very hard, and it was only a few scratches. "I'm a Marine, I can take it," he said. It could have been much worse, for me I mean. Luckily, I got off buying him a six-pack of Mike's Hard Lemonades. Too late I bought the Chuanganzhuo backup camera and monitor kit for about thirty bucks. Boy did I do a good custom install.

NHTSA wasn't so much worried about weeding Marines as the number of children being killed because they were playing behind a car in the driveway when they mandated cameras. About two hundred kids a year die in such accidents. In fact, NHTSA wasn't much worried at all until, as with airbags, distraught parents pushed for the regulation. As of the 2018 model year, all new vehicles must have a backup camera. But during the decade between proposal and implementation, the rule has become an anachronism. It still depends on the driver using the camera at a time when automatic braking systems have become common. The car can look after itself.

Screens are replacing rear-view mirrors and soon may eliminate side-view mirrors as well. Nissan offers a rear-view mirror, as does automotive supplier Gentex, that switches between an actual mirror and a video screen. The screen gives you a hi-def picture and a much wider field of view than a standard reflection can. Trouble is that it's more fun to watch even when what's on the screen is behind you and hence less important than what's in front of your face. Side, or wing, mirrors are going away next in order to reduce drag and thereby improve mileage. They will be replaced by cameras and a screen. In fact, the cameras are already there, although the mirrors persist. I happened to be riding with a friend in her 2017 Honda Pilot. When she'd signal for a lane change, the center display screen would suddenly switch from navigation to a view out the side of the car—the same view afforded by the wing mirror. It felt as if she was channel flipping. I didn't understand the point, but I'm old. Kids love screens.

With the proliferation of cameras, some vehicles now offer a bird's eye view on the screen. You can get one on a high-end Lexus, a mid-market Volvo, or an entry-level Nissan Versa. There's your car, hyper-individualized, as if seen from a bird flying above. They all come with the lawyerly warning: "Check your surroundings for safety." But if I was going to do that, what do I need the camera for? There's no actual bird, of course, not even a drone. The image is a kind of augmented reality, the real world overlaid with computer-generated graphics. It seems like a good idea until they start peppering the image with Pokémons. Or, until the windscreen disappears entirely, replaced by a hi-def simulacrum.

* * * *

EVEN AS THE DRIVING EXPERIENCE becomes mediated through a screen, video screens and the computers behind them are proving quite capable of replicating the real-world experience of driving. In 2011, Jann Mardenborough beat 90,000 other video game players to win a chance to drive a real race car for Nissan Motor Sports. The twenty-six-year-old has been racing for Nissan ever since. I'm not nearly as good.

My only car-guy friend, Bob, invited me to drive his racing simulator. (To protect his identity, I have not used his real name, which is Jonathan.) Divorce is usually a bad thing for everyone involved, unless you're the still married friend of a recent divorcé. Then you get to play with all his new toys. "Any interest in experiencing the state of the art in driving simulation at my dumpy apartment tonight?" Bob asked. "Do I get to drive?" I replied.

I went over late one Wednesday, feeling vaguely naughty for being out on a weeknight. I brought ice cream. Even before the door opened I could smell the Testors aerosol. The intended target was a World War II–era Mustang with a three-foot wingspan. I'd seen the plane before in the correct silver livery with white star on a blue field. Now it was red, all red. A cloud of red still hung in the air. Bob sat on the carpet, oblivious to the paint and the ice cream. I was starting to wonder how well he was taking the divorce. "Come on," I said, "show me the driving game."

I've only driven in a real race once, not counting our timed laps around the Landon School for Boys campus. There I had the fastest time for a 1978 Cutlass. I hit just one bollard and we were able to right it before the headmaster showed up. My only officially sanctioned contest took place in a Detroit parking lot around traffic cones. It was a fairly serious event, as parking lot races around traffic cones go. There was an entrance fee, race officials, timers, and everything. We raced on slicks. I'd been invited by a friend with a vintage Datsun B210. It was sort of a thank you for helping him install an electronic ignition. I did pretty well. In fact, I beat his times, which may be why he never invited me to go racing again.

I didn't do nearly so well in virtual racing. The setup was amazing. Bob had the whole thing wired up to a seat with pedals and a wheel. Modern race car steering wheels are actually square and loaded with buttons and switches—no touch screens at 180 mph. The setup sat a couple of feet from a drive-in-sized screen. From a virtually limitless choice of virtual cars and virtual tracks I chose an old-school open-topped sports car and Watkins Glen, one of the most storied tracks in the country. I lost. So I tried Nürburgring, the track of tracks. Car magazines often reference a model's Nürburgring time as an official measure, akin to horsepower. I did the German track in a Ferrari. After he got tired of watching me, I watched

Bob post an excellent Nürburgring time. Then again, he's divorced and has plenty of time to practice.

The experience left me reflecting on the confluence of real driving and simulated driving. The simulator didn't have a clutch pedal or a stick shift. Instead, behind the square wheel it had a pair of paddle shifters. Pull the left one to shift up, the right, to downshift, without ever taking a hand off the square wheel. They're really nothing more than push buttons that send an electrical signal to the automatic transmission. Pull buttons, to be accurate. Manual transmissions with a foot-pedal clutch and a stick used to offer advantages in terms of fuel economy, ease of repair, and control over the car. Technology has eliminated all of those advantages. The modern automatic shifts faster, with more control, and more efficiently than any human. So the shifter and the manual transmission are going the way of the carburetor on the American automobile. When you use a stick shift, your arm, not your eyes, tells you what gear you're in. Up and to the left, first, down and to the right, fourth. With paddle shifters, you have to look to see what gear you're in.

I try not to blame the kids for all of their screen worship. They're kids after all and anyway I cannot imagine how I would have turned out if instead of five channels plus two snowy ones from Baltimore I had grown up with unlimited "content" on a sixty-three-inch screen in the house, a seventeen-inch screen on my lap, and a six-inch screen in my pocket. I blame the parents. We do try to protect them, limiting "screen time" and haunting them on social media. When it comes to cars, though, our obsession with safety has delivered them into the hands of those evil phones. I speak of the back seat.

In my day we got to sit in the front seat. Sure, the wayback was fun, but the front seat was the winner's circle. "Shotgun!" bands of brothers would yell. "You got it last time." "No, I didn't." "Yesyou-did." "Noididn't." It would go on until a Solomonic parent intervened, "You get it there. You get it on the way home." "Haha." "No fair!" And misery all around. Gauzy nostalgia reminds me of riding on the armrest between my grandparents. Poppa had a boundless Olds '98 in blue on blue with only one catbird seat, and I was in it, gazing down beatifically on Yonkers traffic. Children don't get to gaze through the windshield anymore, beatifically or otherwise. They've been in the back seat since the beginning. The maternity nurse has to check that your baby bucket is properly secured before she'll let you leave the hospital. Kids never get to watch Mom drive, to see the needles move and the lights glow on the instrument panel. The minivan pulls up next to the curb, its wide door slides open like an airlock, and they jump in; they won't look out on the world again until the lock slides open to release them. If Mom drives an SUV (as most moms apparently do now) or Dad drives a four-door pickup (as most dads apparently aspire to do now), the operation is more like ascending a gangplank into the cargo hold. Inside the automotive womb with its high doors and gun-port windows, the little ones might as well be at the bottom of a well. No one gets shotgun, but they still bicker. So giving them screens to watch makes everyone happy, or at least numbed. They are hardly aware of the parents up front; we forget that they are back there. They used to have to ask Mom or Dad, "Are we there yet?" Now they ask the screen. And it knows the answer.

Their banishment began in the 1990s, when airbags started killing children. The story of airbag deaths is worth a brief detour for two reasons. First, it provides yet another example of Detroit's unconscionable response to demands for safer and more environmentally friendly cars. Second, although my interest here is in the way young people have become divorced from the American automobile, I want to acknowledge that that outcome pales in comparison to the loss of life.

On October 15, 1996, Robert Sanders was trying to find the Redskins game on the radio. His daughter Alison, age seven, leaned forward to fiddle with the knobs too. "By the time I looked up, the light turned red," Sanders told a reporter. He braked, but ran into the side of a car that was in the intersection waiting to turn left.

Sanders and his two sons in the back seat were unharmed. Alison suffered massive brain injuries and died the next day. Investigators concluded that the minivan was traveling 9.3 miles an hour at the moment of impact. The airbag that hit Alison was traveling at 200 mph. Sanders couldn't forgive himself for being distracted. But he also told an interviewer, "How was I supposed to know that airbags could kill? I bought the minivan with air bags because I thought they saved lives."

Alison's was not the first airbag death, and by 2007, NHTSA counted 284 confirmed airbag deaths—including 180 children. Automakers blamed NHTSA's requirement that the airbag protect an unbelted "50th percentile male" (five feet, ten inches, and 175 pounds). Smaller drivers, particularly women under five feet, two inches, were at risk because they sat close to the steering wheel air-bag. Similarly, emergency braking sent small passengers, especially children, forward into the path of the airbag. In the language of safety engineering, the occupants were "out of position." Therefore, airbag deaths were not entirely random; as implemented, the tech-nology protected full-sized, unbelted men at the expense of belted or unbelted children. One researcher calculated the issue in stark terms: "Alarmingly, a deploying air bag kills one child for every ten adult passengers it saves." Still, NHTSA defended the technology, crediting airbags with an estimated 24,334 lives saved.

Following his daughter's death, Sanders founded the Parents' Coa-lition for Air Bag Warnings to lobby for action on airbags. Sanders testified passionately before a Senate committee investigating the air-bag crisis. Automakers had known of the danger airbags posed to small occupants, as had NHTSA, since testing began in the 1960s. Furthermore, BMW and Mercedes-Benz had introduced "smart" air-bag technology that could determine the size and position of an occu-pant by the 1980s. Pressed in the hearings by Senator John McCain as to why Detroit had not adopted that technology, representatives of the industry dissembled. They blamed NHTSA's rule. They read from the same script they had used to avoid pollution controls and safety belts: they were working on solutions, but needed time—five years, maybe ten. NHTSA head Ricardo Martinez did not hold the automakers accountable but instead insisted that existing airbags "reduce the chances of fatal injuries for unbelted occupants by more than a third and belted occupants by 20 percent (the actual figures are 14 and 11 percent, respectively). The airbag deaths he attributed to the "speed with which an air bag must inflate." In his testimony, National Transportation Safety Board chairman James Hall diplomatically but firmly disagreed with his NHTSA colleague and supported Sanders. "NHTSA and the industry have been aware of the air bag problem for 25 years, and although they have been working to develop better air bag systems for many years, few vehicles incorporate that technology today," he testified. In fact, studies of airbag deaths showed that sophisticated technology was not needed. Some airbags deployed vertically, against the windshield; others, horizontally, toward the occupant. Only horizontally deploying airbags caused trouble. Nevertheless, NHTSA made no effort to publicize this fact or to identify models with unsafe airbags for consumers. In 1967, NHTSA's first administrator, William Haddon, had declared airbags "the highest priority that the industry and the government . . . should have." Yet after three decades of delay, the agency still deferred to the auto companies and thereby failed to protect the automobile's most vulnerable occupants. Pace Malcolm Gladwell's article *Wrong Turn*, none of this delay was Ralph Nader's fault.

Rather than hold Detroit accountable, NHTSA hurriedly wrote rules allowing dealers to deactivate airbags (either with a switch or permanently) if the driver wrote a nice note to NHTSA explaining why they wanted it done. Eventually, the government formalized the process. To have an on-off switch installed, drivers had to attest to one of the following:

A child age 1 to 12 must ride in the front seat because: My vehicle has no rear seat; Although children ages 1 to 12 ride in the rear seat(s) whenever possible, children ages 1 to 12 sometimes must ride in the front because no space is available in the rear seat(s) of my vehicle; or the child has a medical condition which, according to the child's physician, makes it necessary for the child to ride in the front seat so that the driver can constantly monitor the child's condition.

There were additional affidavits attesting to having read NHTSA's brochure on the subject and waiving liability for the dealer and car maker. The safety agency also put out the message that airbags and seat belts work together. So, the passive safety theory notwithstanding, buckle up.

NHTSA also tried to convince kids that the back seat was cool. In 1997, the agency (working with Chrysler) sent kits to every school to inculcate children into back-seat culture. When they visited a local elementary school that had just received its "back is where it's at" kits, reporters for the *Washington Post* took the pulse of the student body. "Emilia Mahaffey, 10, said although she likes to sit in the front seat because 'you have a better view,' now she will try to sit in back. 'I don't want to get killed,' she said." NHTSA issued warning stickers: "WARNING—DEATH or SERIOUS INJURY can occur. Children 12 and under can be killed by the air bag. The BACK SEAT is the SAFEST place for children." Big Bird did public service announcements, tacked onto the end of Ford minivan commercials. "Remember, kids in the back seat!"

NHTSA finally did require "smart" airbags that sense the weight and position of occupants. But check your sun visor and you will see that the bright yellow warning label is still there. "Even with advanced air bags, children can be killed . . . the back seat is the safest place for children." Never mind that the back seat is the safest place for everyone, the campaign gives parents a choice between following the recommendations or being accused of child endangerment. Strapped in the back seat, entertained by limousine luxuries, why wouldn't they rely on Uber to replace their parental chauffeurs and screens to keep them entertained?

* * * *

IT'S PROM NIGHT. The Jeep is upside down. The Corolla has only a bit of damage to the left front corner but a girl has been ejected. She lies unconscious on its hood. Her prom dress is in remarkably good shape considering she'll be dead in a moment. When the paramedics pull the sheet up over her face, her friend, the driver, wails hysterically. A cop pulls her gently away. A field sobriety test. The handcuffs come out, Miranda is read. As a middle-class white girl, she's been put in the back of the cruiser without the Tasers coming out or the cops shouting profanities. But she was driving drunk and so will be charged with vehicular manslaughter. Call her life ruined. Meanwhile, two other girls are carted off to the hospital in the meat wagon.

Away from the main action, a boy is trapped inside the overturned Jeep. As he tries fruitlessly to wriggle through the window, beer cans spill out almost comically. At first, his friend can only mutter and clasp his hands to his head. Then he gathers himself together and takes a seat among the beer cans. He will buoy the trapped boy's courage until help arrives. From where I'm standing, the trapped boy looks to have only minor injuries and in any case he's feeling no pain. He's a lot luckier than the pair of teens whose young lives have been cut short in this tragedy. Two more, in the prime of life, can look forward to years of rehab before they can walk again.

For all its obvious import, the scene is oddly dull. Collisions between vehicles unleash enormous amounts of energy in a sudden explosive moment. But there's little sign of cataclysm here. In the early 1920s, shards of plate glass would have lacerated everyone. In the 1950s, passengers would have been hurled against chrome knobs and radio grilles, or out an open door, their skin peeled off as they skidded to a stop on the pavement. In the 1970s, a Detroit boat might have torn a Beetle in half. A fuel line might have ruptured and caught fire. Today, the gas stays safely where it belongs and windshields peel away like Tupperware lids. The Corolla's body panels are thin, in part to absorb the impact of a crash. Once the firemen cut the roof support pillars—using a powerful pair of hydraulic scissors hero- ically branded the Jaws of Life—they peel back the roof panel as if it were a can of Maguro. I had high hopes when I first came upon the scene. I'm disappointed that I can't give it more than two stars.

Prom is still two weeks away. Students Against Destructive Deci- sions has decided to stage this car crash in the Swampscott High School parking lot because they are against the kind of destruc- tive decisions that put white girls in the morgue. There's something pathetic about the SADD acronym. It used to stand for Students Against Driving Drunk—a spinoff of sorts from Mothers Against Drunk Driving. The only trouble is, students don't drive drunk much until they're out of high school. But why let a good acronym go to waste? The new organization does things like lobby against marijuana decriminalization (that seems to have backfired). They also lobby for seat belt laws, although every state except "Live Free or Die" New Hampshire already has one.*

The SADD show took a couple of hours away from what in edu- speak is called "time on learning." It was time well spent on a matter of life and death. Or it would have been, if it was having the intended effect on the audience of high schoolers who have shaped up along an embankment. A damp, bone-chilling wind gusts off the ocean at twenty-five miles an hour. Groups of kids are huddled with their backs to the wind and, because of the wind's direction, to this simu- lacrum of a car crash.

The students should return to class SADDER and wiser. Mostly they're just happy to get out of the bitter wind. Did they learn the lesson? Will they stop making Destructive Decisions? Are they con- vinced that the cops will lead them away to jail in handcuffs? "Feh," "Eh," "Mmmm," they vocalize with a shrug. "Allie, I don't want to see you drink and drive," one girl teases another. Granted, kids

---

* Of the forty-nine states with seat belt laws, fifteen do not have "primary enforcement," meaning officers can only issue a ticket if they have stopped the vehicle for another reason. SADD now lobbies to change secondary enforce- ment laws to primary enforcement.

often put a brave face on their fears, but just as likely they've grown inured. The teachers, who spent their own time in the audience destructively deciding to chat among themselves, are unlikely to follow up this powerful lesson. Not to be an apple polisher, but I, for one, did pay attention. The only thing I learned is never to let Molly drive a Jeep. They seem to roll over even idling around the school parking lot.

* * * *

A QUARTER MILE from home, I convince Molly to drive and we switch seats. Some experimentation and a bit of coaching gets the electric seat raised and pitched so she can reach both the pedals and the steering wheel. "Which pedal do I use?"

"The big one is the brake. The little one is the gas."

"I can't see them."

She can't. At four foot ten and three-quarters, her knees are hard against the bolster. I've written the nice note NHTSA requires to get an on-off switch for the airbag. They have sent back official dispensation, but I'm paralyzed by indecision and foreboding.* All she can do is whir the seat back and duck her head underneath. Her left foot finds the brake. I explain that only race car drivers use two feet, but that's what she wants to do. Maybe she's a driving savant. She tries to start the motor. One click (accessories), two clicks (on), then she holds the key against the spring to engage the starter. It turns over once but doesn't start. The Model T is still with us. There's no choke wire running through the minivan radiator and there's no

---

* I find myself in the difficult position of playing the odds with my daughter's life. Like Robert Sanders, I believed NHTSA and thought my minivan safe. Since then I've learned that, given that she always wears a seat belt, the airbag would reduce Molly's risk of injury or death only marginally. What are her chances of being injured by an airbag in a collision that otherwise would have left her unharmed? Life is full of risks, but this is one I'd trusted to the epidemiologists and regulators. The letter will remain in its pile on my desk till I decide my daughter's fate.

danger of a broken thumb, but still she must crank the starter until the explosions take over, just as our forebears did. No more. Newer cars crank themselves at the light touch of a button. Try again. This time she cranks long enough and the smooth Honda motor whispers to life.

I have her move the shift lever down to "D." A dull mechanical clunk passes under us and the van wants to move. Ease up on the brake and we're easing down the road. I am reborn. Driving is new again. A partial transcript of our lesson follows:

"How do you make it go faster?"

"You step on the gas pedal."

"What's the gas pedal?"

"The gas pedal's the one on the right."

"Should I hold the brake down too?"

"No, generally when you use the gas pedal you don't use the brake pedal."

She accelerates and something remarkable happens. She smiles. My Molly never cries when she's hurt, yells when she's angry, or even expresses cheer in my presence. It's actually a bit worrisome. Ah, but at the wheel, a beautiful, shy smile of pure delight breaks through the mask. My closed-lipped little girl exults in her command of the minivan. We haven't shared such joy since budding hormones carried her away. Molly likes to drive. She's not thinking ahead about independence or back on what rules of the road she didn't memorize in driver's ed. Together, we are in the now.

For parents, teaching our children to drive is bittersweet. It's a time of uncommon closeness in the service of letting them fly away. For the first time since Molly learned to make her own waffles, she needs me again. For the first time since I took off her training wheels, there is something I want to teach her that she also wants to learn. And while she's driving, she can sit with me, be with me, without the discomfort of eye contact. I'm right there but she's too scared to take her eyes off the road. I know that one day she'll drive off into the sunset, off to college or with a boy, but for now at least I can hold her to me. The phone sits in the center console and I didn't even have to pry it away.

I know better than anyone that nature has produced nothing so dangerous as a sixteen-year-old behind the wheel. So, I never encouraged Molly to drive; if I had, she probably would have rejected the idea out of hand. It took her over a year to get around to passing her driving test (on the first try). She'll never be a car guy or driving enthusiast of the BMW type. The minivan we've owned for over a decade is good enough for her. She delights in driving just for the sake of it, wandering into the city or out to the coast. I also know better than most how much damage our automotive lifestyle has inflicted on the world. But whatever qualms she may have about contributing to environmental collapse, they're not enough to keep her from filling the tank with gas. Against all of that, I want her to own a car and to take the helm and be the captain. I want her to be in command, to be the one who tells the passive passengers to buckle up and collect the gas money; to say, I know a short cut. And I want driving—the pure experience itself—to rescue her from a life of passive touchscreen consumption. Someday, perhaps, I will apologize to my children, or my grandchildren. I should have done more to protect you, I will say, from the predatory corporations and complicit government that stuffed them into the back seat and screened out the world. For worse, but also for better and of their own accord, generations of Americans have embraced automobility and celebrated ours as an automotive nation. We've been irresponsible and gluttonous to be sure. But we have turned toward ever safer, more efficient, and more luxurious new models year after year. That turning has put our kids on the road to the safest, most efficient, and luxurious cars of all: the car they'll neither own nor drive.

We arrive home, having easily dodged the cars parked along the curb and just barely clipped the tree on the corner with the side mirror (it should buff right out). The final trick is the narrow entrance past the stern of the truck to reach the carriage drive. The curve is as tight as the one below the YMCA and the driveway much narrower.

There's a weeping cherry hard on the left and a mailbox on the right. At least the driveway is flat. Molly does it, slowly, gently, and with growing confidence. She docks the van so the tires are crushing only a small strip of the grass on one side (about as well as her mother does it). Squeezing out of the driver's door, her black gymnastics team bag tangles with the cherry branches. On our way up the front steps I turn over her phone and she clutches it tight again. In a moment she'll be back on the couch, Instagramming, texting, and Snapchatting with her friends. As for me, I hope my baby never quits driving.

Conclusion

CARPETED HIGHWAYS AND BIG YELLOW BIRDS

The author's Saab about to climb onto the Double Arch Bridge and follow the 444-mile-long Natchez Trace Parkway, designated an "All-American Road" and managed by the National Park Service.

I SPENT A LOT OF TIME ON SESAME STREET AS A CHILD, A PLACE where everything was A-OK, and I could meet with friendly neighbors. To be clear, this would have been Sesame Street before Elmo, before Ernie and Bert were enlisted into the culture wars. This was New York before it became a sanitized bodega-less desert of big-box stores. Susan and Bob were young; Mr. Hooper and Jim Henson still lived. It was an integrated neighborhood, black, white, Asian, and Hispanic together. Everything had a lived-in look with a bit of patchwork and beat-up metal trash cans set out. One housed the Grouch. It was how I imagined a New York street, circa 1970, and it made me nostalgic for past I had never known. But my earliest memory is, believe it or not, one of playing cars on the rug. The rug had sinusoidal curves of white against a brown field, tracks just the right width for a Matchbox or a Hot Wheels. The curves intersected in such a way as to make circles, each with four on/off ramps. Inside the circles were squares. I remember the rug as infinite, but I couldn't have been much more than a toddler then, so probably it was finite. I had a Cadillac ambulance that arrived, sirens wooing, whenever there was a crash. Usually it would be a major pileup. Cars often went airborne. The ambulance took only moments to arrive, but there were never any injuries to attend to because the carpeted highways were devoid of people. There were no brownstones, Big Birds, or corner shops like Mr. Hooper's on the rug either. My autonomous cars traced curves through Euclidean space.

Sesame Street was a world of people without cars; my carpeted highway network a world of cars without people. For the last 120 years we have lived in a world that has both. Almost instantly, the car became the ultimate consumer product. Americans bought them the moment they could afford them (and often well before then). Cars offered adventure, independence, social status, and visceral fun. So, we remade our cities, relocated our towns, rearranged our homes, and filled in our open spaces to fit the American automobile. In return, the American automobile provided unprecedented mobility, economic growth, and national prowess. Negotiations between people and cars have not always gone well. Highways tore through the neighborhoods of those too weak to resist them, air became toxic, and people died. There have always been critics and periodic resistance, but as a nation, we mostly embraced automobility.

In the 1970s, however, we Aquarians imagined forcing a no-negotiation, total surrender. I really did think it was end times for cars. Mass transit was cool and a post-oil movie genre was born: *Americathon* (a comedy in which people live in their now permanently parked cars); *Mad Max* and *Mad Max 2* (Mel Gibson rescues a few precious tanks of petrol from a pierced and mohawked gang). In *The Last Chase* Lee Majors and Chris Makepeace race across the country to escape the fascists who have outlawed gasoline. I felt betrayed when automobility not only didn't disappear but metastasized. By the 1990s, Detroit was riding high and mighty on sales of SUVs and pickup trucks.

This time may be different. As consumer values, the nature of work, and our modes of commerce have changed, perhaps the end of the American automobile is nigh. Both Chrysler and GM have already gone essentially bankrupt; Ford might be next. Governments are forcing a switch to EVs. Cities are starting to reverse their car-friendly policies by adding bike lanes and pedestrian spaces. For kids today, getting a license is no longer the universal rite of passage it once was. The death of Detroit and the growing indifference of the young should pave the way for tearing up the pavement. Instead, these changes herald not the end of cars but more, and more brutally efficient, cars.

When we embrace driverless cars, we will surrender our American automobile as an adventure machine, as a tool of self-expression, and the wellspring of our wealth and our defense. We will be left with machines unworthy of love and unable to fill the desires our driven cars now do. Absent the need for Sloanist individuation, these machines will be designed once and churned out by the tens of millions. Yet robot cars will enter an automotive landscape that instantiates myriad moral and political choices made over more than a century and still rehearsed daily.

And make no mistake: the development of driverless cars will flow from the same combination of forces that have carried us from the Model T to the Tesla. Those forces have favored not mobility precisely, but automobility, a system around which we have already remade the world. The tech giants, the Silicon Valley startups, and the global automakers promise that their new driverless machines will not be beholden to those choices, that they will wipe the slate clean. History suggests that they might instead be consumed by them. To paraphrase Marx, "Cars make their own history, but they do not make it as they please."

*   *   *   *

ONE WAY OR ANOTHER, nearly every car eventually meets its end. Most crash, or work their way down the economic ladder until they surrender to the crusher. Recall that when we last saw my, sorry, Keith's Saab it was stuck by a curb in Brooklyn. I feel in my broken heart that it sat up to its hubcaps in blackened New York City slush. After the fiasco with the thirty-six cases of beer, Keith had it towed to a garage. The bill would be $1,000 to keep it running. He faced the brutal tipping point, as when the vet tells you how much it will cost for the dog to get chemo. Is a life worth prolonging just because you can't bear to see it end? The Saab's end of life was even worse for being dragged out needlessly.

He had lost the title, so he couldn't sell or even give the car away. It took several weeks for the state of Massachusetts to get around to sending a duplicate. "During that time the Saab was in the street next to the mechanic's, and twice a week I had to bike down there, in the cold, and sit in the car during alternate side parking so that I wouldn't get a ticket," he tells me. It was like a Swedish debutante from Trollhättan who had traveled to the Big Apple only to end up dead in the gutter with a needle in her arm. When the title finally arrived, he was able to donate the car to a charity, which offered some consolation at least. In the end:

> A guy came with a truck with a huge hook in back. I thought he was going to just stick the hook into the beautiful sky-blue Saab and pick it up that way—I was horrified. But in fact the hook was

for the big chain, which he wrapped around the Saab and onto the hook, and then lifted the Saab. The heavy chain bent the car along the sides as it was lifting it up. The guy got it into the back of his truck and drove away.

I get a small lump in my throat when I imagine that scene. So it has been for millions of car owners over the last 120 years. When a driverless car dies, don't expect anyone to shed a tear.

ACKNOWLEDGMENTS

This book would not exist but for the support and encouragement of my *n + 1* family. I'd like to thank founding editors Keith Gessen and Alison Lorentzen for their encouragement and publisher Mark Krotov for his tireless support. My agent, Edward Orloff, spent many months helping to develop a marketable proposal. My editors at W. W. Norton, Brendan Curry and Nathaniel Dennett, have been endlessly patient and dedicated to the project.

I am especially grateful to friends and colleagues who reviewed drafts, including Professor David N. Gellman, DePauw University, Professor Kevin L. Borg, James Madison University, Professor Ben Gross, Salem State University, and Dr. Daniel Blower, research scientist emeritus, University of Michigan Transportation Research Institute.

Christopher O'Neil of the National Transportation Safety Board, Russ Rader of the Insurance Institute for Highway Safety, Lawrence Gustin of the *Flint Journal,* Todd Gurney, program director of the Massachusetts state Driver Education program, and Ben Hamper, author of *Rivethead*, proved that all the Googling in the world doesn't measure up to a conversation with the right person.

I thank the archivists and librarians at the Hagley Museum and Library, The Henry Ford, GM Heritage Center, Northwestern University Archives, the Ransom Center Archives, the University of Michigan Libraries, Salem State University Library, and the Abbot Public Library.

The following people also provided insights and expertise: Paul Feffer, Sara Harris, Paul Heuper, Monty Hindman, Thomas Imhoff, Jonathan Linde, Alan Ponsford, Robert Schneider, Nicky Tobolski, Sue Vancellete Walker, Pamela Waxman, and Tom and Eva Wedel.

Thank you Rachael, Joey, Molly, and Melissa for your love.

I alone am responsible for any omissions and errors.

NOTES

Introduction: A NATION OF DRIVERS

3   "we borrowed that": Keith Gessen, email message to author, May 27, 2015.

5   14 percent in 2014: Stacy C. Davis and Susan W. Diegel, *Transportation Energy Data Book*, 35th ed. (Oak Ridge, TN: Oak Ridge National Laboratory, 2016), Table 3.12.

6   "South America following along": Daniel Sperling and Deborah Gordon, *Two Billion Cars* (New York: Oxford University Press, 2009).

6   drivers to drive them: Davis and Diegel, Table 8.1.

Chapter 1: THE FIRST REVOLUTION: LET'S REVIEW

16   "and turned a somersault, a complete wreck": Eugene S. Ferguson, *Early Engineering Reminiscences (1815–40) of George Escol Sellers* (Washington, DC: Smithsonian Institution, 1965), 46.

16   still steaming mad: "The Great Race of 1878," Farm Collector, accessed July 8, 2015, http://www.farmcollector.com/steam-traction/the-great-race-of-1878.aspx.

17   "We waited until 1895": quoted in John Bell Rae, *The American Automobile: A Brief History* (Chicago: University of Chicago Press, 1965), 6.

17   "not mechanical inefficiency": Clay McShane, *Down the Asphalt Path* (New York: Columbia University Press, 1995), 97.

17   not the right technology: Rae, 13, 15.

18   "a revolution in the auto industry": Mary Barra, "The Next Revolution in the Auto Industry," World Economic Forum, Jan. 21, 2016, https://

www.weforum.org/agenda/2016/01/the-next-revolution-in-the-car
-industry/.

18 **"we do in about all things else"**: "The Bicycle and Automobile Show,"
New York Times, Jan. 22, 1899.

19 **"a most fascinating pleasure"**: Henry Dey, "Notes on the Show," *The
Horseless Age*, Nov. 7, 1900, 52.

19 **worth a total of $250,000**: "Owned by Five Millionaires," *The Motor
World*, Feb. 26, 1903, 6. See also: Timothy Messer-Kruse, *Tycoons,
Scorchers, and Outlaws: The Class War That Shaped American Auto
Racing* (New York: Palgrave Macmillan, 2013).

19 **wreck and survived**: "Tué Dans Une Course d'Automobiles," *L'Aurore*,
Apr. 2, 1903.

19 **$30,000 a year keeping his ten cars**: "Spend Nearly $30,000 a Year Each
on Autos," *New York Times*, Oct. 10, 1905.

20 **(92 mph) at Daytona, which is nuts**: "Vanderbilt Cup Races (blog)
Translation: May 1902 La Stampa Sportiva: Vanderbilt, Jr., Breaks
the One-Kilometer Land Speed Record," accessed Dec. 7, 2017,
http://www.vanderbiltcupraces.com/blog/article/1902_la_stampa
_sportiva_william_k._vanderbilt_jr._breaks_the_one_kilometer.

20 **"as cocaine is to mortality"**: "A Millionaire's Misery," *Journal*, Aug.
23, 1901, 16.

21 **"through my heart"**: "The Founding and Manifesto of Futurism," *Italian Futurism* (blog), Aug. 22, 2008, https://www.italianfuturism.org
/manifestos/foundingmanifesto/.

21 **"The operator was arrested"**: *Scientific American*, 1896, 377–78.

22 **"through which he recklessly whizzes"**: *New York Times*, May 5, 1902.

24 **women's place in society**: "The Moral Threat of Bicycles in the 1890s,"
JSTOR Daily (blog), Feb. 22, 2016, https://daily.jstor.org/the-moral
-threat-of-bicycles-in-the-1890s/.

24 *A Bicycling Idyll*: H. G. Wells, *The Wheels of Chance: A Bicycling Idyll*
(New York: Macmillan, 1896).

24 **two years later**: Maurice Leblanc, *Voici des ailes* (Paris: Ollendorff,
1898).

24 **"over the ordinary highway"**: Quoted in Rae, 6.

25 **Steamers were all but gone**: Rudi Volti, "Why Internal Combustion?"
Invention & Technology 6, no. 2 (1990): 42.

26 **"like a calf"**: W. Bernard Carlson, *Innovation as a Social Process: Elihu*

Thomson and the Rise of General Electric (New York: Cambridge University Press, 2003), 332.

26 **"fewer than 60 miles":** Volti, 44.

26 **on a single charge:** Gijs Mom, *The Electric Vehicle: Technology and Expectations in the Automobile Age* (Baltimore, MD: Johns Hopkins University Press, 2004), 357.

26 **"places on the main lines of travel":** "Automobile Show," *New York Times*, Nov. 8, 1900.

26 **she won by ten minutes:** Volti, 44.

27 **"a journey fully prearranged cannot give":** *Engineering World* 9, no.2 (1902): 79.

28 **"Christians felt the Cross":** Henry Adams, *The Education of Henry Adams* (Washington, DC: Adams, 1907), 332.

28 **"decided me to sail for America":** "Edison Pioneers," Elihu Thomson Papers, American Philosophical Society Mss. Coll. 74.

29 **"and trolley companies":** Robert H. Wiebe, *The Search for Order, 1877–1920* (Westport, CT: Greenwood Press, 1980); Sam Bass Warner, *Streetcar Suburbs: The Process of Growth in Boston, 1870–1900*, Publications of the Joint Center for Urban Studies (Cambridge, MA: Harvard University Press, 1962).

29 **"to sit over an explosion":** Quoted in Rae, 11.

30 **"We are on the wrong track":** Hiram Percy Maxim, *Horseless Carriage Days* (New York: Harper & Brothers, 1937).

31 **a long-term service contract:** David Kirsch, *The Electric Vehicle and the Burden of History* (New Brunswick, NJ: Rutgers University Press, 2000), 51.

31 **"leave them at their country places":** "Progress of the Electric Vehicle Company," *Horseless Age: The Automobile Trade Magazine*, Jan. 1899, 13.

32 **"force" electrics on a "credulous world":** *Horseless Age,* Nov. 17, 1899, 7.

32 **"floater(s) of watered stock companies":** Mom, 91.

32 **"to give the motive power a black eye irrespective of its real merits":** *Electrical World and the Engineer,* July 19, 1902, 79.

32 **the technology was highly refined:** "1914 Detroit Electric Model 47 Brougham, Personal Car of Clara Ford—The Henry Ford," accessed Dec. 18, 2017, https://www.thehenryford.org/artifact/209957/.

Chapter 2: THE CAR FOR PEOPLE WHO HAVE NONE

35 **"any ordinary inclination":** George B. Selden, Road Engine, 549160, filed May 8, 1879, and issued Nov. 5, 1895.

35 **oversees standardization:** Lawrence Howard Seltzer, *A Financial History of the American Automobile Industry: A Study of the Ways in Which the Leading American Producers of Automobiles Have Met Their Capital Requirements*, Hart, Schaffner & Marx Prize Essays, XLIV (Boston: Houghton Mifflin, 1928), 39–44; Allan Nevins and Frank Ernest Hill, *Ford* (New York: Arno Press, 1976), 1: 293–94.

36 **"Let them try":** Nevins and Hill, 296.

37 **"farm I loved":** Caryn Hannan, *Michigan Biographical Dictionary: A-I* (North American Book Dist LLC, 1998), 250.

37 **"farms of the time":** Henry Ford and Samuel Crowther, *My Life and Work* (Garden City, NY, Doubleday, Page & Company, 1922), 22.

37 **milking her twice a day:** Reynold M. Wik, *Henry Ford and Grass-Roots America*, 1st ed. (Ann Arbor: University of Michigan Press, 1972), 148.

37 **engineer with questions:** Ford and Crowther, 22–23.

38 **to deliver them:** Ford and Crowther, 58–59.

38 **behind his back:** Ford and Crowther, 23.

38 **he moved the family:** Ford and Crowther, 29.

38 **three hundred watches on hand:** Ford and Crowther, 24.

39 **Pennington in *American Machinist*:** John Randol, "The Kane-Pennington Motor," *American Machinist* 18, no. 45 (1895): 881–83+; John Randol, "The Kane-Pennington Motor - II," *American Machinist* 19, no. 2 (1896): 8–11; Nevins and Hill, 1: 142–43.

39 **back to Detroit:** Nevins and Hill, 1: 160–61.

39 **Ford claimed later:** Ford and Crowther, 36.

40 **"if I had it":** Nevins and Hill, 1: 205.

41 **"¢s at Manufacturing":** Sidney Olson, *Young Henry Ford* (Detroit: Wayne State University Press, 1963), 153.

41 **the Springfield Armory:** David A. Hounshell, *From the American System to Mass Production, 1800–1932: The Development of Manufacturing Technology in the United States*, Studies in Industry and Society 4 (Baltimore, MD: Johns Hopkins University Press, 1984), 5.

41 **worked with him:** Nevins and Hill, 1: 192–93.

42 **"'unlimited class'":** "Detroit Races Thrill Thousands of Visitors," *Automobile and Motor Review* 4, no. 34 (1902): 9–12.

42 **"abundance of enthusiasm"**: "Detroit Races," 12.

43 **company's financial position:** Russ Banham, *The Ford Century: Ford Motor Company and the Innovations That Shaped the World* (New York: Artisan Books, 2002). The story of invoice weighing is told often and in different guises. It is one of those stories too good to check.

43 **weight of 2,100 pounds:** Robert D. Dluhy, *American Automobiles of the Brass Era: Essential Specifications of 4,000+ Gasoline Powered Passenger Cars, 1906–1915, with a Statistical and Historical Overview* (Jefferson, NC: McFarland & Company, 2013), 63, 78, 103–4.

43 **"rambled right along":** Billy Murray, Byron Gay, and Walter B. Rogers, "The Little Ford Rambled Right Along," Record (Camden, NJ: Victor, 1915), https://www.loc.gov/item/jukebox.1307/.

44 **until the end:** T. P. Newcomb and R. T. Spurr, *A Technical History of the Motor Car* (Bristol, Eng.: A. Hilger, 1989), 236–37.

46 **brushes the ground:** Floyd Clymer, *Henry's Wonderful Model T, 1908–1927* (New York: McGraw-Hill, 1955), 11.

46 **tremulously disastrous results:** Wik, 108–9 passim.

46 **which was true:** " 'Notice to Dealers, Importers, Agents and Users of Gasoline Automobiles.' Advertisement," *Detroit Free Press*, July 28, 1903.

46 **"third in the United States":** William Greenleaf, *Monopoly on Wheels: Henry Ford and the Selden Automobile Patent* (Detroit: Wayne State University Press, 2011), 116.

47 **garnered enormous press:** David L. Lewis, *The Public Image of Henry Ford: An American Folk Hero and His Company* (Detroit: Wayne State University Press, 1987), 24.

47 **anyone who bought his cars:** Greenleaf, viii; Lewis, 22.

47 **"attend to the tom toms":** Frederick Russell, "Advertising Turned the Tide in the Automobile Industry," *Advertising & Selling*, July 13, 1927; W. R. Hotchkin, "Early Adventures in Advertising: How Advertising Helped Wanamaker during the Fight over the Selden Patents," *Printers' Ink Monthly*, Sept. 1920.

47 **Ford prevailed:** Donna Harris, "Landmark Patent Case Broke Selden's Lock on Auto Industry," *Automotive News*, June 16, 2003; Nevins and Hill, 415–46.

47 *Detroit Free Press*: Lewis, 23–24.

47 **"Love Feast":** "Auto Show Draws Big Society Crowd," *New York Times*, Jan. 13, 1911.

48 **for everybody concerned:** quoted in Nevins and Hill, 2:99.

49 **he boasted:** James Sweinhart, "How 'Wall Street' Saved Henry Ford," *Detroit News*, June 22, 1921.

49 **"other encouraging conditions":** J. L. Garvin, "The Case for Capitalism," *New York Times*, Sept. 12, 1926.

50 **great man in Dearborn:** "Finds Ford Is a Real Study in Contrasts," *Brooklyn Daily Eagle*, Mar. 14, 1932.

50 **"must be broken down":** "The Mussolini of Highland Park," *New York Times*, Jan. 8, 1928; "Urge Ford to Reject German Decoration; Jewish War Veterans Call on Him to Repudiate Nazi Award," *New York Times*, Aug. 7, 1938.

50 **in this instance:** Nevins and Hill, 1:621.

50 **ahead of Mussolini:** Lewis, 215, 232.

50 **"God preserve him":** Wik, 4.

50 **the *New York Times* reported:** "Berlin Hears Ford Is Backing Hitler," *New York Times*, Dec. 20, 1922.

51 **from Hitler's Reich:** "Hitler Acclaimed by 200,000 in Fete; Wild Scenes of Enthusiasm Mark Parade of Athletes at the Breslau Festival; Sudetens Break Ranks 40,000 Swarm Around Stand of Chancellor and Girls Give Flowers in Homage," *New York Times*, Aug. 1, 1938.

51 **Lindbergh got one:** "Ford, at 75, Looks to 'Going Ahead,'" *New York Times*, July 31, 1938.

51 **"of American life":** *The International Jew: The World's Foremost Problem, Being a Reprint of a Series of Articles Appearing in The Dearborn Independent from May 22 to October 2, 1920* (Dearborn, MI: The Dearborn Publishing Co., 1920).

51 **they got home:** "Ford's Anti-Semitism | American Experience | PBS," accessed Feb. 12, 2018, http://www.pbs.org/wgbh/americanexperience/features/henryford-antisemitism/.

51 **a public apology:** Nevins and Hill, 2:317–20.

51 **a baseline anti-Semitism:** Nevins and Hill, 1:618.

51 **cosmopolitan and greedy:** Neil Baldwin, *Henry Ford and the Jews: The Mass Production of Hate* (New York: PublicAffairs, 2002); Ronald R. Stockton, "McGuffey, Ford, Baldwin, and the Jews," *Michigan Historical Review* 35, no. 2 (2009): 85–96.

52 **"white man at the other":** "Portrait of William Perry, circa 1890—The Henry Ford," accessed Feb. 12, 2018, https://www.thehenryford.org/collections-and-research/digital-collections/artifact/338479/.

52 **"we have known":** Wik, 5.

52 **boy's world view:** Norman Pollack, "The Myth of Populist Anti-Semitism," *The American Historical Review* 68, no. 1 (1962): 76–80, https://doi.org/10.2307/1847185.

53 **elements of writing style:** E. B. White and Richard L. Strout, *Farewell to Model T* (New York: G. P. Putnam's Sons, 1936); E. B. White, "Farewell, My Lovely!" *New Yorker*, May 9, 1936, https://www.newyorker.com/magazine/1936/05/16/farewell-my-lovely.

54 **"or Thomas Jefferson":** Wik, 3.

54 **styling and comfort:** "General Motors Corporation—1922," Annual Report, 20.

55 **"the panting tension":** Sinclair Lewis, *Babbitt* (London: Cape, 1922), 13.

Chapter 3: GM'S SLOAN: WE'RE NOT IN KANSAS ANYMORE

57 **opening day in January:** "Optimism Reigns As Auto Show Opens; More Than 350 Cars Viewed by Large Crowd in Grand Central Palace," *New York Times*, Jan. 7, 1923.

58 **"don't cause service problems":** David Conwill, "Copper Cooled Calamity: The 1923 Chevrolet Series C | Hemmings Daily," *Hemmings Motor News*, Apr. 20, 2016, https://www.hemmings.com/blog/2016/04/20/Copper Cooled-calamity-the-1923-chevrolet-series-c/.

59 **"produced in the automobile world":** Quoted in John McDonald, *A Ghost's Memoir: The Making of Alfred P. Sloan's "My Years with General Motors"* (Cambridge, MA: MIT Press, 2002), 45.

60 **"mania for stock speculation":** Quoted in Lawrence R. Gustin, *Billy Durant: Creator of General Motors*, updated, expanded ed. (Ann Arbor: University of Michigan Press, 2012), 29.

61 **"the benefit of cheap transportation":** Gustin, 100.

61 **secured a license:** "Enlivens the Licensed Meeting," *Motor World*, May 13, 1909, 241–42; "Orders Olds's License Cancelled," *Motor World*, Sept. 24, 1908, 897.

63 **"immediately on a profitable basis":** Gustin, 112–13.

63 **"made Shylock crimson with shame":** Nevins and Hill, 1:314.

64 **lieutenant put it:** Alfred P. Sloan Jr., *My Years with General Motors*, edited by John McDonald with Catharine Stevens (New York: Doubleday/Currency, 1990), 11.

64 "we left the room": quoted in Sloan, 32–38.

65 "bear the thought of an automobile": Gustin, 247.

65 "what act I will like best": Quoted in Sloan, 77.

67 "as you could wish for": Sloan, 42.

67 "telling people what to do": Sloan, 54.

67 "an engineering dream": Sloan, 152.

68 "a touch of individuality to the car": H. A. Tarantous, "Big Improvement in 1925 Cars," *New York Times*, Jan. 4, 1925.

68 were now matched with bright exteriors: "Salon Shows Cars of Brighter Hues," *New York Times*, Nov. 29, 1927.

69 "the high water mark in color harmony": "Finds Auto Show Blaze of Beauty," *New York Times*, Jan. 14, 1927.

70 "correct machine for the journey—a Hispano Suiza": Ralph Stein, *The Treasury of the Automobile* (New York: Golden Press, 1961), 152.

71 "see how they take you": Sloan, 270.

71 "'I want you to fix him'": "The Reminiscences of William L. Mitchell," *Automobile in American Life and Society*, accessed Feb. 16, 2018, http://www.autolife.umd.umich.edu/Design/Mitchell/mitchellinterview.htm.

71 "as compared with the new one": Sloan, 265.

72 "and woe to the company which ignores them": Sloan, 265.

74 "glass in the windshield": Joel W. Eastman, *Styling vs. Safety: The American Automobile Industry and the Development of Automotive Safety, 1900–1966* (Lanham, MD: University Press of America, 1984), 178.

74 "expense to buyers of cars": Eastman, 178–80.

76 forward toward commercialization: "Charles F. Kettering and the 1921 Discovery of Tetraethyl Lead," May 18, 2013, http://www.environmentalhistory.org/billkovarik/about-bk/research/cabi/ket-tel/, accessed Sept. 28, 2017.

76 "the poison hazard": Quoted in David R. Farber, *Sloan Rules: Alfred P. Sloan and the Triumph of General Motors* (Chicago: University of Chicago Press, 2002), 82.

77 "hushed, obedient power": "Signal Oil Advertisement," aired during *The Whistler*, Nov. 4, 1951.

77 "a magnificent Stutz": Quoted in Luis Girón Echevarría, "The Automobile as a Central Symbol in F. Scott Fitzgerald," *Revista Alicantina de Estudios Ingleses* vol. 6 (1993), 73.

77 **"sexiest cars of the period"**: Jay Leno's Garage, "1918 Stutz Bearcat—Jay Leno's Garage," YouTube, accessed Aug. 23, 2018, https://www.youtube.com/watch?v=tzr43iLxmmw.

Chapter 4: AUTOMOTIVE ANXIETY DURING THE GREAT DEPRESSION

79 **"brought a smile to their faces"**: John Heidenry, *Theirs Was the Kingdom: Lila and DeWitt Wallace and the Story of the* Reader's Digest (New York: W. W. Norton, 1995), 13.

80 **"flayed off at once"**: J. C. Furnas, "—And Sudden Death: The Reader's Digest Classic," *Reader's Digest* (blog), Aug. 1935, https://www.rd.com/culture/and-sudden-death-readers-digest/.

81 **liability insurance reform:** Arthur A. Ballantine, "After 'Sudden Death,'" *Survey Graphic*, Feb. 1936.

81 **centerpiece of his obituary:** "J. C. Furnas, Wry Historian of American Life, Dies at 95," *New York Times*, June 12, 2001.

81 **the article as a factor in their career:** Franklin Kreml, "Interview with Franklin M. Kreml by Kevin Leonard and Mary Roy," Magnetic Tape (Evanston, IL, 1991), Accession 283: 91–44, Tape 1, Side A, Northwestern University Archives; Patricia Waller in discussion with the author, Apr. 13, 1995; Tom Mahoney, *The Story of George Romney: Builder, Salesman, Crusader* (New York: Harper, 1960), 115; see Mahoney on Ralph Nader and Furnas.

83 **"protection and health"**: Buck v. Bell, 274 US 200 (Supreme Court 292AD).

84 **motor vehicle taxes:** James J. Flink, *The Automobile Age* (Cambridge, MA: MIT Press, 1988), 188.

84 **"reshaping society to fit the automobile"**: Quoted in Flink, 188.

84 **increased by 50 percent between 1929 and 1931:** Wesley C. Mitchell, ed., *Recent Social Trends in the United States: Report of the President's Research Committee on Social Trends, with a Foreword by Herbert Hoover* (New York: McGraw-Hill, 1933), 909.

84 **"so costly as to require a scheme for time payments"**: Daniel J. Boorstin, *The Americans: The Democratic Experience* (New York: Vintage, 1974), 423.

85 **new car sales:** Flink, 191.

85 **"to keep Jim Couzens from making a speech":** Nevins and Hill, 2:11–15.

86 **fell by only 10 percent:** Joseph Interrante, "The Road to Autopia: The Automobile and the Spatial Transformation of American Culture," in *The Automobile and American Culture* (Ann Arbor: University of Michigan Press, 1991), 89–104.

86 **per capita rose slightly:** Flink, 134.

86 **"despite six years of Depression":** Robert Staughton Lynd and Helen Merrell Lynd, *Middletown in Transition: A Study in Cultural Conflicts* (New York: Harcourt, Brace and Company, 1937), 265.

86 **"cling to it as they cling to self respect":** Lynd and Lynd, 26.

86 **$500 for an unexpected car repair:** Jonnelle Marte, "Nearly 30 Percent of Americans Are One Emergency Away from Financial Ruin," *Washington Post*, June 23, 2015, https://www.washingtonpost.com/news /get-there/wp/2015/06/23/a-quarter-of-americans-are-one-emergency -away-from-financial-ruin/; Janna Herron, "Americans Still Lack Savings Despite Bigger Paychecks—Financial Security Index | Bankrate.Com," Bankrate, June 23, 2015, http://www.bankrate .com/banking/savings/americans-still-lack-savings-despite-bigger -paychecks/.

88 **to achieve its ends:** Sloan, 405–6.

89 **worse than useless:** Sloan, 11.

90 **"filtering through continuously":** William P. Eno, "Are Block Lights Worth While?" *The Pathfinder* 17 (Aug. 1929).

90 **"after a thorough trial":** Miller McClintock, *Street Traffic Control* (New York: McGraw-Hill, 1925), 136.

91 **"with his hand on the pile of reports":** Samuel Grafton, "Traffic Engineer," *American Mercury*, July 1933, 335–40.

92 **"which involve violations of the traffic laws":** Curtis Billings, "Traffic Crimes and Criminals," *The Atlantic Monthly*, Oct. 1933.

92 **he pleads guilty and pays a $25 fine:** Russell Holt Peters, "Death on the Highway II," *Forum*, Mar. 1935, 181.

92 **support for stricter enforcement was overwhelming:** George Gallup, *The Gallup Poll: Public Opinion, 1935–1971* (New York: Random House, 1972), 11 (poll taken Jan. 26, 1936); 148 (poll taken Apr. 7, 1939); 1,397 (poll taken Feb. 8, 1956).

92 **traffic psychotechnologist:** A. R. Boone, "Insanity at the Wheel," *Scientific American*, Oct. 1, 1939.

93 **psychophysical tests that "patients" underwent:** Lowell S. Selling, "The Orthopsychiatry of the Young Traffic Offender" (Detroit, 1941?), Recorders Court Psychopathic Clinic; Lowell Sinn Selling, "The Young Traffic Offender," *The American Journal of Orthopsychiatry* 12, no. 2 (1942): 241–50.

93 **was labeled "senile":** Daniel M. Albert, "Primitive Drivers: Racial Science and Citizenship in the Motor Age," *Science as Culture* 10, no. 3 (2001): 327–51; Daniel M. Albert, "Psychotechnology and Insanity at the Wheel," *Journal of the History of the Behavioral Sciences* 35, no. 3 (1999): 291–305.

93 **"not too pleasant looking":** Albert, "Primitive Drivers."

94 **psychologist Harry R. DeSilva:** Harry R. DeSilva, "Applications of Driver Clinics," *The Journal of Psychology* 6 (Oct. 1938): 233–41, https://doi.org/10.1080/00223980.1938.9917600.

94 **were the worst:** Harry R. DeSilva, "Normal Versus Accident Drivers," *The Journal of Psychology* 7, no. 2 (1939): 337–42, https://doi.org/10.1080/00223980.1939.9917640.

94 **"justice and equality":** R. L. Burgess, "Can You Get a Square Deal in Traffic Court?" *American Magazine*, Dec. 19, 1932.

95 **"respect for the law is destroyed":** Thomas Compere, "Telling It to the Judge," *Forum*, 1930; Gerald S. Levin, "Traffic Courts: The Judge's Responsibility," *American Bar Association Journal* 46, no. 2 (1960): 143–224.

95 **traffic violations alone:** Howard James, "Courts for the Common Man," in *Criminal Justice: Law and Politics*, 2nd ed. (North Scituate, MA: Duxbury Press, 1976), 355–71.

95 **"car owning millionaire":** Clay McShane, *Down the Asphalt Path* (New York: Columbia University Press, 1995), 185; see also Peter D. Norton, *Fighting Traffic: The Dawn of the Motor Age in the American City* (Cambridge, MA: MIT Press, 2011) and Tom Vanderbilt, *Traffic* (New York: Vintage, 2008), 11.

95 **"test of its utility":** McClintock, 146.

96 **reprinted and adapted together:** Anedith Nash, "Death on the Ridge Road: Grant Wood and Modernization in the Midwest," *Prospects* 8 (Oct. 1983): 281–301, https://doi.org/10.1017/S0361233300003781.

96 **"simple, elemental existence":** James M. Dennis, *Renegade Regionalists: The Modern Independence of Grant Wood, Thomas Hart Benton, and John Steuart Curry* (Madison: University of Wisconsin Press, 1998); Grant Wood, *Death on the Ridge Road*, 1935, oil on masonite, 81.6 × 99.2 × 3.3 cm, 1935, 47.1.3, Williams College Museum of Art.

Chapter 5: THE HIDDEN HISTORY OF THE SUPERHIGHWAYS THAT TRANSFORMED AMERICA

99 **as drivers ease through them:** See *A Policy on Geometric Design of Highways and Streets*, 7th ed. (Washington, DC: American Association of State Highway Transportation Officials, 2018).

100 **three north-south routes:** "Ted Holmes on Thomas MacDonald and Herbert Fairbank—History of FHWA—Highway History—Federal Highway Administration," accessed Aug. 24, 2018, https://www.fhwa .dot.gov/infrastructure/holmes.cfm.

100 **FDR and the Congress:** *Toll Roads and Free Roads*, 76th Congress, 1st Sess. House. Doc. 272 (Washington, DC: Government Printing Office, 1939), https://catalog.hathitrust.org/Record/001611706.

100 **cut up and encircled:** *Our Cities: Their Role in the National Economy* (Washington, DC: Government Printing Office, 1937), http://hdl .handle.net/2027/mdp.39015002610148.

101 **"good for General Motors, and vice versa":** Wilson has often been misquoted in a way that seems to put GM ahead of the country. Ellen Terrell, "When a Quote Is Not (Exactly) a Quote: General Motors | Inside Adams: Science, Technology & Business," webpage, Apr. 22, 2016, https:// blogs.loc.gov/inside_adams/2016/04/when-a-quote-is-not-exactly -a-quote-general-motors/.

102 **"choices people should make":** George Will, "Why Liberals Love Trains," *Newsweek*, Feb. 27, 2011, http://www.newsweek.com/2011/02/27/high -speed-to-insolvency.html.

102 **sand, cement, and asphalt in the system:** "Materials in Use in U.S. Interstate Highways," fact sheet (Denver, CO: USGS, Feb. 2006), https:// pubs.usgs.gov/fs/2006/3127/2006-3127.pdf.

103 **"planned places of entry":** Paul G. Hoffman and Neil McCullough

Clark, *Seven Roads to Safety: A Program to Reduce Automobile Accidents* (New York: Harper & Brothers, 1939), 37.

103 **"to cause them":** Hoffman and Clark, 39.

104 **"and breathe ozone":** "Firing Thomas H. MacDonald-Twice—History of FHWA—Highway History—Federal Highway Administration," accessed Nov. 28, 2017, https://www.fhwa.dot.gov/infrastructure/firing.cfm.

105 **"no black tie":** Mark Rose, *Interstate: Express Highway Politics 1939–1989* (Knoxville: University of Tenessee Press, 1990), 11.

105 **in that appendix:** *Toll Roads*, x.

106 **"of higher dignity":** *Toll Roads*, 94.

106 **the city to save it:** Daniel Albert, "The Highway and the City," in *City by City: Dispatches from the American Metropolis*, ed. Keith Gessen and Stephen Squibb, 1st ed. (New York: n + 1/Farrar, Straus and Giroux, 2015), 261–76.

107 **"troops to the theater":** "Status of the Nation's Highways, Bridges and Transit: Conditions and Performance: Report to Congress," 2004, https://www.fhwa.dot.gov/policy/2004cpr/.

108 **"idealized political subjectivity":** Cotton Seiler, "Anxiety and Automobility: Cold War Individualism and the Interstate Highway System" (PhD dissertation, University of Kansas, 2002), ii. (As quoted includes part of official dissertation abstract.)

109 **and over rivers:** Joseph F. DiMento and Cliff Ellis, *Changing Lanes: Visions and Histories of Urban Freeways* (Cambridge, MA: MIT Press, 2013); Louis Ward Kemp, "Aesthetes and Engineers: The Occupational Ideology of Highway Design," *Technology & Culture* 27, no. 4 (1986): 759–97; William Brewster Snow, *The Highway and the Landscape* (New Brunswick, NJ: Rutgers University Press, 1959).

Chapter 6: MIDCENTURY FLYING CARS

114 **the American navy:** "Admiral Isoroku Yamamoto," Pearl Harbor Memorials, Aug. 17, 2013, https://pearlharbormemorials.com/admiral-isoroku-yamamoto/; Hiroyuki Agawa, *The Reluctant Admiral: Yama-*

moto and the Imperial Navy, new ed. (Tokyo: Kodansha America, 2000), 221, 268, 329. On Porsche, see Flink, 268.

116 **to get more rations:** "Cars Made 'Trucks' to Evade Rationing," *New York Times,* May 9, 1942.

118 **into the sky:** Thomas E. Stimson, Jr., "Here's Your Helicopter Coupe," *Popular Mechanics,* Feb. 1951.

118 **"a flying car":** "Airbus—Future of Urban Mobility," Future of urban mobility My kind of flyover, accessed Jan. 18, 2017, http://www.airbus group.com/int/en/news-media/corporate-magazine/Forum-88/My-Kind -Of-Flyover.html#. The program has since been rebranded as Vahana.

119 **"rushing like moles":** Quoted in Joseph J. Corn, *The Winged Gospel: America's Romance with Aviation, 1900–1950* (New York: Oxford University Press, 1983), 92.

120 *New York World-Telegram* **reported:** Quoted in Corn, 101.

120 **"For Them, Bombs":** Michael S. Sherry, *The Rise of American Air Power: The Creation of Armageddon* (New Haven, CT: Yale University Press, 1987).

120 **proclaimed GM:** A thematic treatment of car ads is found in V. Dennis Wrynn, *Detroit Goes to War: The American Automobile Industry in World War II* (Osceola, WI: Motorbooks International, 1993).

121 **units *a year*:** Press reports quoted in David L. Lewis, *The Public Image of Henry Ford: An American Folk Hero and His Company* (Detroit: Wayne State University Press, 1987), 348–50.

121 **written in 1943:** Glendon Swarthout, *Willow Run: A Novel* (New York: Thomas Y. Crowell, 1943).

122 **U-turn at sea:** "Jet-Propelled Plane Flies Here from Dayton, 544 Mi., in 62 Min.," *New York Times,* Aug. 2, 1945.

122 **a "blow job":** " 'Fastest Airplane' Revealed by Army," *New York Times,* Aug. 1, 1945.

122 **"as landing fields":** "Future Air Traffic Control," *Flying Magazine,* Feb. 1944, 74.

122 **"dress of tomorrow":** "Trade to Test Helicopter," *New York Times,* Aug. 28, 1944.

123 **what the government did:** American Historical Association, Historical Service Board, and United States Armed Forces Institute, "Will There Be a Plane in Every Garage?" (Washington DC; Government Printing Office, 1945), http://archive.org/details/WillThereBeAplaneInEveryGarage.

123 **definite plans to buy one:** Corn, 108.

123 **the store advertised:** "Macy's Ercoupe" (advertisement), *New York Times*, Sept. 23, 1945, 11.

125 **wound up in prison:** Jim Donnelly, "Three Wheeling—1948 Davis," *Hemmings Motor News*, Apr. 2005, https://www.hemmings.com /magazine/hcc/2005/04/Three-Wheeling---1948-Davis/1280664 .html.

126 **"supplies he needed":** Abigail Tucker, "The Tucker Was the 1940s Car of the Future," *Smithsonian Magazine*, Dec. 2012, http://www .smithsonianmag.com/history/the-tucker-was-the-1940s-car-of-the -future-135008742/.

127 **did their bidding:** Ibid.; Jeff Menne, *Francis Ford Coppola* (Urbana: University of Illinois Press, 2014), 16.

127 **"near its price class":** "Cross Section: Some Stand Out Features," *Consumer Reports*, May 1953, 206.

129 **commented on his failure:** John Brooks, *The Fate of the Edsel and Other Business Adventures* (New York: Harper & Row, 1963), 22–23.

129 **"now complete":** Flink, 277.

131 **"around the family car":** "Key to a Richer Life" (advertisement), *Life*, Aug. 21, 1950, 36–37.

131 **"its use enriching":** Budd Wheel, "Better Family Ties" (advertisement), *National Geographic*, Nov. 1951.

Chapter 7: FOREIGN INVADERS FROM *SPUTNIK* TO THE BUG

135 **Adlai Stevenson told the United Parents Association:** Adlai Stevenson, "Dual Education Problem: School and Home," *New York Times*, Apr. 6, 1958.

136 **"lampshade making and cheer-leading":** Quoted in Edward Andrews Tenney, *The Highway Jungle: The Story of the Public Safety Movement and of the Failure of "Driver Education" in the Public Schools* (New York: Exposition Press, 1962).

137 **"I don't know, but it won't be enough":** The show first appeared as *The Big Rod* on radio in 1954 and then on television in 1958 under the title *The Big Hot Rod*.

137 **"one of America's most serious crimes: auto theft":** "The Indifferent Mother," *This Is Your FBI* (ABC, Dec. 5, 1947), 1:47.

138 **"lives that we can save now":** Virgil M. Rogers and Walter A. Cutter,

"Driver Education: The Case for Life," *The American School Board Journal*, Oct. 1958, 23–28.

138 **"man must be in control":** American Automobile Association, ed., *Sportsmanlike Driving*, 3rd rev. ed. (Washington, DC, 1955), 231.

139 **"the whole world":** American Automobile Association, 361.

139 **"Pedestrian who fails to cooperate":** American Automobile Association, ed., *Sportsmanlike Driving*, 2nd ed. (Washington, DC: 1948), 182, 186.

140 **cars dropped none:** Clay McShane and Joel A. Tarr, *The Horse in the City: Living Machines in the Nineteenth Century* (Baltimore, MD: Johns Hopkins University Press, 2007), 26.

141 **"little harm or good":** "Useful, Progressive, Blunt-Nosed Mechanical Beetles: John Muir's Notes on Cars in Yosemite—Notes—Yosemite, the Southern Sierra Nevada & Death Valley," accessed Apr. 2, 2018, http://www.sierrasurvey.com/notes/useful-progressive-blunt-nosed-mechanical-beetles-john-muirs.html.

142 **"for the first time":** Quoted in Scott Harrison, " 'Smog Sieges' Often Accompanied September Heat from the 1950s to '80s," *Los Angeles Times*, Sept. 9, 2015.

142 **install devices to limit smog-causing emissions:** Quoted in Kevin L. Borg, *Auto Mechanics: Technology and Expertise in Twentieth-Century America* (Baltimore, MD: Johns Hopkins University Press, 2007).

145 **"compact or economy car":** Sloan, 510.

146 **"not very attractive at all":** "Nation's Manpower Revolution: Hearings Before the United States Senate Committee on Labor and Public Welfare, Subcommittee on Employment and Manpower, Eighty-Eighth Congress, First Session," § Subcommittee on Employment and Manpower of the Committee on Labor and Public Welfare (1963), 250–251.

146 **best-selling *The Insolent Chariots*:** John Keats, *The Insolent Chariots* (Philadelphia: Lippincott, 1958).

147 **helping the car track straight in a crosswind:** "Exner Styling and Aerodynamics (1957)," accessed Jan. 5, 2011, http://imperialclub.com/Articles/57Styling/index.htm.

148 **It was to be his father's final insult:** "May I Submit UTOPIAN TURTLE-TOP?" accessed Apr. 2, 2018, http://www.lettersofnote.com/2013/11/may-i-submit-utopian-turtletop.html.

148 **"The mood of 1948 was generally orgiastic":** Keats, 1958.

148 **"was their hair shirt":** John Brooks, "The Edsel II—Epitome," *New*

Yorker, Dec. 3, 1960, https://www.newyorker.com/magazine/1960/11/26/the-edsel-the-e-car-has-faith-in-you-son. Quoted in Joel W. Eastman, *Styling vs. Safety: The American Automobile Industry and the Development of Automotive Safety, 1900–1966* (Lanham, MD: University Press of America, 1984).

149 **he told *Time* magazine:** "Autos: The Dinosaur Hunter," *Time*, Apr. 6, 1959.

151 **"Think of the gas bills!":** "Autos."

151 **"outdrag me at lights":** "Report on the Hillman Minx," *Popular Mechanics*, Jan. 1953, 115.

152 **"all of it bad":** Quoted in Walter Henry Nelson, *Small Wonder: The Amazing Story of the Volkswagen* (Boston: Little Brown, 1970), 169.

Chapter 8: THE AUTOMOTIVE WOMB

161 **passengers did not like them:** Eastman, 181–86.

162 **"in automobile design":** Quoted in Daniel P. Moynihan, "Epidemic on the Highways," *The Reporter*, Apr. 30, 1959, 20.

162 **"the safety belt as used in [commercial airliners]":** Quoted in Eastman, 195.

162 **GM president Harlow H. Curtice:** Eastman, 199.

163 **"will accept these features":** Eastman, 193.

164 **the existing framework:** Ralph Nader, *Unsafe at Any Speed: The Designed-In Dangers of the American Automobile* (New York: Simon & Schuster, 1966), 1978.

164 **but ignored that knowledge:** Nader, 113.

166 **at her apartment:** Walter Rugaber, "Critic of Auto Industry's Safety Standards Says He Was Trailed and Harassed; Charges Called Absurd," *New York*, Mar. 6, 1966.

166 **"But we have to be sure":** Rugaber.

167 **his Connecticut driver's license was still valid:** "Car Safety Crusader; Ralph Nader," *New York Times*, Mar. 3, 1966.

168 **"make safer cars":** Walter Rugaber, "Henry Ford Sees Economic Hazard in Curb on Autos," *New York Times*, Apr. 16, 1966 https://www.nytimes.com/1966/04/16/archives/henry-ford-sees-economic-hazard-in-curb-on-autos-calls-on-congress.html.

168 **sapped engines of power:** Brock Yates, "Big Money Hides Behind a Noble Front," *Car and Driver*, July 2001, http://www.caranddriver

.com/columns/brock-yates-big-money-hides-behind-a-noble-front
-column.

168   "on carefully scheduled trains or buses makes for order": Brock Yates,
        The Decline and Fall of the American Automobile Industry (New
        York: Empire Books, 1983), 254–55.

168   "fear of injury": Yates, *Decline*, 258.

169   "trying to protect": Malcolm Gladwell, "Wrong Turn," *New Yorker*, June
        4, 2001, https://www.newyorker.com/magazine/2001/06/11/wrong-turn.

170   "government . . . should have": Anne Fleming, "Air Bags: A Chronolog-
        ical History of Delay," Congressional Testimony, NHTSA Docket 74-
        14, Notice 20, FMVSS 208, Occupant Crash Protection (Washington,
        DC: Insurance Institute for Highway Safety, Mar. 13, 1981), https://
        www.iihs.org/iihs/topics/bibliography/t/Airbags.

170   "and so forth": quoted in Martin Albaum, *Safety Sells: Market Forces
        and Regulation in the Development of Airbags* (Insurance Institute for
        Highway Safety, 2005).

170   the newly reformed IIHS: "Nader Charges Safety Agency Shows Timid-
        ity," *New York Times*, Mar. 22, 1967; Stan Luger, *Corporate Power,
        American Democracy, and the Automobile Industry* (New York: Cam-
        bridge University Press, 1999), 81.

171   "actively discouraged sales": A. R. Karr, "Saga of the Air Bag, or
        the Slow Deflation of a Car-Safety Idea," *Wall Street Journal*, Nov.
        11, 1976.

171   "Fails to Sell Bags": T. Rowan, "Big Ad Budget Fails to Sell Bags,"
        Automotive News, Oct. 6, 1975.

171   "baby, baby bug-buggies": Richard Nixon et al., "Automobile Safety
        and Air Bag Transcript | Richard Nixon Museum and Library," Cas-
        sette, vol. 488–15 (Segment 7), Nixon Tapes (Washington, DC: White
        House Oval Office, 1971) https://www.nixonlibrary.gov/automobile
        -safety-and-air-bag-transcript.

172   "against it": Richard L. Madden, "A Reporter's Notebook: Governors
        and Seat Belts," *New York Times*, Feb. 1, 1985, sec. N.Y. / Region,
        https://www.nytimes.com/1985/02/01/nyregion/a-reporter-s-notebook
        -governors-and-seat-belts.html.

172   passed the bill 82–60: Wendy Waters, Michael J. Macnabb, and Betty
        Brown, *A Half Century of Attempts to Resolve Vehicle Occupant*

Safety: Understanding Seatbelt and Airbag Technology (New Directions Road Safety Institute, 1998).

174 **"at best, protects itself"**: "Ralph Nader on The Dick Cavett Show 1969," YouTube, accessed January 10, 2018, https://www.youtube.com/watch?v=FccYHPIN8Uo.

174 **"the intent of the act"**: "Automobile Safety and Air Bag Transcript."

Chapter 9: THE ENERGY CRISIS ENDS THE AQUARIAN AGE

177 **"the automobile must go"**: John Jerome, *The Death of the Automobile: The Fatal Effect of the Golden Era, 1955–1970* (New York: W. W. Norton, 1972), 18.

179 **"shape [their] own environment"**: Stewart Brand, "The Purpose of the Whole Earth Catalog," in *The Whole Earth Catalog*, Fall 1968 (Menlo Park, CA: Portola Institute, 1968), accessed Nov. 23, 2019, http://www.wholeearth.com/issue/1010/article/196/the.purpose.of.the.whole.earth.catalog.

179 **"cannot take cars"**: Kenneth R. Schneider, *Autokind vs. Mankind: An Analysis of Tyranny, a Proposal for Rebellion, a Plan for Reconstruction* (New York: W. W. Norton, 1971), 15–16, 251.

180 **"Social Justice and the Auto"**: Ronald A. Buel, *Dead End: The Automobile in Mass Transportation* (Englewood Cliffs, NJ: Prentice-Hall, 1972), 141–56.

180 **"organized car pooling"**: Buel, 155.

181 **"we'll run out of fossil fuels to combust"**: Jerome, 234.

183 **be well understood through an automotive lens**: Raymond A. Mohl, "The Interstates and the Cities: Highways, Housing, and the Freeway Revolt," Research (Poverty and Race Research Action Council, 2002), 54.

184 **"concrete in the East Bronx"**: Frank J. Prial, "The Bruckner Interchange Open at Last," *New York Times*, Dec. 21, 1972, sec. Archives. https://www.nytimes.com/1972/12/21/archives/the-bruckner-interchange-open-at-last.html.

185 **"a junior god"**: Charles Bennett, "Planners Urged to Revive Downtown Expressway," *New York Times*, Apr. 18, 1963.

186 **"Drop Dead"**: "Ford to City: Drop Dead," *New York Daily News*, Oct. 30, 1975.

191 **"not the Republican ethic"**: Daniel Yergin, *The Prize: The Epic Quest for Oil, Money & Power* (New York: Free Press, 2008), 573.

192 **"animals foraging for food"**: "Testing the Tiger," *Time,* Feb. 18, 1974, 35.

192 **"we might as well drive there"**: "News Summary and Index," *New York Times*, Dec. 2, 1973.

196 **"politically inspired scarcity"**: Matthew Huber, "Shocked: 'Energy Crisis' and Neoliberal Transformation in the 1970s" (Berkeley, CA: Environmental Politics Workshop, 2011).

Chapter 10: BANDS OF CITIZENS TAKE ON DICKY, JERRY, AND JIMMY

199 **"his CB listeners"**: "Parma, OH—Jimmy Carter Takes His Campaign to the CB Airways" *Getty Images*, accessed Nov. 26, 2018, https://www.gettyimages.com/detail/news-photo/parma-oh-jimmy-carter-takes-his-campaign-to-the-cb-airways-news-photo/515114494.

199 **"October 4, 1978"**: Jimmy Carter, "10-4 Day Statement by the President," Oct. 2, 1978, https://www.presidency.ucsb.edu/documents/10-4-day-statement-the-president.

199 **"business or personal activities"**: FCC Bulletin No. 81482, Dec. 7, 1959, quoted in Tom Kneitel, *Tomcat's Big CB Handbook* (Commack, NY: CRB Research Books, 1988), 20–21.

200 **"'rag-chewing' activities"**: Kneitel, 20–21.

200 **retail sales by 1976**: Daniel Lewis, "Keeping Up With the Joneses' Cuisinart," *New York Times*, Dec. 30, 1979.

201 **"employee of a large truck line"**: D. Daryl Wyckoff, *The Owner-Operator, Independent Trucker* (Lexington, MA: Lexington Books, 1975).

201 **"towards authority"**: Wyckoff, 55.

202 **"communicating with other drivers"**: Wyckoff, 66.

202 **reported to *Overdrive* magazine**: "The Shutdown," *Overdrive*, Jan. 1974, quoted in Wyckoff.

202 **fifty-seven were women**: D. Daryl Wyckoff, *Truck Drivers in America* (Lexington, MA: Lexington Books, 1979), 77.

202 **harassment and discrimination**: Stephanie Sicard, "Female Truck Driv-

ers: Negotiating Identity in a Male Dominated Environment," *McNair Scholars Journal* 16, no. 1 (2012): 10.

202 **human trafficking:** "Sex Trafficking at Truck Stops" (Polaris Project; US Department of Health and Human Services, n.d.).

206 **"a national catastrophe":** reprinted in Daniel Horowitz, *Jimmy Carter and the Energy Crisis of the 1970s: A Brief History with Documents* (Boston: Bedford/St. Martin's, 2005), 36–42.

207 **"more than a quarter-century":** David Stockman, "The Wrong War? The Case Against a National Energy Policy," *Public Interest*, Fall 1978; reprinted in Horowitz, 43–48.

208 **"comprehensive energy policy":** Joseph Kahn, "Cheney Promotes Increasing Supply as Energy Policy," *New York Times*, May 1, 2001.

209 **to spike nevertheless:** For a complete history, see Yergin.

209 **"I'm a police officer":** NHTSA advertisement, *CBS Radio Mystery Theater*, Apr. 22, 1976.

209 **cost to taxpayers:** "Fifty-Five, A Decade of Experience," Special Report (Transportation Research Board National Research Council, 1984), https://doi.org/10.17226/11373.

210 **traveled on average:** Wyckoff, *Owner-Operator*, 31–32.

210 **"we prefer 'shutdown'":** "Truckers Stall Rush-Hour Traffic on the Long Island Expressway," *New York Times*, June 27, 1979.

211 **"diving for cover":** Dell Upton, *Second Suburb: Levittown, Pennsylvania*, ed. Dianne Harris (Pittsburgh, PA: University of Pittsburgh Press, 2010), 349, http://www.jstor.org/stable/j.ctt83jhq9.

212 **five people unlawful:** "Truckers Abduct and Rob Driver," *New York Times*, June 24, 1979.

212 **middle class American dream:** This history of the gas riot draws on Huber; David M. Anderson, "Levittown Is Burning! The 1979 Levittown, Pennsylvania, Gas Line Riot and the Decline of the Blue-Collar American Dream," *Labor* 2, no. 3 (2005): 47–66.

212 **as the energy crisis:** Horowitz, 83.

213 **"waste and selfishness":** quoted in Horowitz, 89.

214 **"confidence or purpose":** Jimmy Carter, "Energy and National Goals," in *Public Papers of the President of the United States: Jimmy Carter 1977–1981* (Washington, DC: Government Printing Office, 1979), 2:1235–41.

214 **"oil than we did in 1977—never":** Carter, 2:1235–41.

Chapter 11: THE UN-CARS THAT NOBODY LOVED

218 **"build in America":** *TOYOTA GM* (photo), Mar. 3, 1981, Associated Press.

218 **previous year's sales:** Robert Sobel, *Car Wars: The Untold Story* (New York: Dutton, 1984), 299.

219 **since the 1920s:** "Why We Totally Redesigned America's Favorite Car" (advertisement), *Time*, Oct. 4, 1976.

220 **"Detroit's Comeback Kid":** "Detroit's Comeback Kid," *Time*, Mar. 21, 1983, cover.

220 **"listening to Lee":** "America Loves Listening to Lee," *Time*, Apr. 1, 1985, cover.

220 **"one foot in the grave":** Lee Iacocca Chrysler Commercial, 1984, YouTube, https://www.youtube.com/watch?v=nppKMomMP-4&feature=youtu.be.

221 **"automobile in Western society":** Sobel, 171.

222 **five hours in the US:** Sobel, 142–43.

224 **Vancouver film festivals:** Doron P. Levin, "A Film Tweaks G.M. Over Jobless," *New York Times*, Sept. 21, 1989; "AFI Catalog—Roger & Me," accessed Nov. 23, 2018, https://catalog.afi.com/Catalog/MovieDetails/58258.

224 **"out of management's prerogatives":** quoted in Sobel, 302.

225 **"dealer for details":** "Jury Orders G.M. to Pay 10,000 in Switch of Engines," *New York Times*, June 28, 1981, sec. U.S., https://www.nytimes.com/1981/06/28/us/jury-orders-gm-to-pay-10000-in-switch-of-engines.html.

227 **"as firm as Stonehenge":** All quotes from Ben Hamper, *Rivethead: Tales from the Assembly Line* (New York: Warner Books, 1991).

228 **"thousands less":** Lee Iacocca Chrysler Commercial, 1984, YouTube, https://www.youtube.com/watch?v=nppKMomMP-4&feature=youtu.be. Accessed Nov. 23, 2018.

230 **"artifacts in our culture":** Daniel L. Guillory, "Star Wars Style and American Automobiles," in *The Automobile and American Culture*, ed. David Lanier Lewis and Laurence Goldstein (Ann Arbor: University of Michigan Press, 1983), 388.

231 **"pocket calculators":** Guillory, 385.

233 **"the sprawling of America":** "Q&A: Ross Roberts to Ford: Remember Your Strengths," *Automotive News*, June 16, 2003, http://www

.autonews.com/article/20030616/sub/306160802/q%26a%3a-ross-roberts-to-ford%3a-remember-your-strengths.

234 **NHTSA recall:** "U.S. Seeks Firestone 500 Recalls," *Washington Post*, July 9, 1978, https://www.washingtonpost.com/archive/politics/1978/07/09/us-seeks-firestone-500-recalls/4e85c2b3-dc70-4275-a46a-18bf1c2f602e/; "Firestone Hit By New Suit On '500' Tires," *Washington Post*, September 22, 1978, https://www.washingtonpw/archive/business/1978/09/22/firestone-hit-by-new-suit-on-500-tires/5c9274fd-0661-473f-bd12-ec01162a3d5c/; Keith Bradsher, *High and Mighty: The Dangerous Rise of the SUV* (New York: Public Affairs, 2003), Ch. 15, "The Ford Explorer–Firestone Tire Debacle."

234 **called a draw:** Andrew Pollack, "No Clear Winner in Decision In Isuzu vs. Consumer Reports," *New York Times*, Apr. 8, 2000, sec. Business Day, https://www.nytimes.com/2000/04/08/business/no-clear-winner-in-decision-in-isuzu-vs-consumer-reports.html; SUZUKI MOTOR CORPORATION and American Suzuki Motor Corporation, Plaintiff-Appellant, v. CONSUMERS UNION OF UNITED STATES, INC., a non-profit New York Corporation, Defendant-Appellee, No. 00–56043 (United States Court of Appeals, Ninth Circuit May 19, 2003); "Suzuki vs. Consumer Reports," *Washington Post*, May 23, 2003, https://www.washingtonpost.com/archive/business/technology/2003/05/23/suzuki-vs-consumer-reports/28e197ea-a66b-4f01-9b97-5fd68efda053/; James F. Peltz, "Suzuki, Consumer Reports Settle Case," *Los Angeles Times*, July 9, 2004, http://articles.latimes.com/2004/jul/09/business/fi-suzuki9.

235 **"on all fours":** Daniel Kleinman, "Esuvee Safety Campaign: Keep It On All Fours," see https://adage.com/creativity/work/keep-it-all-fours/9379, accessed Nov. 23, 2018.

235 **"look at those calves":** Joe Mathews, "The Hummer and Schwarzenegger: They Probably Won't Be Back," Feb. 28, 2010, http://www.washingtonpost.com/wp-dyn/content/article/2010/02/26/AR2010022603248.html.

236 **crime and violence:** Bradsher, 95–96.

236 **"the public will stand":** Dewey Palmer, "If You Buy a Car," *New Republic*, Apr. 22, 1936, 304–6.

236 **"delusion of grandeur":** Alan R. Raucher, "Paul G. Hoffman, Studebaker, and the Car Culture," *Indiana Magazine of History* 79, no. 3 (1983): 209–30.

238 **muscle through traffic:** "2018 Armada Design | Nissan USA," Nissan, accessed October 18, 2018, https://www.nissanusa.com/vehicles/crossovers-suvs/armada/design.html.

238 **Toyota explains:** "2017 Toyota Sequoia Lives Up to Its Name with Big Power, Roominess, and Capability | Toyota," accessed October 18, 2018, http://toyotanews.pressroom.toyota.com/releases/2017-toyota-sequoia-big-power-roominess-capability.htm.

238 **"it's highly recommended":** Tom Voelk, "Video Review: A Pickup Truck That's Both Primal and Pampering," *New York Times*, Mar. 9, 2017, sec. New Cars, https://www.nytimes.com/2017/03/09/automobiles/auto reviews/video-review-a-pickup-truck-thats-both-primal-and-pampering.html.

239 **$5,100 premium:** Nick Bunkley, "Chevy's Trax Stomps on the Sonic," *Automotive News*, accessed Oct. 18, 2018, http://mexico.autonews.com/article/20170619/RETAIL01/170619758/chevy-trax-sonic-sales-united-states.

Chapter 12: FUTURE VISIONS OF ROBOT CARS

244 **back in one day:** "Let's Talk Self-Driving," accessed Oct. 23, 2017, https://letstalkselfdriving.com/.

246 **"GM! GM! GM!":** Automotive Hall of Fame, "Ralph Nader Acceptance Speech—Automotive Hall of Fame," YouTube, accessed Jan. 10, 2018, https://www.youtube.com/watch?v=vSYZNImEkys.

246 **Great Depression ground on:** Automotive Hall of Fame.

247 **"world of 1960!":** General Motors, *Futurama: Highways and Horizons Exhibit Brochure* (1939), 8, http://www.oldcarbrochures.com/static/NA/GM%20Corporate%20and%20Concepts/1939%20GM%20Futurama/dirindex.html.

247 **the miniature highways:** General Motors, 6.

247 **"Factor in Driving":** Norman Bel Geddes, *Magic Motorways* (New York: Random House, 1940), http://archive.org/details/magicmotorways00geddrich.

249 **by punch card:** Joshua Levin, "Magic Highway USA," YouTube, accessed Nov. 24, 2018, https://www.youtube.com/watch?v=aHjS9YBXzXU.

249 **"made into reflectors":** "Oral-History: Vladimir Zworykin—

Engineering and Technology History Wiki," interview by Mark Heyer, July 4, 1975, Interview #021, IEEE History Center, http://ethw.org /Oral-History:Vladimir_Zworykin.

250 **"all now in operation"**: See Hemmings.com, "GM Tells the Story of the Firebird II | Hemmings Daily." *Hemmings Motor News* for a link to the brochure, accessed Sept. 11, 2018, https://www.hemmings.com/ blog/2016/10/17/gm-tells-the-story-of-the-firebird-ii/.

250 **"a wire in the road"**: Classic Airliners & Vintage Pop Culture, "GM Firebird III Gas Turbine Car Promo Film—1958," YouTube, accessed Apr. 4, 2018, https://www.youtube.com/watch?v=xKOdux6Gjno.

251 **"research in transportation systems"**: Petros Ioannou, ed., *Automated Highway Systems* (Springer Science & Business Media, 2013), 4.

251 **"rather than system building"**: "Public Roads—Creating A Landmark: The Intermodal Surface Transportation Act of 1991, Nov./Dec. 2001," accessed Oct. 26, 2017, https://www.fhwa.dot.gov/publications /publicroads/01novdec/istea.cfm.

253 **a D+ overall:** "ASCE's 2017 Infrastructure Report Card | GPA: D+," ASCE's 2017 Infrastructure Report Card, accessed Nov. 24, 2018, http://www.infrastructurereportcard.org.

253 **"putting wires in the road?"**: Burkhard Bilger, "Has the Self-Driving Car Arrived at Last?" *New Yorker*, Nov. 18, 2013, https://www.newyorker .com/magazine/2013/11/25/auto-correct.

253 **"2,000 decisions a second"**: Reprinted in Imre Szeman and Susie O'Brien, *Popular Culture: A User's Guide* (New York: Wiley, 2017), 306.

255 **sending a note home:** "Darpa Urban Challenge," accessed Oct. 26, 2017, http://archive.darpa.mil/grandchallenge/.

256 **the auto business:** Aswath Damodaran, *Narrative and Numbers: The Value of Stories in Business* (New York: Columbia University Press, 2017), 75.

258 **"along a single wire"**: "Non-Final Office Action," Office Action in Ex Parte Reexamination (USPTO, Mar. 27, 2018), https://www .documentcloud.org/documents/4936885-2018-March-27-Non-Final -Action-90020113-16.html.

258 **factor of ten:** Nick Lucchesi, "Self-Driving Technology Going to Be Surprisingly Cheap," *Inverse*, accessed Jan. 1, 2019, https://www.inverse .com/article/26102-waymo-detroit-auto-show.

259 **offer net earnings:** Sarah Kessler, "This Is How Much Uber and Lyft Drivers Make in Different Cities," *Fast Company*, July 15, 2015,

https://www.fastcompany.com/3048563/this-is-how-much-uber-and -lyft-drivers-make-in-different-cities.

259   **less than minimum wage:** Jacob Bogage, "How Much Uber Drivers Actu-ally Make Per Hour," *Washington Post*, June 27, 2016, sec. The Switch, https://www.washingtonpost.com/news/the-switch/wp/2016/06/27 /how-much-uber-drivers-actually-make-per-hour/.

260   **lasting a year:** Chantel McGee, "Only 4 Percent of Uber Drivers Remain after a Year Says Report," CNBC, Apr. 20, 2017, https://www.cnbc .com/2017/04/20/only-4-percent-of-uber-drivers-remain-after-a-year -says-report.html.

260   **posted to YouTube:** Johana Bhuiyan, "A New Video Shows Uber CEO Travis Kalanick Arguing with a Driver over Fares," *Recode*, Feb. 28, 2017, https://www.recode.net/2017/2/28/14766964/video-uber-travis-kala nick-driver-argument.

260   **"Overhead walks on two legs":** Alan Ponsford, email message to author, "Some Updated Numbers on Costs of Driver/Bus," Mar. 9, 2017.

Chapter 13: THINK OF THE LIVES WE'LL SAVE: THE RHETORICS OF ROBOT CARS

262   **by the side of the road:** Paul Noth, "Does Your Car Have Any Idea Why My Car Pulled It Over?" Dec. 30, 2015, https://www.newyorker.com /cartoon/a19697.

263   **"dangerous instrumentality":** C. P. Berry, *The Law of Automobiles*, 7th ed. (Chicago: Callaghan, 1935).

263   **likely much higher:** "Drowsy Driving—19 States and the District of Columbia, 2009–2010," *Morbidity and Mortality Weekly Report* (Cen-ters for Disease Control and Prevention, Jan. 4, 2013); "Drowsy Driv-ing 2015," *Traffic Safety Facts* (Washington, DC: NHTSA, Oct. 2017).

264   **the intoxicated driver:** "Alcohol-Impaired Driving," *Traffic Safety Facts* (Washington, DC: NHTSA, Oct. 2017). Of 214 children under 14 killed in 2016, 115 were riding with an impaired driver, 61 were in another vehicle, and 36 were pedestrians or cyclists.

264   **"toll of over 25,000":** Michigan State Police v. Sitz, No. 496 U.S. 444 (1990). The 25,000 figure is far higher than estimates by safety experts.

265   **"more people die":** Burkhard Bilger, "Has the Self-Driving Car Arrived

at Last?" *New Yorker*, Nov. 18, 2013, https://www.newyorker.com /magazine/2013/11/25/auto-correct.

265 **"you're killing people"**: Pete Pachal, "Elon Musk to the Media: 'You're Killing People,'" *Mashable*, accessed Apr. 6, 2018, https://mashable .com/2016/10/19/elon-musk-youre-killing-people/.

265 **"marketed vigorously as safe and important to its customers"**: Carol J. Loomis, "Elon Musk Says Autopilot Death 'Not Material' to Tesla Shareholders," *Fortune*, July 5, 2016, http://fortune.com/2016/07/05 /elon-musk-tesla-autopilot-stock-sale/.

265 **"write an article that misleads the public"**: Madison Malone Kircher, "Elon Musk: A Lesson in Never Tweeting," *Select All*, accessed Apr. 8, 2018, http://nymag.com/selectall/2016/07/elon-musk-a-lesson-in-never -tweeting.html.

265 **"90% of the time because of human error"**: Parmy Olson, "Driverless Cars for $10,000? This Startup Is Challenging Google With a Simple Sensor," *Forbes*, accessed Oct. 30, 2017, https://www.forbes.com/sites /parmyolson/2014/06/23/startup-driverless-car-sensors-google/.

265 **to encourage further development of driverless cars**: Elaine Chao, "Remarks as Prepared for Delivery by U.S. Secretary of Transportation Elaine L. Chao Detroit Auto Show," Text, US Department of Transportation, Jan. 14, 2018, https://www.transportation.gov/briefing-room /detroit-auto-show.

266 **"The major factor in 94 percent of all fatal crashes"**: "Automated Driving Systems: A Vision for Safety" (Washington, DC: NHTSA, September 2017).

266 *driver, vehicle, or environment*: "National Motor Vehicle Crash Causation Survey: Report to Congress," Report to Congress, July 2008, https://crashstats.nhtsa.dot.gov/Api/Public/ViewPublication/811059.

267 **"to avoid the crash"**: Daniel Blower, email to the author, "Re: Is the Claim '94% of Crashes Are the Result of Human Error' Supported by Your Research?," Nov. 28, 2017; Daniel Blower and Kenneth L. Campbell, "Large Truck Crash Causation Study" (Ann Arbor: Center for National Truck Statistics, UMTRI, Nov. 2002).

267 **"murkier than you think"**: Patrick Lin, "The Ethics of Saving Lives With Autonomous Cars Is Far Murkier Than You Think," *Wired*, July 30, 2013, https://www.wired.com/2013/07/the-surprising-ethics-of -robot-cars/.

267 **boxes in the first place:** Patrick Lin, "The Ethical Dilemma of Self-Driving Cars," YouTube, accessed Apr. 10, 2018, https://www.youtube .com/watch?v=ixIoDYVfKA0&vl=en.

267 **"for utilitarian cars?":** Jean-François Bonnefon, Azim Shariff, and Iyad Rahwan, "Autonomous Vehicles Need Experimental Ethics: Are We Ready for Utilitarian Cars?" *Science* 352 (2016): 1573–76.

268 **"full of kids":** David Weinberger, "Should Your Self-Driving Car Kill You to Save a School Bus?" *Digital Trends*, Oct. 27, 2015, https://www .digitaltrends.com/cars/self-driving-car-moral-decisions/.

268 **"programmed to kill":** Charlie Sorrel, "In an Accident, Who Will a Driverless Car Be Programmed to Kill?," *Fast Company*, Dec. 17, 2015, https://www.fastcompany.com/3054675/in-an-accident-who-will-a -driverless-car-be-programmed-to-kill.

268 **"Adjustable Ethics Settings":** "The Robot Car of Tomorrow May Just Be Programmed to Hit You," *Wired*, accessed Nov. 24, 2018, https:// www.wired.com/2014/05/the-robot-car-of-tomorrow-might-just-be -programmed-to-hit-you/; "Here's a Terrible Idea: Robot Cars With Adjustable Ethics Settings," *Wired*, accessed Nov. 24, 2018, https:// www.wired.com/2014/08/heres-a-terrible-idea-robot-cars-with -adjustable-ethics-settings/.

268 **"driverless car crash":** "A Driverless Car's Computer Could Decide Who Lives and Dies in a Crash," *CBC News*, Oct. 30, 2015, https:// www.cbc.ca/news/canada/edmonton/computers-could-decide-who -lives-and-dies-in-a-driverless-car-crash-1.3297177.

268 **"Your Car Decide":** Tim Cramton, "Who Lives and Who Dies? Just Let Your Car Decide," Nov. 16, 2015, http://jlpp.org/blogzine/who-lives -and-who-dies-just-let-your-car-decide/.

269 **"decision-making process":** *Handbook of Highway Engineering*, 4–11.

269 **"inevitable or acceptable":** "What Is Vision Zero?" Vision Zero Network, accessed Oct. 31, 2017, https://visionzeronetwork.org/about /what-is-vision-zero/.

270 **did not work:** "We Wanted to Find out Why All Efforts to Date to Tackle Distracted Driving Have Utterly Failed," Center for Health Communication, Apr. 5, 2017, https://www.hsph.harvard.edu/chc/2017/04/05 /professor-behind-designated-drivers-takes-on-distracted-ones/.

271 **"to unusual situations":** "Governor Cuomo Announces Cruise Automation Applying to Begin First Fully Autonomous Vehicle Testing in New

York State," Governor Andrew M. Cuomo, Oct. 17, 2017, https://www
.governor.ny.gov/news/governor-cuomo-announces-cruise-automation
-applying-begin-first-fully-autonomous-vehicle.

271 **"Then I Tried One":** David Leonhardt, "Driverless Cars Made Me Nervous. Then I Tried One," *New York Times*, Oct. 22, 2017, https://www
.nytimes.com/2017/10/22/opinion/driverless-cars-test-drive.html.

271 **"isn't autonomous":** Katie Burke, "When Your 'Self-Driving Car' Isn't
Autonomous," *Automotive News*, accessed Oct. 31, 2017, http://www
.autonews.com/article/20171027/mobility/310279888/when-your-self
-driving-car-isnt-autonomous.

271 **"Magical 'Driverless Car' ":** Lawrence Ulrich, "Terrified *New York
Times* Columnist Confuses Volvo with Magical 'Driverless Car,' " *The
Drive*, accessed Oct. 31, 2017, http://www.thedrive.com/opinion/15393
/terrified-new-york-times-columnist-confuses-volvo-with-magical
-driverless-car.

272 **"semiautonomous driving":** James B. Stewart, "With Tesla in a Danger
Zone, Can Model 3 Carry It to Safety?," *New York Times*, Apr. 5, 2018,
sec. Business Day, https://www.nytimes.com/2018/04/05/business/tesla
-model-3.html.

272 **"in 30 years":** "Autronic-Eye Automatic Headlight Control" (advertisement), *Life*, Mar. 1, 1954.

273 **Cedar Key, Florida:** This account draws on accident investigation reports
from the Florida State Police, NHTSA, and the NTSB. See Daphne Yuncker,
"Traffic Homicide Investigation" (Florida Highway Patrol, November 24,
2016); Kareem Habib, "Office of Defect Investigation Resume" (Washington, DC: NHTSA, January 19, 2017); "Collision Between a Car Operating With Automated Vehicle Control Systems and a Tractor-Semitrailer
Truck Near Williston, Florida May 7, 2016," Highway Accident Report
(Washington, DC: National Transportation Safety Board, September 12,
2017); "Accident ID HWY16FH018 Mode Highway Occurred on May
07, 2016 in Williston, FL United States Last Modified on June 28, 2017
10:06 Public Released on June 19, 2017 11:06 Total 46 Document Items,"
accessed November 1, 2017, https://dms.ntsb.gov/pubdms/search/hitlist
.cfm?docketID=59989&CFID=1126988&CFTOKEN=b1b9a5b7e84
9bb32-88C471C8-01C8-077F-A22C23E2E219927F.

274 **he told Mulligan:** "Human Performance Factors Group Chairman's
Factual Report Attachement 4," Witness Interview (Washington, DC:
National Transportation Safety Board, July 14, 2016).

275 **in the United States was scant:** CGTN, "Shocking Footage: Fatal Tesla Crash in China Triggers Suspicion of Auto-Drive," YouTube, accessed Nov. 24, 2018, https://www.youtube.com/watch?v=CgLE_ZLLaxw.

275 **"allow us to do so":** Neal E. Boudette, "Autopilot Cited in Death of Chinese Tesla Driver," *New York Times*, Sept. 14, 2016, sec. Business Day, https://www.nytimes.com/2016/09/15/business/fatal-tesla-crash-in -china-involved-autopilot-government-tv-says.html.

275 **suing Tesla China:** "Family of Driver Killed in Tesla Crash in China Seeks Court Investigation," *Wall Street Journal*, Sept. 20, 2016, sec. Business, https://www.wsj.com/articles/family-of-driver-killed-in-tesla -crash-in-china-seeks-court-investigation-1474351855. The suit is ongoing.

276 **sixty-four in a thirty-five zone:** NTSB, 6.

276 **tweeted an endorsement:** Joshua Brown, "Autopilot Saves Model S," YouTube, accessed December 22, 2018, https://www.youtube.com/watch?v =9I5rraWJq6E.

276 **a total of twenty-five seconds:** NTSB, 35.

276 **"Cleared in Probe":** "Sigh of Relief for Self-Driving Cars as Tesla Cleared in Probe," Bloomberg.com, Jan. 19, 2017, https://www.bloomberg .com/news/articles/2017-01-19/tesla-escapes-recall-in-probe-of-death -linked-to-autopilot.

276 **"Highlights Technology Strengths":** Daniel Sparks, "NHTSA Drops Tesla Autopilot Investigation, Highlights Technology Strengths," *Motley Fool*, Jan. 19, 2017, https://www.fool.com/investing/2017/01/19 /nhtsa-drops-tesla-autopilot-investigation-highligh.aspx.

276 **"Feds say yay to self-driving":** Jack Stewart, "After Investigating Tesla's Deadly Autopilot Crash, Feds Say Hooray For Self-Driving," *Wired*, Jan. 20, 2017, https://www.wired.com/2017/01/probing-teslas-deadly -crash-feds-say-yay-self-driving/.

276 **reduced crashes by 40 percent:** Elon Musk, "Report Highlight: 'The Data Show That the Tesla Vehicles Crash Rate Dropped by Almost 40 Percent after Autosteer Installation,'" Tweet, *@elonmusk* (blog), Jan. 19, 2017, https://twitter.com/elonmusk/status/822129092036206592?ref _src=twsrc%5Etfw%7Ctwcamp%5Etweetembed%7Ctwterm %5E822129092036206592&ref_url=http%3A%2F%2Ffortune .com%2F2017%2F01%2F19%2Fteslas-autopilot-tech-safer-nhtsa -report%2F. Musk based his claim on a statement by NHTSA in the report that the agency later recanted, "U.S. Safety Agency Says 'Did

Not Assess' Tesla Autopilot Effectiveness," Reuters, May 2, 2018, https://www.reuters.com/article/us-tesla-autopilot-idUSKBN1I334A.

277 **"with the inattentive driver in mind"**: Enforcement Guidance Bulletin 2016-02: Safety-Related Defects and Automated Safety Technologies, 81 Fed. Reg. 65705. with "ODI Resume Investigation PE 16-007" (Washington, DC: NHTSA, Jan. 7, 2017), https://static.nhtsa.gov /odi/inv/2016/INCLA-PE16007-7876.PDF, 11, n. 23.

277 **"action was taken"**: "An Update on Last Week's Accident," Tesla, Mar. 30, 2018, https://www.tesla.com/blog/update-last-week%E2%80%99s -accident.

277 **"when promoting the system"**: "Germany Says Tesla Should Not Use 'Autopilot' in Advertising," Reuters, Oct. 16, 2016, https://www.reuters .com/article/us-tesla-germany-idUSKBN12G0KS.

278 **"in terms of safety"**: "Mobileye Responds to False Allegations," Reuters, accessed Nov. 4, 2017 https://www.reuters.com/article/us-mobileye -tesla/mobileye-says-tesla-was-pushing-the-envelope-in-terms-of-safety -idUSKCN11K2T8; See also "Mobileye Responds to False Allegations" (Mobileye, Sept. 16, 2016), https://static.nhtsa.gov/odi/inv/2016/INLM -PE16007-66309.pdf; "Mobileye Says Tesla Was 'Pushing the Envelope in Terms of Safety,'" Reuters, Sept. 14, 2016, https://www.reuters.com /article/us-mobileye-tesla-idUSKCN11K2T8.

278 **"technology or self-driving car"**: Ibid.

278 **"autopilot is doing everything"**: NTSB, 45.

278 **"aviation and elsewhere"**: "Accident ID HWY16FH018—Board Member Statement," accessed Nov. 1, 2017, https://dms.ntsb.gov/pubdms /search/hitlist.cfm?docketID=59989&CFID=1126988&CFTOKEN= b1b9a5b7e849bb32-88C471C8-01C8-077F-A22C23E2E219927F, 45.

Chapter 14: MY CAR HAS LEFT FOR COLLEGE

281 **national fan club**: Dave Wallace Jr., "They Like the Cars, but Love the Engines," *New York Times*, Oct. 11, 2013, sec. Collectible Cars, https://www.nytimes.com/2013/10/13/automobiles/collectibles/they -like-the-cars-but-love-the-engines.html.

282 **"does not have to think"**: Ford and Crowther, 103.

284 **roughly 17.5 million cars sold**: "2016 Top 150 Dealership Groups," *Automotive News*, Mar. 27, 2017, http://www.autonews.com/article/20170327/

datacenter/170329873/2016-top-150-dealership-groups; John Irwin, "U.S. per-Dealership Sales Rose Again in 2015," *Automotive News*, Feb. 15, 2016, http://www.autonews.com/article/20160215/retail/160219922/u.s.-per -dealership-sales-rose-again-in-2015.

287 **"at moderate cost"**: "1978 Dodge Truck Brochure," accessed Aug. 3, 2018, http://www.lov2xlr8.no/brochures/dodge/78truck/78truck.html. The dealership brochure covers all Dodge trucks. The text is from page 3, which highlights the Adventurer trim package.

289 **dig into the earth:** Newcomb and Spurr, 333.

294 **locates it in class conflict:** Borg, 2.

294 **"more often and more flagrantly than men"**: Roger William Riis and John Patric, *Repair Men May Gyp You* (Garden City, NY: Doubleday, Doran, 1951), 6.

294 **"parts not installed"**: Riis and Patric, 54.

294 **"a crooked explanation"**: Riis and Patric, 52.

295 **every mechanical mystery thrown at him:** "Gus and the Model Garage Archive—Home," accessed Aug. 14, 2018, http://www.gus -stories.org/.

299 **"an understanding of all"**: Robert M. Pirsig, *Zen and the Art of Motor-cycle Maintenance: An Inquiry into Values* (New York: Morrow, 1974), 292.

299 **"more engaging *intellectually*"**: Matthew B. Crawford, *Shop Class as Soulcraft: An Inquiry into the Value of Work* (New York: Penguin Books, 2009), 5.

Chapter 15: KIDS TODAY

305 *New York Times* in 2013: Elisabeth Rosenthal, "The End of Car Culture," *New York Times*, Oct. 19, 2018, sec. Sunday Review, https://www .nytimes.com/2013/06/30/sunday-review/the-end-of-car-culture.html.

305 **Boudette in 2016:** Neal E. Boudette, "Automakers Prepare for an America That's Over the Whole Car Thing," *New York Times*, Dec. 22, 2017, national edition, sec. Automobiles. The quote does not appear in the online version found at https://www.nytimes.com/2016/12/22 /business/automakers-prepare-america-fewer-cars.html.

305 **to eschew driving:** Brandon Schoettle, interview with the author, Jan. 31, 2017; Michael Sivak and Brandon Schoettle, *Recent Decreases*

in the Proportion of Persons with a Driver's License across All Age Groups (Ann Arbor: University of Michigan Transportation Research Institute, Jan. 2016), https://trid.trb.org/view/1480411.

306 **a cultural anthropologist:** Tom Wolfe, *The Kandy-Kolored Tangerine-Flake Streamline Baby* (New York: Farrar, Straus and Giroux, 1965).

309 **see the screen:** "MotorWeek | Retro Review: 1986 Buick Century T-Type & Riviera CRT," YouTube, accessed Jan. 24, 2018, https://www.youtube.com/watch?v=Lkaazk68iGE&t=167s.

315 **"they saved lives":** "Small Victims of a Flawed Safety Device," *Washington Post,* June 2, 1997, https://www.washingtonpost.com/archive/politics/1997/06/02/small-victims-of-a-flawed-safety-device/b25e8a18-96a5-4fae-934e-c6b80c486107/.

315 **"adult passengers it saves":** Lauren Pacelli, "Asleep at the Wheel of Auto Safety? Recent Air Bag Regulations by the National Highway Traffic Safety Administration," *Journal of Contemporary Health Law & Policy* 15, no. 2 (1999): 739–77. Note that not every airbag deployment saves a life.

316 **11 percent, respectively:** Charles Kahane, *Fatality Reduction by Air Bags: Analyses of Accident Data through Early 1996* (Washington, DC: NHTSA, Aug. 1996), 1, 6. https://crashstats.nhtsa.dot.gov/Api/Public/ViewPublication/808470.

317 **"monitor the child's condition":** "Request for Air Bag On-Off Switch" (Washington, DC: National Highway Traffic Safety Administration), https://www.nhtsa.gov/sites/nhtsa.dot.gov/files/documents/airbagswitchrequestform_03012017_v3.pdf.

317 **"'get killed,' she said":** "Chrysler Campaign Steers Children to the Back Seat," *Washington Post,* Feb. 14, 1997, https://www.washingtonpost.com/archive/business/1997/02/14/chrysler-campaign-steers-children-to-the-back-seat/e3fb94cd-2710-41b4-9aab-8891bcd35d22/.

317 **"kids in the back seat!":** Ford Windstar Commercial, 1997, YouTube, accessed Jan. 2, 2019, https://www.youtube.com/watch?v=cYLNBpFCmTY.

ILLUSTRATION CREDITS

INDEX

Page numbers in *italics* indicate illustrations. Page numbers followed by *n* indicate footnotes.